The Modern RPG Language

With Structured Programming

The Modern RPG Language

With Structured Programming

Fourth Edition
March 1993

Robert Cozzi, Jr.
Cozzi Research

Dedication

To Jacqueline Caroline, the joy of my life

And, to Nana, who taught me to think, question, and wonder

Cozzi Research, Warrenville, Illinois 60555

First Published February 1989
-Reprinted July 1989, March 1990 and April 1990
Second Edition Published September 1990
Third Edition Published April 1991, Reprinted August 1991
-Updated and reprinted July 1992
Fourth Edition Published March 1993
-Updated and reprinted October 1993

Printed in the United States of America

ISBN 0-9621825-0-8

Contents

Forward

In the four years since I first wrote this book, the RPGIII language has been enhanced more frequently and with more function than in the past 25 years.

It would be inconsiderate of me not to mention the work put into improving the RPGIII language by the planners, team leaders and, specifically, the programmers at the IBM Canada, Ltd. Toronto Laboratory in North York, Ontario, Canada and at the IBM Rochester Minnesota Laboratory. The Toronto Lab personnel have received an inordinate amount of persuasion over the past several years from the RPGIII community. Their results, so far, have been encouraging.

Now a new language definition for RPG is being developed. This new definition is being referred to as *RPGIV*, and should eliminate many shortcomings in the current language definition. Many new features will be added to the language, including natural expressions, longer variable names, easier substring handling, local variables, pointer support, keyword functions, multi-dimensional arrays, and decimal data error transparency. I look forward to writing "*RPGIV: The Next Generation*" as soon as this new RPG is released.

Robert Cozzi, Jr.

Preface

In 1974, at the request of my father who had a friend in the computer industry since the early '60s, I signed up for an introduction to computer programming course. The first semester of the course was spent discussing the financial benefits of being in the computer industry over other types of business. I debated with the instructor quite often, arguing that money isn't everything and that becoming an Astronaut was what I really wanted to do.

Needless to say, the instructor felt I was unqualified to attend the second semester. However, after six months of negotiating with the instructor (I think my mother called him), I attended the second semester of the course during the next school year.

In that course, I was exposed to the syntax of COBOL. It looked simple, similar to English, but then again, maybe not.

I spent hours, days, even weeks carefully drawing flowcharts and diagrams as well as keypunching COBOL statements into 80-column cards on an IBM 029 keypunch machine. It wasn't the greatest way to complete your homework, but it was the only way we had.

Even back then everyone was required to backup their programs. The only way for a student to backup a program (since no disk space was allocated to the students) was to use the duplicator to punch a second set of 80-column cards. Carrying all that paper meant toting your homework around in a wheelbarrow (I think COBOL programs punched onto 80-column cards is what started the green house effect). Imagine the frustration I had the day I spilled my 1000-line COBOL program made up of 80-column cards.

In 1976 I signed up for two computer language classes, "FORTRAN IV with WATFOR and WATFIV", and "RPG with RPGII for S/370 and S/3". The FORTRAN class was the most interesting—scientific formulas, mathematical expression, subprograms and brevity—a pleasant change from COBOL. On the other hand, I considered the RPG class as an "it's a language, so I'll take it" experience. After all, by knowing FORTRAN and COBOL I was set for life!

Shortly after classes began, I took a job as a Computer Operator working with the IBM System/32. I was awed that, unlike my college courses, businesses could actually run programs without compiling them each time! "What power!" I thought naively. Since the IBM System/32 used RPG as its primary language, I figured that it must be *the* greatest language to use for business, so I began reading the System/32 RPGII reference manual.

From my FORTRAN and COBOL background, I quickly recognized the perform subroutine (EXSR) operation and used it for all of the assignments in my college course. When I turned in one of my assignments, it included a single "main-line" calculation—the EXSR operation—the remainder of the program was written with subroutines and the RPG cycle. The instructor was baffled by my self-indulged modular programming. His first question was "What's that?" as he pointed to the EXSR operation, followed by "Why did you use it?"

That day, I learned that people who are authorities or who are perceived to be authorities on various subjects, often know far less than we think they do. If someone is considered an "authority" or "expert", that simply means that they are (a) a person who has practiced the subject or profession long enough for others in the profession to notice, or (b) a person who is willing to act as a cornerstone for building and sharing knowledge on the subject. It doesn't mean they know everything about the subject.

Textbooks contain the knowledge of an individual or group of people (authors) on a specific subject. Typically, subject matter authorities are involved in the creation of textbooks. Textbooks can assist you in the act of gathering knowledge by presenting the knowledge of others. The art of learning is up to you.

The Evolution of RPG

In 1960, someone had the inspiration to develop a computer language that would replace manually wired jumper boards of an IBM 1400 business machine. The jumper boards were column oriented; the developers used this as an element in designing the language. The language that resulted was the Report Program Generator language or RPG.

In 1964, RPG was upgraded to a more usable language. This improvement coincided with the announcement of the IBM 360 model 20. RPG did a fine job of handling 80-column cards, however it couldn't handle tape or disk processing, not to mention display devices, which were just being introduced.

The RPG cycle (the processes in which an RPG program automatically reads a record and performs certain routines) was at the heart of file processing. Unlike other high-level languages, RPG did not require extensive file declarations for opening and closing files, nor did it require a complex list of instructions to simply print data—the RPG cycle took care of that for the programmer.

In 1969, RPGII was announced, along with a new mini-computer called the IBM System/3. RPGII had all the features of the original RPG, plus disk processing. Later, limited support for workstation devices (i.e., dumb terminals) was added to for System/3 workstation display devices and a newly available System/34 computer.

In 1978, RPGIII was announced for a new mini-computer, the IBM System/38. The System/38 was a replacement for the IBM System/3. The System/38 was the most advanced general purpose computer of its day. It was the first with a built-in relational-like database management system.

RPGIII added a host of new functions to RPG, among them a nearly complete set of structured programming operations (e.g., IF-THEN-ELSE, DO). With these new features, the benefit of the RPG cycle grew thin. Today, the RPG cycle exists more for compatibility with older systems. The use of the cycle is typically avoided because of structured and modular programming practices.

In 1985, RPGIII was enhanced to include support for AND/OR logic within IF and DO operations. This support greatly enhanced program readability and greatly decreased programmer frustration levels.

In 1988, the IBM AS/400 was announced and with it a new compiler called the *AS/400 RPG/400 compiler*. The RPG/400 compiler supports four versions of the RPG language: (1) System/38-compatible RPGIII; (2) System/36-compatible RPGII; (3) SAA RPG Level 1; and (4) AS/400-compatible RPGIII.

The initial AS/400 RPG/400 compiler added few new features to the RPGIII language, including SQL host language coupling (i.e., embedded SQL statements), the REDPE (read prior record with equal key) operation, 30-digit numeric fields, and a few other subtle changes.

In late 1988, IBM introduced SAA RPG Level 1, a specification of guidelines for writing application programs that may be ported across multiple computers. The SAA RPG Level 1 specification is a subset of RPGIII that includes most RPGII primitives, such as calculation specifications, input specifications, data structures and embedded SQL (structured query language). Missing, however, are several operation codes such as ACQ, EXFMT, READC, FREE, FEOD, REL, and TESTZ.

The industry has all but ignored the SAA RPG Level 1 specification. As of this writing, IBM is preparing SAA RPG Level 2, which I have dubbed "RPGIV". Said to be to RPGIII what RPGIII was to RPGII. Just what the future holds for RPG is any body's guess, but with more programmers using the RPG language on IBM mid-size general purpose computers than any other, the RPG language is here to stay.

This text provides the person who has some programming experience with a high-level language, such as PL/I, COBOL, FORTRAN or any version of RPG, with a comprehensive explanation of the modern RPG language. The concepts and terminology are directed at persons with moderate exposure to data processing.

The RPG language explained in this text is that implemented by the IBM Corporation on the IBM AS/400 and System/38 mid-size computers. A subset of this language is also available on other IBM systems such as the IBM System/36 mini-computer and the IBM Personal Computer under OS/2. Under Personal Computer DOS (PC-DOS and MS-DOS), the RPG language is available from several third party software vendors. RPG is also available from Bull, Data General and Hewlett Packard for their mid-size computer systems.

This text discusses only RPGIII implementations of the RPG language. Chapter 3, however, details the RPG cycle. The RPG cycle is no longer considered a productive method for programming, and is included here for reference purposes. The modern RPG programmer avoids using the RPG cycle. In its place, structured programming constructs are used.

Remember, the current AS/400 RPG compile package is named the *IBM AS/400 RPG/400 compiler*. It contains three different RPG compilers: (1) System36 compatible RPGII; (2) System/38 compatible RPGIII; (3) and AS/400 RPGIII. There is no "RPG/400" language per se, only AS/400 RPGIII. Often I'm asked "does this book cover the RPG/400 language?" When what really should be asked is, "does this book cover AS/400 RPGIII?" And the answer to that question is yes!

Chapter 1

Introduction

RPG is a column-oriented language. This means that certain information, such as control codes and field names, must be placed into specific columns of the RPG program statements. Failure to fulfill this obligation will result in an error message.

For example, in a free-form procedure language such as COBOL, the value of one variable (or "field") could be copied to another by specifying the following statement:

```
MOVE  FIELDA  TO  FIELDB.
```

Most high-level languages use the MOVE instruction to *copy* data. There is no documentation as to how this tradition started, but it's taken for granted now. The COBOL statement above, copies each character from the memory location of the first field, "FIELDA," to the memory location of the second field, "FIELDB".

The same program statement written in PL/I would look like this:

```
FIELDA=FIELDB;
```

In RPG, the same program statement would look like this:

```
*... ... 1 ... ... 2 ... ... 3 ... ... 4 ... ... 5 ... ... 6
     C                      MOVE FIELDA    FIELDB
```

The MOVE instruction appears in columns 28 to 32 (column 32 is blank). These columns contain the program instruction or operation code, commonly referred to as *OpCode.*

The field that is being copied, called the source field, appears in columns 33 to 42. The field that will receive the copied data, called the target or Result field, appears in columns 43 to 48.

The letter "C" must appear in column 6 of the RPG "calculation" statement. Different letters are used to identify the various type of program statements, or specifications. There are specifications for file descriptions, input specification, data structures, array specification, calculations and output specifications. (See Figure 1-2 on page 7.)

Ordinarily, an editor is available that provides prompting for "fill in the blank" coding of the different RPG specifications. Consequently, the programmer need not be concerned with remembering column positions. However, a thorough knowledge of the various specification types would, obviously, greatly improve efficiency.

Another example of the column-oriented structure of RPG follows.

Suppose three account totals need to be accumulated. In a free format procedure language such as PL/I, the program statements would look like this:

```
IF ACCT = '01' THEN
            TOTAL1 = TOTAL1 + AMOUNT;
ELSE IF ACCT = '02' THEN
            TOTAL2 = TOTAL2 + AMOUNT;
ELSE IF ACCT = '03' THEN
            TOTAL3 = TOTAL3 + AMOUNT;
```

In RPG, the equivalent program would look like this:

```
*... ... 1 ... ... 2 ... ... 3 ... ... 4 ... ... 5 ... ... 6
     C           ACCT      IFEQ '01'
     C                     ADD  AMOUNT    TOTAL1
     C                     ELSE
     C           ACCT      IFEQ '02'
     C                     ADD  AMOUNT    TOTAL2
     C                     ELSE
     C           ACCT      IFEQ '03'
     C                     ADD  AMOUNT    TOTAL3
     C                     ENDIF
     C                     ENDIF
     C                     ENDIF
```

In this example, the IFEQ (if equal) operation is used to compare the field ACCT to three numbers then the value of the field AMOUNT is added to one of three total fields.

RPG requires an associated "ENDIF" operation for each IFEQ operation. This is because IFxx operations are treated as an "IF THEN DO" structure. This allows several statements to be conditioned and performed for each IFxx operation. As a by-product, the program's complexity is reduced. However, when IFxx statements are nested too deeply (usually more than 3 levels deep), the program's readability is reduced. Readability can be greatly improved, however, through the use of the CASE operation. The CASE operation is explained in Chapter 4.

Column-Oriented Program Specifications

As mentioned earlier, for ease in writing RPG programs, various pre-printed specification forms may be available. These forms allow an application program to be written, making certain the correct columns are used. The source statements that make up an application program are transferred to the computer for compilation. This is known as "desk coding" and was very popular before the onslaught of desk-top personal computers and their full-screen editors, as well as the full-screen editors available on most computers.

The supplier of the RPG compiler usually provides programming specification forms free of charge. However, it seems that no one uses these specifications anymore. Consequently, they are not readily available.

Since very little desk coding is done anymore, programmers usually write pseudo code (a free-format English-like logic-based language that is not compiled), then that pseudo code is translated, by hand, into a high-level language. Pseudo code strongly resembles PL/I. When translating pseudo code into a high-level language, such as RPG, a full-screen editor is used to provide a more productive environment with fewer typing errors. This usually results in fewer errors being placed into the source program.

Most full-screen editors provide simple prompts that allow program statements to be typed without regard for columns and form types. The editor correctly formats the program statement to match the RPG specification. There are RPG source editors that exist today that run on the AS/400, System/36 and PC (under both OS/2 and MS-Windows).

A programmer who has experienced writing RPG programs using 80-column cards on an IBM 029 or 129 keypunch machine will appreciate using an on-line full-screen editor that syntax-checks the statements as they are typed into the computer. A novice programmer normally makes a few mistakes anyway and will benefit from the assistance of the full-screen editor.

A Brief Language

One of the first things anyone should learn about RPG is that it is a brief language. Only a few statements are needed to read a record, change the data in that record, then update it. With other languages, such as COBOL, dozens of lines of code are required to perform this function.

Other languages, such as the C language, are often thought to be brief, but the truth is, RPG is the briefest of all higher-level languages.

For example, to read a file containing orders, then multiply the quantity ordered by the price and update the file with the new information, only four RPG statements are required. For example:

```
*... ... 1 ... ... 2 ... ... 3 ... ... 4 ... ... 5 ... ... 6
0010 FORDERS  UPE E                     DISK
0020 C            QTYORD    MULT PRICE     EXTEND
0030 OORDRCD  D  1    N1P
0040 O                          EXTEND
```

On line 10 of the above example, the file ORDERS is defined as the primary file (indicated with the letter "P" in column 16). The file is declared as an update file (indicated by the letter "U" in column 15). Each record that is read will be modified on line 20 by multiplying the quantity ordered by the price, giving the extended price. Each record is automatically updated (i.e., rewritten with the new value) on lines 30 and 40 by the RPG cycle. (Line 30 contains the name of the record format for the file ORDERS, line 40 contains the name of the fields that will be updated.)

As can be seen in this example, RPG is one of the fastest programming languages to write with. Once a programmer has learned the essentials, and you add in the benefit of prompting source code via an on-line editor, the RPG language can be the easiest language to use and the most productive for general-purpose business applications.

Specification Types

RPG programs consist of one or more specification types. The most common specifications include:

Specification Type	Identification	Common or Alternate Name
Control	"H" in column 6	Header spec or "H" spec.
File Description	"F" in column 6	File spec or "F" spec.
Array	"E" in column 6	Array spec or "E" spec.
Line Counter	"L" in column 6	"L" spec.
Input	"I" in column 6	Input specs or "I" specs.
Calculation	"C" in column 6	Calc specs or "C" specs.
Output	"O" in column 6	Output specs or "O" specs.

Although no specification is required, when more than one type is used, as is normally the case in an RPG program, they must appear in this sequence. A list of all RPG specifications and the correct sequence is featured in Figure 1-1 The definition of each specification is featured in Figure 1-2 beginning on page 7.

Header Specification
File Specifications
Extension Specifications
Line Counter Specifications
Input Specifications
Calculation Specifications
Output Specifications
**
File Translation Table
**
Alternate Collating Sequence
**
Compile-time Array Data

Figure 1-1: RPG Specification Sequence

Even the quasi-required "H" specification is not needed in the source program because the compiler uses a default "H" specification.

Column 6	Description
H	Header Specification. This specification is used very little, and if omitted, a default will be used. However, if it is specified, it must be the first statement in the program. The header specification was used in older versions of RPG to control various system functions. Nowadays, most system functions can be controlled directly by the program or outside the program through a system function. Column 15 of the Header specification is used to enable the DUMP OpCode. If column 15 contains the number 1, the DUMP OpCode will produce a formatted dump report. If column 15 contains a blank, the DUMP OpCode is ignored. Placing the number 1 into column 15 not only enables the DUMP OpCode, it also causes all internal compiler-generated variables to be listed when a formatted dump is generated. This additional function comes at the cost of slightly larger program size. This feature should be used in development versions of the program, then removed when the application program is placed into a production environment.
F	File Description Specification. This specification is used to define each input and output device file to the program. The type of device on which the file is or will be located, (e.g., DISK, PRINTER or WORKSTN,) and the type of access that is required (e.g., input, output, update, or delete) are among the items defined by the "F" specification.
E	Extension Specification. This specification defines all tables and arrays to the program, with the exception of multiple occurring data structures, which are defined on the input specification. There are three types of tables and arrays. (1) compile-time, (2) run-time, and (3) prerun-time. Extension specifications are also used to describe *limits files* and *record-address files*.

Figure 1-2: Specification Description and Sequence (1 of 2)

Column 6	Description
L	Line Counter Specification. This specification defines the number of lines per page and the overflow line number for printer files. Because system functions can perform this task more easily and can override the entries of the "L" specification, the usefulness of the "L" specification is lost. For the most part, when a program contains one or more "L" specifications, it has probably been converted from an older system.
I	Input Specification. This specification describes input file record formats, input field locations, data structure names and data structure subfield locations. "I" specifications are also used to describe "feedback" information fields, such as file I/O status, error indications, program status and error information fields.
C	Calculation Specification. This specification describes the calculations (computations) that are to be performed. The order and the conditions under which the calculations are to be performed are also specified here.
O	Output Specification. This specification describes the output file record formats, output field locations and printer file control (i.e., spacing and skipping).

Figure 1-2: Specification Description and Sequence (2 of 2)

For more information on each specification form, see Chapter 2 beginning on page 35.

RPG Components

Every RPG program is made up of components. Each component is defined through one or more RPG specification. A description of some of the components follows.

Files: The names of files that will be accessed by the RPG program.

Input: The information read and processed by the program.

Fields, Arrays, Data Structures, and Named Constants: The names of the variables—called "fields" in RPG—and constants, that will be used to store, compare and process information within the program.

Labels: The names assigned to BEGSR, ENDSR, KLIST, PLIST, EXCPT and TAG identifiers. They are used to label subroutines, access data files, pass parameters between programs, control output and act as the target of a GOTO, respectively.

Calculations: The computations (e.g., math, field manipulation, decisions and array searching) performed on the information within the program.

Output: The results of the program. The processed data is written to a printer, written or rewritten (updated) to a data file, or presented to a user through a workstation device.

RPG Limitations

Like all high-level languages, RPG has a set of restrictions. The three primary data types described below. Figure 1-3 on page 10 contains a list of RPG limits.

> ***Character*** (alphanumeric) fields may be any length when used as externally described data file input, however, the System/34, System/36, System/38 and AS/400 impose a restriction of 256 characters for all other character fields. When not used as input from an externally described file, character fields cannot exceed 256 characters, unless they are also the name of a data structure.
>
> ***Numeric*** fields may be up to 30 digits in length with up to 9 decimal positions. The System/34, System/36, System/38 and SAA versions of RPGII and RPGIII impose a restriction of 15 digits with 9 decimal positions.

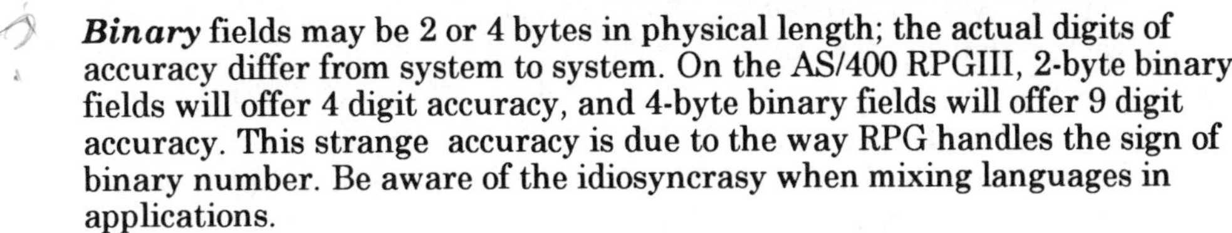

> ***Binary*** fields may be 2 or 4 bytes in physical length; the actual digits of accuracy differ from system to system. On the AS/400 RPGIII, 2-byte binary fields will offer 4 digit accuracy, and 4-byte binary fields will offer 9 digit accuracy. This strange accuracy is due to the way RPG handles the sign of binary number. Be aware of the idiosyncrasy when mixing languages in applications.

Feature	Limit
AN/OR (columns 7-8 of Calc Spec)	7 per operation
Array elements	9,999 per array/table
Arrays and tables	200 per program
Compile-time array or table length	80 positions
Data structure length	9,999 positions
Data structure occurrences	9,999 per data structure
Edit word length	Literal: 24 positions; Named Const: 115 positions
Field length	Char: 256 positions; Numeric: (30 9)
Field name	6 characters
Files	50 per program
File key length (program described)	99 positions
File key length (externally described)	2,000 positions
Hexadecimal literal values	256 positions[1] (512 hexadecimal characters)
Lines per page (program described)	Minimum of 2; maximum of 112
Lines per page (externally described)	Minimum of 1; maximum of 118
Matched fields (combined length)	256 positions
Named constants	Char: 256 positions; Numeric: (30 9)
Nested IF, DOxxx, SELECt groups	100 levels
Primary files	1 per program
Printer files	8 per program
Program status data structure	1 per program
Record address files (ADDROUT)	1 per program
Record format length	9,999 positions
Subroutines	254 per program

Figure 1-3: RPG Language Limitations

1 The actual limitation is based on the location where the hexadecimal literal is used. In Calculation specifications, for example, hexadecimal literal values are limited to the 10 columns available for Factor 1 and Factor 2. (Actually 9 positions: 3 for the X'' and 6 for the hexadecimal characters).

Naming Conventions

The RPG language has more restrictive naming conventions than most other languages. However, programmer verboseness is often more confusing than brevity. Figure 1-4 contains the criteria for each component of an RPG program. Unless otherwise noted, all names must be unique, for example, the name of a data structure cannot be the same as that of a KLIST (key list).

Name	Naming Convention
All Names	The first character must be A-Z, @, #, or $. Subsequent characters can be A-Z, @, #, $ or 0-9. If @, # or $ is used as the first character of a name, at least one other character must be specified. No embedded blanks, underscores or periods are allowed. If the name's length is less than the maximum allowed, it must be left justified and padded to the right with blanks, except for array names which can be suffixed with an array index. All names are global to all areas of the program.
File	A file name must be 1 to 8 characters in length. A file name cannot be the same as a (record) format name.
Format	A (record) format name must be 1 to 8 characters in length. Format names cannot be the same as that of a file name.
Field	A field name must be 1 to 6 characters in length. Field names can be the same as a data structure or data structure subfield name, but not both.
Structure	A structure name, called data structure in RPG, must be 1 to 6 characters in length. A data structure name can be the same as that of an input (data file) field name; it can be manipulated the same as any field and can be specified as a parameter.

Figure 1-4: Naming Conventions (1 of 2)

Name	Naming Convention
Array Index	An array index name must be 1 to 6 characters in length and follow the rules and restrictions for field names, with the following exceptions: An array index must be a numeric field that contains zero decimal places. The array index can be a field of type packed, zoned, or binary. Although binary is the most efficient, packed decimal is most commonly used. A structure name, called data structure, must be 1 to 6 characters in length. A data structure name can be the same as that of an input (data file) field name; it can be manipulated the same as any field and can be specified as a parameter.
Label	A label must be 1 to 6 characters in length. A label is the target of a branch or GOTO operation. A label is defined with either the TAG or ENDSR operation.
Literal	A literal value can be a quoted character string (using apostrophes as quotes), numeric value that can include a decimal and sign, or a hexadecimal literal. Literal values can be as long as permitted by the area in which they are being used. For example, in Factor 1 of the calculation specification, a character literal can be up to 8 positions plus the quotes.
Named Constant	The name of a named constant must be 1 to 6 characters in length. It cannot be the same as any other name. A named constant is used to assign a name to a literal value, that is used repeatedly throughout the program.

Figure 1-4: Naming Conventions (2 of 2)

Indicators

Indicators are logical variables or *switches* that are either on or off; that is, they contain a value of '1' or '0'. Indicators are used to control program logic, program termination, output, signal conditions and communicate with device files.

For example, when an indicator is used to condition the ADD operation, the indicator is tested before the ADD operation is performed. If the indicator test is true, the ADD operation is performed. If the indicator test is false, the ADD operation is bypassed and the program goes to the next statement.

```
SeqNoCLOn01n02n03Factor1+++OpCodFactor2+++ResultLenDXHiLoEq
     C            AREA      COMP '1401'                   38
     C      38              ADD  100       COST
     C            SALES     SUB  COST      PROFIT
```

Logically, this program would be illustrated as follows:

```
          Clear Indicator(38)
          If AREA = '1401' Set On Indicator(38)

Test1:    If Indicator(38) is OFF, Goto EndTest1;

          Add 100 to COST;

EndTest1:
          Substract COST from SALES giving PROFIT;
```

Prior to RPGIII, structured constructs did not exist in the RPG language; consequently, the use of indicators proliferated. The modern RPG programmer avoids the use of indicators except where it is impossible to ignore them. In place of indicators, structured operation codes are used to control program logic. Today, the use of indicators is all but eliminated.

Indicatorless RPG Code

The example on the previous page, if written with structured RPG operation codes would appear as follows:

```
SeqNoCLOn01n02n03Factor1+++OpCodFactor2+++ResultLenDXHiLoEq
     C           AREA      IFEQ '1401'
     C                     ADD  100       COST
     C                     ENDIF
     C           SALES     SUB  COST      PROFIT
```

In pseudo code, this program would be illustrated as follows:

```
If AREA = '1401' Then
   Add 100 to COST;
EndIf
Subtract COST from SALES giving PROFIT;
```

Notice how concise and readable the program becomes when structured operations are used properly. A side effect of the use of structured operations is that programs tend to run more efficiently than they do when indicators control the logic. This is a by-product of the AS/400 RPGIII compiler and not inherent in compilers in general.

Figure 1-5 on page 15 contains a list of indicator definitions.

Indicator	Description
1P	**First Page Indicator.** This indicator is set on as part of the "first time through" routine and is set off just prior to the first detail time routine. It is traditionally used to print a forms alignment character.
01 to 99	**General Purpose Indicators.** Used for various tasks.
H1 to H9	**Halt Indicators.** These indicators are used to signal a severe error. When a halt indicator is set on and program ends, and "abnormally termination" message is issued.
KA to KY	**Function Key Indicators.** These indicators correspond to 24 function keys on most keyboard. F1 - F14 are represented by KA - KN respectively, F15 - F24 are represented by KP - KY respectively.
L1 to L9	**Level-Break Indicators.** These indicators are used in conjunction with the RPG cycle. They are set on when their corresponding input field is changed when a record is read via the RPG cycle.
L0	**Level Zero Indicator.** This indicator is, by definition, always on and therefore never tested at run-time. It is normally used during "total-time" phase of the RPG cycle.
LR	**Last Record Indicator.** When this indicator is set on, and the end of program is cause by the RETRN operation or the end of cycle, the program will terminate, and its storage will be released. If LR is off and the program ends, the program's storage is saved, and the program is still considered to be active.
M1 to M9	**Match Field Identifiers.** These identifiers are not indicators. They are flags used to control the sequencing of primary/secondary file processing, and to signal a matching record condition (which will set on the MR indicator). Matching record processing is part of the RPG cycle.
MR	**Matching Record Indicator.** This indicator is set on when all the match fields of a secondary file match all the match fields of the primary file. This function is part of the RPG cycle.
OA to OG and OV	**Overflow Indicators.** These indicators are normally associated with a specific printer file. They are set on when printed output reaches the designated overflow line (normally line 60 for a 66 line form, or line 80 for an 88 line form).
RT	**Return Indicator.** When this indicator is set on, it indicates that when the end-of-calculation specification is reached (i.e., the end of this RPG cycle), or the RETRN operation code is performed, the program should return to its caller and remain active (provided that indicator LR is off).
U1 to U8	**External User Indicators**. These indicators or *switches* are used to communicate between the RPG program and the external operating environment. They can be used to condition the opening of a file or to control calculations.

Figure 1-5: Indicator Definitions

Indicator Usage

Indicators were used extensively in early RPG programming to control program logic, identify input, condition output, detect errors and signal certain "events". Due to support for structured programming constructs, extensive use of indicators is no longer an endorsed programming practice. There are, however, several hundred thousand application programs that were written prior to (and unfortunately, since) the time when structured constructs were added to RPG. These programs will have to be maintained. When maintaining these applications, try to convert as much of the application as possible to structure programming. This can ordinarily be accomplished without affecting the program's overall design.

Nowadays, a typical application program will utilize fewer than four indicators, unless communicating with a device file necessitates using more. My recommendation for each of the four indicators follows.

1. ***"Trash" Indicator***. Used for just about anything, for example, to condition the END statement of a DO..END loop construct, or to indicate the result of various operations such as LOKUP, COMP, SCAN, TESTB, MULT and DIV.

2. ***Error Indicator***. Used to signal error conditions such as record locking, device file time out or other errors.

3. ***File Status Indicator***. Used to signal various file conditions such as record not found, end of file or beginning of file. In some cases, such as with small programs, the indicator used as the file indicator can also be used as the error indicator.

4. ***Program Termination Indicator***. Normally, the Last Record indicator (LR) or ReTurn indicator (RT) is used as the program termination indicator. LR is used as a signal that the program should terminate upon reaching the end of calculation specifications, or when the return (RETRN) operation is performed. RT, when used independently, signals that the program should end but remain active in memory at the completion of the calculation specifications.

When communicating with a workstation, printer or telecommunications device file the number of indicators being used can increase. This is primarily due to limitations in the technology being used for device file definition. Also, each function key (i.e., special keys on every keyboard that normally causes an immediate reaction by the program) can result in the use of an additional indicator.

Workstation Function Key Response Indicators

Standard indicators can be established and used as response indicators for workstation function keys. This can help invite consistency between programs. Figure 1-6 contains a list of most function keys for IBM 5250-type workstations along with recommendations for resulting indicators assignments. The indicator assignments listed in Figure 1-6 are not hard and fast standards, but are guidelines. It is more important to implement a standard for function key response indicators than to use these specific suggestions.

Group 1	
DDS Keyword (Function Key)	**Suggested Resulting Indicator**
VLDCMDKEY	70
F1	71
F2	72
F3	73
F4	74
F5	75
F6	76
F7	77
F8	78
F9	79
F10	80
F11	81
F12	82

Group 2	
DDS Keyword (Function Key)	**Suggested Resulting Indicator**
F13	83
F14	84
F15	85
F16	86
F17	87
F18	88
F19	89
F20	90
F21	91
F22	92
F23	93
F24	94
ROLLUP	95
ROLLDOWN	96
HOME	97
HELP	98
PRINT	99

Figure 1-6: Standard Function Key Resulting Indicators

Function Key Attention Identification Byte

An alternative to assigning function key response indicators is being used more frequently. This method avoids assigning indicators and uses the *Function identification byte* (FIB) in position 369 of the workstation device information data structure. Figure 1-7 illustrates how the FIB can be interpreted.

Function Key	FIB ID Value	Bit Mask for BITON OpCode
F1	X'31'	'237'
F2	X'32'	'236'
F3	X'33'	'2367'
F4	X'34'	'235'
F5	X'35'	'2357'
F6	X'36'	'2356'
F7	X'37'	'23567'
F8	X'38'	'234'
F8	X'39'	'2347'
F10	X'3A'	'2346'
F11	X'3B'	'23467'
F12	X'3C'	'2345'
F13	X'B1'	'023457'
F14	X'B2'	'0236'
F15	X'B3'	'02367'
F16	X'B4'	'0235'
F17	X'B5'	'02357'
F18	X'B6'	'02356'
F19	X'B7'	'023567'
F20	X'B8'	'0234'
F21	X'B9'	'02347'
F22	X'BA'	'02346'
F23	X'BB'	'023467'
F24	X'BC'	'02345'
CLEAR	X'BD'	'023457'
ENTER	X'F1'	'01237'
HELP	X'F3'	'012367'
Roll Down	X'F4'	'01235'
Roll Up	X'F5'	'012357'
Print	X'F6'	'012356'
Rec'd Bksp	X'F8'	'01234'
Auto Enter	X'3F'	'234567'

Figure 1-7: FIB Identification Values (Position 369 of the WSDS)

Indicator Classification

Depending on the type of RPG specification used, indicators have various definitions. A list of the various indicator classifications and definitions follows.

Overflow Indicator: An indicator that is specified in columns 33 and 34 of the File Description specification for a printer device file is called an overflow indicator. An overflow indicator is set on automatically when the overflow line for a printer file is printed.

Record Identifying Indicator: An indicator that is specified in columns 19 and 20 of the input specifications is called a record identifying indicator. A record identifying indicator is automatically set on by RPG when a record is read that matches the record type for the record identifying indicator.

Control-Level and Level-Break Indicator: An indicator that is specified in columns 59 and 60 of the input specifications is called a level-break indicator. In addition, an indicator specified in columns 7 and 8 of the calculation specification is called a control-level indicator. A control-level or level-break indicator is set on automatically by the RPG cycle when the cycle reads a record and the value of the field that is associated with the level break indicator changes. If the RPG cycle is avoided—as is normally the case with new application programs—and the READ and CHAIN operation codes are used to access data files, level-break indicators are not changed and become less useful.

Field-Record Relation Indicator: An indicator specified in columns 63-64 of the input specifications is called a field-record relation indicator. A field-record relation indicator identifies an input field with a specific input record format. For example, when a file contains multiple record-identifying indicators, the fields within the record are identified (i.e., associated with the record format containing the record-identifying indicator) with a field-record relation indicator. RPG initializes the field only when its corresponding record-identifying indicator is on.

Field Indicator: An indicator specified in columns 65-66, 67-68 or 69-70 of the input specifications is called a field indicator. A field indicator is set on or off automatically by RPG when a record is read. A numeric field can be assigned up to three field indicators. The field indicator in columns 65-66 is set on if the numeric field to which it is assigned is greater than zero. The field indicator in columns 67-68 is set on if the numeric field to which it is assigned is less than zero. The field indicator in columns 69-70 is set on if the numeric field to which it is assigned is equal to zero, or if the character field to which it is assigned is equal to blanks.

Controlling and Conditioning Indicator: An indicator specified in columns 10 to 11, 13 to 14 or 16 to 17 of the calculation specifications is called a controlling or conditioning indicator. It controls the logic flow of the calculation specifications. For example, on indicator 01, the program might add an amount field to a total field; on another, it may zero-out the total field. In structured programming, conditioning indicators are not a viable programming tool and therefore should be avoided. The test condition for the indicator can be reversed by specifying an N prior to the indicator, in column 9, 12, and 15 respectively.

Resulting Indicator: An indicator specified in columns 54-55, 56-57 or 58-59 of the calculation specifications is called a resulting indicator. The purpose of a resulting indicator is to signal various conditions as the result of a calculation operation. For example, if the CHAIN OpCode is used to attempt to access a database record, and that CHAIN operation is unsuccessful, the resulting indicator specified in positions 54-55 will be set on, signaling a "record not found" condition. In RPGIII and later, resulting indicators are set off before the OpCode is performed. (See Chapter 3 for a description of each OpCode's resulting indicators.)

First Page Indicator: The single first page indicator, 1P, is set on at the beginning of the RPG program, then set off by the cycle just prior to the first detail cycle.

Last Record Indicator: The last record indicator, LR, is used in old-style RPG to signal that the RPG cycle had read the last record from a primary or secondary input file (which contained the "end of file" indication on the "F" specification). This indicates that the program will end after the current cycle is completed. In modern RPG, the LR indicator is used to cause program termination (i.e., to return to its calling program.) Normally, the LR indicator is explicitly set on in the program.

Matching Record Indicator: The matching record indicator, MR, is set on by the RPG cycle when all matching fields of a secondary file match all the matching fields in the primary file. Match fields are identified by specifying the match field identifiers M1 to M9 in columns 61 to 62 of the "I" specifications.

Indicator Variables: Indicator variables allow the RPG programmer to use indicators as data. Indicators are addressed using the convention *INxx where xx is the indicator being addressed. For example, *IN01 is indicator 01 and *INOF is the overflow indicator OF

Indicator Array: The indicator array is a 99-element array that allows the programmer to manipulate indicators 01 to 99 as an array or array element. The indicator array is addressed like any other array or array element, with the convention *IN,xx where xx is the indicator being addressed. For example, *IN,38 addresses indicator 38. If no array index is used, the reference is to the entire 99-element array. For example, *IN refers to the entire indicator array.

Indicators to Avoid

The modern RPG programmer avoids using level-break indicators L1-L9, matching record indicator MR, conditioning indicators (of any kind) and the default function key indicators KA-KY. In a perfect world, all indicators would be avoided.

Level-break Indicators (L1-L9) are of no use when the RPG cycle is avoided. There is a design requirement that would allow level-break indicators to be set on if the content of a field changes when a READ operation is performed on a file. The current version of RPG, however, does not support this construct.

Matching Record Indicator and match field identifiers (MR and M1-M9) also are of no use in cycle-less programming. There are system functions outside of high-level languages that perform the equivalent of matching record indicators, as well as more sophisticated functions. For example, the database management system data manipulation language (DML) most often talked about is *Structured Query Language* (SQL). It provides support for organizing data such that *Matching Record* processing is no longer necessary.

On certain computer systems, a DML other than SQL may be available. For example, on the IBM AS/400 a programmer has four options: (1) SQL; (2) a system function called Open Query File; (3) an interactive query utility; and (4) the database SORT utility. One or more of the secondary options are available on computer systems that do not support SQL.

Conditioning Indicators have been replaced with structured operations. Conditioning indicators tend to make programs more difficult to read and more difficult to maintain. Avoid using conditioning indicators. In their place, use the IFxx, CASxx, DO, DOWxx and DOUxx operation codes. This will result in programs that are easier to read and easier to maintain.

Default Function Key Indicators (KA-KY) are a carry over from the System/32/34/36 RPGII compiler. It is not feasible to use these indicators with the modern RPG language because Kn indicators bind a requested function to a function key rather than to the function itself. For example, KG means EXIT when the indicator is bound to the function, but EXIT means EXIT when the function requested equals the function to be performed.

Another reason to avoid using Kn indicators is that not all function keys support Kn indicators. The ROLLUP, ROLLDOWN, HELP, HOME and PRINT keys are a few examples. Using function key indicators to control the process of an application is not recommended in this text. Instead, programming by function is encouraged.

Constants and Literal Values

Constants are verbatim values placed in the program. It is often advantageous to specify a value as a literal or constant. For example, when comparing a balance due for an account, to zero.

The length of literal values can be as long as the specification column where they are being used permits. When a literal value is assigned a name, it is referred to as a *Named Constant* and is often shorted to the simpler *constant*. The length of a character constant cannot exceed 256 characters, however, and numeric constants cannot exceed 32 characters (30 digits, plus the decimal notation and sign), and hexadecimal literal values cannot exceed 515 positions (512 hexadecimal characters, plus the leading X and the two apostrophes).

There are three types of constants:

1. Figurative Constants
2. Named Constants
3. Literal Values

Figurative constants represent compiler-defined values. Named constants and literal values, however, can be one of the following:

1. Character literal value
2. Numeric literal value
3. Hexadecimal literal value

Character literal values must be enclosed in apostrophes, for example:

```
'This is a literal value'
```

Numeric literal values are not enclosed in apostrophes, and may contain decimal notation and a sign. If a sign is specified it must appear to the left of the numeric value, for example:

```
-3.1415962
```

Hexadecimal literal values begin with a capital letter X and must be enclosed in apostrophes. There must be an even number of hexadecimal characters enclosed in apostrophes. The hexadecimal characters can be A, B, C, D, E, F, or a, b c, d, e, f, or 0, 1, 2, 3, 4, 5, 6, 7, 8, 9. For example:

```
X'1Face2Face'
```

When the actual literal value includes an apostrophe, as in the literal `O'clock`, two consecutive apostrophes must be specified and the entire literal must be enclosed in single apostrophes. For example, the literal value `O'clock` would be specified as `'O''clock'`. By doubling the apostrophe `O''clock` and enclosing the literal value in apostrophes, the resulting value specified in the program should be `'O''clock'`.

Numeric constants referenced for their numeric value can contain a decimal notation character. In the United States, the period (.) is used; in other countries the comma (,) is used for decimal notation. Column 21 of the Header specification is used to specify the decimal notation character. The sign for numeric constants must precede the constant. For example -12 is a valid negative numeric constant.

The following examples illustrate several valid and invalid literal values.

Literal Value	Description
123456.78	Eight-digit numeral with two decimals
-55555	Five-digit negative numeral
'O''clock'	Seven position character constant O'clock
'1'	One position character constant 1
'Banyan'	Five position character constant Banyan
X'F100B1'	Hexadecimal literal

Example Valid Literal Values

Literal Value	Description
O'clock	Missing apostrophes. Should be 'O''clock'
100.00-	Invalid sign. Should be -100.00
Deforestation	Missing apostrophes. Should be 'Deforestation'.
32,767.00	Thousands notation is not allowed in numeric literal values.

Example Invalid Literal Values

Figurative Constants

Figurative Constants are special built-in names that have a predefined value associated with them. For example *BLANKS can be used in place of quoted blanks, and *ZEROS can be used in place of zeros. All figurative constant names begin with an asterisk (*).

Figurative constants can be specified in Factor 1 and Factor 2 of calculation specifications. The value that a figurative constant represents is implied, and will be equal to that of the complementary field. For example, if *ZEROS is used with a 7-digit numeric field, its implied value is 0000000. If *ZEROS is used with a 5-position character field, its implied value is '00000'. The implied value is unique to the program statement using the figurative constant. A description of each figurative constant is listed in Figure 1-8.

Figurative Value	Type of Value	Description
*ALL'...'	Figurative Constant	Repeating pattern. Automatically adjusts to the size of the corresponding field that it is being compared with or moved to. For example: *ALL'abcd' moves 'abcdabcd' etc. to the Result field for the length of the Result field.
*ALLX'...'	Figurative Constant	Repeating hexadecimal pattern. Automatically adjusts to the size of the corresponding field that it is being compared with or moved to. For example: *ALLX'00' moves binary zeros to the Result field for the length of the Result field.
*BLANK *BLANKS	Figurative Constant	Blanks. Automatically adjusts to the size of corresponding field that it is being compared with or moved to.
*HIVAL	Figurative Constant	Represents the highest possible value for the corresponding data type that it is being compared with or moved to.
*LOVAL	Figurative Constant	Represents the lowest possible value for the corresponding data type that it is being compared with or moved to.
*OFF	Figurative Constant	Logical off ('0'). Functionally similar to *ALL'0'. Typically, *OFF is used with the IFxx and MOVE operations to test or set the status of an indicator.
*ON	Figurative Constant	Logical on ('1'). Functionally similar to *ALL'1'. Typically, *ON is used with the IFxx and MOVE operations to test or set the status of an indicator.
*ZERO *ZEROS	Figurative Constant	Used to represent zeros. Can be used with all data types.

Figure 1-8: Figurative Constants

Named Constants

Named Constants are programmer-defined literal values with a unique name assigned to them. The name allows long literal values to be used in places like Factor 1 and Factor 2 of the calculation specification (where only 10 positions are available). The value represented by a named constant cannot be changed when the program is run—the value is *constant*. The name assigned to the constant is specified in positions 53 to 58 (field name) of the input specification. The field type (position 43) must contain the letter C, the field attribute for constants.

Named constants allow a name to be assigned to literal character values and numeric values. Character named constants up to 256 characters and numeric named constants of up to 32 positions (including a sign and decimal point) are supported. Named constants can be specified in Factor 1 and Factor 2 of calculation specifications, in the output field positions (32 to 37) and output constant positions (45 to 70) of output specifications. (See example on page 26.) An attribute of CONST is assigned to named constants.

The constant value is specified in positions 21 to 41. This provides up to 20 characters per line for a character constant and 21 positions for numeric constants. Character constants must be left-justified and enclosed in apostrophes. When a constant is continued onto subsequent lines, a minus sign (-) must appear to the right of the constant (see Figure 1-9.) When a character constant is continued onto subsequent lines, each new line must contain an apostrophe in column 21. The last line of a character constant must contain a closing apostrophe.

Named constants are not restricted to the length of the locations where the constant is used. For example, a named constant representing a 256-character literal can be used in Factor 1 or Factor 2 of the calculation specifications. See Figure 1-9.

```
SeqNoI..............Constant++++++++++++++C.........CONST+........
0001 I              'This is a short one'  C         MSG

0002 I              -9999999.99999         C         NEGNBR

0003 I              12345.67               C         SHORT#
0004 I              X'21'                  C         REVIMG

0005 I              12345678901234567 8-   C         LONG#
0006 I              901.123456789

0007 I              'This is a named -     C         LNGMSG
0008 I              'constant.  It -
0009 I              'contains quotes -
0000 I              'and it''s very, -
0011 I              'very long.'

SeqNoCSRn01n02n03Factor1+++OpCodFactor2+++ResultLenDXHILOEQ
0012 C                     Z-ADDNEGNBR    VALUE  155
0013 C                     Z-ADDLONG#     BIGNBR 309
0014 C                MSG  DSPLY
                            .
                            .
                            .
SeqNoOFilenameEFBASBSAn01n02n03Field+EBEnd+POutputconstant++++++++++
0101 OQPRINT  E  1
0102 O                            SHORT#J +  2 '$'
0103 O                                    +  2 LNGMSG
```

Figure 1-9: Named Constant Example

In the example featured in Figure 1-9, six named constants are defined. Line 1 defines the named constant MSG (message). Line 2 defines the named constant NEGNBR (negative number), which includes a negative sign and decimal notation. Line 3 defines a simple 7-digit numeral with 2 decimal places. Lines 4 defines a hexadecimal value named REVIMG (reverse image). Line 5 defines the named constant LONG# (long number), which contains decimal notation. And, lines 7 to 11 define the long named constant LNGMSG (long message).

In this example, the Z-ADD operation; is used to move the named constant NEGNBR to the field VALUE (line 12). The named constant LONG# is moved to the field BIGNBR (line 13). The named constant MSG is used as Factor 1 of the DSPLY (display) operation (line 14). The named constant SHORT# is used as output with numeric editing (line 102). And, the named constant LNGMSG is used as an output constant (line 103).

Reserved Names

Reserved field names are predefined fields that contain specific data such as the date. Some reserved fields begin with an asterisk and some do not. Reserved fields that begin with an asterisk cannot be modified, all other reserved fields can be changed by an RPG program. See Figure 1-10 for a description of each reserved field name.

Reserved Field	Description
PAGE	Page number. This 4-digit numeric field is used as a page counter. It is incremented each time it is output.
PAGE*n*	Additional page counters. These 4-digit numeric fields are used as additional page counters. PAGE*n*, where *n* can be 1 to 7, offers 7 additional page counters for a total of 8 available page counters.
UDATE[2]	Session date. This numeric field is initialized to the run-date when the program is started.
UDAY	Session day. This 2-digit numeric field contains the day of the month.
UMONTH	Session month. This 2-digit numeric field contains the month.
UYEAR	Session year. This 2-digit numeric field contains the year.

Figure 1-10: Reserved Field Names

2 Also see *DATE, *MONTH, *DAY and *YEAR reserved words on page 24.

Reserved Words

The number of reserved field names in RPG is less than that in most other languages. This is primarily due to the columnar nature of RPG. There are, however, many different classifications of reserved words, including the following:

1. Reserved Fields: Special field names containing a specific value. Typically, these values can be changed at runtime.
2. Figurative Constants: Special field names whose value is constant or is established at prerun-time. The content of these fields cannot be changed.
3. Control Values: Special values that control operation code function or Output specification results.
4. Routines: Special routines within the RPG cycle.

Figure 1-11 through Figure 1-14 contain the various reserved names and special names supported by RPGIII.

Special Name	Description
*DATE	Used to retrieve the current date. This date value represents the date with 8 positions. For example, if the date format is MDY, *DATE will contain *mmddccyy*, where *cc*=century; *yy*=year; *mm*=month; *dd*=day. Unlike UDATE, *DATE cannot be modified at program runtime.
*DAY	Used to retrieve the current day. This date value represents the day of the month in *dd* format, where *dd*=day of the month.
*MONTH	Used to retrieve the current month. This date value represents the month in *mm* format. Where *mm*=month.
*YEAR	Used to retrieve the current century and year. This date value represents the year in *ccyy* format, where *cc*=century; *yy*=year.

Figure 1-11: Special Reserved Names

Control Value	Operation Codes	Description
*ENTRY	PLIST	The *ENTRY parameter list identifies the parameter list used to pass parameters into and return parameters from the program.
*INZSR	BEGSR	The *INZSR subroutine, if specified in the program, is called by the RPG cycle before 1P output.
*LIKE	DEFN	The *LIKE DEFN operation code is used to define a new field, based on the attributes of another field. The types of fields that can be defined with *LIKE DEFN are character and packed decimal.
*LOCK	IN OUT	The *LOCK IN operation code is used to read a data area, then place an object-lock on that data area. The *LOCK OUT operation code is used to write a data area and retain the object-lock.
*LDA	DEFN	The *NAMVAR DEFN *LDA operation code is used to assign a variable to receive the contents of the local data area.
*PDA	DEFN	The *NAMVAR DEFN *PDA operation code is used to assign a variable to receive the program initialization parameters.
*NAMVAR	DEFN	The *NAMVAR DEFN operation code is used to declare the entry in Factor 2 as a data area. An optional field name can be specified in the Result field. If Factor 2 is not specified, the field name in the Result field is used as the data area name.
	IN	The IN *NAMVAR operation code is used to read all data areas defined in the program. If *LOCK IN *NAMVAR is specified, all data areas defined in the program are read and an object-lock is placed on each one.
	OUT	The OUT *NAMVAR operation is used to write (i.e., output) all data areas defined in the program. If *LOCK OUT *NAMVAR is specified, all data areas are written and any object-locks are retained.
*PSSR	BEGSR	The *PSSR subroutine, if specified in the program, is called by the RPG exception/error handling routine whenever an unmonitored error occurs.

Figure 1-12: Control Values Used in Calculation Specifications

Control Field	Description
*ALL	Output all fields. This control field causes all fields from an externally described file to be output. It is used on Output specifications controlled by an EXCPT operation code.
*PLACE	Asterisk-Place. This control field replicates Output specifications, within the specific output line up to the position of the *PLACE. The replicated output is positioned at the end position specified for the *PLACE. *PLACE is (or more accurately, "was") used in label printing programs to print 2-, 3-, and 4-up labels. It was created primarily to automate printed output from 80-column card-based programs. It is virtually worthless today considering the on-line source editors available.

Figure 1-13: Control Fields Used in Output Specifications

Routine	Description
*CANCL	Cancel the program.
*DETC	Return to detail-time calculations.
*DETL	Return to detail-time lines (i.e., detail output).
*GETIN	Return to the next "get in" cycle.
*OFL	Return to the overflow output-time portion of the cycle.
*TOTC	Return to total-time calculations.
*TOTL	Return to total-time lines (i.e., total-time output).
blanks	If the *PSSR or INFSR subroutines were called by the EXSR or CASxx operation, control returns to the statement following the EXSR or CASxx operation. If the RPG exception/error handler called the subroutine, the following applies: • If the error status code is 1121 to 1126 control returns to the operation where the error occurred. • Any other error status code causes an exception to be issued and the requester is notified (i.e., a message is sent to the user or system operator.)

Figure 1-14: *PSSR and INFSR Subroutine Return Points

Directives

Directives are controls that are placed into a source program. Two types of directives exist: (1) Compiler directives; and (2) Preprocessor directives. All directives begin in column 7 of the RPG statement.

Compiler directives control various functions of the compile process, such as, page printing and inclusion of external source code.

Preprocessor directives are processed by preprocessors. A preprocessor is a program that reads the RPG source code and performs some work, possibly altering the RPG source code, before calling the RPG compiler. The RPG compiler and SQL preprocessor directives provide functions to alter the RPG program listing and to include the SAA SQL database manager.

The program listed in Figure 1-15 illustrates the use of several RPG compiler directives as well as SQL preprocessor directives.

```
 /TITLE Example RPG Source with Directives
FQPRINT  O   F     132     OV      PRINTER
F/SPACE
I                '0(   )&   -    '     C          EDTPHN
IHSTVAR       DS
I                                         01  050CUSTNO
I                                         06  35 CSTNAM
I                                         36  450PHNNBR
 /COPY QINCSRC,STDDCL
C                      Z-ADD1207      KEYVAR  50
C/SQL EXEC
C+          SELECT custnbr,custnam,phone FROM CUSTMAST
C+            WHERE custnbr = :KEYVAR
C+            INTO :HSTVAR
C/END-EXEC
C                      TIME           TIME    60
C                      Z-ADD*DATE     DATE    90
C                      EXCPT
C                      MOVE *ON       *INLR
C/EJECT
OQPRINT  E  1
O                                 +  0 'Customer:'
O                         CUSTNOZ +  2
OQPRINT  E  1
O                                 +  0 'Name:'
O                         CSTNAM  +  2
OQPRINT  E  1
O                                 +  0 'Phone:'
O                         PHONE   +  2 EDTPHN
OQPRINT  E  1
O                                 +  0 'Date/Time:'
O                         DATE  Y +  2
O                         TIME    +  2 '0  :  :  '
```

Figure 1-15: Example Use of RPG Compiler Directives

With the exception of the /COPY compiler directive, most compiler directives offer little additional function. The /COPY compiler directive allows external source members to be included at compile-time. Although, /COPY directives cannot be nested, they do provide substantial support for program source modularity. Figure 1-16 contains a summary of the compiler and preprocessor directives.

Directive	Description
/COPY [[*library/*]*file*,]*member*	Causes the compiler to include source code contained in a separate source member. Any RPG source code can be included using the /COPY directive.
/COPY [*file*[.*library*],]*member*	Causes the compiler to include source code contained in a separate source member. Any RPG source code can be included using the /COPY directive. This syntax is valid for RPG on the System/38 and in the System/38 environment on the AS/400.
/EJECT	Causes the compiler to skip to the top of the next page when the compiled program is printed.
/TITLE *text*	Causes the compiler to print the *text* on the top of each page of the printed compiler list. Subsequent /TITLE directives override previous /TITLE.
/SPACE [*n*]	Causes the compiler to print *n* blank lines. If no *n* value is specified, 1 is assumed.
/EXEC SQL [*sql statement*]	This SQL preprocessor directive starts an SQL statement. The SQL statement can begin on this line or on a subsequent line.
+ *continued-sql statement*	This SQL preprocessor directive indicates the continuation of the SQL statement that began with /EXEC SQL.
/END-EXEC	This SQL preprocessor directive ends the SQL statement that followed the previous /EXEC SQL.

Figure 1-16: Preprocessor/Compiler Directives

TIP1: Specify the /EJECT directive just before the first subroutine in the program; this provides a simple way to isolate subroutines from the rest of the program.

TIP2: Use /COPY to include standard routines, data structures, and named constants. For example, a source member named STDDCL can be used to store frequently used constants, while another named PSDS can be used to store the program status data structure.

Chapter 2

Specification Formats

RPG is a rigid language—it is not a free-form language like PL/I, COBOL or C. With RPG, each area of a program, (e.g., file descriptions, data structures, computations, output etc.) requires a different format for the program statement. These formats are known as RPG specification forms.

When writing RPG programs, a general knowledge of each type of specification form is necessary. A specification form is used to guide the programmer in writing specific areas of the RPG program. Most other languages, such as PL/I, COBOL, and C require only one, free-form specification; RPG requires several. This chapter describes each RPG specification form type.

Specification Types

Chapter 1 introduced the various RPG specification forms. A summary of the RPGIII specifications follows.

Specification Type	Identification	Common, or Alternate Name
Control	"H" in column 6	Header spec or "H" spec.
File Description	"F" in column 6	File spec or "F" spec.
Array	"E" in column 6	Array spec or "E" spec.
Line Counter	"L" in column 6	"L" spec.
Input	"I" in column 6	Input specs or "I" specs.
Calculation	"C" in column 6	Calc specs or "C" specs.
Output	"O" in column 6	Output specs or "O" specs.

RPG source programs can contain any number of specifications. When more than one specification form is used, they must appear in the order illustrated in Figure 2-17.

Header Specification
File Specifications
Extension Specifications
Line Counter Specifications
Input Specifications
Calculation Specifications
Output Specifications
**
File Translation Table
**
Alternate Collating Sequence
**
Compile-time Array Data

Figure 2-17: RPG Specification Sequence

If the specifications do not appear in this order, the RPG compiler will generate a severe error and the program will not be created.

As illustrated in Figure 2-17, after the final specification, additional information about tables, array, collating sequencing, and file translation can be included in the program.

Double asterisks in columns 1 and 2, indicate the beginning of a File translation table, Alternate collating sequence table, or what's called "user table or array" data. Nearly 99% of all RPG program that use this area of the program, include only user table or array data. The area is used to store the compile-time data for an array or table defined on the E specifications.

Header (Control) Specification

The Control specification, more commonly referred to as the Header specification, is used to control various features and options of the program. For example, column 19 can be used to specify the format of the UDATE (user date) field as year-month-day, month-day-year or day-month-year. One header specification is allowed per program.

Figure 2-18 illustrates the header specification. The header specification form is normally combined with the File Description specification form.

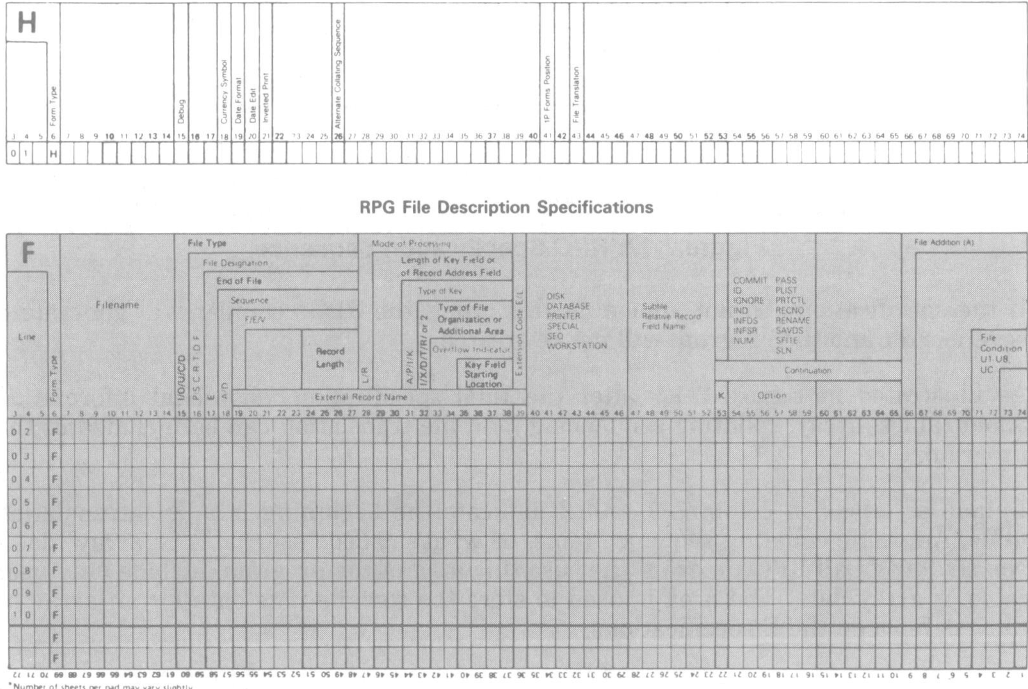

Figure 2-18: Header (Control) Specification Form

Header (Control) Specification Summary

Column	Title	Value	Description
6	Form Type	H	Identifies the statement as a Header (control) specification.
7-14			Not used with RPGIII and later.
15	Debug	blank	The DEBUG and DUMP operation codes are ignored.
		1	The DEBUG and DUMP operation codes are functional.
16-17			Not used by RPGIII.
18	Currency symbol	blank	The default currency symbol ($) is used.
		any symbol	The specified symbol is used as the currency symbol. This entry cannot be any of the following symbols: (0) zero; (*) asterisk; (,) comma; (.) period; (&) ampersand; (–) minus; and the letters C and R.
19	Date format	Blank	The date format is derived from column 21 of the Header specification. If column 21 is blank, the date format is *mmddyy* for UDATE and mmddccyy for *DATE. If column 21 contains the letters D, I, or J the date format is *ddmmyy* for UDATE and *ddmmccyy* for *DATE.
		M	The date format is month-day-year (MDY) for UDATE, and month-day-century-year (MDCY) for *DATE.
		D	The date format is day-month-year (DMY) for UDATE, and day-month-century-year (DMCY) for *DATE.
		Y	The date format is year-month-day (CYMD) for UDATE, and century-year-month-day (CYMD) for *DATE.
20	Date separator	Blank	The separator is derived from column 21 of the Header specification.
		&	Blanks are used as the separator for the Y edit code.
		any symbol	The symbol specified is used as the date separator for the Y edit code.

Header (Control) Specification Summary (continued)

Column	Title	Value	Description
21	Decimal notation	blank	Numeric fields use the period for decimal notation and the comma for thousands notation. If column 19 of the Header specification is blank, the date format is *mmddyy* for UDATE and *mmddccyy* for *DATE. If column 20 is blank, the slash (/) is used as the date separator for the Y edit code.
		I	Causes the comma (,) to be used as the decimal position notation and the period (.) to be used to separate units of a thousand (European format). If position 20 contains a blank, then the period is used for the date edit code.
		J	Causes the comma (,) to be used as the decimal position notation and the period (.) to be used to separate units of a thousand (European format). If position 20 contains a blank, then the period is used for the date edit code. In addition, when an edit code causes zero balances to print, a zero will be printed to the left of the leftmost comma (e.g., 0100 yields 0,100).
		D	Causes the period (.) to be used as the decimal position notation and the comma (,) to be used to separate units of a thousand (U.S.A format). The date edit code uses the slash (/) as the separator.
22-25			Not used by RPGIII.
26	Collating sequence	blank	Normal collating sequence is used.
		S	An alternate collating sequence is used. The alternate collating sequence must be specified before any compile-time tables and arrays, and after any file translation records.
27-39			Not used by RPGIII.
40	Sign Handling	blank	This entry is not used by RPGIII, but a default value of "Force Sign" is implied. No other value is available for this entry.

Header (control) Specification Summary (continued)

Column	Title	Value	Description
41	1P Forms Alignment	blank	No forms alignment is generated by RPG. However, the operating system can override this value and generate its own forms alignment routine.
		1	The forms alignment routine is generated and the system operator is prompted to verify printed output forms alignment. The output lines that are printed for this alignment are those conditioned by the 1P indicator.
42			Not used by RPGIII.
43	File Translation	blank	No file translation is performed.
		F	File translation is performed. File translation uses the file translation tables specified and the end of the program, but prior to any alternate collating sequence entries, or tables and arrays.
44-56			Not used by RPGIII.
57	Transparency Check	blank	Double-byte and multi-byte character sets are not checked for transparency.
		1	Double-byte character sets are checked for transparency.
58-74			Not used by RPGIII.
75-80	Program name	blanks	This entry is, by convention, not used in RPGIII.

File Description Specification

The File Description specification is used to declare each file used by the program (except for SQL tables and views which are accessed through SQL statements). Each file must have its own File Description specification. Optionally, each file may have one or more File Continuation specification, which is also specified with a File Description specification.

While most applications written today use externally described files, this section also highlights program described file descriptions.

Figure 2-19 illustrates the File Description specification. The File Description specification form is normally combined with the header specification form.

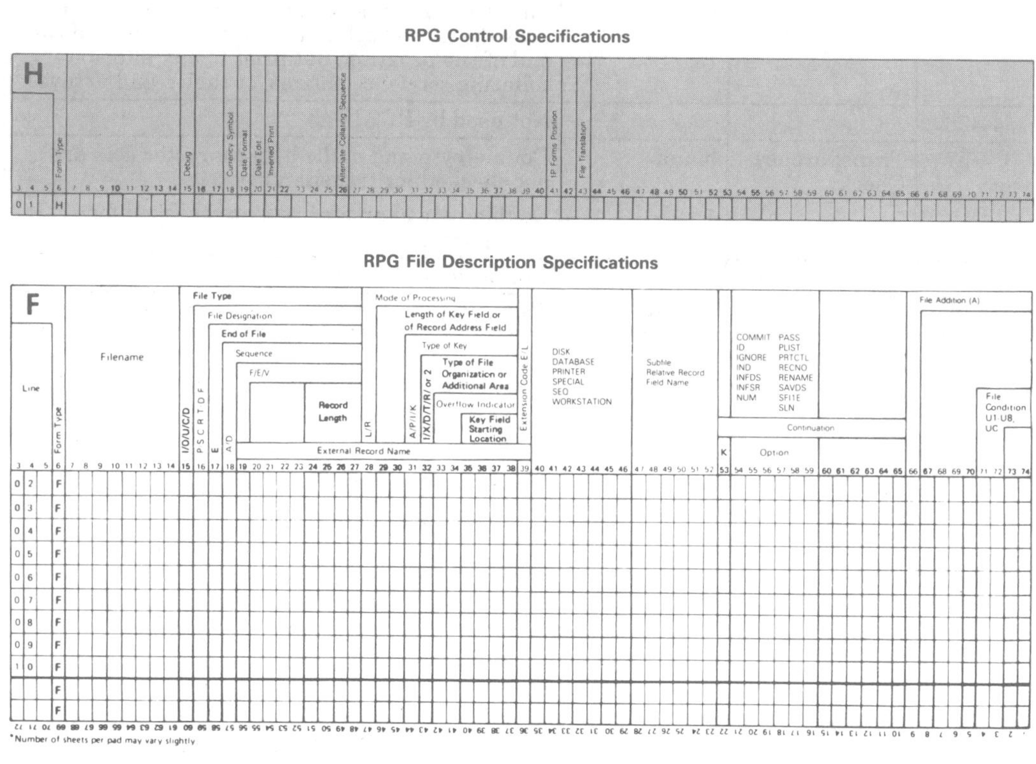

Figure 2-19: File Description Specification Form

File Description Specification Summary

Column	Title	Values	Description
6	Form Type	F	Identifies the statement as a File Description specification.
7 - 14	File Name	blanks	The statement is a file continuation.
		file name	The name of a file to be used by this program.
15	File Type	I	The file is opened for input processing.
		O	The file is opened for output processing.
		U	The file is opened for update (read, change, delete) processing.
		C	The file is opened for combined (read, write) processing. Valid for WORKSTN files only.
16	File Designation	blank	The file is an output file. Blank is the only valid entry for output files.
		P	The file is the *Primary* file. There can be only one primary file in an RPG program.
		S	The file is a *Secondary* file. There can be 0, 1, or more than 1 secondary file in an RPG program.
		R	The file is a record address (ADDROUT) file.
		T	The file is a prerun-time table. The file will be "read into" the array specified on the Extension specifications when the program is called.
		F	The file is a full procedural file. That is, the file is processed only through procedural RPG file operation codes, such as READ and WRITE in the Calculation specifications. The RPG cycle does nothing more than automatically open and close the file.
17	End of File	blank	If all files contain a blank entry in this column, then all records in all files will be processed before the RPG cycle will set on the LR indicator.
		E	When all the records from this file have been processed, the RPG cycle will set on the LR indicator. If more than one file uses this option, all records from each file containing the end-of-file indication will be processed before the RPG cycle sets on the LR indicator. The end-of-file indication applies only to files specified as Primary or Secondary. It does not apply to Full procedural files.

File Description Specification Summary (continued)

Column	Title	Values	Description
18	Sequence	blank or A	The sequence for matching record fields is ascending order.
		D	The sequence for matching record fields is descending order.
19	Format	F	The file is program described. Input specifications are used to define the record format for this file.
		E	The file is externally described. The record format for the file is imported by the RPG compiler.
20 - 23	Blocking	blank	File blocking is controlled by the operating system—outside the RPG program.
		1 to 9999	File blocking size (in bytes). Note: This entry is ignored by RPGIII.
24 - 27	Record Length	blank	Valid when the file is an externally described file. The record length will be imported by the compiler.
		1 to 999	The length used by RPG for the file. The actual record length may be different from this value; RPG will pad or truncate the record as required.
28	Mode of Processing	blank	The mode of processing is controlled by the entries in the File Designation and the Record Address Type.
		L	The mode of processing is sequential within limits; meaning the file is an ADDROUT file.
29 - 30	Length of Key Fields	blanks	The key is established outside the RPG program; or the file is not keyed.
		1 to 99	The length of the key for a program described file.
31	Record Address Type	blank	The file processing (access) is sequential or by relative record number.
		A	The file is keyed and the key fields are character (for program described files only).
		P	The file is keyed and the key fields are packed decimal data (for program described files only).
		K	The externally described file is keyed.

File Description Specification Summary (continued)

Column	Title	Values	Description
32	File Organization	blank	The file is not keyed (for program described files). For externally described files, this entry must be blank.
		I	The program described file is "indexed" that is, it is a keyed file.
		T	The program described file is a record address file (ADDROUT) file containing relative record numbers to be used for sequencing file input.
33 - 34	Overflow Indicator	OA to OG, or OF	For program described PRINTER device files only; the indicator is set on when the line specified as the file's overflow line is printed.
		01 to 99	For externally described PRINTER device files only; the indicator is set on when the line specified as the file's overflow line is printed.
		blank	For PRINTER devices files, overflow processing control is not given to the program. For all other device file types these positions must be blank.
35 - 38	Key Field Location	blank	On the System/38 and AS/400 this entry is always ignored, regardless of its content. On other systems it is required for keyed files.
		1 to 9999	The starting position, within the file's record, of the key fields. (This entry is ignored on the AS/400 and System/38.)
39	Extension	blank	No Extension specification is used to further define the file.
		E	The file is a prerun-time table or array, or it is an ADDROUT file. The file is described further by an Extension specification.
		L	The PRINTER device file is further described by a Line Counter specification. The overflow line, and number of lines per page may be specified.

File Description Specification Summary (continued)

Column	Title	Values	Description
40 - 46	Device Type	DISK	The file is a database (disk) file.
		PRINTER	The file is a printer file, and can be written to.
		WORKSTN	The file is an interactive workstation.
		SEQ	The file is a sequential files that can be processed with the READ, WRITE, OPEN and CLOSE operations (depending on the File Type specified for the file).
		SPECIAL	The file is processed via a special device "driver". A device driver is a program (such as another RPG program) that handles the input and output requests from this program. The named of the device driver program is specified in columns 54 o 59.
47 - 52			Not used by RPGIII.
53	File Continuation	blank	Normal File Description specification; not a File Continuation specification.
		K	A File Continuation keyword is included on this File Description specification. For more information, see File Continuation Keyword summary beginning on page 50.
54 - 59	Exit Program	blank	No File Continuation keyword and no exit program are specified on this statement.
		program name	The name of the program to be call to perform file operations. Valid for SPECIAL device files only. A program name can only be specified when the File Continuation ID (column 53) is blank.
		keyword	File Continuation keyword. For more information on the valid keywords, see File Continuation Keyword Summary beginning on page 50. The entry can be any File Continuation keyword except the following: SFILE, RENAME, PLIST and IGNORE.
60 - 65	Keyword Parameter	blanks	These columns must be blank unless a File Continuation keyword is specified.
		any value	If the File Continuation ID is specified (K in column 53), then these positions contain the parameter for the File Continuation keyword specified in columns 54 to 59.

File Description Specification Summary (continued)

Column	Title	Values	Description
66	Allow Add to File	blanks	For input and update files (I or U in column 15) no records can be added (i.e., written) to the file. The compiler will generate an error if WRITE or EXPCT with ADD operations are used.
		A	For input and update files (I or U in column 15) the WRITE and EXCPT with ADD operations are allowed. This allows new records to be added to the file.
			For output files, the entry in this column is ignored.
67 - 70			Not used by RPGIII.
71 - 72	File Open Control	blank	The RPG cycle is used to automatically open and close the file.
		UC	The RPG cycle does not open the file. The file must be opened by an OPEN operation, or have been previously opened outside the RPG program. The file must be a full procedural file (i.e., an F must appear in column 16) to take advantage of this function.
		U1 to U8	The file is opened by the RPG cycle only when the UPSI switch indicator is on. Otherwise the file is not opened.

File Continuation Specification

The File Continuation specification (continuation line) is used to define additional information about the file being declared. More than one continuation specification can be specified for each file. Continuation lines must immediately follow the File Description specification for the file or be included on the same specification line.

A Continuation line is specified with the letter K in column 53 of the File Description specification. Figure 2-20 illustrates the RPG file continuation specification form.

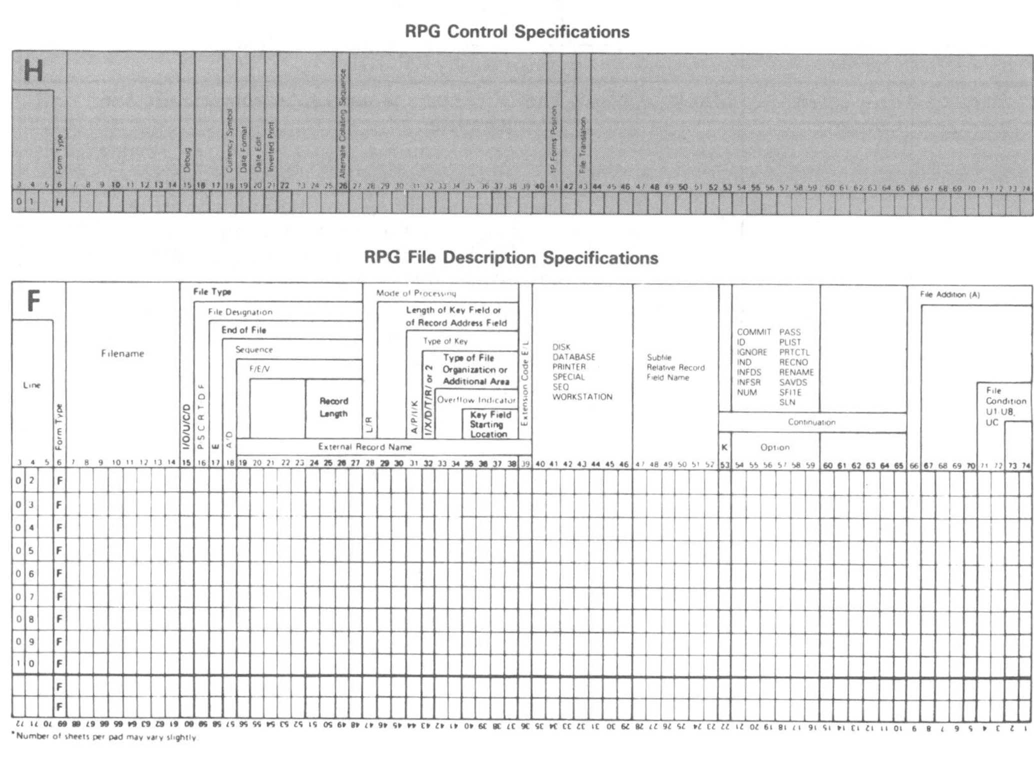

Figure 2-20: File Continuation Specification Form

File Continuation Specification Summary

Column	Title	Values	Description
6 - 7	Form Type	Fƀ	The identifies the statement as a File Continuation specification.
7 - 18		blank	These columns must be blank for a File Continuation specification.
19 - 28	External Format Name	format name	Name of an externally described file record format. The format name can be used by the RENAME or IGNORE keywords.
29 - 46			These columns must be blank for a File Continuation specification.
47 - 52	Subfile Record Number	field name	The name of the field that will be used as the subfile relative record number. The value in the field will be updated by RPG when the subfile is read and must be set by the program when the subfile is written to or updated. The keyword SFILE must be specified in columns 54-59.
53	Continuation ID	K	Redundantly identifies the statement as a File Continuation keyword.
54 - 59	Keyword Name	keyword	The name of a File Continuation keyword. For a list of valid keywords, see File Continuation Summary beginning on page 50.
60 - 65	Keyword Parameter	parameter value	The entry in these columns is used by the keyword specified in columns 54 to 59. For a list of valid keyword parameters, see File Continuation Summary beginning on page 50.
60 - 67	Keyword Parameter (Alternate)	parameter value	These columns are similar to columns 60 to 65, except 2 additional columns are provided. This allows full names (e.g., format names) to be specified.

File Continuation Keyword Summary

Columns		
54 to 59	**60 to 65**	**Description**
COMIT	blank	The file is under commitment control. COMIT and ROLBK operations can be used to control changes made to the file.
ID	field name	A ten-position character field that contains the device name for ACQ, NEXT and FORCE operations.
IND	01 to 99	Valid for WORKSTN device files only. Indicates the number of indicators from 01 to 99 that will be saved for each attached device input/output operation. The IND keyword was used in MRT (multiple requesting terminal) programs, which were written for the SSP (System/36) operating system.
INFDS	Data Structure Name	The name of the file information data structure. The INFDS contains information about the file and the input/output operations associated with it.
INFSR	Subroutine Name	The name of the file exception/error handling subroutine that will be called automatically by RPG when an unmonitored exception/error occurs. If *PSSR is specified, the default RPG exception/error handling routine is called. If a user written *PSSR subroutine is present in the program, then the subroutine will be called.
NUM	01 to 9999	Valid for WORKSTN device files only. Specify the maximum number of devices that can be acquired by this program. (See the ACQ operation in Chapter 4 on page 145 for information on acquiring devices.) For workstation time-out via the INVITE workstation keyword, a value of at least 01 must be specified.
PASS	*NOIND	Valid for WORKSTN device files only. RPG avoids passing indicators to the workstation device file. This is primarily used when converting programs from the IBM System/34 and System/36 to the IBM System/38 or IBM AS/400.

File Continuation Keyword Summary (continued)

Columns		
54 to 59	**60 to 65**	**Description**
PLIST	parameter list name	The name of a named parameter list (named PLIST) to be used by the SPECIAL device file I/O routine. The named PLIST is passed (in addition to the parameter list that follows) to the program specified as the SPECIAL device file I/O routine. The parameters from the named PLIST are added to the following parameter list: OPCODE CHAR(1) /* Operation */ O = Open the file C = Close the file R = Read from the file W = Write to the file D = Delete the current record U = Update the current record RTNCOD CHAR(1) /* Return code */ 0 = Normal completion 1 = End or Beginning of file 2 = Exception/error occurred ERRCOD ZONED(5,0) /* Error code */ Returned to the *RECORD subfield of the INFDS data structure for the file. BUFFER CHAR(*) /* Data from or for the record */ The data for the record is placed into this parameter and returned to the input record format of the SPECIAL device file. The actual length of this parameter, as passed to the program, is equal to the file length specified for the SPECIAL device file. This parameter list is automatically generated by RPG in the program that contains the SPECIAL device file. In the program being used as the SPECIAL device file's I/O routine, however, this parameter list must be specified.

File Continuation Keyword Summary (continued)

<table>
<tr><th colspan="2">Columns</th><th></th></tr>
<tr><th>54 to 59</th><th>60 to 65</th><th>Description</th></tr>
<tr><td>PRTCTL</td><td>Data Structure Name</td><td>Valid for PRINTER device files only. The data structure is used to control the skipping and spacing of printed output. The data structure must be at least nine positions in length. It is normally comprised of the following five fields.
<table>
<tr><th>Name</th><th>Type</th><th>Description</th><th>Values</th></tr>
<tr><td>SPACEB</td><td>Char(1)</td><td>Spacing before</td><td>ƀ, 0, 1, 2, 3</td></tr>
<tr><td>SPACEA</td><td>Char(1)</td><td>Spacing after</td><td>ƀ, 0, 1, 2, 3</td></tr>
<tr><td>SKIPB</td><td>Char(2)</td><td>Skipping before</td><td>ƀ, 01 to 99
A0 to A9
B0 to B2</td></tr>
<tr><td>SKIPA</td><td>Char(2)</td><td>Skipping after</td><td>ƀ, 01 to 99
A0 to A9
B0 to B2</td></tr>
<tr><td>CURLIN</td><td>Zoned(3)</td><td>Current Line</td><td>n/a</td></tr>
</table>
The PRTCTL data structure is typically formatted as follows:
<pre>
IDSName.......DS...   TFromTo++DField+
IPRTCTL   DS
I   1   1 SPACEB
I   2   2 SPACEA
I   3   4 SKIPB
I   5   6 SKIPA
I   7   90CURLIN
</pre></td></tr>
<tr><td>RECNO</td><td>field name</td><td>Valid for DISK device files only. The RECNO field is used when writing to a direct file. The relative record number of the record to be written must be placed into the RECNO field.

The relative record number of the record just accessed by an OPEN, READ and SETLL operation will be placed into this field. If the file uses blocked input/output (normally specified outside of the RPG program), the value in this field will be invalid most of the time.</td></tr>
<tr><td>SAVDS</td><td>Data Structure Name</td><td>The name of a data structure to be saved and restored for each device input/output operation. This applies to programs that "attach" themselves to multiple workstation devices.</td></tr>
<tr><td>SLN</td><td>field name</td><td>A numeric field that is used as the variable starting line number for a WORKSTN device file output operation. The DDS for the file must contain the SLNO(*VAR) keyword. Also, if the field name is not defined, RPG defines it as a 2-position numeric field with 0 decimal positions.</td></tr>
</table>

File Continuation Keyword Summary (continued)

Columns		
54 to 59	**60 to 67**	**Description**
SFILE	subfile record format	Valid for external WORKSTN device files only. Specify the name of the subfile record format. A subfile relative record number field must also be specified in columns 47-52. Each subfile must have its own file continuation line. The subfile record format name must appear in columns 60 to 67.
IGNORE	format name	Name of the record format that will be ignored by the program. Formats that are ignored are not imported into the program by the compiler. This keyword is valid only for externally described files, and is typically used only with WORKSTN device files.
RENAME	new format name	Specify the new name for an externally described file record format. The original format name must appear in columns 19 to 28 of this statement.

Extension and Line Counter Specification

The Extension specification is used to declare record address files, tables and arrays to the program. A maximum of 200 tables and arrays can be defined in a single program.

Figure 2-21 illustrates the RPG extension specification form. The extension specification form is normally combined with the line counter specification form.

RPG EXTENSION AND LINE COUNTER SPECIFICATIONS

Extension Specifications

E Line (3-5)	Form Type (6)	(7-8)	Record Sequence of the Chaining File / Number of the Chaining Field (9-10)	From Filename (11-18)	To Filename (19-26)	Table or Array Name (27-32)	Number of Entries Per Record (33-35)	Number of Entries Per Table or Array (36-39)	Length of Entry (40-42)	P/B/L/R (43)	Decimal Positions (44)	Sequence (A/D) (45)	Table or Array Name (Alternating Format) (46-51)	Length of Entry (52-54)	P/B/L/R (55)	Decimal Positions (56)	Sequence (A/D) (57)	Comments (58-74)
0 1	E																	
0 2	E																	
0 3	E																	
0 4	E																	
0 5	E																	
0 6	E																	
0 7	E																	
0 8	E																	
	E																	
	E																	

Line Counter Specifications

L Line (3-5)	Form Type (6)	Filename (7-14)	1 Line Number (15-17)	1 FL or Channel Number (18-19)	2 Line Number (20-22)	2 OL or Channel Number (23-24)	3 Line Number (25-27)	3 Channel Number (28-29)	4 Line Number (30-32)	4 Channel Number (33-34)	5 Line Number (35-37)	5 Channel Number (38-39)	6 Line Number (40-42)	6 Channel Number (43-44)	7 Line Number (45-47)	7 Channel Number (48-49)	8 Line Number (50-52)	8 Channel Number (53-54)	9 Line Number (55-57)	9 Channel Number (58-59)	10 Line Number (60-62)	10 Channel Number (63-64)	11 Line Number (65-67)	11 Channel Number (68-69)	12 Line Number (70-72)	12 Channel Number (73-74)
1 1	L																									
1 2	L																									
	L																									

*Number of sheets per pad may vary slightly.

Figure 2-21: Extension (Array) Specification Form

Extension Specification Summary

Column	Title	Values	Description
6	Form Type	E	Identifies this statement as an Extension specification.
7 - 10			Not used by RPGIII.
11 - 18	From File	blank	No input database file is used by this Extension specification.
		file name	The file is automatically loaded into array or table when the program is activated.
		RAF name	Name of the record address file (ADDROUT) that will be used to control the file processing of the file specified in columns 19 to 26.
19 - 26	To File	blank	No output database file is used by this Extension specification.
		RAF controlled file name	Name of the file whose processing is controlled by the record address file (ADDROUT) file specified in columns 11 to 18.
		Output file	Name of a file that is automatically replaced with the contents of the array or table specified in columns 27 to 32 when the program ends.
27 - 32	Array Name	name	The name of the array or table being defined.
33 - 35	Entries per source line	blank	The array is loaded through Calculation statements, or through Input specifications.
		1 to 999	Number of array or table elements that are specified on each source statement that is specified at the bottom of the source program.
36 - 39	Entries per Array	1 to 9999	Number of elements in the array dimension. (RPG arrays and tables are single dimensioned.)
40 -42	Length of an Entry	1 to 256	Length of a single array element. For character type elements, this value can be 1 to 256; for numeric elements, this value can be 1 to 30.
43	Data Type	blank	If column 44 contains a blank, the data type is character. If column 44 contains a 0 to 9 the data type is numeric.
		P	The data type is packed decimal.
		B	The data type is AS/400 database binary.
		L	The data type is zoned numeric with a leading plus or minus sign.
		R	The data type is zoned numeric with a trailing plus or minus sign.

Extension Specification Summary (continued)

Column	Title	Values	Description
44	Decimal Pos.	blank	The data type is character.
		0 to 9	The data type is numeric with the number of decimal positions specified.
45	Sequencing	blank	The array or table is not specifically sequenced.
		A	The array or table is in ascending order.
		D	The array or table is in descending order.
46 - 51	Alternate Array or Table	blank	No alternate array or table is specified.
		name	Name of the alternate array or table. The alternate array or table will have the same number of elements as the primary array or table (named in columns 27 to 32).
52 - 54	Length of an Entry	1 to 256	Length of the alternate array or table element. Character type elements can be 1 to 256; Numeric elements can be 1 to 30.
55	Data Type	blank	If column 56 contains a blank, the data type is character. If column 56 contains a 0 to 9 the data type is numeric.
		P	The data type is packed decimal.
		B	The data type is AS/400 database binary.
		L	The data type is zoned numeric with a leading plus or minus sign.
		R	The data type is zoned numeric with a trailing plus or minus sign.
56	Decimal Pos.	blank	The data type is character.
		0 to 9	The data type is numeric with the number of decimal positions specified.
57	Sequencing	blank	The array or table is not specifically sequenced.
		A	The array or table is in ascending order.
		D	The array or table is in descending order.

Line Counter Specification

Line Counter specifications are used to define the number of lines per page and the overflow line number of program defined printer files. A File Description specification for a printer file is associated with the line counter specification by placing the letter L into column 39 of the printer file's File Description specification.

Figure 2-22 illustrates the RPG line counter specification form. The line counter specification form is normally combined with the extension specification form.

RPG EXTENSION AND LINE COUNTER SPECIFICATIONS

Extension Specifications

E Line	Form Type	Record Sequence of the Chaining File	Number of the Chaining Field	From Filename	To Filename	Table or Array Name	Number of Entries Per Record	Number of Entries Per Table or Array	Length of Entry	P/B/L/R	Decimal Positions	Sequence (A/D)	Table or Array Name (Alternating Format)	Length of Entry	P/B/L/R	Decimal Positions	Sequence (A/D)	Comments
3 4 5	6	7 8	9 10	11 12 13 14 15 16 17 18	19 20 21 22 23 24 25 26	27 28 29 30 31 32	33 34 35	36 37 38 39	40 41 42	43	44	45	46 47 48 49 50 51	52 53 54	55	56	57	58 59 60 61 62 63 64 65 66 67 68 69 70 71 72 73 74
0 1	E																	
0 2	E																	
0 3	E																	
0 4	E																	
0 5	E																	
0 6	E																	
0 7	E																	
0 8	E																	
	E																	
	E																	

Line Counter Specifications

L Line	Form Type	Filename	1 Line Number	1 FL or Channel Number	2 Line Number	2 OL or Channel Number	3 Line Number	3 Channel Number	4 Line Number	4 Channel Number	5 Line Number	5 Channel Number	6 Line Number	6 Channel Number	7 Line Number	7 Channel Number	8 Line Number	8 Channel Number	9 Line Number	9 Channel Number	10 Line Number	10 Channel Number	11 Line Number	11 Channel Number	12 Line Number	12 Channel Number
3 4 5	6	7 8 9 10 11 12 13 14	15 16 17	18 19	20 21 22	23 24	25 26 27	28 29	30 31 32	33 34	35 36 37	38 39	40 41 42	43 44	45 46 47	48 49	50 51 52	53 54	55 56 57	58 59	60 61 62	63 64	65 66 67	68 69	70 71 72	73 74
1 1	L																									
1 2	L																									
	L																									

*Number of sheets per pad may vary slightly

Figure 2-22: Line Counter Specification Form

Line Counter Specification Summary

Column	Title	Values	Description
6	Form Type	L	Identifies this statement as a Line Counter specification.
7 - 14	Print File Name	name	Name of the PRINTER device file being controlled by this Line Counter specification.
15 -17	Lines per page	2 to 112	Number of printable lines per page. Note: Program described files are restricted to a minimum of 2 lines per page and a maximum of 112 lines per page. Externally described printer files, however, can use as few as 1 line per page and as many as 122 lines per page. Line Counter specifications cannot be used for externally described files.
18 - 19	Forms Length ID	FL	The letters FL must be specified.
20 - 22	Overflow Line Number	2 to 112	A line number that, when printed upon, will cause the overflow indicator specified in columns 33-34 of the File Description specification to be set on.
23 - 24	Overflow ID	OL	The letters OL must be specified.

Input Specification

Input specifications are used to describe program described file formats, rename externally described file fields, define data structures and data areas, and assign match field, level-break and field indicators to fields.

Program described files require that their formats be defined via input specifications. Columns 7 to 42 are used to identify the formats of program described files. These specifications are known as *Record Identifying Entries*. They contain identifying codes that allow a record format to be associated with an indicator. For example, *If column 6 contains the letter H and column 12 contains the number 1, then indicator 20 is set on.*

Externally described files do not require input specifications. The RPG compiler generates the equivalent of input specifications based on the external definition of the file. However, each file format can be associated with a record-identifying indicator by specifying the format name in columns 7 to 14 and the record-identifying indicator in columns 19 and 20.

Additionally, externally described files can have their field names changed by specifying the external field name in columns 21 to 30, and the new name—the one used by the RPG program—in columns 53 to 58.

Data structures are defined with input specifications. A data structure can be program defined, externally described or a combination of both. A file format is used for externally described data structures. That file, however, need not be used elsewhere in the program.

Data area, data structures can be defined with input specifications, similar to data structures. Data area, data structures are identified by specifying the letter U in column 18 of the data area, data structure input specification.

The Input specifications form is featured in Figure 2-23 on page 60.

RPG INPUT SPECIFICATIONS

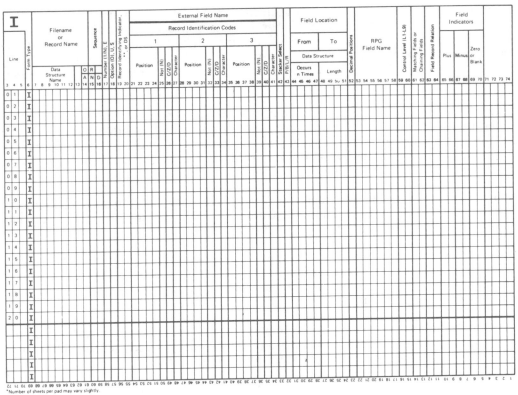

I

Line

Form Type

Filename or Record Name

Data Structure Name

OR

AND

Sequence

Number (1/N), E

Option (O), U, S

Record Identifying Indicator, **, or DS

External Field Name

Record Identification Codes

1 Position | Not (N) | C/Z/D | Character

2 Position | Not (N) | C/Z/D | Character

3 Position | Not (N) | C/Z/D | Character

Stacker Select

P/B/L/R

Field Location: From | To

Data Structure: Occurs n Times | Length

Decimal Positions

RPG Field Name

Control Level (L1-L9)

Matching Fields or Chaining Fields

Field Record Relation

Field Indicators: Plus | Minus | Zero or Blank

Lines: 01 02 03 04 05 06 07 08 09 10 11 12 13 14 15 16 17 18 19 20

*Number of sheets per pad may vary slightly.

Figure 2-23: Input Specification Form

Input Specification Summary

Program Described Files

Program described files are seldom used with the modern RPG language. Typically, when this type of file exists in a program, the program has either been converted from an older system or it is some kind of system utility.

Column	Title	Values	Description
6	Form Type	I	Identifies the statement as an Input specification.
7 - 14	File Name	blank	If columns 14 to 16 are blank, the statement is a field description. If columns 14 to 16 contain AND or OR, the statement is a continued record format entry. If column 14 is blank and columns 15 to 16 are not blank, the statement is a record format description.
14 - 16	Format Entry Continuation	AND	The record identifying entries (columns 21 to 41) are continued from the previous statement. The AND indicates that both the preceding line's and this line's record-identifying codes must be satisfied for the record-identifying indicator (columns 19 and 20) to be set on.
		OR	The record identifying entries (columns 21 to 41) are continued from the previous statement. The OR indicates that the preceding line's or this line's record-identifying codes must be satisfied for the record-identifying indicator (columns 19 and 20) to be set on.
15 - 16	Sequencing	Any letters	Alphabetic characters indicate that no special record sequencing is required. Typically, the letters NS are used to indicate *no sequence*.
		01 to 99	Special record sequencing is desired. Depending on the entries in columns 17 to 18 of this statement, the record may or may not be required.
17	Sequence Requirement	blank	A blank is required when columns 15 to 16 contain no sequencing characters.
		1	One record of this type, per sequence, is required. More than one record of this type, per sequence, generates an error.
		N	One or more records of this type, per sequences, are allowed.

Program Described File Descriptions (continued)

Column	Title	Values	Description
18	Option	blank	A blank is required when columns 15 to 16 contain no sequencing characters. If columns 15 to 16 contain a numeric sequence entry, the sequence entry is required.
		O	Valid when columns 15 to 16 contain a numeric sequence entry. The O option indicates that the sequence entry is optional.
19 - 20	Record Identifying Indicator	Indicator	Any valid indicator except overflow (OA to OF, OV), first page (1P) and RPGII function key (KA to KY) can be specified as a record identifying indicator. When a record of the type specified is read, the indicator is set on.
		**	Two asterisks indicate that the statements that follow are *look ahead fields*. Look ahead fields are used for viewing the information in the next record in the file when processing a file via the RPG cycle. For example, if a file contains 100 records, and the RPG cycle just processed the 39th record, look ahead allows the contents of the 40th record to be interrogated before that record is actually retrieved. Look ahead fields function with input files only. With other types of files such as update and combined files, look ahead fields contain the same data as the record just read.
21 - 41	Record Type Identifying Codes	Position and character value	Up to three record-identifying codes can be specified for each record-identifying entry. If more than three record-identifying codes are required, specify an AND/OR entry in columns 14-16 to extend the codes.

Program Described File Descriptions (continued)

Column	Title	Values	Description
21 - 24	Position	blank	No record identifying code is specified.
		1 to 9999	Position within the record of the value specified in column 27.
25	Not	blank	The character specified in column 27 must exist in the record at the position specified in columns 21 to 24.
		N	The character specified in column 27 must NOT exist in the record at the position specified in columns 21 to 24.
26	Comparison Type	blank	No record identifying code is specified.
		C	The value specified in column 27 is a character and the full value is used for the record identifying code comparison.
		Z	The upper four bits of the character specified in column 27 is used as the record identifying code comparison. This allows comparisons for numeric values of positive or negative value, for example.
		D	The lower four bits of the character specified in column 27 are used for the record identifying code.
27	Record Identifying Value	any character	If entries in columns 21 though 26 exist, this column contains a record-identifying code. Any character (including a blank) can be used as a record-identifying code.
28 - 34	Record Identifying Code #2		Same structure as columns 21 to 27
35 - 41	Record Identifying Code #3		Same structure as columns 21 to 27.
24 - 74			Not used by RPGIII.

Program Described File Field Descriptions

Column	Title	Values	Description
6	Form Type	I	Identifies this statement as an Input specification.
7 - 42			Not used by RPGIII.
43	Data Type	blank	If column 52 contains a blank, the field being defined is *character*. If column 52 contains a 0 to 9, the field being defined is *zoned*.
		P	The field being defined is packed decimal.
		B	The field being defined is RPG binary.
		L	The field being defined is zoned decimal with a preceding sign value.
		R	The field being defined is zoned decimal with a trailing sign value.
44 - 47	Start Position of Field	1 to 9999	The starting position within the file's record of the field.
48 - 51	Ending Position of Field	1 to 9999	The ending position within the file's record of the field. Positions 44 to 47 and 48 to 51 are collectively referred to as the FROM and TO columns.
52	Decimal Positions	blank	The field data type is character unless the following applies: The field is an array or array element. In which case the data type is specified by the array definition.
		0 to 9	Number of decimal positions (i.e., positions to the right of the decimal point) for the field. If the field named in columns 53-58 is a numeric array or numeric array element, this entry must match the entry in column 44 of the Extension specification for the array. It can also be blank, which causes the compiler to default to the value specified in column 44 of the Extension specification.
53 - 58	Field Name	name	The name of the field being defined. In addition to a symbolic name an array name, array element, data structure name, indicator variable, indicator array element or PAGEn can be specified.

Program Described File Field Descriptions (continued)

Column	Title	Values	Description
59 - 60	Control Field	blanks	The field is not a control field.
		L1 to L9	The field is a control field. When a record is read by the RPG cycle, if the contents of the field change, the level-break indicator will be set on. If more than one field contains the same level-break indicator, the indicator will be set on when any of the fields change. When a specific level break indicator is set on, all low level break indicators are also set on. For example, if indicator L4 is set on, L3, L2 and L1 are also set on.
61 - 62	Match Field	blanks	The field is not a matched field.
		M1 to M9	The field is a matched field and has a corresponding matched field in another file.
63 - 64	Field Record Relation	blank	No field/record relationship exists.
		record identifying indicator	The indicator that associates this field with a specific record identifying entry code and indicator for this file.
65 - 66	Field Status Indicator (PLUS)	blank	No indicator is set on.
		indicator	The indicator is set on when a record is read and the contents of this field is greater than zero.
67 - 68	Field Status Indicator (MINUS)	blank	No indicator is set on.
		indicator	The indicator is set on when a record is read and the contents of this field is less than zero.
69 - 70	Field Status Indicator (Blank/Zero)	blank	No indicator is set on.
		indicator	The indicator is set on when a record is read and the contents of this field is equal to zero (for numeric fields), or blanks (for character fields).

Externally Described files

Externally described files are the rule when writing new applications with the modern RPG language. External definitions allow the programmer to avoid specifying lengthy record format descriptions and allows the programmer to easily take advantage of modern operation codes.

Column	Title	Values	Description
6	Form Type	I	Identifies this statement as an Input specification.
7 - 14	Record Format Name	name	The name of a record format from an externally described file.
15 - 18			Not used by RPGIII.
19 - 20	Record Identifying Indicator		Any valid indicator except overflow (OA to OF, OV), first page (1P) and RPGII function key (KA to KY) can be specified as a record identifying indicator. When a record of the type specified is read, the indicator is set on. Note: The Look Ahead Field codes (**) are supported by externally described data, but the look ahead field entries must be program described.
21 - 74			Not used by RPGIII.

Externally described Field Descriptions

Externally described files need no input specifications. The RPG compiler automatically generates record format(s) from the external definition. Externally described files can, however, rename their external field names and assigned level-break, match field and field indicators.

Most RPGIII compilers generate a data structure with the same name as any input fields that exceeds 256 characters.

Column	Title	Values	Description
6	Form Type	I	Identifies this statement as an Input specification.
7 - 20			Not used by RPGIII.
21 - 30	External Field Name	blank	The name of the externally described field is used as the name of the field in the program—referred to as the *internal name*.
		name	Name of the externally described file's field being renamed to the field name specified in columns 53 to 58.
31 - 52			Not used by RPGIII.
53 - 58	Internal Field Name	name	Internal name used for the external name specified in columns 21 to 30. If columns 21 to 30 are blank, the field name specified here is also the external name being referenced.

Externally described Field Descriptions (continued)

Column	Title	Values	Description
59 - 60	Control Field	blanks	The field is not a control field.
		L1 to L9	The field is a control field. When a record is read by the RPG cycle, if the contents of the field change, the level-break indicator will be set on. If more than one field contains the same level-break indicator, the indicator will be set on when any of the fields change. When a specific level break indicator is set on, all low level break indicators are also set on. For example, if indicator L4 is set on, L3, L2 and L1 are also set on.
61 - 62	Match Field	blanks	The field is not a matched field.
		M1 to M9	The field is a matched field and has a corresponding matched field in another file.
63 - 64	Field Record Relation	blank	No field/record relationship exists.
		record identifying indicator	The indicator that associates this field with a specific record identifying entry code and indicator for this file.
65 - 66	Field Status Indicator (PLUS)	blank	No indicator is set on.
		indicator	The indicator is set on when a record is read and the contents of this field is greater than zero.
67 - 68	Field Status Indicator (MINUS)	blank	No indicator is set on.
		indicator	The indicator is set on when a record is read and the contents of this field is less than zero.
69 - 70	Field Status Indicator (Blank/Zero)	blank	No indicator is set on.
		indicator	The indicator is set on when a record is read and the contents of this field is equal to zero (for numeric fields), or blanks (for character fields).

Data Structure Specification

Data structures provide what is commonly referred to as working storage, or work-fields. Data structures can be used for a variety of situations such as field decomposition, parameter passing and setting initial values for fields.

Column	Title	Values	Description
6	Form Type	I	Identifies this statement as an Input specification.
7 - 14	Data Structure Name	blanks	The name of the data structure is not referenced in the RPG program. The compiler generates a random data structure name.
		name	The name of the data structure. The name is optional for single occurrence data structure and is required for multiple occurrence data structures or when the data structure is initialized (i.e., column 18 contains the letter I).
16			Not used by RPGIII.
17	Externally Described Indication	blank	The data structure is program described.
		E	The data structure is externally described and is based on the file specified in columns 21 to 30 of this statement.
18	Type of Data Structure	blank	The data structure is of no special type. It is a normal data structure.
		I[1]	The data structure subfields are initialized in the sequence in which they appear in the data structure—according to their field attribute. Numeric subfields are initialized to zeros and character subfields are initialized to blanks. For more information see CLEAR and RESET operations in Chapter 4, on pages 169 and 264.
		S	The data structure is used as the Program Status data structure (PSDS). Which has special predefined field locations and values.
		U	The data structure is a data area data structure. The information stored in the data structure is retrieved from a data area—stored outside the RPG program and retained after the program ends.

[1] All occurrences of multiple occurrence data structures are initialized to the same value. To initialize indiviual occurrences of a data structure, the OCUR operation can be used during the *INZSR subroutine.

Data Structure Specification (continued)

Column	Title	Values	Description
19 - 20	Data Structure ID	DS	The letters DS are required to identify the beginning of a new data structure.
21 - 30	Data Structure Format File	blank	No external file is used to format this data structure.
		file name	The name of the file that is used as the format for this data structure. If an external file is used to define the data structure format, additional "program defined" fields can be appended to the data structured. Also, column 17 must contain the letter E to enable the external format name.
31 - 43			Not used by RPGIII.
44 - 47	Occurrence	blanks	The data structure is a single occurrence data structure.
		1 to 9999	The data structure is a multiple occurrence data structure. The OCUR operation can be used to set and retrieve the data in each specific occurrence.
48 - 51	Length	blanks	The overall length of the data structure is derived from the data structure subfields. If the data structure name is also an input field, its length is the same as the input field. If the data structure is not also an input field name, the length of the data structure is the same as the largest ending position for a subfield with the data structure.
		1 to 9999	The length of the data structure.
52 - 74			Not used by RPGIII.

Data Structure Subfield Specification

Data structure subfields provide working storage for a program. Unlike conventional fields from an input file, overlapping data structure subfields actually overlap in memory. For example, if one subfield is located in positions 1 to 10 and a second subfield is located in positions 8 to 20, both subfields share positions 8, 9 and 10 within the data structure. Therefore, if position 8, 9 or 10 is altered, the contents of both subfields are affected.

Column	Title	Values	Description
6	Form Type	I	Identifies this statement as an Input specification.
7			Not used by RPGIII.
8	Initialization	blank	If columns 21 to 42 are blank, no user-specified initial value exists for this subfield, and the subfield will default to blanks, unless its initial value is overridden elsewhere in the program. If columns 21 to 42 are not blank, this is either a continuation of the initial value for a data structure subfield or a rename of a field name of an external file.
		I	The value specified in columns 21 to 42 of this input specification is used as the initial value for the data structure subfield specified in columns 53 to 58. If columns 21 to 42 contain no initial value then the initial value for the subfield will default to one of the following: for numeric subfields, the initial value is zero; for character subfields, the initial value is blanks.
9-20			Not used by RPGIII.
21-30	External Field Name	blank	The external field name is not specifically referenced, the name in columns 53 to 58 is used as the externally name reference.
		Field name	The external field name be referenced by this statement. (Used when renaming an external field name from the externally described file whose format is used for the data structure. The external name is renamed to an alternate internal name.)
31-42			Not used by externally described input fields.

Data Structure Subfield Specification (continued)

Column	Title	Values	Description
21-42	Initial Value	blank	If column 8 also contains a blank, no initial value is specified for this data structure subfield. If column 8 contains the letter I and columns 21-42 are blank, the initial value for the data structure subfield will be based on the attribute of the subfield; numeric subfields are initialized to zero, character subfields are initialized to blanks.
		initial value	The initial value for the data structure subfield. To specify a value in these columns, the letter I must appear in column 8 of this data structure subfield input specification. An initial value can be a literal constant enclosed in apostrophes (e.g., '*YES'), a numeric value (e.g., 3.1415926), or a named constant. The value specified here can be overridden by specifying moving another value into the subfield during the initialization subroutine (*INZSR).
43	Data Type	blank	For externally described data structures the subfield is of the same attributes as the external definition. This column must be blank for externally described subfields. For program defined subfields, the subfield named in columns 53 to 58 is either character or zoned numeric. If column 52 contains a 0 to 9, the subfield is zoned. If column 52 is blank, the subfield is character.
		P	The subfield is packed decimal.
		B	The subfield is RPG binary.

Data Structure Subfield Specification (continued)

Column	Title	Values	Description
44 - 47	Starting Position	blank	The subfield is an externally described subfield, and its position within the data structure is based on its external location.
		1 to 9999	Starting position of the subfield within the data structure.
48 - 51	Ending Position	blank	The subfield is an externally described subfield, and its position within the data structure is based on its external location.
		1 to 9999	Ending position of the subfield within the data structure.
52	Decimal Positions	blank	The subfield's data type is character, or it is an array or array element.
		0 to 9	Number of decimal positions (i.e., positions to the right of the decimal point) for the subfield. If the subfield is a numeric array or numeric array element, this entry must match the entry in column 44 of the extension specification for the array. It can also be blank, which causes the compiler to default to the value specified in column 44 of the extension specification.
53 - 58	Subfield Name	blank	The subfield name must be blank when the statement is a continuation of the previous statement. This normally occurs when the initial value for a subfield is continued onto a second line or when the subfield is renamed, and an initial value is specified.
		name	Name of the data structure subfield. If columns 21 to 30 contain an external name, that subfield is renamed to this name. Otherwise this is a new subfield.

Special PSDS Data Structure Subfields

Special Built-In Field Locations for the Program Status Data Structure (PSDS)

These special values are used in place of from and to positions. They represent built-in positions that contain special values. They are part of the Program Status Data Structure (PSDS). The PSDS is used to store both runtime and error specific information. Many of these fields are set when the program starts, other are set when an error occurs.

Column	Title	Values	Description
44 - 51	Special Locations	*FILE	Name of the file being processed.
		*OPCODE	The RPG operation code being performed when an exception/error occurred.
		*PARMS	Number of parameters passed to the program.
		*ROUTINE	Name of the RPG routine (via the RPG cycle) that was being performed when an exception/error occurred.
		*RECORD	Name of the record format being processed when an exception/error occurred.
		*PROGRAM	Name of the program (determined at runtime.)
		*STATUS	Status or *error code*. For a description of status codes see Chapter 4

Special INFDS Data Structure Subfields

Special Built-In Field Locations for the File Information Data Structure (INFDS)

These special values are used in place of from and to positions. They represent built-in positions that contain special values. They are part of the file information input/output feedback data structure (INFDS). The INFDS is used to store information about a file being processed. Each file declared in the program can have its own INFDS.

Column	Title	Values	Description
44 - 51	Special Locations	*FILE	File being processed, that is the external name for the opened file.
		*INP	A 2-digit numeric field containing the DBCS (double-byte character set) indicator. A value of 0 indicates that a non-DBCS keyboard is being used. A value of 10 indicates that a Katakana or DBCS keyboard is being used. This value applies to WORKSTN device files only.
		*OUT	A 2-digit numeric field containing the output DBCS (double-byte character set) indicator. A value of 0 indicates that a non-DBCS output device is being used. A value of 10 indicates that a Katakana or DBCS output is being used. This value applies to WORKSTN device files only.
		*OPCODE	A 6-position field containing the RPG operation code being performed when an exception/error occurs. The 6th position of this field contains one of the following status flags: F The operation was performed on a file name R The operation was performed on a record format I The operation was an implicit file name. For example that CHAIN operation would appear as CHAINR (chain to a record format).

File Input/Output Feedback Data Structure (continued)

Column	Title	Values	Description
		*MODE	A 2-digit numeric field that indicates the type of session. A value of zero indicates a non-DBCS session. A value of 10 indicates that this is a DBCS session. This value applies to WORKSTN device files only.
		*RECORD	For externally described files, this eight-byte character field contains the name of the record format being processed when an exception/error occurred. For program described files, the record-identifying indicator of the record just processed is placed left-adjusted into the field.
		*ROUTINE	An 8-position character field containing the name of the RPG cycle routine that was running when an exception/error occurred. This field will contain one of the following routines: *INIT=program initialization *DETL=detail-time output *GETIN=get-in *TOTC=total-time calculations *TOTL=total-time output *DETC=detail calculations *OFL=overflow output *TERM=program termination. If the exception error occurs during another program—as is normally the case when a SPECIAL file is being processed—this field will contain the first eight characters of that program name.
		*SIZE	A 4-digit numeric field containing the number of characters that can be sent to the display device in its current mode.
		*STATUS	Status or *error* code. For a description of error codes, see Chapter 4.

Named Constant Specification

Named constants provide a method for assigning a name to a literal value. The literal value can be numeric, character or hexadecimal. A named constant can be used anywhere a literal value can be used. In addition, it can also be used in the Output field columns of the Output specification.

Column	Title	Values	Description
6	Form Type	I	Identifies this statement as an Input specification.
7 - 20			Not used by RPGIII.
21 - 42	Constant Value	number	The numeric value assigned to the named constant. Numeric values must be left justified in columns 21 to 42. If a sign is required, the sign must precede the numeric value. To continue a long numeric literal onto a second line, a minus sign must be used after the rightmost digit of the first line.
		'quoted character value'	For character named constants, the constant must begin in column 21 with an apostrophe (single quote). An apostrophe must also appear to the right of the character closing the named constant. When a constant is continued onto subsequent lines, a minus sign (-) must be placed to the right of the portion of the constant that is on the current line. This indicates that the constant is continued onto the next line. Each subsequent line must begin with a single quote and end with the continuation symbol (the minus sign), except the final line of the named constant, which must end with a closing single quote.
		X'hex value'	For hexadecimal named constants, the constant must begin in column 21 with a capital letter X, immediately followed by a single quote. The named constant can be any valid hexadecimal characters (0 to 9, A to F, and a to f). The continuation rules are the same as for quoted character value named constants.

Named Constant Specification (continued)

Column	Title	Values	Description
43	Data Type	blank	The line is a continuation of the previous named constant.
		C	The data type is C for named Constant. The name of the named constant must appear in columns 53 to 58 of this statement.
44 - 52			Not used for Named Constants.
53 - 58	Named Constant	blank	The line is a continuation of the previous named constant.
		name	The name assigned to the named constant.
59 - 74			Not used for Named Constants.

Calculation Specification

Calculation specifications comprise 90 percent of modern RPG programming. All operations, including but not limited to file processing, computations and data manipulation, are performed with Calculation specifications.

The Calculation specification supports only one format. However, to the use of compiler and preprocessor directives, multiple calculation formats exist. This section will mention the compiler and preprocessor directives, but will focus on the traditional calculation specification form.

Figure 2-24 illustrates the Calculation specification form.

RPG CALCULATION SPECIFICATIONS

Line (3–5)	Form Type (6)	Control Level (L0-L9, LR, SR, AN/OR) (7–8)	Indicators: Not (9), (10–11)	And: Not (12), (13–14)	And: Not (15), (16–17)	Factor 1 (18–27)	Operation (28–32)	Factor 2 (33–42)	Result Field: Name (43–48)	Result Field: Length (49–51)	Decimal Positions (52)	Half Adjust (H) (53)	Resulting Indicators — Arithmetic: Plus / Compare: 1 > 2 / Lookup (Factor 2) is: High (54–55)	Arithmetic: Minus / Compare: 1 < 2 / Lookup: Low (56–57)	Arithmetic: Zero / Compare: 1 = 2 / Lookup: Equal (58–59)	Comments (60–74)
01	C															
02	C															
03	C															
04	C															
05	C															
06	C															
07	C															
08	C															
09	C															
10	C															
11	C															
12	C															
13	C															
14	C															
15	C															
16	C															
17	C															
18	C															
19	C															
20	C															
	C															
	C															
	C															
	C															
	C															

*Number of sheets per pad may vary slightly.

Figure 2-24: Calculation Specification Form

Calculation Specification Summary

Column	Title	Values	Description
6	Form Type	C	Identifies this statement as a Calculation specification.
7	Control Code	*	The statement is ignored (it is a comment).
		/	The statement contains either a compiler directive, such as /COPY or a preprocessor directive, such as /EXEC SQL.
		+	The statement is a preprocessor continuation specification that began with /EXEC SQL on a previous line.
7 - 8	Control Level Indicator or Subroutine Notation	blank	The statement is a normal statement or normal subroutine statement. No special controlling is specified.
		AN / OR	The indicator conditioning (columns 9 to 17) on the previous statement is continued onto this line. The indicator condition of the previous line and/or the indicator condition of this line must be met before the operation code can be performed. When AN/OR is used, the operation code must be specified on the last statement of the AN/OR group. No more than 7 AN/OR lines can be specified in RPGIII.
		L0	Total-time calculation. Level zero (L0) is always on; therefore, this controlling level indicator will always test true.
		L1 to L9	Total time calculation. The control level indicators are tested at total time (level-break).
		LR	Total time and Last Record processing. The calculation statement is performed during total time processing—after the last record indicator is set on.
		SR	Optional documentary notation to indicate a subroutine statement. Typically, SR is used only on the first and last statements of each subroutine to better identify the beginning and ending of the subroutine.

Calculation Specification Summary (continued)

Column	Title	Values	Description
9 - 17	Conditioning Indicators	blank	No conditioning indicators are used to control whether or not this statement is performed. There should never be an entry in these columns if proper programming practices are followed.
		any valid indicator(s)	The specified indicator(s) control the running of this calculation. If more than three indicators are required, the conditioning can be continued on subsequent calculation specifications by specifying an AN or OR in columns 7 and 8 of the next calculation line. All valid indicators are allowed.
18 - 27	Factor 1	blank	No Factor 1 entry is specified. Several operation codes support an entry in Factor 1, while others do not require Factor 1.
		any characters	The entry is used by the operation code specified in columns 28 to 32. The entry must match the requirements of the operation code. All entries in Factor 1 must be left justified.
28 - 32	Operation Code or *OpCode*	Valid Operation Code	The name of the RPG instruction (OpCode) that is to be performed. Most opcodes use one or more of Factor 1, Factor 2, and the Result field.
33 - 42	Factor 2	blank	No Factor 2 entry is specified. Several operation codes support an entry in Factor 2, while others do not require Factor 2.
		any characters	The entry is used by the operation code specified in columns 28 to 32. The entry must match the requirements of the operation code. All entries in Factor 2 must be left justified.
43 - 48	Result field	blank	No Result field entry is specified. Several operation codes support an entry in the Result field, while others do not require the Result field.
		variable name	The entry is used by the operation code specified in columns 28 to 32. The entry must match the requirements of the operation code. All entries in Result field must be left justified. The Result field is normally used as the target of the operation code. For example, it is the target of a MOVE operation, the contents of Factor 2 is copied to the field named in the Result field.

Calculation Specification Summary (continued)

Column	Title	Values	Description
49 - 51	Result field length	blank	The Result field is defined elsewhere in the program or it is not a definable value (such as a label or subroutine name).
		1 to 30	For numeric fields, the length of the Result field.
		1 to 256	For character fields, the length of the Result field.
		-99 to +99	Relative length of the Result field based on the field specified for Factor 2 for a *LIKE DEFN operation. The Result field's length is the length of the field specified in Factor 2, plus or minus the value specified.
52	Decimal Positions	blank	If the Result field is specified, and a Result field length is also specified, the new field's data type is character. If the Result field length is blank, then these columns must also be blank. For the *LIKE DEFN operation, the Result field decimal positions must be blank.
		0 to 9	Number of decimal positions for the Result field. (Valid only for numeric Result fields.)
53	Operation Extender	blank	No operation extender is specified.
		H	Half Adjust. For numeric operations, the result of the calculation is rounded up to the specified decimal position.
		N	No Lock. If the file being processed by the operation is opened for update, the record is read but not locked. This operation extender is only valid for operation codes that perform record input.
		P	Pad. The Result field's contents are replaced by the operation. Logically, the Result field is padded with blanks or zeros—depending on the result of the operation—hence the 'P' extender.
54 - 59	Resulting Indicators	blank	No resulting indicators are set on as a result of the operation code.
		any valid indicator	The resulting indicators are set according to the results of the operation code specified in columns 28-32. All but the following can be specified as resulting indicators: 1P, MR.
60 - 74	Comments	any characters	These columns can be used to document the individual Calculation program statement.

Output Specification

Output specifications are used to define the output of the program. In the modern RPG language, output specifications are used for two purposes: (1) defining program defined printer files and (2) releasing database record locks.

Figure 2-25 illustrates the output specifications form.

RPG OUTPUT SPECIFICATIONS

Figure 2-25: Output Specification Form

Program Described Output File Control Entries

Column	Title	Values	Description
6	Form Type	O	Identifies this statement as an Output specification.
7 - 14	Output File Name	blank	The name used is the same as the more recently specified output file name.
		file name	Any file opened for output can be specified.
15	Output Type	H	Heading records. For documentation purposes only. The H in this column is functionally equivalent to placing a D in this column. Heading records usually contain report column titles, page numbers and date information.
		D	Detail records. Usually, detail records contain information that will be repeated on subsequent output records such as a printed report. Additionally, detail records are used to write and update records in program defined data files.
		T	Total time records. Usually, total time records are used to output the results of the program.
		E	Exception records. Exception records are written via the EXCPT operation code. Exception records can be conditioned by indicators and/or an Exception name. Exception names appear in columns 32 to 37 of the output specification.
14 - 16	Conditioning Continuation Controls	AND / OR	The indicator conditioning in columns 23 to 31 is a continuation of the previous line. The indicator condition on the previous line AND/OR the indicator condition on this line must be satisfied for the output line to be written.

Program Described Output File Control Entries (continued)

Column	Title	Values	Description
16 - 18	File Addition and File Deletion	ADD	For database (DISK) files only. Records are added to the file. The letter A must appear in column 66 of the File Description specification for the file being written.
		DEL	For database (DISK) files only. The record is deleted from the file; it will no longer be accessible. The letter U (update) must appear in column 15 of the File Description specification for the file being deleted.
16	Output Control	blank	No special controlling is specified for this output statement.
		F	Fetch overflow. When fetch is specified, RPG checks for overflow after each printed line. If the overflow indicator for this printer file is on and fetch has been specified, any detail and heading lines that are conditioned by that indicator will be printed before this line.
		R	Release WORKSTN device. When release is specified, the WORKSTN file specified in columns 7 to 14 is released from the program. This is functionally equivalent to the REL operation code. See the REL operation code in Chapter 4 for more information on release.
17	Line Spacing Before Printing	blank	For PRINTER files only. The printer will not advance before printing the output line.
		Ø to 3	The printer will advance Ø, 1, 2, or 3 lines before printing the output line.
18	Line Spacing After Printing	blank	For PRINTER files only. The printer will advance 1 line after printing the output line.
		Ø to 3	The printer will advance Ø, 1, 2, or 3 lines after printing the output line.

Program Described Output File Control Entries (continued)

Column	Title	Values	Description
19 - 20	Line Skipping Before	blank or Ø	For PRINTER files only. The printer will not advance before printing the output line.
		Ø1 to 99	The printer will advance to the line on the current page before printing. If the current print line is beyond the line specified, the printer will eject the current page, and advance to the line on the next page before printing.
		AØ to A9 or BØ to B2	The function for AØ to A9 and BØ to B2 is the same as for Ø1 to 99, except the line numbers represented by AØ to A9 are 1ØØ to 1Ø9 and by BØ to B2 110 to 112 respectively.
21 - 22	Line Skipping After	blank or Ø	For PRINTER files only. The printer will not advance after printing the output line.
		Ø1 to 99	The printer will advance to the line on the current page after printing. If the current print line is beyond the line specified, the printer will eject the current page, and advance to the line on the next page after printing.
		AØ to A9 or BØ to B2	The function for AØ to A9 and BØ to B2 is the same as for Ø1 to 99, except the line numbers represented by AØ to A9 are 1ØØ to 1Ø9 and by BØ to B2 110 to 112 respectively.
23 - 31	Controlling Indicators	blank	No indicators condition this output line.
		1P	First page indicator (valid for heading and detail output only). Output lines conditioned with the 1P indicator are printed after the *INZSR subroutine is performed. during program start.
		indicator	Any valid indicator (up to three) can be specified to control the output line. If more than three indicators are required, the continuation controls can be specified. (AND/OR in columns 14 to 16.)
32-37	Except Name	blank	No exception name controls the output line.
		name	This line is controlled by an exception name (column 15 contains the letter E). If conditioning indicators are specified, their condition must be satisfied for the line to be output. Except names are used in conjunction with the EXCPT operation code.
38-74		Blank	These columns are not used.

Program Described Output File Field Description

The advanced support for externally described files has lead RPG programmers to rarely use program described files. But while the use of program defined WORKSTN and DISK files is virtually nonexistent, it is quite common to find program described PRINTER output files. This is probably due to the advanced support RPG has for printed output—which is a principle design element in the original RPG.

Column	Title	Values	Description
6	Form Type	O	Identifies this statement as an Output specification.
7 - 22			Not used for program defined output fields.
23 - 31	Controlling Indicators	blank	The output field is always written whenever the controlling output specification is written.
		1P	The output field is written only once—at first page output time (1P).
		any valid indicator (up to three)	The output field is included in the output operation only when the test of the controlling indicators is true.
32 - 37	Output Field Name	name	The name of the field to be output when the controlling output specification is written. The field name must have already been defined in the program.
		name constant	The name of the named constant to be output when the controlling output specification is written.

Program Described Output File Field Description (continued)

Column	Title	Values	Description
32 - 37 (cont'd)		PAGE, or PAGE1 to PAGE7	The current page number is output. The various PAGE fields include PAGE and PAGE*n* where *n* is 1 to 7. Conditioning indicators condition the resetting, not the printing, of the page number fields. When the indicator condition is met, the PAGEn field is reset to zero. When the indicator condition is not met, the PAGEn field value is printed normally.
		*IN*xx*	The value of the indicator *xx* is output to the record. *xx* can be any valid RPG indicator.
		*IN,*xx*	The value of the indicator *xx* is output to the record. *xx* can be any general purpose indicator (Ø1 to 99).
		*PLACE	This reserved word causes the data that has been specified up to the first *PLACE to be repeated to the right of that same data. For example, if 4-UP labels for the same name and address are required, the output specification would contain the field for the name, followed by three *PLACE entries.
38	Edit Code	blank	No edit code is used for this output field.
		1 to 9 A, B, C, D, J, K, L, M, N, O, P, Q, X, Y, Z	The predefined edit code is used to mask the output field. The output field must be a numeric variable or numeric named constant. For more information on edit codes and edit words, see Edit Code Summary beginning on page 99.
39	Blank After	blank	The field is output and no other action is taken.
		B	The field is output, then it is cleared. Numeric fields are set to zero and character fields are set to blanks.

Program Described Output File Field Description (continued)

Column	Title	Values	Description
40 - 43	Output Positions (Ending or rightmost location)	blank	The output field is output to a relative position of +0. That is, it is output adjacent to the previous output field's rightmost character.
		1 to 9999	The ending (rightmost) position of the output field.
		+ Ø to +999	The field is output relative to the previous field's ending position. That is, the value of the relative position represents the number of spaces between the first character of this field and the last character of the previous field. For example, an ending position of +001 will put one space between this field and the previous field. The plus sign (+) must appear in column 40, while the relative value must be left justified in columns 41 to 43.
		– 1 to –999	The field is output relative to the previous field's ending position. That is, the value of the relative position represents the number of spaces that this output field will overlap the previous field. For example, an ending position of -001 will overlap the first character of this field with the last character of the previous field. The minus sign (–) must appear in column 40, while the relative value must be left justified in columns 41 to 43.
		K1 to K8	For program defined workstation device files, the K1 to K8 entry represents the length of the format name specified in columns 45 to 54. For example, if the name of a WORKSTN device record format is ORDENTRY, the value K8 must be specified in columns 40 and 41 and the format name 'ORDENTRY' must be specified in columns 45 to 54 (quotes are required).

Program Described Output File Field Description (continued)

Column	Title	Values	Description
44	Data Type	blank	The output field is written as zoned decimal (if it is a numeric data type) or character.
		P	The output field is written as packed decimal.
		B	The output field is written as RPG binary.
		L	The output field is written as zoned numeric with a leading sign. That is the sign appears in the first (leftmost) position of the output field.
		R	The output field is written as zoned numeric with a trailing sign. That is the sign appears in the last (rightmost) position of the output field.
45 - 70	Output Constant or Edit Word	blank	No constant or edit work is used with this output field. These columns must be blank when a non-numeric value is being output.
		'quoted literal', named constant, or numeric literal	If an output field (columns 32 to 37) is not specified, the value specified here is output as a literal. That is, it is written to the output file as it is specified here. If a numeric output field is specified in columns 32 to 37, the quoted literal or a named constant is used as an edit word to mask the numeric output. For more information see Edit Words beginning on page 95.
		format name	The name of a format for a WORKSTN file. The name of the format must be left-adjusted and enclosed in single quotation marks. Also, an entry of K*n* (were *n* is the number of charters in the format name) must be specified in columns 40 and 41.

Externally Described Output File Control Entries

Externally described output files can be controlled with RPGIII operation codes such as WRITE, UPDAT, DELET and EXCPT or by the RPG cycle. In addition, externally described files opened for update can be released from a record lock by using the EXCPT operation to an empty output format.

Column	Title	Values	Description
6	Form Type	O	Identifies this statement as an Output specification.
7 - 14	Format Name	blank	The name used is the same as that of the previous output file control entry.
		format name	The name of an externally described file's format to be output.
15	Type	H or D	Heading output. Heading entries are typically used to output column headings, page numbers and title page data.
		D	Detail output. Functionally the same as the H entry, the D (detail) entry is provided for documentation purposes only.
		T	Total-time output. Total-time records are output during the level-break processing (total-time) of the RPG cycle.
		E	Exception output. Exception records are written via the EXCPT operation code. Exception records can be conditioned by indicators and/or an exception name. Exception names can be specified in columns 32 to 37 of the output statement.
14 - 16	Conditioning Continuation	AND / OR	The indicator conditioning in columns 23 to 31 is a continuation of the previous line. The indicator condition on the previous line AND/OR the indicator condition on this line must be satisfied for the output line to be written.

Externally Described Output File Control Entries (continued)

Column	Title	Values	Description
16 - 18	File Addition and File Deletion	ADD	For database (DISK) files only. Records are added to the file. The letter A must appear in column 66 of the File Description specification for the file being written.
		DEL	For database (DISK) files only. The record is deleted from the file; it will no longer be accessible. The letter U (update) must appear in column 15 of the File Description specification for the file being deleted.
16	Output Control	blank	No special controlling is specified for this output statement.
		F	Fetch overflow. When fetch is specified, RPG checks for overflow after each printed line. If the overflow indicator for this printer file is on and fetch has been specified, any detail and heading lines that are conditioned by that indicator will be printed before this line.
		R	Release WORKSTN device. When release is specified, the WORKSTN file specified in columns 7 to 14 is released from the program. This is functionally equivalent to the REL operation code. See the REL operation code in Chapter 4 for more information on release.
17	Line Spacing Before Printing	blank	For PRINTER files only. The printer will not advance before printing the output line.
		Ø to 3	The printer will advance Ø, 1, 2, or 3 lines before printing the output line.
18	Line Spacing After Printing	blank	For PRINTER files only. The printer will advance 1 line after printing the output line.
		Ø to 3	The printer will advance Ø, 1, 2, or 3 lines after printing the output line.

Externally Described Output File Control Entries (continued)

Column	Title	Values	Description
19 - 20	Line Skipping Before	blank or Ø	For PRINTER files only. The printer will not advance before printing the output line.
		Ø1 to 99	The printer will advance to the line on the current page before printing. If the current print line is beyond the line specified, the printer will eject the current page, and advance to the line on the next page before printing.
		AØ to A9 or BØ to B2	The function for AØ to A9 and BØ to B2 is the same as for Ø1 to 99, except the line numbers represented by AØ to A9 are 1ØØ to 1Ø9 and by BØ to B2 110 to 112 respectively.
21 - 22	Line Skipping After	blank or Ø	For PRINTER files only. The printer will not advance after printing the output line.
		Ø1 to 99	The printer will advance to the line on the current page after printing. If the current print line is beyond the line specified, the printer will eject the current page, and advance to the line on the next page after printing.
		AØ to A9 or BØ to B2	The function for AØ to A9 and BØ to B2 is the same as for Ø1 to 99, except the line numbers represented by AØ to A9 are 1ØØ to 1Ø9 and by BØ to B2 110 to 112 respectively.
23 - 31	Controlling Indicators	blank	No indicators condition this output line.
		1P	First page indicator (valid for heading and detail output only). Output lines conditioned with the 1P indicator are printed after the *INZSR subroutine is performed. during program start.
		indicator	Any valid indicator (up to three) can be specified to control the output line. If more than three indicators are required, the continuation controls can be specified. (AND/OR in columns 14 to 16.)
32-37	Except Name	blank	No exception name controls the output line.
		name	This line is controlled by an exception name (column 15 contains the letter E). If conditioning indicators are specified, their condition must be satisfied for the line to be output. Except names are used in conjunction with the EXCPT operation code.
38-74		Blank	These columns are not used.

Externally Described Output File Field Description

Externally described file output fields can be used to specify that only certain fields be output and they can also be used to assign the blank-after function to an externally described output field.

Column	Title	Values	Description
6	Form Type	O	Identifies this statement as an Output specification.
7 - 22			Not used for output fields.
23 - 31	Controlling Indicators	blank	The output field is always written whenever the controlling output specification is written.
		1P	The output field is written only once—at first page output time (1P).
		any valid indicator (up to three)	The output field is included in the output operation only when the test of the controlling indicators is true.
32 - 37	Output Field Name	name	The name of the field to be output when the controlling output specification is written. The field name must have already been defined in the program.
		*ALL	All fields are output to the file.
			Output field specifications are optional for the WRITE, UPDAT, and EXCPT operations to externally described files.
		blank	An EXCPT operation to an exception output label with no output fields specified causes the current record lock (if any) to be released.
38			Not used by externally described output fields.
39	Blank After	blank	The field is output and no other action is taken.
		B	The field is output, then it is cleared. Numeric fields are set to zero and character fields are set to blanks.
40 - 74			Not used by externally described output fields.

Editing Numeric Output

Edit Words

Edit words are patterns or *masks* that are specified in RPG Output specifications. They are used to create ad hoc edits for numeric values such as phone numbers, social security numbers, sales figures and the time-of-day. Figure 2-26 illustrates various edit word masks.

Description	Edit Word `*...v....1....v...`	Unedited Value	Edited Output
Large value	`'   ,   . '`	00654321	6,543.21
Stop zero-suppression	`'   , 0 . '`	00000027	0.27
Time-of-day	`'0  :  : '`	071223	07:12:23
Social Security number	`'0   -  -    '`	023456789	023-45-6789
Phone number	`'0(   )&   -    '`	8005529404	(800) 552-9404
Floating currency symbol	`'  ,   , $0. '`	000009402	$94.02

Figure 2-26: Example Edit Word Usage

The number of blanks plus the zero suppression control code (i.e., the leading zero or asterisk), within an edit word must be greater than or equal to the number of digits for the field or named constant being edited.

Since editing a numeric value often changes the overall size of the value, RPG uses ending positions for the output location of fields in the Output specification. This allows the right sides of numeric values to be aligned properly after editing.

TIP: To prevent zero suppression of output, specify a leading zero in the first (i.e., leftmost) position of the edit word. This is typically used for editing values such as phone numbers where zero suppression is not desired.

Edit Word Construction

The currency symbol and zero suppression character do not displace numbers within the edit word. The currency symbol, however, requires an additional position. This additional position is usually allocated as the leftmost position of the edit word. Figure 2-27 illustrates the edit mask required to edit a numeric field with a floating currency symbol, commas, a decimal point and zero suppression. The size of this numeric field is 9 positions with 2 decimal positions.

Output positions ☞		CS	1		2	3	4		5	6	7		8	9	
Edit Word mask ☞	‘	ƀ	ƀ	,	ƀ	ƀ	ƀ	,	ƀ	$	0	.	ƀ	ƀ	’
Unedited value ☞						7	6	5	4	3	2	1	2	1	
Output value ☞		$	7	,	6	5	4	,	3	2	1	.	2	1	

Figure 2-27: Edit Mask with Floating Currency Symbol

Figure 2-31 on page 101 illustrates how to specify any symbol as the currency symbol used by the RPG program.

Edit words consist of four optional elements:

1. The *Body*. The area of the edit word where the numeric value will be positioned.
2. The *Status*. The area of the edit word consisting of the letters CR or a minus sign (–). It is used to indicate whether the value is negative or positive.
3. The *Expansion*. The area following the body and status (usually literal values).
4. *Literal values*. Literal values can appear anywhere in the edit word. Literal values are included in the output only when significant digits appear to the left of the literal value. Note: While a named constant can be used as an edit word, named constants cannot be used within (that is, as part of) the edit word itself.

Edit Word Control Codes

There are several control codes that can be inserted into an edit word to control zero suppression, leading asterisks, floating currency symbol, blanks and decimal notation. The first occurrence of a *control* code is used as the control code. Subsequent occurrences are treated as literal values except for the ampersand (&), which is always used as a control code. Figure 2-28 contains a description of the edit word control codes that can be used in an edit word.

Control Code	Description
$	***Currency symbol:*** If the currency symbol is followed immediately by a zero, the currency symbol will precede the first significant digit. This is referred to as a *floating currency sign*. If the currency symbol is not followed by a zero, the currency symbol's position is fixed. When using the floating currency symbol, an available blank position is displaced. Typically, the displaced blank is shifted to the left of the currency symbol. The character used as the currency symbol is specified in column 18 of the Header specification.
*	***Asterisk***: Leading zeros are replaced with asterisks to the position of the asterisk. Zero suppression ends at the position of the asterisk.
&	***Ampersand***: Always replaced with a blank when output.
0	***Zero***: Ends zero suppression at the position of the zero. The zero used as one of the output positions for digits to appear.
. or ,	***Decimal notation***: These characters are not actual control codes, they are treated as literal values. They are traditionally used for decimal and thousands notation.
b̸	***Blanks***: Identifies available positions for the numeric value.
CR	***Status***: The literal value CR is output if the value is negative.
–	***Status***: The minus sign (-) is output if the value is negative.

Figure 2-28: Edit Word Control Codes

Edit Words and Named Constants

To use an edit word, place the desired edit word—left-justified—into columns 45 to 70 of the Output specification for the field being edited. The RPG Output specification accepts edit word literal values of up to 26 positions. For edit words that exceed 26 positions, a Named Constant can be used. Named constant edit words can be up to 115 positions in length and can be specified—left justified—in columns 45 to 50 of the Output specification. Figure 2-29 contains examples of edit word usage.

```
SeqNoI..............NamedConstant+++++++++C.........Const+
     I              '0(   )&   -    '     C         EDTPHN

SeqNoCSRn01n02n03Factor1+++OpCodFactor2+++ResultLenDXHILOEQ
     C                     TIME           TIME    60
     C                     Z-ADD*DATE     DATE    90
     C                     Z-ADD8005551212PHONE  100
     C                     Z-ADD654321    SALES  102
     C                     MOVE 023456789 SSNBR   90
     C                     EXCPT
     C                     SETON                        LR

SeqNoOFilenameEFBASBSAn01n02n03Field+EBEnd+POutputconstant++++++++++++
     OQPRINT  E  1
     O                                +  0 'Soc Sec Nbr:'
     O                        SSNBR   +  2 '0   -  -    '
     OQPRINT  E  1
     O                                +  0 'Phone Nbr:'
     O                        PHONE   +  2 EDTPHN
     OQPRINT  E  1
     O                                +  0 'Date/Time:'
     O                        DATE   Y+  2
     O                        TIME    +  2 '0  &  &  '
     OQPRINT  E  1
     O                                +  0 'Salary:'
     O                        SALES   +  2 '$   ,   ,  *. CR'
```

Figure 2-29: Example Edit Word Usage

TIP: Be careful when using literal values in an edit word. Literal values can be any characters, including the letters CR. The first occurrence of the letters CR is interpreted as the *status* code and will not appear when the number is positive.

Edit Codes

Edit codes are single–character codes that represent predefined editing patterns. These edit patterns are simply specific edit word masks that automatically adapt to the size of the numeric field or named constant being edited. This allows numeric fields of any size to be edited without concern for the particular semantics involved in using edit words.

To edit using an edit code, place the desired edit code into column 38 of the Output specification for the field to be edited.

Edit codes can be combined with special edit characters, such as the floating currency symbol ($) and leading asterisk (*), to further edit numeric output. These special characters can be specified—left justified—columns 45 to 70 of the Output specification. The characters must be enclosed in single quotes (i.e., apostrophes), and only one of these characters can be specified for a field edited with an edit code.

To illustrate the output of numeric values edited with edit codes, three versions of edited output are illustrated in Figure 2-30. The first uses only the edit code, the second uses the edit code and the floating currency symbol, and the third uses the edit code with leading asterisks.

In each example, the data being output is a nine-digit numeric field with two decimal positions. For positive numbers, the value 0004567.89 is used; for negative output, the value -0004567.89 is used; and for zero output, the value 0000000.00 is used.

Edit Code	Thousands Notation	Output Zeros	Negative Sign	Positive Output	Negative Output	Zero Output
1	Yes	Yes	No	4,567.89	4,567.89	.00
1 $				$4,567.89	$4,567.89	$.00
1 *				****4,567.89	****4,567.89	*********.00
2	Yes	No	No	4,567.89	4,567.89	
2 $				$4,567.89	$4,567.89	
2 *				****4,567.89	****4,567.89	************
3	No	Yes	No	4567.89	4567.89	.00
3 $				$4567.89	$4567.89	$.00
3 *				****4567.89	****4567.89	*********.00
4	No	No	No	4567.89	4567.89	
4 $				$4567.89	$4567.89	
4 *				****4567.89	****4567.89	**********

Figure 2-30: RPGIII Edit Codes (1 of 2)

Edit Code	Thousands Notation	Output Zeros	Negative Sign	Positive Output	Negative Output	Zero Output
A A $ A *	Yes	Yes	Yes CR	4,567.89 $4,567.89 ****4,567.89	4,567.89CR $4,567.89CR ****4,567.89CR	.00 $.00 *********.00
B B $ B *	Yes	No	Yes CR	4,567.89 $4,567.89 ****4,567.89	4,567.89CR $4,567.89CR ****4,567.89CR	************
C C $ C *	No	Yes	Yes CR	4567.89 $4567.89 ****4567.89	4567.89CR $4567.89CR ****4567.89CR	.00 $.00 *******.00
D D $ D *	No	No	Yes CR	4567.89 $4567.89 ****4567.89	4567.89CR $4567.89CR ****4567.89CR	************
J J $ J *	Yes	Yes	Yes -	4,567.89 $4,567.89 ****4,567.89	4,567.89- $4,567.89- ****4,567.89-	.00 $.00 *********.00
K K $ K *	Yes	No	Yes -	4,567.89 $4,567.89 ****4,567.89	4,567.89- $4,567.89- ****4,567.89-	************
L L $ L *	No	Yes	Yes -	4567.89 $4567.89 ****4567.89	4567.89- $4567.89- ****4567.89-	.00 $.00 *******.00
M M $ M *	No	No	Yes -	4567.89 $4567.89 ****4567.89	4567.89- $4567.89- ****4567.89-	************
N N $ N *	Yes	Yes	Yes -	4,567.89 $4,567.89 ****4,567.89	-4,567.89 -$4,567.89 ****-4,567.89	.00 $.00 *********.00
O O $ O *	Yes	No	Yes -	4,567.89 $4,567.89 ****4,567.89	-4,567.89 -$4,567.89 ****-4,567.89	************
P P $ P *	No	Yes	Yes -	4567.89 $4567.89 ****4567.89	-4567.89 -$4567.89 ****-4567.89	.00 $.00 *******.00
Q Q $ Q *	No	No	Yes -	4567.89 $4567.89 ****4567.89	-4567.89 -$4567.89 ****-4567.89	************
X	No	Yes	No	000456789	00045678R	000000000
Y	No	Yes	N/A	45/67/89	N/A	0/00/00
Z	No	No	No	456789	456789	

Figure 2-30: RPGIII Edit Codes (2 of 2)

Custom Currency Symbol

The RPG Header specification is used to control global editing values. The currency symbol, date format, date separator and decimal notation are all controlled by the Header specification (see Figure 2-18 on page 38).

The character used as the currency symbol is controlled by column 18 of the Header specification. The character specified in column 18 is used as the currency symbol and can be with edit words and edit codes. For example, if the "at" sign (@) is specified in column 18, then the @ symbol must be used wherever the currency symbol is normally used. Figure 2-31 illustrates the use of the @ symbol as the currency symbol.

```
*...v....1....v....2....v....3....v....4....v....5....v....6....v....7.
     H           @
     OQPRINT E
     O                                  +  0 'Salary:'
     O                         WAGE     +  2 '   ,   , @0.  '
```

Figure 2-31: Example Custom Currency Symbol Use

Date Edit Code Control Summary

Figure 2-32 contains various examples that illustrate how the RPG Header specification effects the date edit code (Y). Specific references to columns 19, 20 and 21 of the Header specification are included in the figure.

The date: 21 June, 1988 (or June 21, 1988 for those who live in the U.S.A.) is the basis for the examples used in this chart. For a description of the columns of the Header specification referred to in Figure 2-32, see the Header specification beginning on page 38.

Type of Date	Date Separator	Decimal Notation	Date Format Column 19 of the Header Specification			
See note[2]	Column 20	Column 21	Blank	M	D	Y
UDATE	Blank	Blank	6/21/88	6/21/88	21/06/88	88/06/21
UDATE	Blank	D	21/06/88	6/21/88	21/06/88	88/06/21
UDATE	Blank	I or J	21.06.88	6.21.88	21.06.88	88.06.21
UDATE	–	Blank	6-21-88	6-21-88	21-06-88	88-06-21
UDATE	–	D	21-06-88	6-21-88	21-06-88	88-06-21
UDATE	–	I or J	21-06-88	6-21-88	21-06-88	88-06-21
*DATE	Blank	Blank	6/21/1988	6/21/1988	21/06/1988	1988/06/21
*DATE	Blank	D	21/06/1988	6/21/1988	21/06/1988	1988/06/21
*DATE	Blank	I or J	21.06.1988	6.21.1988	21.06.1988	1988.06.21
*DATE	–	Blank	6-21-1988	6-21-1988	21-06-1988	1988-06-21
*DATE	–	D	21-06-1988	6-21-1988	21-06-1988	1988-06-21
*DATE	–	I or J	21-06-1988	6-21-1988	21-06-1988	1988-06-21

Figure 2-32: Controlling Date Editing with the Header Specification

---

TIP: To avoid zero-suppression of the leading zero in a date field, (e.g., to output the date as 06/21/88 instead of 6/21/88) use a 7 or 9 position numeric field for output instead of UDATE or *DATE. The Y edit code, by definition, zero-suppresses only the first zero in the output field. Moving UDATE or *DATE to a larger field avoids zero suppression of the leading digit in the date.

---

2 The UDATE field is a 6 position numeric field with zero decimal positions. The *DATE field is an 8 position numeric field with zero decimal positions.

Table and Array Specification

Tables and arrays are placed after the last specification form and are identified by placing asterisks in columns 1 and 2 and leaving column 3 blank. The table or array data must begin on the line following the table and array specification. If multiple tables or arrays are required, they must follow each other. For example, the following program contains two compile-time arrays.

```
SeqNoFFileNameIPE.E....RLEN...K.OV.....Device+RcdNbrKOptionEntry+
     FPRINTER O   F     132      OV      PRINTER
SeqNoE....FromfileTofile..ArrnamEPRDim+LenPDAAltnamLenPDA
     E                    CODE    3   6  3
     E                    DESC    1   3 80
SeqNoCLOn01n02n03Factor1+++OpCodFactor2+++ResultLenDXHiLoEq
     C                     DO   6         X       50
     C          X          COMP 3                      3030
     C                     EXCPTDETAIL
     C                     END
     C                     MOVE *ON       *INLR
SeqNoOFilenameEFBASBSAn01n02n03Field+EBEnd+POutputconstant+++++++++++
     OPRINTER E  1             DETAIL
     O                                +  0 'Index/value:'
     O                         X     Z +  1
     O                         CODE,X  +  2
     O                    30   DESC,X  +  2
**      This is the CODE array.
A01B02C03
D04E05F06
**      This is the DESC array.
Code Group Alpha
Code Group Beta
Code Group Gamma
```

When this program is run, the following output is generated.

```
*... ... 1 ... ... 2 ... ... 3 ... ... 4 ... ... 5 ... ... 6 ... ...
Index/value:  1  A01  Code Group Alpha
Index/value:  2  B02  Code Group Beta
Index/value:  3  C03  Code Group Gamma
Index/value:  4  D04
Index/value:  5  E05
Index/value:  6  F06
```

Chapter 3

The RPG Program Cycle

The RPG program cycle is a built-in mechanism through which RPG programs can process data. RPG was originally designed to generate reports, hence the name Report Program Generator. Today, however, RPG is used for much more. Interactive programs featuring sophisticated inquiry, financial and manufacturing processes are the norm for RPG programs.

The RPG cycle provides support for:

1. Primary and secondary file processing. The method used to implicitly read, write and/or update data files.
2. Matching record processing. A technique used to control the input sequence of primary and secondary files.
3. Level break processing. A technique used to indicate when the contents of one or more fields changes between records, and to control total-time calculations.
4. Detail and total time processing. Used to control when calculations are performed and when certain output lines, are written.

The cycle is a complex high-function feature of RPG. It is seldom used, however, in the modern RPG language. Instead, structured programming constructs, modular programming and several modern RPG OpCodes make the RPG cycle a feature that is more complex than functional.

In this chapter the components of the RPG cycle are illustrated. For additional information on the RPG cycle, consult the RPG programming reference manual for the system being used. The IBM System/3 RPGII Programmer Reference manual contains the most correct and clear description of the RPG cycle. However, this manual is no longer in print and is difficult to obtain.

On the pages that follow several flowcharts are used to illustrate the RPG cycle. Figure 3-33 on page 107 includes a description of the *INZSR subroutine. Figure 3-34 on page 108, contains a detailed flowchart of the entire RPG cycle.

Program Initialization

After the *INIT routine of the RPG cycle is performed, if an initialization subroutine (*INZSR) exists in the program, it will be called. The *INZSR subroutine can be used to initialize fields, data structures, arrays, indicators, etc. The *INZSR subroutine is specified by coding the subroutine and naming it *INZSR. See Figure 3-33. Note: The RESET operation cannot be specified within the *INZSR subroutine, nor can it be used in any subroutine that is called by *INZSR.

*INZSR Subroutine

The *INZSR subroutine is the first user-specified subroutine to be run after a program is started—before 1P (first page) output. All RPG operation codes, except RESET, can be specified in the *INZSR subroutine. Normally, *INZSR is used to set initial values for fields, data structures, data structure subfields and arrays. It can also be used to retrieve date and time information for 1P output and to set unique initial values for specific occurrences of multiple occurrence data structures.

Upon exiting *INZSR, RPG sets up a save area containing the value of the fields that are referenced by a RESET operation anywhere in the program. This save area is a mirror image of the field value after *INZSR is performed. It is used by the RESET operation to reset the field, data structure, array, etc. to its initial value.

Figure 3-33 illustrates the use of the *INZSR subroutine.

```
SeqNoIDSName....IUDSInitialValue++++++++++PFromTo++DField+
     IINVOIC      DS
     I                                        1   50INVNBR
     I                                      P 6   82PRICE
     I                                        9  12 ITEM

SeqNoCLOn01n02n03Factor1+++OpCodFactor2+++ResultLenDXHiLoEq
                           .
                           .
                           .
     CSR         *INZSR    BEGSR
     C                     Z-ADD1000      INVNBR
     C                     Z-ADD0         PRICE
     C                     MOVEL'AS'      ITEM
     CSR                   ENDSR
```

Figure 3-33: Example *INZSR Subroutine

In the example illustrated in Figure 3-33, the data structure subfield INVNBR is set to 1000, the subfield PRICE is set to zeros and the subfield ITEM is set to 'AS' by the *INZSR subroutine. Since the field values are set by the *INZSR subroutine, these values become the *initial values* for the fields. Consequently, whenever a RESET operation is performed on the data structure INVOIC or the individual fields, the initial values (i.e., 1000, 0 and 'AS') will be moved into the fields.

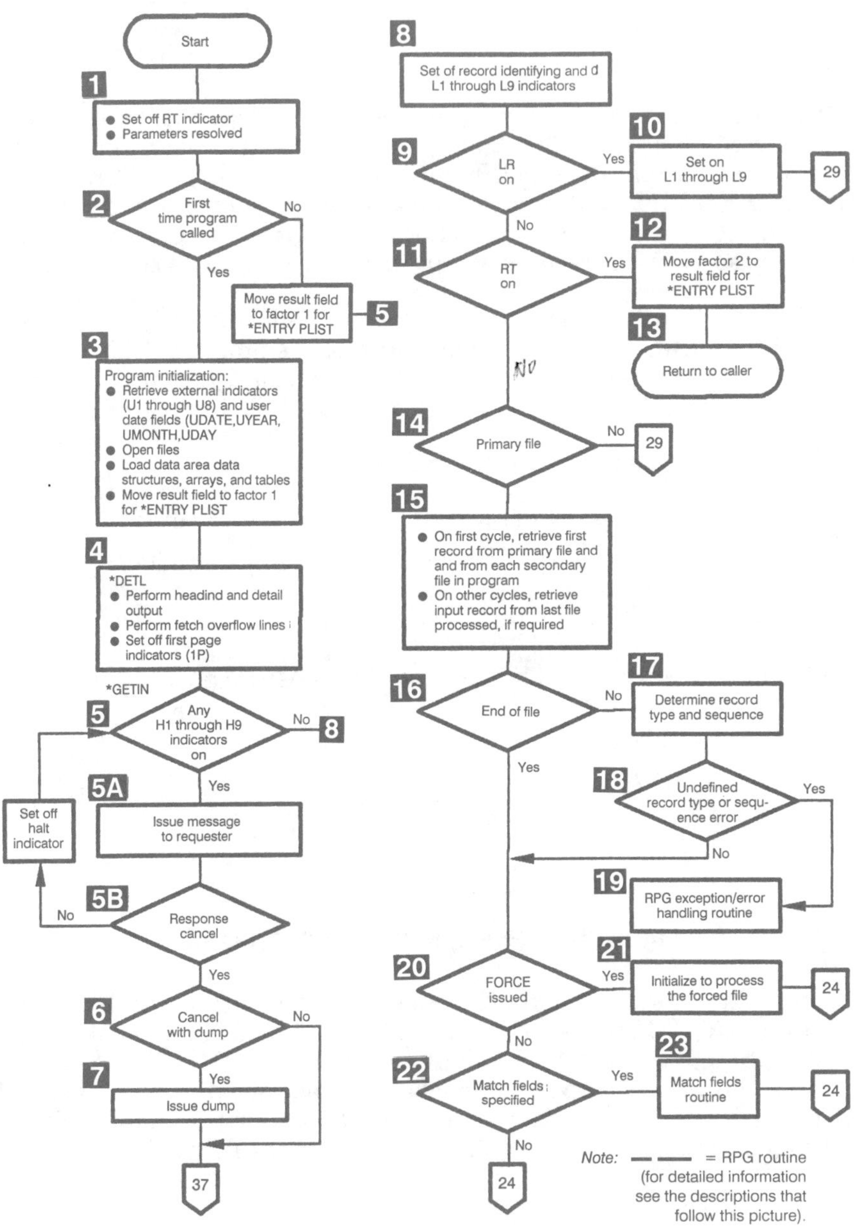

Figure 3-34: Detailed RPG Program Cycle (1 of 2)

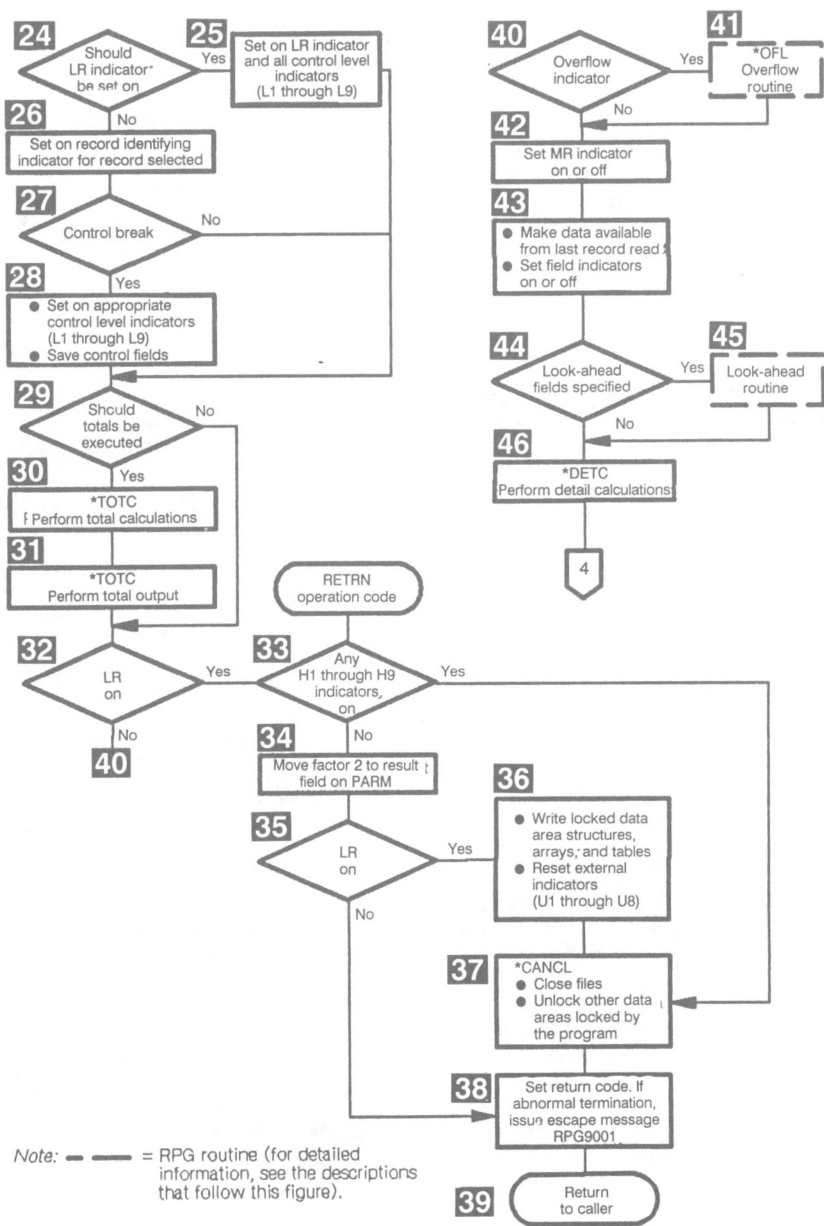

Figure 3-34 : Detailed RPG Program Cycle (2 of 2)

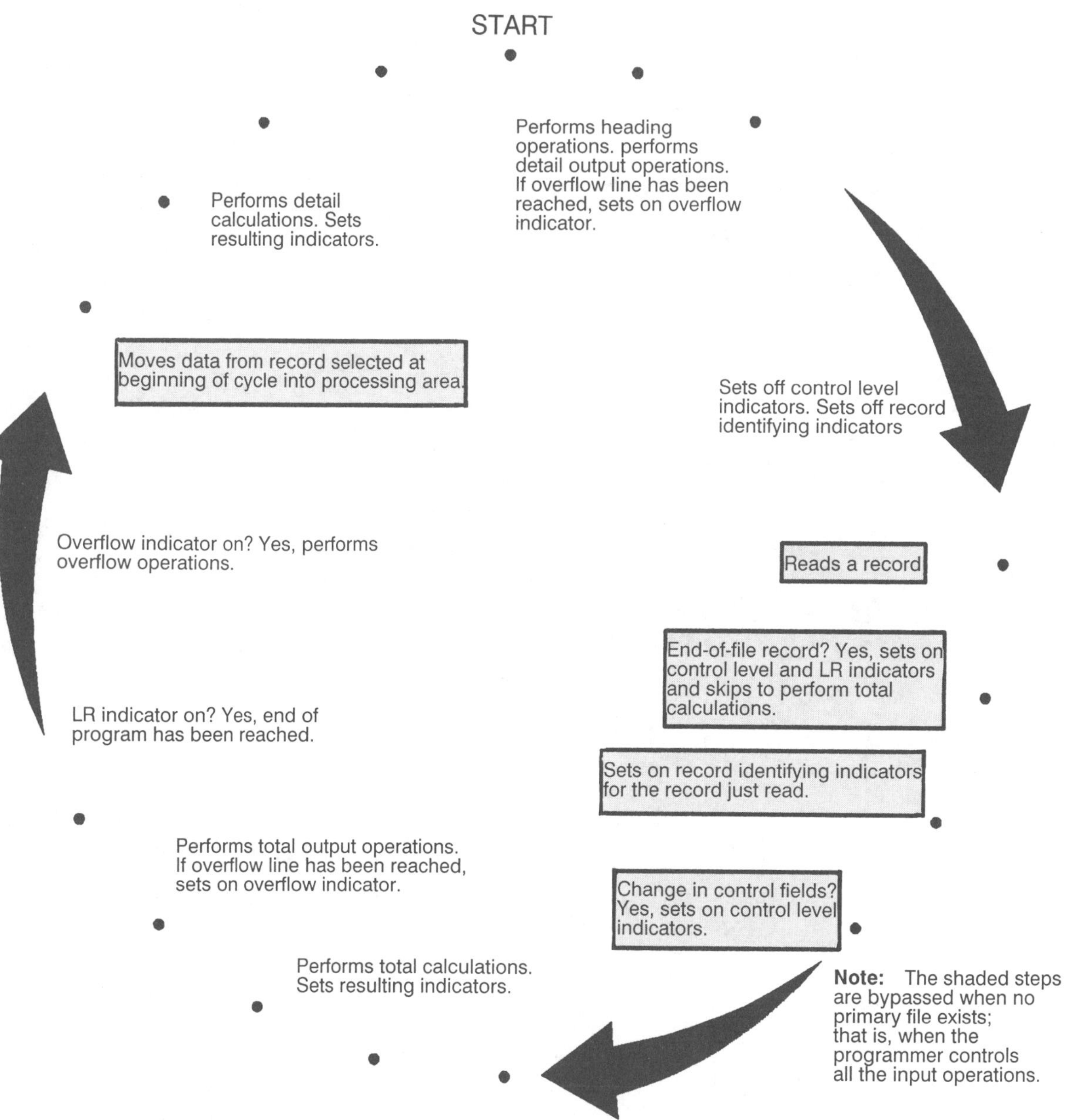
START
Performs heading operations. performs detail output operations. If overflow line has been reached, sets on overflow indicator.
Performs detail calculations. Sets resulting indicators.
Moves data from record selected at beginning of cycle into processing area.
Sets off control level indicators. Sets off record identifying indicators
Overflow indicator on? Yes, performs overflow operations.
Reads a record
End-of-file record? Yes, sets on control level and LR indicators and skips to perform total calculations.
LR indicator on? Yes, end of program has been reached.
Sets on record identifying indicators for the record just read.
Performs total output operations. If overflow line has been reached, sets on overflow indicator.
Change in control fields? Yes, sets on control level indicators.
Performs total calculations. Sets resulting indicators.
Note: The shaded steps are bypassed when no primary file exists; that is, when the programmer controls all the input operations.

Figure 3-35: RPG Logic Cycle

Detailed RPG Program Cycle Description

Figure 3-34 illustrates the specific steps in the detailed flow of the RPG program cycle, while Figure 3-35 provides an overview of the RPG logic cycle. The item numbers on the pages that follow refer to the numbers in Figure 3-34. Other routines, such as the overflow and exception/error routines, appear in subsequent flowcharts starting on page 116.

1. Indicator RT is set off. RPG determines whether an *ENTRY PLIST is specified. If so, parameters are resolved.

2. RPG checks for the first invocation of the program. If it is the first invocation, RPG continues the program initialization (step 3), then calls the program initialization subroutine (*INZSR) if one exists in the program. If it is not the first invocation of the program, RPG moves the input parameters (Result fields) to Factor 1 in the PARM statement of the *ENTRY PLIST and branches to step 5.

3. The program is initialized. RPG sets up the external indicators (U1 to U8) and user date fields (UDATE, UYEAR, UMONTH, and UDAY), opens the files, loads all data area data structures and arrays, and moves the Result fields to Factor 1 in the PARMS statement of the *ENTRY PLIST.

4. Heading and detail lines (identified by an H or D in position 15 of the output specifications) are written before the first record is read. Heading and detail lines are always processed at the same time. If conditioning indicators are specified, the proper indicator setting must be satisfied. If fetch overflow logic is specified and the overflow indicator is on, the appropriate overflow lines are written. File translation, if specified, is done for heading and detail lines and overflow output. This step is the return point in the program if Factor 2 of an ENDSR operation contains a field name of a constant with the value *DETL.

5. RPG tests the halt indicator (H1 to H9). If all halt indicators are off, the program branches to step 8. Halt indicators can be set on anytime during the program. This step is the return point in the program if Factor 2 of an ENDSR operation contains a field name or a constant with the value *GETIN.

5a. If any halt indicators are on, a message is issued to the requester. For an interactive job, the message goes to the requester. For a batch job, the message goes to the system operator; if the system operator is not available (i.e., not in break mode,) the default response is issued.

5b. If the response is to continue, the halt indicator is set off, and the program returns to step 5. If the response is to cancel, the program goes to step 6.

6. If the response is to cancel with a dump, the program goes to step 7; otherwise, the program branches to step 37.

7. The program issues a dump operation and branches to step 37 (abnormal ending).

8. RPG sets off all record identifying, 1P (first page) and control level (L1 to L9) indicators. All overflow indicators (OA to OG and OV) are set off unless they have been set on during the preceding detail calculations or detail output. Any other indicators that are on, remain on.

9. RPG determines whether the LR (last record) indicator is on. If it is on, the program continues with step 10. If it is not on, the program branches to step 11.

10. RPG sets the appropriate control level (L1 to L9) indicators on and branches to step 29.

11. RPG determines whether the RPG indicator is on. If it is on, the program continues with step 12; otherwise, the program branches to step 14.

12. If an *ENTRY PLIST is specified, RPG moves Factor 2 of the PARM operation to the Result field of the *ENTRY PLIST.

13. If the RT indicator is on, the called program returns to the caller.

14. RPG determines whether the program contains a primary file. If a primary file is specified, the program continues with step 15; otherwise, the program branches to step 29.

15. During the first program cycle, RPG reads the first record from the primary file and from each secondary file in the program. In other program cycles, RPG reads a record from the last file processed. If this file is processed by a record address (ADDROUT) file, the data in the record address file defines the record to be retrieved. If look-ahead fields are specified in the last record processed, the record may already be in storage; therefore, no read may be performed at this time.

16. RPG determines whether end of file has occurred on the file just read. If it has not occurred, the program continues with step 17; otherwise, the program branches to step 20.

17. If RPG has read a record from the file, the record type and record sequence (columns 15 though 18 of the input specification) are determined.
18. RPG determines whether the record type is defined in the program, or if the record sequence is correct. If the record type is undefined or the record sequence is incorrect, the program continues with step 19; otherwise, the program branches to step 20.
19. The RPG exception/error handling routine receives control. (For more information on this routine, see the flowchart on this routine featured later in this chapter, and "Exception/error handling" in Chapter 9.)
20. RPG determines whether a FORCE operation was processed on the previous cycle. If a FORCE operation was processed, the program selects that file for processing (step 21) and branches around the processing for matched fields (steps 22 and 23). The branch is processed because all records processed with a FORCE operation are processed with the matching record (MR) indicator off.
21. If FORCE was issued on the previous cycle, the program selects the forced file for processing after removing any match fields from the file just read. If the file FORCEd is at end of file, normal, primary or secondary multifile logic selects the next record for processing and the program branches to step 24.
22. RPG determines whether match fields are specified. If match fields are specified, the program continues with step 23; otherwise, the program branches to step 24.
23. The match fields routine receives control. (For more information on this routine, see the flowchart on this routine featured later in this chapter.)
24. RPG sets on the LR indicator when all records are processed from the files that have an E specified in column 17 of the File Description specification and all matching secondary records have been processed. If indicator LR is not set on, processing continues with step 26.
25. RPG set on the LR indicator and all control level indicators; processing continues with step 29.
26. RPG sets on the record identifying indicator for the record selected for processing.

27. RPG determines whether the record selected for processing caused a control break. A control break occurs when the value in the control fields of the record being processed differs from the value of the control fields of the last record processed. If a control break has not occurred, the program branches to step 29.

28. When a control break occurs, RPG sets on the appropriate control level indicator. This causes all lower level control indicators to be set on. The program saves the contents of the control field(s).

29. RPG determines whether the total-time calculations and total-time output should be done. Totals are bypassed on the first cycle if control levels are not specified in the input specifications. After the first cycle, totals are processed on every cycle. If control levels are specified in the input specifications, totals are bypassed until after the first record containing control fields has been processed. Totals are always processed when the LR indicator is on.

30. RPG processes all total-time calculations conditioned by a control level entry (columns 7 and 8 of the calculation specifications). This step is the return point in the program if Factor 2 of the ENDSR operation contains a field name or constant with the value *TOTC.

31. RPG processes all total-time output. If fetch overflow logic is specified and an overflow indicator (OA to OG or OV) is on, the overflow lines are written. File translation, if any, is done for all total output and overflow lines. This step is the return point in the program if Factor 2 of the ENDSR operation contains a field name or a constant with the value *TOTL.

32. If indicator LR is on, the program continues with step 33; otherwise, the program branches to step 40.

33. RPG tests the halt indicators. If any halt indicators are on, the program branches to step 37 (abnormal ending). If the halt indicators are off, the program continues with step 34. If the RETRN operation is used, the program branches to step 33 upon processing that operation.

34. RPG moves the Factor 2 fields in the PARM statements of the *ENTRY PLIST to the Result fields of the PARM statements.

35. If indicator LR is on, the program continues with step 36; otherwise, the program branches to step 38.

36. RPG writes all arrays and tables for which a file name is specified in columns 19 to 26 of the extension specifications and translates them, if necessary. All locked data area data structures are written, and the external indicators (U1 to U8) are reset.

37. RPG closes all open files. If Factor 2 of the ENDSR operation contains a field name or constant with the value *CANCL, the return point in the program is here and includes steps 37 to 39. RPG also unlocks all data areas that have been locked (*LOCK IN) but not unlocked.
38. The internal return code is set. RPG issues an escape message that the program is ending abnormally.
39. RPG returns control to the calling program.
40. RPG determines whether any overflow indicators are on. If an overflow indicator is on, the program continues with step 41; otherwise the program branches to step 42.
41. The overflow routine receives control. (For more information on the overflow routine, see the flowchart on this routine featured later in this chapter.) This step is the return point in the program if Factor 2 of an ENDSR operation contains a field name or a constant with the value *OFL.
42. Indicator MR is set on and remains on for the complete cycle that processes the matching record if this is a multifile program and if the record to be processed is a matching record. Otherwise, indicator MR is set off.
43. Data from the last record read is made available for processing. RPG sets field indicators on, if specified.
44. RPG determines whether look-ahead fields are specified. If so, the program continues with step 45; otherwise, the program branches to step 46.
45. The look-ahead routine receives control. (For more information on the look-ahead routine, see the flowchart on this routine featured later in this chapter.)
46. RPG processes detail calculations. This step is the return point in the program if Factor 2 of the ENDSR operation contains a field name or constant with the value *DETC. The program branches to step 4.

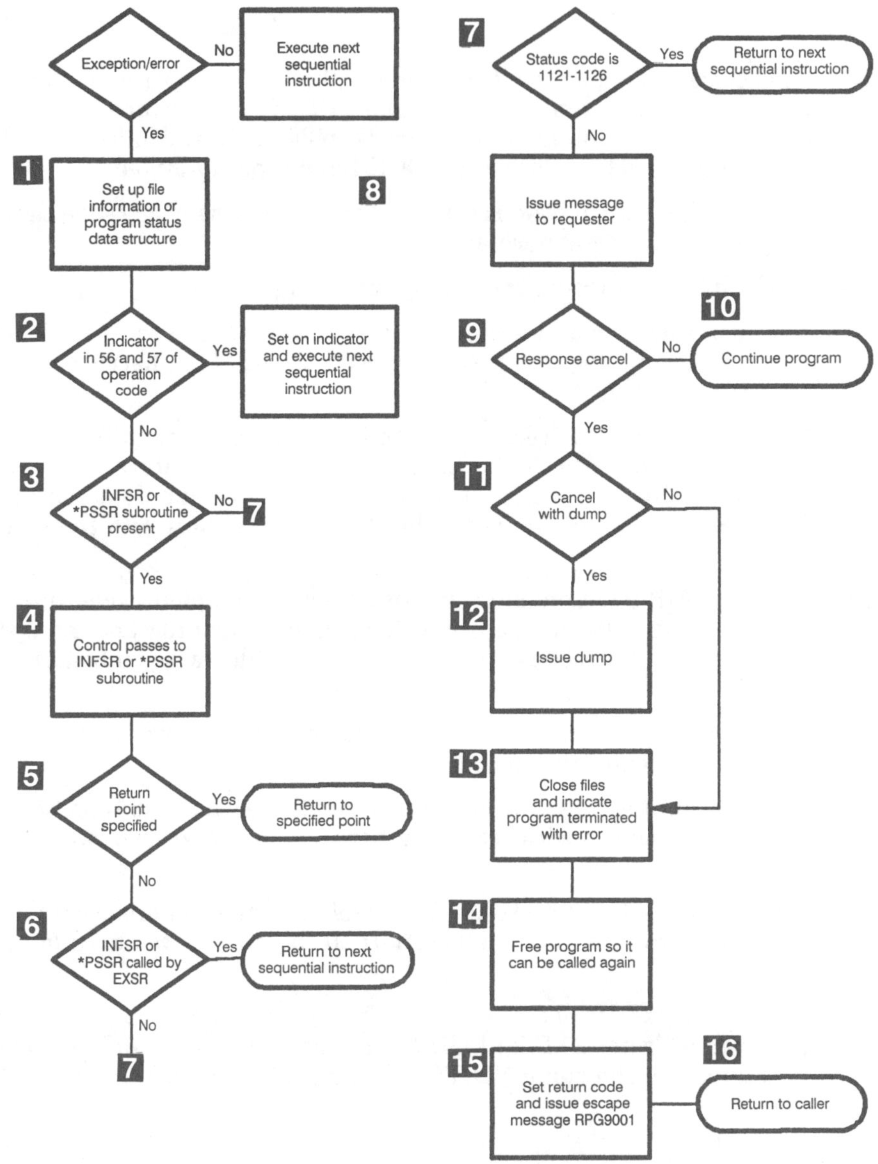

Figure 3-36: Exception/Error Handling Routine

Exception/Error Handling Routine Description

The exception/error handling routine, illustrated in Figure 3-36 is described in the steps that follow.

1. Set up the file information or program status data structure, if specified, with status information.
2. If the exception/error occurred on an operation code that has an indicator specified in position 56 and 57 of the calculation specifications, RPG sets the indicator and control returns to the next sequential instruction in the calculations.
3. RPG determines whether the appropriate exception/error subroutine (INFSR or *PSSR) is present in the program.
4. Control passes to the exception/error subroutine (INFSR or *PSSR).
5. RPG determines whether a return point is specified in Factor 2 of the ENDSR operation for the exception/error subroutine. If a return point is specified, the program goes to the specified return point. If a return point is not specified, the program goes to step 6. If a field name is specified in Factor 2 of the ENDSR operation and the content is not one of the RPG-defined return points (such as *GETIN or *DETC), the program goes to step 6. No error is indicated, and the original error is handled as though the Factor 2 entry were blank.
6. If the exception/error subroutine was called explicitly by the EXSR operation, the program returns to the next sequential instruction. If not, the program continues with step 7.
7. If the STATUS code is 1121 to 1126 (see "Program Status Codes" in Chapter 4 for a list of available status codes,) control returns to the next sequential instruction. If not, the program continues with step 7.
8. A message is issued. For an interactive program, the message is sent to the requester (e.g., the workstation user). For a batch program, the message is sent to the computer system operator. If the computer system operator is not available, a default response is used.
9. RPG determines whether the response is to cancel the program. If the response is to cancel, the program branches to step 11. If not, the program continues with step 10.
10. The program continues processing at *GETIN.

11. RPG determines whether the response is to cancel with a dump. If the response is to cancel with a dump, the program continues with step 12. If not, the program branches to step 13.
12. RPG issues a formatted dump operation.
13. RPG closes all files and sets the return code to indicate that the program ended with an error.
14. RPG frees the program so that it can be called again, and control returns to the calling program.
15. The return code is set, and an error message is issued.
16. Control returns to the calling program.

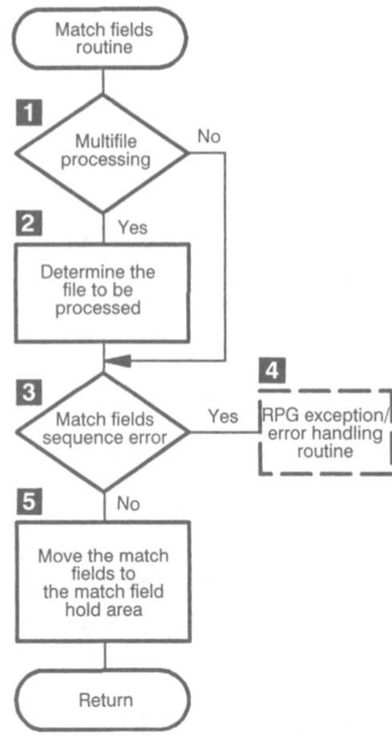

Figure 3-37: Match Fields Routine

Match Fields Routine Description

1. RPG determines whether multifile processing is being used. IF multifile processing is being used, processing continues with step 2; otherwise, the program branches to step 3.
2. RPG tests the value of the match fields in the hold area to determine which file is to be processed next.
3. RPG extracts the match fields from the match files and performs match file sequence checking. If the match fields are in sequence, the program branches to step 5.
4. If the match fields are not in sequence, the RPG exception/error handling routine receives control. See flowchart on page 116.
5. RPG moves the match fields to the hold area for the respective file. A hold area is provided for each file that has match fields. The next record is selected for processing based on the value in the match fields.

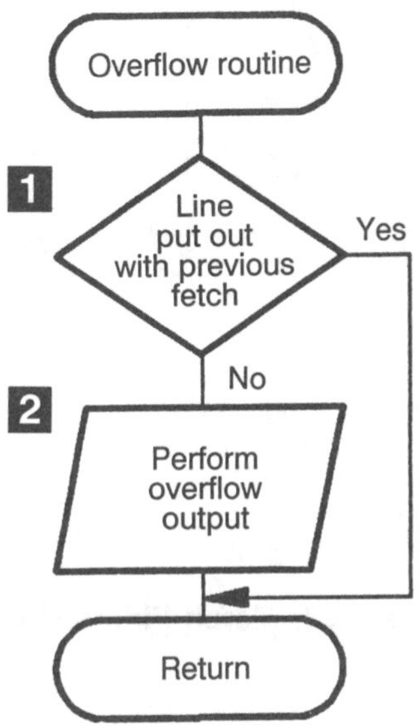

Figure 3-38: Overflow Routine

Overflow Routine Description

1. RPG determines whether the overflow lines were written previously using fetch overflow logic. If the overflow lines were written previously, the program branches to a specified return point; otherwise, processing continues with step 2.
2. RPG tests all output lines conditioned with an overflow indicator and writes the conditioned overflow lines.

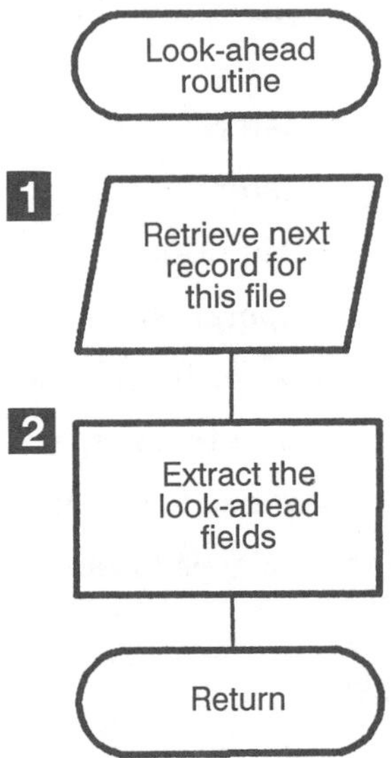

Figure 3-39: Look-Ahead Routine

Look-Ahead Routine Description

1. RPG reads the next record for the file being processed. However, if the file is a combined or update file (identified by a C or U, respectively, in column 15 of the File Description specification), RPG extracts the look-ahead fields from the current record being processed.
2. RPG extracts the look-ahead fields.

If the program does not contain a primary file, the program must end through one of the following methods:

- By setting on the LR indicator
- By setting on the RT indicator
- By setting on an H1 to H9 indicator
- By performing a RETRN operation
- By allowing an exception/error to end the program, if:
  - No exception/error subroutine is specified
  - No return point is specified for an exception/error subroutine
  - The response to a message is to cancel the program

Program Controlled File Processing

Specify a full procedural file (F in column 16 of the File Description specification) to control the input for a program. A full procedural file indicates to the compiler that input is controlled by program-specified calculation operation. When both full procedural files and a primary file (P in column 16 of the File Description specification) are specified in a program, some of the input is controlled by the program, and other input is controlled by the RPG cycle. The program cycle exists when a full procedural file is specified; however, file processing occurs with RPG operation codes at detail or total calculation time.

File operation codes can be used for program control of input and output. These file operation codes and all operation codes are discussed in Chapter 4.

Chapter 4

Operation Codes

The RPG language contains a rich set of operation codes commonly referred to as *OpCodes*. These OpCodes provide a wide variety of processes within an application program. The programmer specifies these OpCodes, left justified, in columns 28 to 32 of the Calculation specifications.

Before describing each operation code, let's review the terms used when referring to the areas of the RPG Calculation specification.

When referring to columns 7 to 8, the term ***control-level indicator*** is used.

When referring to columns 9 to 17, the term ***conditioning indicator*** is used.

When referring to columns 18 to 27, the term ***Factor 1*** is used.

When referring to columns 28 to 32, the term ***OpCode*** or ***operation*** is used.

When referring to columns 33 to 42, the term ***Factor 2*** is used.

When referring to columns 43 to 48, the term ***Result field*** is used.

When referring to columns 49 to 51, the term ***field length*** is used.

When referring to column 52, the term ***decimal positions*** is used.

When referring to column 53, the term ***operation extender*** is used.

Previously, the term *half adjust* was used for column 53.

When referring to columns 54 to 55, the term ***resulting indicator 1*** is used.

When referring to columns 56 to 57, the term ***resulting indicator 2*** is used.

When referring to columns 58 to 59, the term ***resulting indicator 3*** is used.

When referring to columns 54 to 59 the term ***resulting indicator(s)*** is used.

These terms are used in place of column numbers to easily identify the areas of a calculation program statement.

Figure 4-40 contains a list of RPG operation codes, along with their descriptions.

Operation Code Summary

OpCode	Description
ACQ	Acquire a program device.
ADD (H)	Add two values together.
ANDxx	Extends IFxx, DOWxx, DOUxx and WHxx conditioning.
BEGSR	Begin a subroutine.
BITOF	Set off individual bits with a field.
BITON	Set on individual bits with a field.
CABxx	Compare two values then branch to a label.
CALL	Calls another program.
CASxx	Compare two values then call a subroutine.
CAT (P)	Concatenate Factor 1 to Factor 2.
CHAIN (N)	Random file access by index.
CHECK	Verify the data in Factor 2 against Factor 1 (from left to right).
CHEKR	Verify the data in Factor 2 against Factor 1 (from right to left).
CLEAR	Clear data structure, variable or record format.
CLOSE	Close a file.
COMIT	Commitment control, commit group.
COMP	Compare two values and set on/off resulting indicators.
DEBUG	Print a debug statement.
DEFN	Define one field like another field.
DELET	Delete a database record.
DIV (H)	Divide two values.
DO	Begin Do-loop with an optional counter.
DOUxx	Begin Do-until loop.
DOWxx	Begin Do-while loop.
DSPLY	Displays a message at the workstation.
DUMP	Print a formatted dump.
ELSE	Else clause, used in conjunction with the IFxx operation.
END	Ends a DO, DOWxx, DOUxx, CASxx, IFxx or SELEC group.
ENDCS	End a CASxx group.
ENDDO	End a DO, DOWxx or DOUxx group.
ENDIF	End an IFxx group.
ENDSL	End a SELEC group.
ENDSR	End of a subroutine.
EXCPT	Writes a program defined or externally described record format.
EXFMT	Writes and then reads a workstation device.
EXSR	Calls an intra-program subroutine.
FEOD	Causes a file "cursor" reset, frees locked records.
FORCE	Forces input priority alteration.
FREE	Deactivates a program that was left active with RETRN or RT.
GOTO	Performs an unconditional branch to a label.
IFxx	Compares two values and performs a block of code.
IN	Retrieves an external data area's data.
ITER	Iterate a DO, DOWxx or DOUxx loop.
KFLD	Defines a key field of a key list.
KLIST	Defines a key list used to access an indexed file.
LEAVE	Leave a DO, DOWxx or DOUxx loop.

Figure 4-40: Alphabetic Operation Code Table (1 of 2)

OpCode	Description
LOKUP	Searches an array or table for like or unlike elements.
MOVE (P)	Copy data, right-justified, from a field or constant to field.
MOVEA (P)	Copy data, left-justified, to all successive array elements.
MOVEL (P)	Copy data, left-justified, from a field or constant to a field.
MULT (H)	Multiply two values.
MVR	Copy the remainder of a preceding division to a field.
NEXT	Force the next input cycle to read input from a specific device.
OCUR	Set/Get the occurrence of a multi-occurrence data structure.
OPEN	Open a file.
ORxx	Extend IFxx, DOWxx, DOUxx and WHxx conditioning.
OTHER	Otherwise clause of a SELECT/WHEN group.
OUT	Update an external data area.
PARM	Define a parameter field within a parameter list.
PLIST	Define a parameter list.
POST	Retrieve and post device-specific information to a data structure.
READ (N)	Read from a file.
READC	Read next changed subfile record.
READE (N)	Read the next data file record with equal key index.
READP (N)	Read previous data file record.
REDPE (N)	Read previous data file record with equal key index.
REL	Release an acquired program device.
RESET	Reset a variable to its initial value.
RETRN	Return to calling program.
ROLBK	Commitment control, roll back group.
SCAN	Scan argument for search pattern and return position.
SELEC	Begin an inline SELECT/WHEN case group.
SETGT	Set the file cursor greater than the specified index.
SETLL	Set the file cursor less than the specified index.
SETOF	Set an indicator off.
SETON	Set an indicator on.
SHTDN	Test for system shut down.
SORTA	Sort an array.
SQRT (H)	Compute the square root of a number.
SUB (H)	Subtract one value from another.
SUBST (P)	Copy substring value in Factor 2 to the Result field.
TAG	Define the location and name of a label.
TESTB	Test bit pattern.
TESTN	Test character field for numeric data.
TESTZ	Test the zone of the rightmost position of a field.
TIME	Retrieve the system time and date.
UNLCK	Unlock an external data area.
UNLCK	Unlock a record.
UPDAT	Update a file.
WHxx	When select condition is true, then do.
WRITE	Write to a file.
XFOOT (H)	Cross foot (sum up) an array.
XLATE (P)	Translate Factor 2 using translate data in Factor 1.
Z-ADD (H)	Zero and add numeric.
Z-SUB (H)	Zero and subtract numeric.

Figure 4-40: Alphabetic Operation Code Table (2 of 2)

Unconditionable Operation Codes

The operation codes listed in Figure 4-41 do not support conditioning indicators. Most of these operation codes permit, but are not affected by, control-level indicators. The BEGSR and ENDSR operations do not support control-level indicators.

OpCode	Description
ANDxx	Continuation of the IFxx, DOWxx, DOUxx and WHxx operations.
BEGSR	Begin subroutine.
DEFN	Define variable; Data area declaration.
ELSE	Else operation of the IFxx operation.
ENDIF	End IFxx.
ENDCS	End CASxx.
ENDSL	End SELECt.
ENDSR	End subroutine.
KFLD	Index key field declaration.
KLIST	Index key list declaration.
ORxx	OR continuation of the IFxx, DOWxx, DOUxx and WHxx operations.
OTHER	Otherwise clause of a SELECt/WHEN case group.
PARM	Parameter.
PLIST	Parameter list.
TAG	Target of a CABxx or GOTO operation.
WHxx	When compare clause of a Select CASE group.

Figure 4-41: Operation Codes Not Supporting Conditioning Indicators

Abbreviation Legend

This chapter contains an alphabetized description of each RPG operation code. All descriptions include a syntax diagram for the operation code as well as an example of its use. Throughout this chapter and within the syntax diagrams, certain abbreviations are used. These abbreviations are listed in Figure 4-42.

Abbreviation	Description
[0 or ƀ]	The result of the operation is zero or blank.
[+]	The result of the operation is positive.
[–]	The result of the operation is negative.
[0]	The result of the operation is zero.
[ ]	Brackets denote optional values.
bof	The result of the operation produces a beginning-of-file condition.
eof	The result of the operation produces an end-of-file condition.
[full]	The WRITE operation has filled up the subfile specified in Factor 2.
[ind*n*]	Indicator *n*, where *n* is 1, 2 or 3. ind1 is columns 54 and 55, ind2 is columns 56 and 57, and ind3 is columns 58 and 59.
[mix]	The result of a TESTB operation is some bits on and some off; the result of a TESTN operation is some characters are numeric and some are not.
[num]	The result of the TESTN operation is all numeric.
[other]	The result of the TESTZ operation indicates that the zone of the Result field is neither positive or negative, it is unknown.
1<2	Factor 1 is less than Factor 2.
1=2	Factor 1 equals Factor 2.
1>2	Factor 1 is greater than Factor 2.
char value	Character value—that is, a character variable, literal, or named constant.
char variable	Character variable—that is, a character field, array, array element, data structure or data structure subfield.
data struct	Data structure name.
dec	Decimal digits (i.e., the number of digits to the right of the decimal point)
n / f	The result of the operation produces a Not Found condition.
num value	Numeric value—that is, a numeric variable, literal, or named constant.
num blanks	Number of blanks.
num variable	Numeric variable—that is, a numeric field, array, array element, or data structure subfield.
plist	Parameter list name.

Figure 4-42: Glossary of Abbreviations Used in this Chapter

Operation Code Syntax Diagram Summary

Figure 4-43 contains a table of RPG operation codes and their parameters, (i.e., Factor 1, Factor 2, Result field, and Resulting indicators).

Factor 1	OpCode	Factor 2	Result	Length	Dec	Ext	Resulting Ind.		
workstn device ID	ACQ	workstn file name						[error]	
[numeric value]	ADD	numeric value	sum	[size]	[dec]	[H]	[+]	[–]	[0]
compare value 1	ANDxx	compare value 2							
[subroutine name]	BEGSR								
	BITOF	'bit nums to set off	char variable	[size]					
	BITON	'bit nums to set on'	char variable	[size]					
compare value 1	CABxx	compare value 2	[label]				[1>2]	[1<2]	[1=2]
compare value 1	CAB	compare value 2	[label][1]				[1>2]	[1<2]	[1=2]
	CALL	program name	[plist]					[error]	[LR]
[compare value 1]	CASxx	[compare value 2]	subroutine				[1>2]	[1<2]	[1=2]
[operand 1]	CAT	operand 2[:num blanks]	char variable	[size]		[P]			
key value or rec num	CHAIN	record format				[N]	n/f	[error]	
key value or rec num	CHAIN	file name	[data struct]			[N]	n/f	[error]	
check list	CHECK	base value[:start]	[position(s)]	[size]	[dec]			[error]	[found]
check list	CHEKR	base value[:start]	[position(s)]	[size]	[dec]			[error]	[found]
[*NOKEY]	CLEAR	variable to clear							
	CLOSE	file name						[error]	
	CLOSE	*ALL						[error]	
[boundary]	COMIT							[error]	
compare value 1	COMP[2]	compare value 2					[1>2]	[1<2]	[1=2]

Figure 4-43: RPG OpCode Summary (1 of 6)

1 If the Result field (label) is not specified, at least one resulting indicator is required.

2 At least one resulting indicator is required.

Factor 1	OpCode	Factor 2	Result	Length	Dec	Ext	Resulting Ind.		
[descriptive text]	DEBUG	[printer file]	[print value]						
*LIKE	DEFN	based-on variable	new variable	[±] [size]	[dec]				
*NAMVAR	DEFN	[data area name][3]	assignment	[size]	[dec]				
[key value]	DELET	file name					[n/f]	[error]	
[key value]	DELET	record format					[n/f]	[error]	
[numerator]	DIV	denominator	result	[size]	[dec]	[H]	[+]	[–]	[0]
[starting value]	DO	[maximum iterations]	[counter]	[size]	[dec]				
compare value 1	DOUxx	compare value 2							
compare value 1	DOWxx	compare value 2							
[message ID]	DSPLY	[*EXT]	[response]	[size]				[error]	
[message ID]	DSPLY	[message queue]	[response]	[size]				[error]	
[descriptive text]	DUMP								
	ELSE								
	END	[increment]							
	ENDxx	[increment][4]							
[label]	ENDSR	[return point]							
	EXCPT	[except output label]							
	EXFMT	record format						[error]	
	EXSR	subroutine							

Figure 4-43: RPG Operation Code Summary (2 of 6)

3 If Factor 2 is not specified, the Result field is used as the name of the data structure.

4 The increment value is valid for END and ENDDO operations associated with a DO, DOWxx and DOUxx operation code.

Factor 1	OpCode	Factor 2	Result	Length	Dec	Ext	Resulting Ind.		
	FEOD	file name						[error]	
	FORCE	file name							
	FREE	program name						[error]	
	GOTO	label							
compare value 1	IFxx	compare value 2							
[*LOCK]	IN	data area						[error]	
[*LOCK]	IN	*NAMVAR						[error]	
	ITER								
	KFLD		key field	[size]	[dec]				
key list name	KLIST								
	LEAVE								
search pattern	LOKUP	array [,elem number]					[high]	[low]	[equal]
search pattern	LOKUP	table 1	[table 2]				[high]	[low]	[equal]
	MHHZO	source	char variable	[size]					
	MHLZO	source	char variable	[size]					
	MLHZO	source	char variable	[size]					
	MLLZO	source	char variable	[size]					
	MOVE	source	target	[size]	[dec]	[P]	[+]	[–]	[0 or b̸]
	MOVEA	source	target	[size]	[dec]	[P]	[+]	[–]	[0 or b̸]
	MOVEL	source	target	[size]	[dec]	[P]	[+]	[–]	[0 or b̸]
[numeric value]	MULT	numeric value	product	[size]	[dec]	[H]	[+]	[–]	[0]
	MVR		remainder	[size]	[dec]		[+]	[–]	[0]
workstn device ID	NEXT	workstn file name						[error]	

Figure 4-43: RPG Operation Code Summary (3 of 6)

Factor 1	OpCode	Factor 2	Result	Length	Dec	Ext	Resulting Ind.		
[occurrence to set to]	OCUR	data structure	[occurrence]	[size]	[dec]			[error]	
	OPEN	file name						[error]	
compare value 1	ORxx	compare value 2							
	OTHER								
[*LOCK]	OUT	data area						[error]	
[*LOCK]	OUT	*NAMVAR						[error]	
[input value]	PARM	[output value]	parameter	[size]	[dec]				
parameter list name	PLIST								
[workstn device ID]	POST	workstn file name[5]	[infds]					[error]	
	READ	record format				[N]		[error]	eof
	READ	file name	[data struct]			[N]		[error]	eof
	READC	subfile record format						[error]	eof
[key value]	READE	record format				[N]		[error]	eof
[key value]	READE	file name	[data struct]			[N]		[error]	eof
	READP	record format				[N]		[error]	bof
	READP	file name	[data struct]			[N]		[error]	bof
[key value]	REDPE	record format				[N]		[error]	bof
[key value]	REDPE	file name	[data struct]			[N]		[error]	bof
workstn device ID	REL	workstn file name						[error]	
[*NOKEY]	RESET	variable to reset						[error]	
	RETRN								
	ROLBK							[error]	

Figure 4-43: RPG Operation Code Summary (4 of 6)

5 Factor 2 is optional when an INFDS data structure name is specified for the Result field.

Factor 1	OpCode	Factor 2	Result	Length	Dec	Ext	Resulting Ind.		
search pattern[:length]	**SCAN**	search variable[:start]	[position(s)][6]	[size]	[dec]			[error]	[found]
	SELEC								
key value	**SETGT**	file name					[n/f]	[error]	
key value	**SETGT**	record format					[n/f]	[error]	
key value	**SETLL**	file name					[n/f]	[error]	[found]
key value	**SETLL**	record format					[n/f]	[error]	[found]
	SETOF						[ind1]	[ind2]	[ind3]
	SETON						[ind1]	[ind2]	[ind3]
	SHTDN						yes		
	SORTA	array							
	SQRT	numeric value	square root	[size]	[dec]	[H]			
[numeric value]	**SUB**	numeric value	difference	[size]	[dec]	[H]	[+]	[–]	[0]
[length of source][7]	**SUBST**	source variable[:start]	char variable	[size]		[P]		[error]	
label	**TAG**								
	TESTB	'bit numbers to test'	char variable	[size]			[xor]	[mix]	[equal]
	TESTN		char variable	[size]			[num]	[mix]	[blank]
	TESTZ		char variable	[size]			[+]	[–]	[other]
	TIME		num variable	[size]	[dec]				

Figure 4-43: RPG Operation Code Summary (5 of 6)

6 If the Result field is omitted, resulting indicator 3 is required.

7 Optional under OS/400 version 2 release 2 and later; required under earlier releases.

Factor 1	OpCode	Factor 2	Result	Length	Dec	Ext	Resulting Ind.		
	UNLCK	data area						[error]	
	UNLCK	***NAMVAR**						[error]	
	UNLCK	file name						[error]	
	UPDAT	record format						[error]	
	UPDAT	file name	[data struct]					[error]	
compare value 1	**WHxx**	compare value 2							
	WRITE	record format						[error]	[full][8]
	WRITE	file name	[data struct]					[error]	
	XFOOT	numeric array	sum of array	[size]	[dec]	[H]	[+]	[–]	[0]
from value : to value	**XLATE**	source[:start]	char variable	[size]		[P]		[error]	
	Z-ADD	numeric value	num variable	[size]	[dec]	[H]	[+]	[–]	[0]
	Z-SUB	numeric value	num variable	[size[	[dec]	[H]	[+]	[–]	[0]

Values in square brackets [ ] are optional: For example: **[*NOKEY]** means ***NOKEY** is optional. The square brackets can not be included when specifying these values.

Values in lowercase are variable values. For example: *compare value 2* means that a literal or variable (i.e., field) can be specified.

Values in uppercase are constants: for example, ***LOCK**

The word 'value' generally means any field or literal value can be specified.

The word 'variable' generally means any field, data structure, array, or array element can be specified. For example: *char variable*

In all cases where an operation code accepts an operation extender ("half adjust" column 53), the operation extender is optional.

Figure 4-43: RPG Operation Code Summary (6 of 6)

8 Resulting indicator 3 [full] is only valid for WRITE operations to a subfile detail record format.

Boolean Operations

Boolean operators can be specified for the *xx* portion of several operations. When an operation code contains *xx* as part of its name, any of the following boolean operators can be substituted for the *xx*.

EQ	Factor 1 is equal to Factor 2.
GE	Factor 1 is greater than or equal to Factor 2.
GT	Factor 1 is greater than Factor 2.
LE	Factor 1 is less than or equal to Factor 2.
LT	Factor 1 is less than Factor 2.
NE	Factor 1 is not equal to Factor 2.
blank	Unconditional comparison (for CASxx and CABxx only).

Listed in Figure 4-44 are the operation codes that support these Boolean operators.

Factor 1	OpCode	Factor 2	Result	Length	Dec	Ext	Resulting Ind.		
compare value 1	**ANDxx**	*compare value 2*							
compare value 1	**CABxx**	*compare value 2*							
compare value 1	**CASxx**	*compare value 2*							
compare value 1	**DOUxx**	*compare value 2*							
compare value 1	**DOWxx**	*compare value 2*							
compare value 1	**ORxx**	*compare value 2*							
compare value 1	**WHxx**	*compare value 2*							

Figure 4-44: Operations that Support Boolean Operators

Operation Extender Cross Reference

Until recently, column 53 of the RPG Calculation specification was referred to as the *Half Adjust* column. Now, new options have been added to control the results of several operation codes. These new options are called *Operation Extenders*. Consequently, the Half Adjust column is now referred to as the *Operation Extender*.

Listed in Figure 4-45 are the operation extenders and each operation code that supports the operation extender.

Operation Extender	Operation Codes	Description
H	ADD SUB MULT DIV[9] Z-ADD Z-SUB SQRT XFOOT	Half Adjust. Used to round the result up to the nearest decimal value. This is accomplished by adding $5 * 10^{-(n+1)}$ to the absolute value of the result. Where *n* = number of decimal positions. For a DEC(5,2) field, the following applies: 1.006 will half adjust to 1.01 -1.006 will half adjust to -1.01
N[10]	CHAIN READ READP READE REDPE	Read without locking. Used when accessing database records from files that are opened for update. This operation extender allows records to be read, but avoids placing a record-lock on the record.
P	CAT MOVE MOVEA MOVEL SUBST XLATE	Pad result with blanks. Used to replace the data in the Result field. The P operation extender allows a single operation to replace the contents of the Result field.

Figure 4-45: Operation Extender to Operation Code Cross Reference

[9] The half adjust (H) operation extender is valid for independent DIV operations; that is, it cannot be used on a DIV operation that is followed by a MVR (move remainder) operation.

[10] In addition to the N operation extender, the UNLCK (unlock) operation code can be used to release a record previously locked by one of the database input operations.

Program Status Codes

Most operation codes support a *status* error code. When an operation code generates an exception/error, the program-information data structure field *STATUS is updated. In addition, if the operation code supports an error indicator (resulting indicator 2, in columns 56 and 57), that indicator is set on when an error is generated. The program status error codes are listed in Figure 4-46 on page 138.

For operation codes that do not support the error indicator (e.g., SQRT, ADD, SUB, MULT, DIV, MOVE and MOVEA), the program exception/error subroutine (*PSSR) is automatically performed (if it exists in the program).

Example 1 — Program Status Data Structure used to detect a divide by zero error.

```
SeqNoIDSName....EUDSExternalname..........PFromTo++DField+
0010 IPSDS       SDS
0020 I                                     *STATUS  STATUS

SeqNoCLOn01n02n03Factor1+++OpCodFactor2+++ResultLenDXHiLoEq
0030 C                     Z-ADD5         FACT1   30
0040 C                     Z-ADD0         FACT2   30
0050 C           FACT1     DIV  FACT2     ANSWER  30
0060 C                     MOVE *ON       *INLR
0070 CSR         *PSSR     BEGSR
0080 C           STATUS    IFEQ 0102                          n/Zero?
0090 C                     Z-ADD999ANSWER
0100 C                     ENDIF
0110 CSR         ENDPSR    ENDSR
```

Code	Description of Conditions
00000	No exception/error occurred.
00001	Called program ended with indicator LR on.
00100	String operation had range or subscript error.
00101	Square root of a negative number.
00102	Divide by zero.
00121	Invalid array index.
00122	OCUR operation outside of data structure range.
00202	Called program failed with indicators H1 to H9 off.
00211	Program specified on CALL or FREE operation not found.
00221	Called program tried to access a parameter that was not passed to it.
00231	Called program failed with halt indicator (H1 to H9) on.
00232	Halt indicator (H1 to H9) on in current program.
00233	Halt indicator on when RETRN operation performed.
00299	RPG formatted dump failed.
00333	Error occurred during DSPLY operation.
00401	Data area specified for IN/OUT operation not found.
00402	*PDA not valid for prestart job.
00411	Attributes of data area specified for IN/OUT operation does not match actual data area.
00412	Data area specified for OUT operation was not locked.
00413	Error occurred during IN/OUT operation.
00414	Security authorization to access data area failed.
00415	Security authorization to change data area failed.
00421	Error occurred during UNLCK operation.
00431	Data area is locked by another program and/or job.
00432	Data area is locked by another program in this job.
00907	Decimal data error.
00970	Compiler level does not match run-time subroutine level.
09998	Internal failure in RPG or generated run-time subroutines.
09999	Program exception in an operating system routine.

Figure 4-46: Runtime Program Status Message Codes

Note: These codes apply to RPGIII on the IBM AS/400 and may differ with other compilers.

File Status Error Codes

In addition to program status error codes, there are also file exception/error status codes. This code indicates when an error condition has been encountered after a file-specific operation is performed, for example, the CHAIN operation, where a record time-out error could occur.

Most operation codes set on resulting indicator 2 (located in columns 56 and 57) when an exception error is detected. If the programmer has specified this error indicator, the indicator is set on and control passes to the next RPG operation. If resulting indicator 2 is not specified, and a file exception/error subroutine is specified, control automatically transfers to that subroutine. At that point, the *STATUS code can be interrogated. If resulting indicator 2 is not specified and a file exception/error subroutine is not specified, the RPG general exception/error handling subroutine receives control. The user or workstation operator will usually be issued an error message at this point.

Example 2 — Detect a record lock/time-out condition.

```
SeqNoFFileNameIPE.E....RLEN...K.OV.....Device+RcdNbrKOptionEntry+
0010 FCUSTMASTIF  E            K        DISK           KINFDS INFDS
0020 F                                                 KINFSR INFSR

SeqNoIDSName....EUDSExternalname..........PFromTo++DFie1d+
0030 IINFDS       DS
0040 I                                        *STATUS  STATUS

SeqNoCLOn01n02n03Factor1+++OpCodFactor2+++ResultLenDXHiLoEq
0050 C           1234567   CHAINCUSTMAST              54
0060 C                     MOVE *ON       *INLR
0070 CSR         INFSR     BEGSR
0080 C           STATUS    IFEQ 01218
0090 C                     MOVE 'TIME-OUT'MSG     12
0100 C                     ENDIF
0110 CSR         ENDPSR    ENDSR
```

A list of file status error codes is featured in Figure 4-48 on page 141.

Figure 4-47 contains the definitions for the abbreviations used to describe the type of devices that are referred to in Figure 4-48.

Abbreviation	Device type	Description
WS	WORKSTN	Workstation device file. Used to access display files and ICF (communications) files.
DSK	DISK	Disk file. Used to access database Physical, Logical, or Joined-logical files. Also, Save files can be access through this device type.
PRT	PRINTER	Printer file. Used to output printed data to a print device. Typically, the data is spooled (stored on disk) for a time, then printed later.
SEQ	SEQ	Sequential file. Used to access Diskette, Tape and Save files. That is files can be opened, read, written to, and closed, but not updated.
SPC	SPECIAL	Special file. Used to support user-written device file drivers. A device file driver is a user-written program that handles the file access requests, such as open, close and read and write.

Figure 4-47: Device Type Abbreviation Glossary

Code	Devices	Description of Conditions
00000		No exception/error occurred.
00002	WS	Function key used to input display.
00011	WS,DSK,SEQ	End of file detected on a READ (input) operation.
00012	WS,DSK,SEQ	No-record-found condition for a CHAIN SETLL or SETGT operation.
00013	WS	Subfile is full.
01011	WS,DSK,SEQ	Undefined record type (identifying indicators do not match record).
01021	WS,DSK,SEQ	Attempted to write to an existing record or duplicate index value.
01031	WS,DSK,SEQ	Matching record match field data out of sequence.
01041		Array/table load sequence error.
01051		Too many array/table entries.
01052		Clearing of table prior to dump of data failed.
01071	WS,DSK,SEQ	Numeric sequence error.
01121	WS	PRINT key pressed with no resulting indicator.
01122	WS	ROLLUP (PAGEDOWN) key pressed with no resulting indicator.
01123	WS	ROLLDOWN (PAGEUP) key pressed with no resulting indicator.
01124	WS	CLEAR key pressed with no resulting indicator.
01125	WS	HELP key pressed with no resulting indicator.

Figure 4-48: File Status (Error) Code Descriptions (1 of 2)

Code	Devices	Description of Conditions
01126	WS	HOME key pressed with no resulting indicator.
01201	WS	Workstation record mismatch detected on input.
01211	all	I/O operation to a closed file.
01215	all	OPEN operation issued to a file that was already opened.
01216	all	Error on an implicit OPEN/CLOSE operation (cycle oriented).
01217	all	Error on an explicit OPEN/CLOSE operation.
01218	DSK,SEQ	Unable to allocate record (record locked by another program).
01221	DSK,SEQ	Update operation without a prior successful read.
01231	SPC	Error on SPECIAL file.
01235	PRT	Error in PRTCTL data structure spacing or skipping entries.
01241	DSK,SEQ	ADDROUT record not found.
01251	WS	Permanent workstation I/O error detected.
01255	WS	Workstation session or device error occurred (recovery possible).
01261	WS	Attempted to exceed maximum number of acquired devices.
01281	WS	Operation to an acquired device.
01282	WS	Job ending (canceled) with controlled option.
01285	WS	Attempted to acquire an already acquired device.
01286	WS	Attempted to open shared file with SAVDS or IND file continuation.
01287	WS	Response indicators overlap IND continuation option indicators.
01299	WS,DSK,SEQ	Miscellaneous I/O error.
01331	WS	Wait-for-record time exceeded for READ or EXFMT operation.

Figure 4-48: File Status (Error) Code Descriptions (2 of 2)

Standards and Conventions Used in this Chapter

The following pages of this chapter contain examples for each RPG operation code. The examples use certain conventions and standard field names. The following statements are assumed to be included in each example.

```
SeqNoCLOn01n02n03Factor1+++OpCodFactor2+++ResultLenDXHiLoEq
     C                     MOVE *OFF      EOF   1
     C                     MOVE *OFF      BOF   1
     C                     MOVE *OFF      NF    1
```

To improve clarity and reduce complexity in the examples, some fields, data structures and arrays are used without explicit declaration. When a data element is used without being defined, it should be assumed that the attribute of the data element is what is necessary to perform the specific operation. For example, if 1 is added to the field COUNT, it should be assumed that COUNT is a numeric field.

Nested Code Illustration

Nested DO, DOWxx, DOUxx, SELEC/WHxx and IFxx/THEN/ELSE levels appear in several examples. Occasionally a graphic is used to illustrate the nesting levels. The source code is also indented for clarity. Figure 4-49 illustrates the graphic and the indenting.

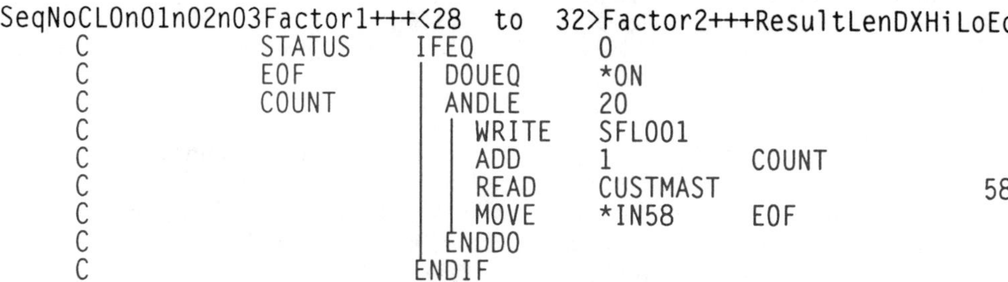

```
SeqNoCLOnO1nO2nO3Factor1+++<28  to  32>Factor2+++ResultLenDXHiLoEq
     C            STATUS    IFEQ      0
     C            EOF        | DOUEQ     *ON
     C            COUNT      | ANDLE     20
     C                       |  | WRITE  SFL001
     C                       |  | ADD    1         COUNT
     C                       |  | READ   CUSTMAST                   58
     C                       |  | MOVE   *IN58     EOF
     C                       | ENDDO
     C                      ENDIF
```

Figure 4-49: Graphic Illustration of Nesting

ACQ (Acquire)

The ACQ operation is used to grab or capture the program device (workstation/display station) specified in Factor 1.

Factor 1	OpCode	Factor 2	Result	Length	Dec	Ext	Resulting Ind.		
workstn device ID	ACQ	*workstn file name*						[error]	

Factor 1 must contain a constant or a field that contains the name of the program device (workstation/display station) that will be acquired by the program.

Factor 2 must contain the name of the workstation file that will be used to acquire the program device.

When resulting indicator 2 is set on by the ACQ operation, one of the following conditions exists: (1) the device has already been acquired by another application (a user may have "signed on" to the system using that device); (2) the device is already acquired by the device file specified in Factor 2; (3) the device specified in Factor 1 does not exist.

Resulting Indicator Legend			
Columns	**Ind.**	**Usage**	**Set On Condition**
54 - 55	1	N/A	Not used by this operation.
56 - 57	2	[error]	An error occurred during the operation.
58 - 59	3	N/A	Not used by this operation.

Once a device has been acquired, the program may read from the device or write to the device. To identify which device a program will access, move the name of the device into the field specified for the program device ID. This field is specified on the File Description Continuation specification. The maximum number of program devices a program can acquire is equal to the number of program devices specified for the File Description Continuation specification value NUM.

Note: The NUM value can be overridden outside of the program; however, a program can never acquire more than NUM program devices.

More about ACQ

Example 3 — Acquire a workstation device.

```
SeqNoFFileNameIPE.E....RLEN...K.OV.....Device+RecNbrKOptionEntry+
0010 FGLENTRY CF  E                    WORKSTN      KNUM      3
0020 F                                              KID    WSID

SeqNoCLOnO1nO2nO3Factor1+++OpCodFactor2+++ResultLenDXHiLoEqComments
0030 C           'DSP01'   ACQ  GLENTRY                 56
0040 C           *IN56     CASEQ*ON       *PSSR
0050 C                     END
0060 C                     MOVEL'DSP01'   WSID
0070 C                     EXFMTPROMPT
```

In this example, Line 10 contains the File Description specification for the workstation display file GLENTRY (G/L Entry). The 'K' in column 53 of the File Description specification indicates that a file continuation entry is present. The NUM keyword is used to indicate the maximum number of devices that may be acquired by the program for the GLENTRY workstation display file. In our example, three devices can be acquired. This value may be overridden to a lesser number outside of the program through a system function.

Line 20 contains the continuation line for the ID keyword. This is used to identify which device has just been processed by the program and controls which device will be read on the next I/O operation.

Line 30 uses the constant 'DSP01' as the name of the device that will be acquired by the program. GLENTRY is the workstation file that will acquire DSP01.

Line 60 moves the constant 'DSP01' into the field WSID to force the EXFMT (write/read format) operation on line 70 to write to and then read from the DSP01 device. Note: Line 70 uses a record format name 'PROMPT' in place of the workstation file name.

ADD (Add Numeric)

The ADD operation is used to produce the sum of two values.

Factor 1	OpCode	Factor 2	Result	Length	Dec	Ext	Resulting Ind.		
[numeric value 1]	ADD	*numeric value 2*	*sum*	[size]	[dec]	[H]	[+]	[–]	[0]

If Factor 1 is specified, Factor 1 and Factor 2 are added together producing a sum that is returned to the Result field. If Factor 1 is omitted, Factor 2 and the Result field are added together, and the sum is placed into the Result field.

The operation extender H can be specified to cause the result to be half adjusted, that is, rounded up.

Resulting Indicator Legend			
Columns	**Ind.**	**Usage**	**Set On Condition**
54 - 55	1	[+]	The Result field is greater than zero.
56 - 57	2	[–]	The Result field is less than zero.
58 - 59	3	[0]	The Result field is equal to zero.

```
SeqNoCLOn01n02n03Factor1+++OpCodFactor2+++ResultLenDXHiLoEq
0010 C            A         ADD  B         C
0020 C                      ADD  1         C              545658
```

If the previous example was written in traditional mathematical expressions, it would appear as follows:

```
A + B = C
C + 1 = C
```

In this example, fields A and B are added together, and the result is placed into field C. Then, field C is incremented by 1.

After the second ADD operation, if field C is greater than zero (i.e., a positive number), resulting indicator 1 (indicator 54) is set on; if field C is less than zero (i.e., negative), resulting indicator 2 (indicator 56) is set on; and if field C equals zero, resulting indicator 3 (indicator 58) is set on.

ANDxx (And Condition)

The ANDxx operation is used in conjunction with the IFxx, DOWxx, DOWxx and WHxx operations. ANDxx complements these other operations in that their conditioning is extended through the use of the ANDxx.

Conditioning indicators are not allowed for this operation. Resulting indicators are not valid for this operation.

Factor 1	OpCode	Factor 2	Result	Length	Dec	Ext	Resulting Ind.		
compare value 1	**ANDxx**	*compare value 2*							

Factor 1 is required and must contain a field, literal value, array element or figurative constant. Factor 1 is compared to Factor 2 using the AND operation Boolean operator.

Factor 2 is required and must contain a field, literal value, array element or figurative constant. Factor 2 is compared to Factor 1 using the ANDxx operation Boolean operators (EQ, GE, GT, LE, LT and NE). See page 135 for details.

Factor 1 and Factor 2 must be the same type.

Example 4 — ANDLE used to extend the DOWxx operation.

```
SeqNoCLOn01n02n03Factor1+++OpCodFactor2+++ResultLenDXHiLoEq
0010 C             *IN58     DOWEQ*OFF
0020 C             C         ANDLE10
0030 C                       ADD  1        C      30
0030 C                       READ CUSTMAST                 58
0040 C                       ENDDO
```

In this example, indicator 58 is compared to the field off. If indicator 58 is off, field C is compared to the constant 10. If it is less than or equal to 10, the ANDLE extension is satisfied, and the Do while loop will be performed.

BEGSR (Begin Subroutine)

The BEGSR operation marks the beginning of a subroutine. Factor 1 must contain a unique name for the subroutine. That unique name is used as the target of the EXSR (perform subroutine) and CASxx (compare Factor 1 and Factor 2, then perform subroutine) operations. If Factor 1 contains *PSSR, the subroutine is the program status subroutine and is called before the RPG exception/error handling routine is called to handle runtime exceptions. If Factor 1 contains *INZR, the subroutine is the initialization subroutine and is called immediately after the RPG cycle completes the *INIT routine—before first page (i.e., 1P) output is performed.

Control level break indicators (L1-L9) are not valid for this operation. Resulting indicators are not valid for this operation.

Factor 1	OpCode	Factor 2	Result	Length	Dec	Ext	Resulting Ind.		
subroutine name	**BEGSR**								

Factor 1 is required and must contain a unique subroutine name.

The control-level indicator (columns 7-8) can contain the subroutine identifying letters SR. This identifier is optional with most of today's RPG compilers; however, the beginning and end points of a subroutine are often identified by the SR identifier.

Example 5 — Perform a subroutine.

```
SeqNoCLOn01n02n03Factor1+++OpCodFactor2+++ResultLenDXHiLoEq
0010 C                     EXSR COUNT
0020 CSR         COUNT     BEGSR
0030 C                     READ FILE                  58
0040 C           *IN58     IFEQ *OFF
0050 C                     ADD  1         C
0060 C                     ENDIF
0070 CSR         ENDCNT    ENDSR
```

In this example, the subroutine COUNT is called from the "main line" calculations through the use of the EXSR operation. The subroutine COUNT is delimited with the BEGSR operation on line 20 and the ENDSR (end subroutine) operation on line 70.

BITOF (Set Bits Off)

The BITOF operation causes the bits specified by Factor 2 to be set to '0' in the Result field. Bits that are not referenced in Factor 2 are unchanged in the Result field.

This operation is normally used in conjunction with the BITON (set bits on) operation to build character values that are less than X'40'. It is also often useful for converting upper case letters to lower case.

Resulting indicators are not valid for this operation.

Factor 1	OpCode	Factor 2	Result	Length	Dec	Ext	Resulting Ind.		
	BITOF	*'bit nums to set off'*	*char variable*	[size]					

Factor 2 can contain a *bit pattern* (see example). The bit pattern can be a named constant containing bit numbers or a one-position character field. If a field is specified for Factor 2 then the bits that are on in Factor 2 will be set off in the Result field. Bits that are off in Factor 2 are not changed in the Result field.

The Result field must contain a one-position character field or array element.

For more information on bit patterns, see the TESTB operation on page 286 in this chapter.

Example 6 — Convert the contents of an array to lower case letters.

```
SeqNoE....FromfileTofile..ArrnamEPRDim+LenPDAAltnamLenPDA
0010 E                    NAME       35  1

SeqNoCLOn01n02n03Factor1+++OpCodFactor2+++ResultLenDXHiLoEq
0020 C                         DO    35         X
0030 C                         BITOF'1'         NAME,X
0040 C                         ENDDO
```

In this example, bit 1 in the first 35 elements of the array NAME are set off. If the array NAME contains some text, this routine would convert that text to lower case.

BITON (Set Bits On)

The BITON operation causes the bits indicated in Factor 2 to be set to '1' in the Result field. Bits that are not referenced in Factor 2 are unchanged in the Result field.

This operation is normally used in conjunction with the BITOF (set bits off) operation to build character values that are less than X'40'. It can also be used to convert lower case letters to upper case, however, the XLATE operation provides a more portable method of conversion.

Resulting indicators are not valid for this operation.

Factor 1	OpCode	Factor 2	Result	Length	Dec	Ext	Resulting Ind.		
	BITON	*'bit nums to set on'*	*char variable*	[size]					

Factor 2 can contain a *bit pattern* (see example). The bit pattern can be a named constant or a literal value containing bit numbers, a one-position character field, or a hexadecimal literal value. If a field name or hexadecimal literal value is specified for Factor 2 then the bits that are on in Factor 2 will be set on in the Result field. Bits that are off in Factor 2 are not changed in the Result field.

The Result field must contain a one-position character field or array element.

For more information on bit patterns, see the TESTB operation on page 286.

Example 7 — Convert the contents of an array to upper case letters.

```
SeqNoE....FromfileTofile..ArrnamEPRDim+LenPDAAltnamLenPDA
0010 E                    ITEM       35  1

SeqNoCLOn01n02n03Factor1+++OpCodFactor2+++ResultLenDXHiLoEq
0020 C                     DO   35        X
0030 C                     BITON'1'       ITEM,X
0040 C                     ENDDO
```

In this example, bit 1 in the first 35 elements of the array ITEM are set on. If the array ITEM contains some text, this routine would convert that text to upper case.

More about BITON and BITOF

If Factor 2 contains a bit pattern literal value, it must conform to the following guidelines:

- It must be left justified in Factor 2.
- It must be enclosed in single quotation marks.
- It must contain one or more unique numerals ranging from 0 to 7.

Bits 0-3 are the top half of the byte. Bits 4-7 are the bottom half of the byte. Bits that are not referenced in Factor 2 go unchanged. The bit pattern for Factor 2 is described below.

Bit numbers that can be set ☞ **0123 4567**

Value of bits that are set ☞ **8421 8421**

More Examples:

```
SeqNoCLOn01n02n03Factor1+++OpCodFactor2+++ResultLenDXHiLoEq
     *  Set off all the bits in FLDA.
0010 C                     BITOF'01234567'FLDA
     *  Set on all the bits in FLDB.
0020 C                     BITON'01234567'FLDB
     *  Change field ATTR to x'22' (two operations required).
0030 C                     BITOF'013457'  ATTR
0040 C                     BITON'26'      ATTR
     *  Set on bits 0 to 3 in HEXVAL.
0050 C                     BITONX'F0'     HEXVAL
```

Line 10 sets off all the bits in field FLDA. Line 20 sets on all the bits in the field FLDB. Line 30 sets off bits 0,1,3,4,5 and 7 in the field ATTR. Line 40 sets on bits 2 and 6 in field ATTR. Line 50 set on bits 0, 1, 2 and 3 (the mask for x'F0'). Bits 4,5,6, and 7 are not changed.

The use of the BITON and BITOF operations has been substantially reduced since the introduction of hexadecimal literal values to the language. BITON and BITOF have traditionally been used to created characters whose value is less than X'40' (a blank). With hexadecimal literal values, a simple MOVE or MOVEL accomplishes the same task and is much more readable.

CABxx (Compare and Branch)

The CABxx operation compares Factor 1 to Factor 2. If the relationship test is true, then a branch is performed to the label specified in the Result field and any resulting indicators are set on accordingly.

Factor 1	OpCode	Factor 2	Result	Length	Dec	Ext	Resulting Ind.		
compare value 1	CABxx	*compare value 2*	*[label]*				[1>2]	[1<2]	[1=2]

The Result field is optional and contains the label of a TAG or ENDSR statement that will be the target of the branch. If the Result field is omitted, at least one resulting indicator must be specified.

Resulting indicators are optional unless no Result field (label) is specified or when *xx* of the CAB*xx* operation is blank. Under these situations, at least one resulting indicator is required.

Resulting Indicator Legend			
Columns	**Ind.**	**Usage**	**Set On Condition**
54 - 55	1	[1>2]	Factor 1 is greater than Factor 2.
56 - 57	2	[1<2]	Factor 1 is less than Factor 2.
58 - 59	3	[1=2]	Factor 1 is equal to Factor 2.

Example 8 — Branch to certain labels based on the contents of various fields.

```
SeqNoCLOn01n02n03Factor1+++OpCodFactor2+++ResultLenDXHiLoEq
     C                     Z-ADD100       A       30
     C                     Z-ADD200       B       30
0010 C           A         CABEQB         LAB1
0020 C           A         CABLTB         LAB2          545658
0030 C           A         CAB  B         LAB3          545658

0040 C           LAB1      TAG
0050 C           LAB2      TAG
0060 C           LAB3      TAG
```

On line 10, the result of the relationship test is false; therefore, a branch to LAB1 is not performed. The result of line 20 is true; therefore, a branch to LAB2 is performed and consequently, line 30—which is an unconditional branch—will never be reached with A and B set as they are, line 30, therefore, will not be performed.

CALL (Call Another Program)

The CALL operation temporarily interrupts the program, then loads and runs another program.

Factor 1	OpCode	Factor 2	Result	Length	Dec	Ext	Resulting Ind.		
	CALL	*program name*	*[parm list]*					[error]	[LR]

Factor 2 must contain the name of the program to be run. Factor 2 can be either a quoted literal value, named constant, field, array element, data structure or data structure subfield name.

The Result field is optional and may contain the name of a parameter list (PLIST) label. The parameter list is used to pass parameters between the programs. If the parameter list is omitted and parameters are required, the CALL operation may be immediately followed by the PARM operation to identify the parameters.

Resulting Indicator Legend			
Columns	**Ind.**	**Usage**	**Set On Condition**
54 - 55	1	N/A	Not used by this operation.
56 - 57	2	[error]	The call ends in error.
58 - 59	3	[LR]	The called program ended with its LR indicator set on.

Example 9 — Call a program, passing two parameters.

```
SeqNoCLOnO1nO2nO3Factor1+++OpCodFactor2+++ResultLenDXHiLoEq
0010 C                     CALL 'CUSTINQ'             56
0020 C                     PARM           SEARCH
0030 C                     PARM           CSTNBR
```

In this example, the program CUSTINQ is called and is passed two parameters: a customer number and some search data. Since the program CUSTINQ accepts parameters and those parameters are defined immediately following the CALL operation, a parameter list (PLIST) is not needed in the Result field of the CALL operation.

More about CALL

Example 10 — Call a program, passing a data structure name as the parameter.

```
SeqNoIDSName....EUDSExternalname.........PFromTo++DField+
0010 IPARMDS      DS
0020 I                                   P    1    40CSTNBR
0030 I                                        5   54 SCHDTA
0040 I                                       55   55 RTNCOD
0050 I             'OELIB/CUSTINQ'       C           PGM

SeqNoCLOn01n02n03Factor1+++OpCodFactor2+++ResultLenDXHiLoEq
0060 C                     CALL PGM                     56
0070 C                     PARM           PARMDS
```

The program name CUSTINQ is defined by a named constant (line 50) and is used by the CALL operation (line 60) to call the program CUSTINQ in the library OELIB. Since the data structure PARMDS is passed as the parameter (line 70) , the data contained in all subfields within the data structure will be accessible by the *called* program. The *called* program CUSTINQ should contain a parameter similar to PARMDS to receive the data. (For more information on parameters and parameter lists, see the PARM and PLIST operation codes on pages 243 and 247.

Qualified Program Name

A called program can be qualified to a library by appending the library to the program name. If a library name is omitted, the library directory is searched for the program name. Typically, a program is qualified to a library using one of the following methods:

1. Using the OS/400 convention: **library/program** The forward slash is used to qualify the library to the program; the library name is followed by the program name.
2. Using the System/38 convention: **program.library** The period is used to qualify the program to the library; the program name is followed by the library.
3. Using the OS/2 convention: **d:\directory\program** The back slash is used to qualify the program name to a directory or subdirectory. Also, a colon can be used to qualify the disk drive on which the program resides.

UNIX, AIX, PC-DOS and SSP release 6 (System/36) operating systems do not support qualified program names for the RPGII CALL operation.

CASxx (Compare and Perform Subroutine)

The CASxx operation compares Factor 1 to Factor 2. If the comparison indicated by the *xx* Boolean operator is true, one or both of the following occurs: (1) the subroutine (internal call) named in the Result field is performed, and (2) any resulting indicators are set on.

Factor 1	OpCode	Factor 2	Result	Length	Dec	Ext	Resulting Ind.		
[compare value 1]	CASxx	*[compare value 2]*	*subroutine*				[1>2]	[1<2]	[1=2]

Factor 1 can contain any valid data type.

Factor 2 must contain a value with attributes similar to Factor 1. For example, if Factor 1 contains a numeric field, Factor 2 must contain a numeric value, such as another numeric field, a numeric literal value or a figurative constant.

The *xx* is optional and can be any valid Boolean operator (EQ, GE, GT, LE, LT, NE or blanks). See page 135 for details. The Boolean operator controls the comparison and whether the subroutine specified in the Result field is called.

At least one resulting indicator must be specified when the *xx* operator is blank. The resulting indicator(s) will be set on base on the result of the comparison. If Factor 1 and Factor 2 are not specified, then no resulting indicators can be specified.

Resulting Indicator Legend			
Columns	**Ind.**	**Usage**	**Set On Condition**
54 - 55	1	[1>2]	Factor 1 is greater than Factor 2.
56 - 57	2	[1<2]	Factor 1 is less than Factor 2.
58 - 59	3	[1=2]	Factor 1 is equal to Factor 2.

If the comparison between Factor 1 and Factor 2 is met, the subroutine specified in the Result field will be called. Upon completion of the subroutine, control passes to the END or ENDCS statement associated with this CASxx group. If the comparison is not met, control passes to the next sequential CASxx operation. If no additional CASxx operations are specified for this CASxx group, control passes to the END or ENDCS statement associated with this CASxx group.

More about CASxx

If *xx* is blank, the subroutine named in the Result field is performed unconditionally, after any comparison is made. This form of CASxx (the CAS operation) is often used as a catch-all routine at the end of a CASxx group.

The IFxx and SELEC/WHxx/OTHER operations provide an in-line form of the CASE group. Whereas CASxx calls a subroutine, these other operation codes control operations that immediately follow them. When using the IFxx operation, try to avoid nesting them more than three levels deep. If further nesting is required, the CASxx and SELEC/WHxx/OTHER operations provide better readability. For more information on in-line CASE groups see the IFxx operation on page 208 and the SELEC operation on page 271.

The CASE group of a CASxx operation is a list of one or more consecutive CASxx statements that conditionally perform (i.e., call) an internal subroutine. The CASE group is ended with a single END statement. An END statement must be used to close the CASE group, regardless of the number of CASxx statements.

Example 11 — Test for less than, equal and a catch all situation.

```
SeqNoCL0n01n02n03Factor1+++OpCodFactor2+++ResultLenDXHiLoEq
0010 C           QTYORD    CASLTQTYOH     SHIP
0020 C           ORDSTS    CASEQSHPSTS    BILL          545658
0030 C                     CAS            POST
0040 C                     END
```

In this example, assume the fields are set to the following values:

```
QTYORD=100, QTYOH=200

ORDSTS='S', SHPSTS='S'
```

The result of the comparison (line 10) is true; therefore, subroutine SHIP is called.

After subroutine SHIP has completed, control returns to the END statement associated with the CASE group (line 40); lines 20 and 30 will not be performed.

More about CASxx

The following illustrates the logic of the two CASE constructs.

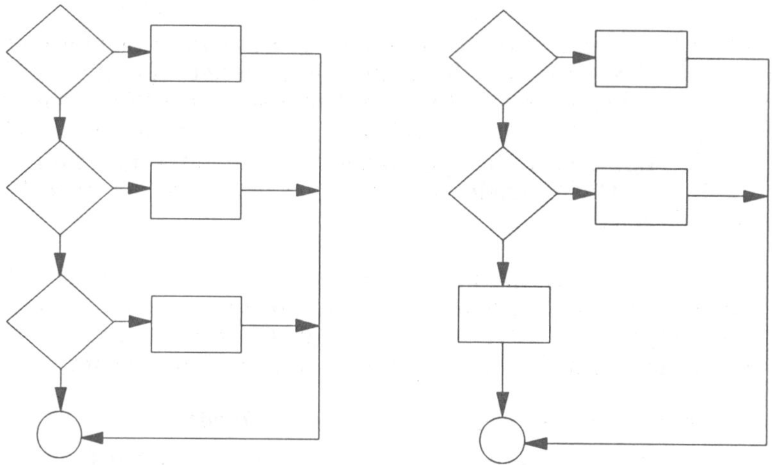

Figure 4-50: The Two Forms of CASE

The leftmost flowchart in Figure 4-50 illustrates the traditional CASE construct—a relationship test followed by a process; another relationship test followed by a process, repeated as needed.

The rightmost flowchart in Figure 4-50 illustrates an alternative form of the CASE construct—a relationship test followed by a process; another relationship test followed by a process; then a default process which is performed when all of the CASE relationship tests are false.

Only one process of a CASE group is performed when the CASE group is entered. After a process is performed, control passes to the corresponding END statement for the CASE group.

CAT (Concatenation)

The CAT operation concatenates Factor 1 and Factor 2, placing the concatenated string in the Result field.

Factor 1	OpCode	Factor 2	Result	Length	Dec	Ext	Resulting Ind.		
[string 1]	CAT	*string 2:[num blanks]*	*result*	[size]		[P]			

Factor 1 is optional and can contain any character variable, constant or named constant. If Factor 1 is omitted, the Result field is used in place of Factor 1. Factor 2 is required and can contain any character variable, constant or named constant.

Factor 2 accepts one optional parameter: BLANK-COUNT. This parameter is used to specify the number of blanks that will be inserted between the last non-blank character of Factor 1 and the first non-blank character of Factor 2. If the BLANK-COUNT parameter is omitted, Factor 2 is concatenated to the end of Factor 1. BLANK-COUNT can be a literal value, named constant, numeric field or numeric data structure subfield.

The Result field must be a character field, array element, data structure or data structure subfield. If the length of the Result field is less than the sum of the result of the CAT operation, the concatenated value is stored left justified in the Result field.

The operation extender P can be specified to cause the result to be padded with blanks, that is the Result field is replaced.

Example 12 — Concatenate Two Values.

```
SeqNoCLOn01n02n03Factor1+++OpCodFactor2+++ResultLenDXHILOEQ
0010 C             'RPG     ' CAT  'Lang'     NAME1  12 P
0020 C             'RPG     ' CAT  'Lang':0   NAME2  12
0030 C             'RPG     ' CAT  'Lang':1   NAME3  12
0040 C                        CAT  'III':0    NAME3
```

In this example, the constant: `'RPG     '` is concatenated with: `'Lang'`.

After line 10 is performed, NAME1 contains: `'RPG     Lang'`

After line 20 is performed, NAME2 contains: `'RPGLang     '`

After line 30 is performed, NAME3 contains: `'RPG Lang    '`

After line 40 is performed, NAME3 contains: `'RPG LangIII'`

More about CAT

The CAT operation is typically used to build proper salutations, such as 'Dear President Kennedy,' or to format an address, such as 'Washington, DC 20500'.

In the example that follows, the following fields are initialized as indicated.

```
Positions: *...v... 1 ...v... 2 ...v... 3
FNAME     =  'John                          '
MIDDLE    =  'F'
LNAME     =  'Kennedy                       '
ADDR      =  '1600 Pennsylvania Ave         '
CITY      =  'Washington                    '
STATE     =  'DC  '
ZIP       =  '20500     '
```

Example 13 — Use CAT to Build an Address Line.

```
SeqNoI..............Constant++++++++++++++C.........Const+
     I               'President'           C          PRES

SeqNoCLOn01n02n03Factor1+++OpCodFactor2+++ResultLenDXHILOEQ
      *  First, build address line 1.
     C           PRES      CAT  FNAME:1   ADDR1   35 P
     C           MIDDLE    IFNE*BLANKS
     C                     CAT  MIDDLE:1  ADDR1
     C                     CAT  '.':0     ADDR1
     C                     ENDIF
     C                     CAT  LAST:1    ADDR1
      *  Second, simply move in the street address.
     C                     MOVELADDR      ADDR2   35 P
      *  Third, build the city, st zip line.
     C           CITY      CAT  ',':0     ADDR3   35 P
     C                     CAT  STATE:1   ADDR3
     C                     CAT  ZIP:2     ADDR3
```

The output from Example 13 would be as follows:

```
President John F. Kennedy
1600 Pennsylvania Ave
Washington, DC  20500
```

CHAIN (Random Record Access/Read)

The CHAIN operation retrieves a single record based on the key-index or relative record number specified in Factor 1 from the file represented in Factor 2.

Factor 1	OpCode	Factor 2	Result	Length	Dec	Ext	Resulting Ind.		
key value or rec num	**CHAIN**	*format name*				[N]	n/f	[error]	
key value or rec num	**CHAIN**	*file name*	*[data struct]*			[N]	n/f	[error]	

Factor 1 is required and must be a constant index, a constant relative record number, a field containing an index, a field containing a relative record number or a key list.

Factor 2 is required and must conform to the following rules:

1. For an externally described file, a file or record format name may be specified.
2. For a program described file, only a file name may be specified.
3. For a workstation file, only the name of a subfile record format may be specified.

The Result field can be specified for a program described file only. The Result field can contain the name of a data structure into which the retrieved record's data is placed. When a record is retrieved, the data is placed directly into the data structure.

The operation extender N can be used when a file is opened for update. This causes the record to be retrieved but avoids locking the record.

Resulting Indicator Legend			
Columns	**Ind.**	**Usage**	**Set On Condition**
54 - 55	1	n/f	The record identified by the key value or record number in Factor 1 does not exist in the file specified in Factor 2.
56 - 57	2	[error]	An error occurred during the operation.
58 - 59	3	N/A	Not used by this operation.

More about CHAIN

The following characteristics apply when a record is accessed with the CHAIN operation.

- For INPUT files, the record is retrieved, but no record-locking occurs.
- For OUTPUT-only files, this operation is not valid.
- For UPDATE files, if no operation extender is specified, the record is retrieved and locked until it is released via one of the following:
    1. Another READ, READE, READP, REDPE or CHAIN operation.
    2. The record is updated by an UPDAT or EXCPT operation.
    3. The record is deleted by a DELET or EXCPT with DEL operation.
    4. The record is implicitly released by one of the following operations:
        - Except to an empty output format: EXCPT
        - Unlock the record: UNLCK
        - Set lower limit: SETLL
        - Set greater than: SETGT
        - Force end of data: FEOD
        - Close file: CLOSE

Example 14 — Access an externally described file using a key list.

```
SeqNoCLOn01n02n03Factor1+++OpCodFactor2+++ResultLenDXHiLoEq
0010 C           PART      KLIST
0020 C                     KFLD           PRTNBR
0030 C                     KFLD           DTESLD

0040 C           PART      CHAINPARTFMT              54

0050 C                     MOVE *IN54     NF
0060 C           NF        CASEQ*ON       ERROR
0070 C                     CAS            UPDATE
0080 C                     END
```

In Example 14, the key list PART contains two key fields; the part number (PRTNBR) and the date sold (DTESLD). The key list PART is used to retrieve a record from the record format PARTFMT.

More about CHAIN

If a record does not exist with a matching index, resulting indicator 1 (indicator 54) is set on. That indicator is then placed into the field NF (line 50), which is subsequently used to control the flow of the program's logic.

Example 15 — Read a program described file into a data structure.

```
SeqNoCL0n01n02n03Factor1+++OpCodFactor2+++ResultLenDXHiLoEq
0010 C                     MOVELPRTNBR    INDEX
0020 C                     MOVE DTESLD    INDEX

0030 C           INDEX     CHAINPARTMST   PARTDS        54

0040 C                     MOVE *IN54     NF
0050 C           NF        CASEQ*ON       ERROR
0060 C                     CAS            UPDATE
0070 C                     END
```

In Example 15, a program described file is accessed by the key field INDEX. The index value is assembled using the fields PRTNBR (part number) and DTESLD (date sold). Then the CHAIN operation is used to access the file PARTMST. If a record exists with an index value that matches Factor 1, the data from that record is moved into the data structure PARTDS. Resulting indicator 1 (indicator 54) will remain off.

Graphically, a CHAIN operation to the index 'THX1138' would position the file cursor as illustrated below.

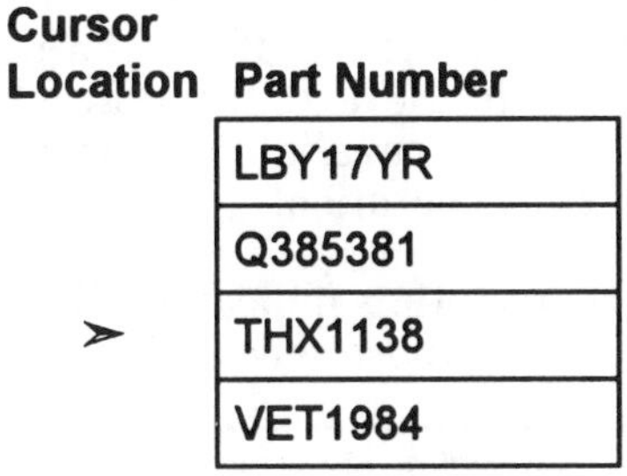

Cursor Location	Part Number
	LBY17YR
	Q385381
➢	THX1138
	VET1984

CHECK (Verify a Character String)

The CHECK operation verifies that each character of Factor 2 is one of the list of characters in Factor 1. This is accomplished by comparing the characters of Factor 2, character by character, to the list of characters in Factor 1 until a difference is detected or until the end of Factor 2 is reached. If a difference is detected, its position is returned to the Result field.

Factor 1	OpCode	Factor 2	Result	Length	Dec	Ext	Resulting Ind.		
check list	CHECK	*base value[:start]*	*[position(s)]*	[size]	[dec]			[error]	[found]

Factor 1 is required and must contain a character field, data structure, data structure subfield, array element, constant or named constant. Factor 1 contains a list of one or more characters that will be used to verify Factor 2.

Factor 2 is required and can contain a field, data structure, data structure subfield, array element, constant or named constant that will be verified against Factor 1.

Factor 2 accepts one optional parameter: START-POSITION. This parameter is used to specify the starting position of Factor 2 where the verification begins. If the START-POSITION parameter is omitted, verification begins in position one of Factor 2. START-POSITION can be a literal value, named constant, numeric field or numeric data structure subfield.

The Result field is optional and can contain a numeric field, array or array element. The CHECK operation returns the position within Factor 2 that is not contained in the list of characters located in Factor 1. If all the characters of Factor 2 match Factor 1, zero is returned to the Result field. If the Result field contains an array, the positions of as many occurrences of invalid characters as there are array elements can be returned with one CHECK operation.

If no Result field is specified, resulting indicator 3 is required, and can be used to signal when a character other than those specified in Factor 1 is found in Factor 2.

Resulting Indicator Legend			
Columns	**Ind.**	**Usage**	**Set On Condition**
54 - 55	1	N/A	Not used by this operation code.
56 - 57	2	[error]	The operation ended in error.
58 - 59	3	[found]	A character other than those specified in Factor 1 is found in Factor 2.

More about CHECK

The CHECK operation is primarily used for two functions: (1) To find the first character position of Factor 2 that is not in Factor 1. For example, to find the first non-blank character position of the field in Factor 2. And (2) to verify that Factor 2 contains valid characters—those specified in Factor 1. For example, to verify that Factor 2 contains only numbers or only lower case alphabetic characters.

Example 16 — Verify Factor 2 against a list of characters.

```
SeqNoI...............NamedConstant+++++++++C.........Const+
0001 I               '1234567890ABCDEF-     C         HEXCHR
0002 I               'abcdef'

SeqNoCLOn01n02n03Factor1+++OpCodFactor2+++ResultLenDXHiLoEq
0003 C            HEXCHR    CHECKINPUT     POS   30
0004 C            POS       CASGTO         ERROR
0005 C                      END
```

In Example 16, the character field INPUT is verified against the named constant HEXCHR. If INPUT contains any characters other than those specified for HEXCHR, the position within INPUT of the invalid character will be returned in the field POS.

Before:

```
          *...v... 1 ...v... 2 ...v... 3
INPUT =  'FDE6GE7B'
POS   =   0
```

After:

```
          *...v... 1 ...v... 2 ...v... 3
INPUT =  'FDE6GE7B'
POS   =   5
```

Example 17 — Use CHECK to left adjust a field.

```
SeqNoCLOn01n02n03Factor1+++OpCodFactor2+++ResultLenDXHiLoEq
0001 C            ' '       CHECKLSTNAM    S         50
0002 C                      SUBSTLSTNAM:S  LSTNAM     P
```

More about CHECK

In Example 17, the CHECK operation is used to locate the first non-blank position in the field LSTNAM. Then, the SUBST (substring) operation is used to left justify the value. The operation extender P is used in conjunction with the SUBST operation. This causes the SUBST operation to replace the Result field. Below is the before and after values of the LSTNAM field.

Before:

```
              *...v... 1 ...v... 2 ...v... 3
LSTNAM   =   '    Kennedy                    '
```

After:

```
              *...v... 1 ...v... 2 ...v... 3
LSTNAM   =   'Kennedy                        '
```

Example 18 — Use CHECK to build a proper salutation.

```
SeqNoCLOn01n02n03Factor1+++OpCodFactor2+++ResultLenDXHiLoEq
0001 C           ' '       CHECKLSTNAM    S        50
0002 C                     SUBSTLSTNAM:S  LSTNAM     P
0003 C           FSTNAM    CAT  LSTNAM:1  NAME    30 P
```

Example 18 begins by locating the first non-blank position of the LSTNAM field. Then, using the SUBST operation, the value is left justified. Finally, the CAT operation is used to build the concatenated salutation.

Before:

```
              *...v... 1 ...v... 2 ...v... 3
FSTNAM   =   'Robert                         '
LSTNAM   =   '    Kennedy                    '
NAME     =   '                               '
```

After:

```
              *...v... 1 ...v... 2 ...v... 3
FSTNAM   =   'Robert                         '
LSTNAM   =   'Kennedy                        '
NAME     =   'Robert Kennedy                 '
```

CHEKR (Verify Right to Left)

The CHEKR operation verifies that each character of Factor 2 is contained in the list of characters in Factor 1. This is accomplished by comparing each character in Factor 2, starting with its rightmost character, to the list of characters specified in Factor 1. The verification stops when a difference is detected or the first position of Factor 2 is reached. If a difference is detected, its position is returned to the Result field. Also see CHECK operation on page 164.

Factor 1	OpCode	Factor 2	Result	Length	Dec	Ext	Resulting Ind.		
check list	CHECKR	*char value[:start]*	*[position(s)]*	[size]	[dec]			[error]	[found]

Factor 1 is required and must contain a character value. The character value identifies the valid characters that can appear in Factor 2.

Factor 2 is required and must contain a character variable. This character value is verified against the list of characters specified in Factor 1. Verifications begins with the rightmost character in Factor 2 or, if specified, with the *start position.*

Factor 2 accepts one optional parameter: START-POSITION: This parameter is used to specify the starting position, in Factor 2, for the verification to begin. If the START-POSITION is omitted, verification begins in the rightmost position of the value specified for Factor 2. The START-POSITION can be any numeric value.

The Result field is optional and, if specified, must contain the name of a numeric field, array or array element. The CHEKR operation returns the rightmost position of Factor 2 that is not listed in Factor 1 to the Result field. Multiple unmatching positions can be located with a single CHEKR operation by specifying a numeric array in the Result field. If an array is specified for the Result field, the operation is repeated until all available array elements have be filled or until the beginning of Factor 2 is reached.

Resulting Indicator Legend			
Columns	**Ind.**	**Usage**	**Set On Condition**
54 - 55	1	N/A	Not used by this operation code.
56 - 57	2	[error]	The operation ended in error.
58 - 59	3	[found]	A character other than those specified in Factor 1 is found in Factor 2.

More about CHEKR

If the Result field is not specified, resulting indicator 3 is required, and is used to signal when a character is found in Factor 2 that is other than those specified in Factor 1.

The CHEKR operation is the complement of the CHECK operation. The CHECK operation begins checking from the left, continuing to the right. The CHEKR operation begins checking on the right, continuing to the left.

The CHEKR operation is useful for determining the length of the data in a field. When variable length data is used in an RPG program, the program must maintain the length of the data. The CHEKR operation can be used to retrieve the length of the data, then store that length as a 2-byte binary field that precedes the variable length field's data.

For example, by specifying a blank in Factor 1, the CHEKR operation will return the position of the last non-blank in Factor 2. This position is the length of the data in the field specified for Factor 2.

Example 19 — Find the length of data for a variable length field.

```
SeqNoIDSName.....UDSInitialValue++++++++++TFromTo++DField+
0001 ITEXT         DS
0002 I                                        B   01  020LENGTH
0003 I                                             3 512 TITLE
SeqNoCLOn01n02n03Factor1+++OpCodFactor2+++ResultLenDXHILOEQ
0004 C           'Presi'   CAT  'dent':0  TITLE
0005 C                     CAT  'John':1  TITLE
0006 C                     CAT  'F.':1    TITLE
0007 C                     CAT  'Ken':1   TITLE
0008 C                     CAT  'nedy':0  TITLE
0009 C           ' '       CHEKRTITLE     LENGTH
```

After the CAT operations on lines 1 to 5 are performed, the field LENGTH is set to 25 and the field TITLE contains the following:

```
 *...v....1....v....2....v....3....v
'President John F. Kennedy          '
                         ↑          ↑
                         |          CHEKR starts in position 35.
                         |
                         Position (25) returned to LENGTH.
```

CLEAR (Clear Data Set)

The CLEAR operation sets Factor 2 to blanks, zeros or '0' depending on its attribute. The CLEAR operation is primarily used to clear all the subfields of a data structure or all the fields of a display file record format.

Factor 1	OpCode	Factor 2	Result	Length	Dec	Ext	Resulting Ind.		
[*NOKEY]	CLEAR	*variable to clear*							

Factor 1 is optional, and can contain constant *NOKEY when Factor 2 contains a record format of a keyed database (DISK) file. This indicates that the key fields of the record are to be preserved (i.e., not cleared) when the record format is cleared.

Factor 2 is required and can contain a field, data structure, data structure subfield, record format, array, array element, table or named indicator.

If Factor 2 contains a record format, the corresponding file must be opened for update, output-only or combined (input/output) processing, and must be used in the program with an output operation code or cycle output. The CLEAR operation cannot be used on a record format of a file that is opened for input-only. Only fields defined as output or input/output are cleared. Input-only fields are not cleared.

If Factor 2 contains an array, the entire array (every element) is cleared. When Factor 2 contains an array element, (e.g., ARR,3) only that element is cleared.

If Factor 2 contains a multiple occurrence data structure, the current occurrence of the data structure is cleared. When Factor 2 contains a data structure, each subfield is cleared in order of its appearance in the data structure. The sequence in which the subfields appear in the input specifications, not the relative offset within the data structure, control the sequence of the clearing.

CLEAR and Initial Values

The CLEAR operation ignores initial values—it moves either blanks or zeros into a variables based on the variable's attribute. If the application requires resetting a variable to its initial value, the RESET operation should be used. For more information, see the RESET operation on page 264.

More about CLEAR

It should be pointed out that the default initial value for all data structure subfields is blanks. Unlike the RESET operation which moves the initial value into the variable, the CLEAR operation will move blanks to character variables, and zeros to numeric variables, regardless of their initial value.

The initial value for data structure subfields can be set to reflect the subfield's attribute by specifying the letter I in column 18 of the data structure specification. Character subfields are initialized to blanks and numeric subfields are initialized to zeros. Specific subfields can be initialized based on the subfield attribute by specifying the letter I in column 8 of the subfield specification with no value in columns 21 to 42.

When the CLEAR operation is performed within the *INZSR subroutine, the *cleared* value becomes the initial value. For data structures, this provides a result similar to specifying the letter I in column 18 of the data structure specification.

Example 20 — Clear a Data Structure.

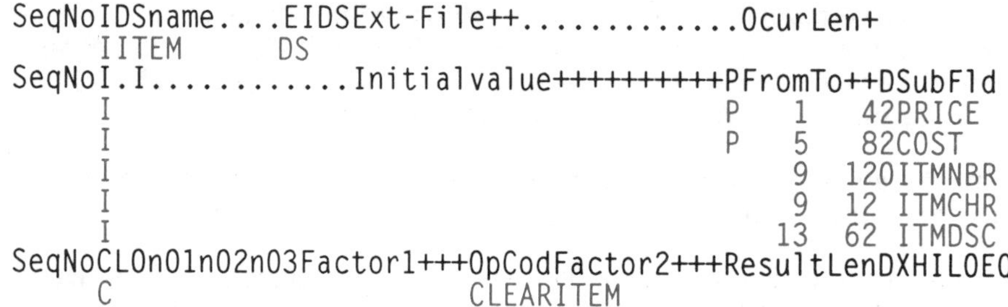

```
SeqNoIDSname....EIDSExt-File++.............OcurLen+
     IITEM       DS
SeqNoI.I............Initialvalue++++++++++PFromTo++DSubFld
     I                                    P    1    42PRICE
     I                                    P    5    82COST
     I                                         9   120ITMNBR
     I                                         9   12 ITMCHR
     I                                        13   62 ITMDSC
SeqNoCL0n01n02n03Factor1+++OpCodFactor2+++ResultLenDXHILOEQ
     C                     CLEARITEM
```

In this example, the subfields of the data structure named ITEM are cleared as follows:

1. Zeros are moved to the subfield PRICE.
2. Zeros are moved to the subfield COST.
3. Zeros are moved to the subfield ITMNBR.
4. Blanks are moved to the subfield ITMCHR—overlaying the zeros moved into the previous subfield.
5. Blanks are moved to the subfield ITMDSC.

CLOSE (Close a File)

The CLOSE operation closes the file specified in Factor 2 and optionally closes all opened files when *ALL is specified for Factor 2.

Factor 1	OpCode	Factor 2	Result	Length	Dec	Ext	Resulting Ind.		
	CLOSE	*file name*						[error]	
	CLOSE	*ALL						[error]	

Factor 2 must contain the name of the file being closed or *ALL. If Factor 2 contains the figurative constant *ALL, all files currently opened in the program are closed.

When a file is closed, it is disconnected from the program and can no longer be accessed by the program. If the file must be accessed again—in the same program—it must be opened with the OPEN operation.

A prerun-time table or array file name (indicated by a T in column 16 of the "F" specification) cannot be specified in Factor 2. An output table or array (indicated by the file name appearing in positions 19 to 26 of the "E" specification) can be specified in Factor 2, however, its records are not written out to disk until the program ends with the LR indicator on.

Resulting Indicator Legend			
Columns	**Ind.**	**Usage**	**Set On Condition**
54 - 55	1	N/A	Not used by this operation.
56 - 57	2	[error]	An error occurred during the operation.
58 - 59	3	N/A	Not used by this operation.

Example 21 — Close a data file by naming the file.

```
SeqNoCLOn01n02n03Factor1+++OpCodFactor2+++ResultLenDXHiLoEq
0010 C                     CLOSECUSTMAST                56
```

In this example, the file CUSTMAST is closed. If the CLOSE operation does not complete successfully, resulting indicator 2 (indicator 56, in our example) will be set on, signaling that the close attempt failed.

COMIT (Commit)

The COMIT operation is a relational database management function. It performs the commitment function of the Relation Model by making all modifications that have been made since the previous COMIT or ROLBK operation permanent (see the ROLBK operation later in this chapter).

Factor 1	OpCode	Factor 2	Result	Length	Dec	Ext	Resulting Ind.		
[boundary]	COMIT							[error]	

Factor 1 is optional and can contain a value that will be used as a boundary identification. This identification can be used by a recovery process after an abnormal system termination occurs. The boundary identifier will be logged to one of many optional locations, such as a data file, message queue, or data area, one of which can be specified outside the RPG program to a system function.

Resulting Indicator Legend			
Columns	**Ind.**	**Usage**	**Set On Condition**
54 - 55	1	N/A	Not used by this operation.
56 - 57	2	[error]	An error occurred during the operation.
58 - 59	3	N/A	Not used by this operation.

The commit operation is performed on all files that are currently under commitment control for a process (i.e., job) regardless of whether they are actually defined in the program performing the COMIT operation.

When the COMIT operation is performed, all records that have been locked during and by the commit process are released (including records that have been committed outside of the domain of the current program).

Example 22 — Commit with a boundary identifier.

```
SeqNoFFileNameIPE.E....RLEN...K.OV.....Device+RecNbrKOptionEntry+
0010 FCUSTMASTIF  E                    DISK            KCOMIT

SeqNoCLOn01n02n03Factor1+++OpCodFactor2+++ResultLenDXHiLoEq
0020 C                     MOVE 'POST03'  BNDRY
0030 C           BNDRY     COMIT                          56
```

COMP (Compare)

The COMP operation compares Factor 1 to Factor 2. Resulting indicators 1, 2 and 3 are set on according to the outcome of the comparison.

As least one resulting indicator must be specified. If three resulting indicators are specified, no more than two may be the same indicator.

Factor 1	OpCode	Factor 2	Result	Length	Dec	Ext	Resulting Ind.		
compare value 1	COMP	*compare value 2*					[1>2]	[1<2]	[1=2]

Factor 1 can contain any RPG variable, including a literal value, field, data structure, data structure subfield, array, array element or figurative constant such as *BLANKS.

Factor 2 must contain a value with attributes similar to Factor 1. For example, if Factor 1 contains a numeric field, Factor 2 must be a numeric field, a numeric constant or a numeric figurative constant (such as *ZEROS). If Factor 1 is character, Factor 2 must also be character.

Resulting Indicator Legend			
Columns	**Ind.**	**Usage**	**Set On Condition**
54 - 55	1	[1>2]	Factor 1 is greater than Factor 2.
56 - 57	2	[1<2]	Factor 1 is less than Factor 2.
58 - 59	3	[1=2]	Factor 1 is equal to Factor 2.

Example 23 — Compare fields to constants.

```
SeqNoCL0n01n02n03Factor1+++OpCodFactor2+++ResultLenDXHiLoEq
0010 C           STATE     COMP 'IL'                     58
0020 C           AMOUNT    COMP 5000.00              545658
```

In this example, the field STATE is compared to the constant 'IL' on line 10. If STATE is equal to 'IL', resulting indicator 3 (indicator 58, in our example) is set on. On line 20 the numeric field AMOUNT is compared to the constant 5000.00 and sets on the appropriate indicators.

DEBUG (Print Debug Statement)

The DEBUG operation provides a simple means of debugging an RPG program. Indicator settings, KLIST, array, table and data structure contents can be printed or displayed with this operation by specifying the name of the field, KLIST, array, table or data structure in the Result field.

Resulting indicators are not valid for this operation.

With today's interactive debug tools, this operation is of limited use. Its main function is to provide compatibility with older systems.

Factor 1	OpCode	Factor 2	Result	Length	Dec	Ext	Resulting Ind.		
[descriptive text]	DEBUG	*[printer file name]*	*[print value]*						

Factor 1 can contain a literal value, field array element, or a data structure name, the contents of which will be printed or displayed when the DEBUG operation is performed.

Factor 2 can contain the name of the file to which the output from the DEBUG operation is sent. The file must be at least 80 bytes in length. If Factor 2 is blank, the output is sent to the display device associated with the job. If the job is a batch job (i.e., one with no associated workstation device file), the output is sent to the default printer.

The Result field can contain the name of a field, the contents of which will be sent to the output device specified in Factor 2.

Example 24 — Debug sent to a printer file with a constant.

```
SeqNoCLOnO1nO2nO3Factor1+++OpCodFactor2+++ResultLenDXHiLoEq
0010 C                     MOVE ARR,7     FIELDA
0020 C           'BRK01'   DEBUGPRTFILE   FIELDA
```

In this example, the seventh array element of the array ARR is copied to the field FIELDA. Then, the DEBUG operation prints the constant 'BRK01' and the contents of FIELDA to the printer file named PRTFILE.

DEFN (Define a Field or Data Area)

The DEFN operation defines a variable to the program. The variable can be based on the attributes of another variable (i.e., character or numeric) or it can be associated with a data area.

The DEFN operation can be specified anywhere in a program's calculations including detail, total-time or subroutine calculations.

Conditioning indicators are not valid for this operation. Result indicators are not valid for this operation.

Factor 1	OpCode	Factor 2	Result	Length	Dec	Ext	Resulting Ind.		
*LIKE	**DEFN**	*based-on variable*	*variable*	[±][size]	[dec]				
*NAMVAR	**DEFN**	*[data area name]*	*variable*	[size]	[dec]				

The first form of DEFN defines a derived field. That is a field based-on the attributes of another field. Only the length, and high-level type (i.e., character or numeric) can be inherited .

The second form of DEFN assigns a field to an external data area. That is when the field is referenced by the IN, OUT or UNLCK operations, the data area assigned to the variable is read, written or unlocked.

Factor 1 is required and can contain one of the following:

Factor 1	Description
*LIKE	Defines a derived field. The field specified in the Result field inherits the attributes of character or numeric and the length of the variable specified for Factor 2. The numeric subtype, (i.e., packed, zoned or binary) is not inherited. All numeric variables are assigned the type of packed data.
*NAMVAR	Defines a field as a data area. The data in Factor 2 is assigned to the field. When the variable specified in the Result field is referenced by the IN, OUT or UNLCK operations, the data area specified in Factor 2 is accessed.

More about DEFN

If *LIKE is specified for Factor 1, the following conditions apply:

1. Factor 2 must contain the name of a field, data structure, array or array element that will be used as a basis for a derived field.
2. If Factor 2 contains an array name, an element of the array is used as the basis for the derived field.
3. The Result field must contain the name of the field that will be derived based-on Factor 2.
4. The derived field's length will be equal to the length of the field specified in Factor 2. The field's derived length can be overridden by specifying a relative or absolute field length in the Result field length (columns 49 to 51).

Relative length allows a longer or shorter length for the derived field to be specified. To make the derived field longer than the based-on field, place a plus sign (+) into the first position of the Result field length (i.e., column 49) and indicate the additional number of positions for the field, right-justified, in the Result field length (columns 50 and 51 of the calculation specification). To make the derived field shorter than the based-on field, place a minus sign (-) into the first position of the Result field length, and indicate the number of positions to reduce the derived field by, right-justified, in columns 50 and 51.

Example 25 — Define three derived fields.

```
SeqNoCL0n01N02n03Factor1+++OpCodFactor2+++ResultLenDXHiLoEq
0010 C           *LIKE     DEFN CSTNBR    ACTNBR+ 3
0020 C           *LIKE     DEFN CSTNBR    OLDACT- 2
0030 C           *LIKE     DEFN CSTNBR    SAVCST
```

On line 10, the field ACTNBR is defined and is three positions longer than the field CSTNBR. Line 20 defines the field OLDACT with a length of two positions less than CSTNBR, and line 30 defines the field SAVCST with the same attributes (i.e., length and type) as CSTNBR.

More about DEFN

If *NAMVAR is specified for Factor 1, the following conditions apply:

1. Factor 2 may optionally contain the name of an external data area. If the system supports a Local Data Area, *LDA may be specified in Factor 2. If the system supports the program information parameters data area, *PDA may be specified for Factor 2. If Factor 2 is omitted, then the value specified in the Result field is used as the name of the external data area.
2. The Result field is required and must contain the name of a field, data structure, data structure subfield or data area data structure. The entry in the Result field is used to access the external data area's data. The Result field is "assigned" to the data area and is used by the IN and OUT operations.
3. The length of the field being assigned to the data area may be specified in the Result field length (columns 49 to 52).

An external data area can be retrieved (read) and rewritten (updated) with the IN and OUT operations. (See IN and OUT operations later in this chapter.)

Example 26 — Define an external data area and assign the data area to the field named.

```
SeqNoCLOnO1NO2nO3Factor1+++OpCodFactor2+++ResultLenDXHiLoEq
0010 C           *NAMVAR   DEFN CONTROL   CTRL     70
0020 C                     IN   CTRL                   56
```

Line 10 defines the external data area CONTROL and assigns it to the field CTRL. In this example, the attributes (i.e., length and type) of CTRL are defined as a seven-digit packed numeric. However, the Result field can be a field, data structure, or data structure subfield.

Line 20 retrieves (i.e., reads) the external data area CONTROL into the field CTRL. The data in the field CTRL can be used (moved, copied, changed or deleted) without affecting the data contained in the external data area. The data in the external data area is not affected until an OUT operation to CTRL is performed.

Resulting indicator 2 (indicator 56 in our example) is set on by the IN operation on line 20 if the data area does not exist, or if it has been locked by another process.

DELET (Delete Data File Record)

The DELET operation deletes a single record from the file specified in Factor 2. Factor 2 can be a file name or a record format name.

Factor 1	OpCode	Factor 2	Result	Length	Dec	Ext	Resulting Ind.		
[key value]	`DELET`	*file name*					[n/f]	[error]	
[key value]	`DELET`	*format name*					[n/f]	[error]	

For keyed access files, Factor 1 may contain the following: (1) blanks, which causes the DELET operation to delete the record currently locked by the program; (2) a field or data structure name containing the key value; (3) a key list name whose key fields contain the key or partial key value; (4) a constant representing the key value.

For files accessed by relative record number, Factor 1 may contain the following: (1) blanks, which will cause the DELET operation to delete the record currently locked by the program; (2) a numeric field with zero decimal positions that contains a positive non-zero number; (3) an integer constant (e.g., 27 for record number 27).

For externally described files, Factor 2 can be either the name of the file containing the record that will be deleted, or the name of a file's record format whose record will be deleted.

The file represented in Factor 2 must be declared as an update file (i.e., the letter U must appear in position 15 of the file's File Description specification) to allow the DELET operation to function.

When Factor 1 is used to access the record, resulting indicator 1 must be specified to signal a record-not-found condition.

Resulting Indicator Legend			
Columns	**Ind.**	**Usage**	**Set On Condition**
54 - 55	1	[n/f]	Record Not Found.
56 - 57	2	[error]	Error occurred during the operation.
58 - 59	3	N/A	Not used by this operation code.

More about DELET

The examples that follow use the file ORDERS. The file ORDERS contains a record format name of HEADER. The file's index is made up of the key fields CSTNBR and ORDNBR. Access by CSTNBR is all that is needed in our examples.

Example 27 — Delete record by specifying a key-list in Factor 1.

```
SeqNoFFileNameIPE.E....RLEN...K.OV.....Device+RecNbrKOptionEntry+
0010 FORDERS  UF  E             K         DISK

SeqNoCLOn01N02n03Factor1+++OpCodFactor2+++ResultLenDXHiLoEq
0030 C*  Key list by customer number only.
0040 C              CSTKEY    KLIST
0050 C                        KFLD           CSTNBR
0060 C*  Delete first order for customer = 200
0070 C                        Z-ADD200       CSTNBR
0080 C              CSTKEY    DELETHEADER                 5456
```

In this example, the key list CSTKEY is used by the DELET operation to access the file ORDERS by key. If a matching key is found, its corresponding record will be deleted. If no matching key is found, resulting indicator 1 will be set on. If the record exists but could not be allocated, resulting indicator 2 will be set on. Factor 2 of the DELET operation contains the record format name HEADER. This is the name of the record format for the file named ORDERS.

Optionally, resulting indicator 2 may be used to signal errors that might occur during the attempt to delete the record. Possible errors that would set on resulting indicator 2 are: record allocation time-out or lack of proper authority to delete records from the file. The *STATUS variable should be checked to identify the error that caused resulting indicator 2 to be set on. (See *File Status Error Codes* on page 142 for specific error codes.)

More about DELET

Example 28 — Delete a record using CHAIN/DELET combination.

```
SeqNoFFileNameIPE.E....RLEN...K.OV.....Device+RecNbrKOptionEntry+
0010 FORDERS  UF  E            K        DISK

SeqNoCLOn01N02n03Factor1+++OpCodFactor2+++ResultLenDXHiLoEq
0030 C*  Key list by customer number.
0040 C             CSTKEY    KLIST
0050 C                       KFLD           CSTNBR
0060 C*  Retrieve 1st order for customer = 200
0070 C                       Z-ADD200       CSTNBR
0080 C             CSTKEY    CHAINHEADER                 5456
0090 C             *IN56     IFEQ *ON
0100 C                       EXSR TIMOUT
0110 C                       ELSE
0120 C             *IN54     IFEQ *OFF
0130 C                       DELETORDERS
0140 C                       ENDIF
0150 C                       ENDIF
```

In this example, the key list CSTKEY is used to access the file ORDERS through the CHAIN operation on line 80. If a record is found, the DELET operation on line 130 will delete the record from the file.

Note: The file ORDERS is accessed through the record format HEADER on line 80 and deleted through its file name on line 130. The DELET will delete the last record read by the program. Also, line 130 avoids using resulting indicator 2 because the CHAIN operation retrieves and locks the record for update.

Unlike the CHAIN, READ, and READP operations, the DELET operation does not copy the contents of a file's fields to the input buffer. Therefore, when the index of a record is known to the program, using only the DELET operation with Factor 1 specified yields better performance.

When the DELET operation deletes a record, that record is permanently erased from storage. Also, a subsequent READ operation will read the record following the deleted record, a subsequent READP operation will read the record prior to the deleted record.

DIV (Divide)

The DIV operation is used to produce the quotient (result) of a divide operation in the form *Factor 1 divided by Factor 2* (F1/F2)—long form, or *Result field divided by Factor 2* (RF/F2)—short form.

Factor 1	OpCode	Factor 2	Result	Length	Dec	Ext	Resulting Ind.		
dividend	DIV	divisor	quotient	[size]	[dec]	[H]	[+]	[-]	[0]
	DIV	divisor	quotient and dividend	[size]	[dec]	[H]	[+]	[-]	[0]

If Factor 1 contains a value, Factor 1 is the dividend, Factor 2 is the divisor and the Result field is the quotient. If Factor 1 is blank, the Result field is used as the dividend, Factor 2 is the divisor, and the Result field is the quotient.

The operation extender H can be specified to cause the result to be half adjusted—that is, rounded up. If the DIV operation is immediately followed by the MVR operation, the operator extender cannot be specified for the DIV operation.

Resulting Indicator Legend			
Columns	**Ind.**	**Usage**	**Set On Condition**
54 - 55	1	[+]	The Result field is greater than zero.
56 - 57	2	[–]	The Result field is less than zero.
58 - 59	3	[0]	The Result field is equal to zero.

If the dividend (Factor 1, long form; Result field, short form) is 0, the result is 0. If the divisor (Factor 2) is 0, a "divide by zero error" occurs. In this case, the default exception/error handling subroutine will receive control. Therefore, the exception/error handling subroutine must be coded in the program, or Factor 2 must be tested before performing the divide operation. Normally the program would compare the divisor (Factor 2) to zero before the DIV operation is performed, thus avoiding a divide-by-zero error.

To capture the remainder of a DIV operation, the MVR (move remainder) operation must immediately follow the DIV operation. If MVR is specified, the remainder from the DIV operation is placed into the Result field of a MVR operation; the H operation extender (half adjust) cannot be specified for the DIV operation. For more information see the MVR operation on page 232.

More about DIV

Example 29 — Long and short forms of division.

```
SeqNoCLOn01n02n03Factor1+++OpCodFactor2+++ResultLenDXHiLoEq
0010 C           B         IFNE 0
0020 C           A         DIV  B         C
0030 C                     DIV  B         C         545658
0040 C                     ENDIF
```

In Example 29, the first DIV operation divides field A by field B, and the quotient is placed in field C. In the second DIV operation, field C is divided by field B, and the quotient replaces the value in field C. Also, if the quotient is greater than zero (i.e., a positive number), resulting indicator 1 is set on. If the quotient is less than zero (i.e., a negative number), resulting indicator 2 is set on. If the quotient is equal to zero, resulting indicator 3 is set on.

Example 30 — Long form division with remainder.

```
SeqNoCLOn01n02n03Factor1+++OpCodFactor2+++ResultLenDXHiLoEq
0010 C           A         DIV  B         C
0020 C                     MVR            REMDR
```

In Example 30, the remainder of A / B is stored into the field REMDR. If A = 5 and B = 3, then as a result of the calculations in Example 30, C = 1 and REMDR = 2.

Example 31 — Division with rounding (half adjust).

```
SeqNoCLOn01n02n03Factor1+++OpCodFactor2+++ResultLenDXHiLoEq
0010 C           A         DIV  B         C         H
```

In Example 31, the H that appears in operation extender (column 53) causes the quotient (Result field) to be rounded. For example, if A = 7 and B = 4, then A / B = 1.75; with half adjust in effect, the quotient will be C = 2. The quotient will vary based on the number of decimal positions of the Result field. For example, if the quotient is defined with one decimal position, the result of the calculation would be C = 1.8 (rounding to the tenths position).

DO (Begin Do Loop)

The DO operation begins a DO..ENDDO Loop. The code between the DO and the ENDDO statement is called the Do group and is performed a number of times. The END or ENDDO statements close a DO..ENDDO loop.

The DO operation is a structured programming construct. It contributes to, but does not cause, structured programming.

Factor 1	OpCode	Factor 2	Result	Length	Dec	Ext	Resulting Ind.		
[starting value]	DO	*[limit]*	*[counter]*	[size]	[dec]				

The structure of the DO..ENDDO loop appears below.

```
SeqNoCLOn01n02n03Factor1+++OpCodFactor2+++ResultLenDXHiLoEq
     C  in1       Start     DO   Limit      Count
     C                       .
      *        Do group code goes here.
     C                       .
     C  in2                 ENDDOIncrement
```

Start is an optional starting value of *Count*. When the Do loop is entered, the value of *Start* is place into *Count*. If *Start* is omitted, 1 is used as the starting value.

Limit is the optional upper limit of the number of times the Do loop will be performed. *Limit* is compared to *Count* at the "top" of the Do loop. If *Count* is greater than *Limit*, the Do group is NOT performed. If *Limit* is omitted, 1 is used as the upper limit value.

Count is the index or counter of the Do loop. *Count* is increased by *Increment* at the end of each pass through the Do loop. At the top of each pass of the Do loop, *Count* is compared to *Limit*. If *Count* is greater than *Limit*, the Do loop is ended. If *Count* is omitted, an internal variable is used for the counter.

Increment is Factor 2 of the ENDDO statement, which contains the value that will be added to *Count* when the ENDDO statement is encountered. If *Increment* is not specified, a value of 1 is used as the *Increment*.

More about DO

IN1 is an optional indicator or set of indicators that controls the entry into the Do loop. If the conditioning indicator test is met when the Do loop is encountered, the Do loop will be entered. If the conditioning indicator test is not met, the program branches to the statement following the ENDDO statement.

IN2 is an optional indicator that controls the unnatural exit from the Do loop. When the ENDDO statement is encountered and one or more conditioning indicators are present, the indicator conditions are tested. If the condition is met, the ENDDO statement is performed and control passes back up to the DO statement. If the condition is not met, control passes to the statement following the ENDDO statement, and the Do loop is exited.

The ENDDO statement is the Do loop's "end marker." It defines the end of the block of code controlled by the Do operation. When used in conjunction with the DO statement, ENDDO adds *Increment* to *Count*, then branch to the top of the Do loop.

Example 32 — Perform a Do group multiple times.

```
SeqNoCLOn01n02n03Factor1+++<28  to  32>Factor2+++ResultLenDXHiLoEq
0010 C                          DO        12        X         50
0020 C            ARR,X          | IFEQ      'Q38'
0030 C                           | | MOVEL   'Midrange'ARR,X
0040 C                           | ENDIF
0050 C                          ENDDO
```

More about DO

In Example 32, line 10 begins the Do loop. Factor 2 of line 10 indicates that the DO loop will be performed 12 times. The Result field on line 10 defines the field X as the *count* field of the Do loop. Each pass through the Do group will increment the X by 1. Line 20 uses X as an index of the array ARR.

Each time the Do loop is encountered (i.e., each time the program flow causes the Do loop to be processed,) the count field is automatically initialized to the value specified in Factor 1 of the DO operation.

Example 33 — Nested DO..END groups.

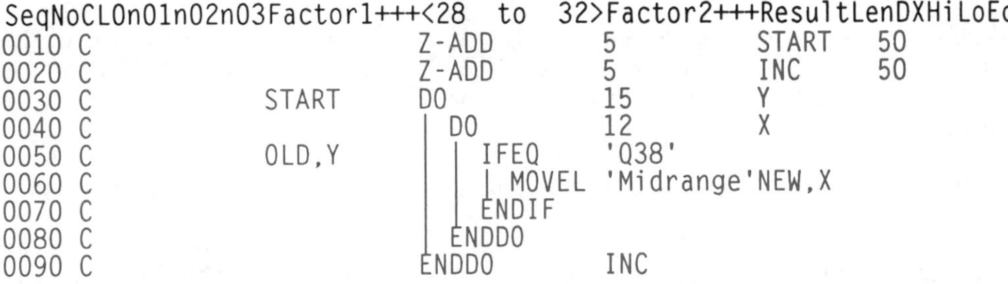

```
SeqNoCLOn01n02n03Factor1+++<28  to  32>Factor2+++ResultLenDXHiLoEq
0010 C                    Z-ADD      5          START   50
0020 C                    Z-ADD      5          INC     50
0030 C           START    DO         15         Y
0040 C                    | DO       12         X
0050 C           OLD,Y    | | IFEQ   'Q38'
0060 C                    | | | MOVEL 'Midrange'NEW,X
0070 C                    | | ENDIF
0080 C                    | ENDDO
0090 C                    ENDDO      INC
```

In Example 33, lines 10 and 20 set the outer DO..END loop *start* and *increment* fields to 5. When the DO group is started, Y will be set to 5, then increased by 5 during each pass through the Do loop. Since the limit for the outer loop is 15, the Do group will be performed three times. Then inner loop, (lines 40 to 80) will be performed 12 times the number of times the outer Do loop is performed. Therefore, the inner Do loop will be performed 36 times.

DOUxx (Begin Do Until-Loop)

The DOUxx operation begins a Do until loop. The code between the DOUxx and the ENDDO statement is called the Do group and is always performed at least once.

The DOUxx operation is a structured operation. It contributes to, but does not cause, structured programming.

Factor 1	OpCode	Factor 2	Result	Length	Dec	Ext	Resulting Ind.		
compare value 1	DOUxx	*compare value 2*							

The DOUxx operation requires a relationship test *xx*, where *xx* may be any one of the Boolean operators (EQ, GE, GT, LE, LT and NE). See page 135 for details. Factor 1 is compared to Factor 2 based-on the *xx* operator. Factor 1 and Factor 2 must be similar data types.

Conditioning indicators, if specified, are tested before entry into the Do until group.

The Do until construct logically tests the xx Boolean operation at the bottom of the Do loop (i.e., when the ENDDO statement is encountered) and, therefore, always performs its Do group at least once. The ENDDO statement can be conditioned by indicators. If the indicator condition is true, the ENDDO is performed normally. If the indicator condition is false, the ENDDO is not performed, and control passes the statement following the ENDDO.

The DOUxx test can be extended with the ANDxx or ORxx operations. ANDxx allows compound conditions to be tested, ORxx allows distinct conditions to be tested.

Example 34 — DOUxx with ANDxx extension.

```
SeqNoCLOnO1n02n03Factor1+++OpCodFactor2+++ResultLenDXHiLoEq
0010 C               A         DOUEQB
0020 C               D         ANDGTC
0030 C                         ADD  1         B
0040 C                         ADD  2         D
0050 C                         ENDDO
```

In Example 34, the Do group is performed until A is equal to B and D is greater than C, but it is always performed at least once.

More about DOUxx

Example 35 — DOUxx with ORxx extension to fill a subfile or list panel with 20 records.

```
SeqNoCLOn01n02n03Factor1+++<28  to  32>Factor2+++ResultLenDXHiLoEq
0010 C              CSTNBR    CHAIN     DATAFILE              54
0020 C                        MOVE      *IN54     EOF
0030 C              EOF       IFEQ      *OFF
0040 C                        | Z-ADD   0         RELNO   30
0050 C              EOF       | DOUEQ   *ON
0060 C              RELNO     | ORGE    20
0070 C                        | | ADD   1         RELNO
0080 C                        | | WRITE SUBFILE
0090 C                        | | READ  DATAFILE                  58
0100 C                        | | MOVE  *IN58     EOF
0110 C                        | ENDDO
0120 C                        ENDIF
```

In Example 35, the database file named DATAFILE is accessed on line 10 with the CHAIN operation. If an index exists for the key value contained in CSTNBR, the record is retrieved and the field EOF is set off. The DOUEQ, ORGE pair control the Do until group. The END operation on line 110 is where the actual relationship test is performed.

DOWxx (Begin Do While-Loop)

The DOWxx operation begins a Do while loop. The code between the DOWxx and the END statement is called the Do group and is performed a number of times.

The DOWxx operation is a structured operation. It contributes to, but does not cause structured programming.

Factor 1	OpCode	Factor 2	Result	Length	Dec	Ext	Resulting Ind.		
compare value 1	DOWxx	*compare value 2*							

The DOWxx operation requires a relationship test xx, where xx may be any one of the Boolean operators (EQ, GE, GT, LE, LT, or NE). See page 135 for details.

As with all structured operations, conditioning indicators control entry into the structure and are tested before entry into the Do while group.

The Do while construct logically tests the *xx* Boolean operation at the top of the Do loop and, therefore, always performs its Do group only when the Boolean test is true.. The ENDDO statement can be conditioned by indicators. If the indicator condition is true, the ENDDO is performed normally. If the indicator condition is false, the ENDDO is not performed, and control passes the statement following the ENDDO.

The DOWxx test can be extended with the ANDxx or ORxx operations. ANDxx allows compound conditions to be tested, ORxx allows additional, but separate conditions to be tested.

Example 36 — DOWxx with ORxx extension.

```
SeqNoCLOn01n02n03Factor1+++OpCodFactor2+++ResultLenDXHiLoEq
0010 C            A         DOWEQB
0020 C            C         ORNE D
0030 C                      ADD  1         B
0040 C                      ADD  2         D
0050 C                      ENDDO
```

In Example 36, the Do loop is performed while A is equal to B or C is not equal to D.

More about DOWxx

Example 37 — DOWxx with ANDxx extension to fill a subfile with 20 records.

```
SeqNoCLOn01n02n03Factor1+++<28  to  32>Factor2+++ResultLenDXHiLoEq
0010 C           CSTNBR    CHAIN       CUSTMAST                54
0020 C                     MOVE        *IN54      EOF
0030 C                     Z-ADD       0          RELNO   30
0040 C           EOF       DOWEQ       *OFF
0050 C           RELNO     ANDLT       20
0060 C                     | ADD       1          RELNO
0070 C                     | WRITE     SUBFILE
0080 C                     | READ      CUSTMAST                    58
0090 C                     | MOVE      *IN58      EOF
0100 C                     ENDDO
```

In Example 37, the database file named CUSTMAST is accessed on line 10 with the CHAIN operation. If an index exists for the key value contained in CSTNBR, the record is retrieved and the field EOF is set off.

The DOWEQ ANDLT operations control entry into the Do group. First, the field RELNO (subfile relative record number) is increased on line 60, then a subfile (or tabular list panel) detail record named SUBFILE is written. Finally, the database file CUSTMAST is read, and the Do loop is performed again. If end-of-file is reached or RELNO is equal to 20 the Do loop ends.

Normally, when processing a database file with this operation, the file is positioned to the first record to be processed before entering into the Do while group.

DSPLY (Display Workstation Message)

The DSPLY operation provides a primitive form of message-level communication between the workstation operator or the system operator and the RPG program. The message can be sent so that it returns an operator response, it can also be sent without returning a response.

Factor 1	OpCode	Factor 2	Result	Length	Dec	Ext	Resulting Ind.		
[message text]	`DSPLY`	*[message queue]*	*[reply value]*	[size]				[error]	

Factor 1 is optional and can contain a message ID, a literal value or a field with information to be displayed. If a message ID is specified, it must conform to one of the following formats:

1. *Myyyy—Where *M is constant and yyyy is a user-defined message ID. For example *M10 would generate user message USR0010. The yyyy message ID must be 1 to 4 characters in length, left justified against the *M constant.
2. *Mxxxyyyy—Where xxx is a message prefix such as USR, RPG or MCH, and yyyy is a user-defined message ID. For example, *MRPG400 would generate user message RPG0400. The xxx must be 3 characters in length, left justified against the *M constant. The yyyy message ID must be 1 to 4 digits in length, left justified against the *Mxxx constant.

Factor 2 is optional and can contain the name of the message queue that will receive the message. For example, 'QSYSOPR' would cause the message to be sent to the system operator, and '*EXT' would cause the message to be sent to the workstation operator. For interactive jobs, Factor 2 will default to '*EXT'. For batch jobs, Factor 2 will default to 'QSYSOPR'.

The Result field can contain the name of a field that will receive the workstation or system operator's reply. If the Result field is omitted, the operator will not be allowed to type in a reply.

Resulting Indicator Legend			
Columns	**Ind.**	**Usage**	**Set On Condition**
54 - 55	1	N/A	Not used by this operation.
56 - 57	2	[error]	An error occurred during the operation.
58 - 59	3	N/A	Not used by this operation.

More about DSPLY

If Factor 1 contains a message ID, RPG retrieves the message text of the message ID from the message file named QUSERMSG. This message file name can be overridden to some other name by running the OS/400 command OVRMSGF. This command can be run outside of the RPG program, or by calling a system command processing program (such as QCMDEXC on AS/400) from within RPG and passing it a string containing the OVRMSGF command.

The message ID text, constant or field specified in Factor 1 will be displayed at the workstation or system operator message queue, along with any data that is contained in the Result field when the DSPLY operation is performed.

If Factor 1 is blank and the Result field is specified, only the data contained in the Result field will be displayed. If the Result field is blank and Factor 1 is omitted, nothing is displayed.

Example 38 — Display a message at the workstation.

```
SeqNoCLOn01n02n03Factor1+++OpCodFactor2+++ResultLenDXHiLoEq
0010 C              *MUSR010  DSPLY'*EXT'    REPLY
0020 C              REPLY     IFEQ 'C'
0030 C                        MOVE *ON       *INLR
0040 C                        RETRN
0050 C                        ENDIF
```

In this example, the user-defined message USR0010, indicated by *MUSR010 in Factor 1, is sent to the workstation operator indicated by the constant '*EXT' in Factor 2.

Any response the workstation operator types in will be returned to the program in the field REPLY, which is specified in the Result field.

DUMP (Print Formatted Dump)

The DUMP operation generates a list of all fields, data structures, indicators, internal fields, pointers, storage areas, tables and arrays.

The DUMP operation valid only when position 15 of the Header specification contains the number 1. Resulting indicators are not valid for this operation.

Factor 1	OpCode	Factor 2	Result	Length	Dec	Ext	Resulting Ind.		
[descriptive text]	DUMP								

Factor 1 is optional and may contain a dump identifier that will be printed on the generated dump listing. The dump listing is quite similar to the formatted dump generated by the operating system.

Example 39 — Produce a dump when divide-by-zero occurs.

```
0010 H         1

SeqNoIDSName....EUDSExternalname..........PFromTo++DField+
0020 I                SDS
0030 I                                      *STATUS   STATUS

SeqNoCLOn01n02n03Factor1+++OpCodFactor2+++ResultLenDXHiLoEq
0040 C                       Z-ADD123       TOTAL    70
0050 C                       Z-ADD0         ORDQTY   70
0060 C                 TOTAL      DIV  ORDQTY     UNIT     52H
0070 C                       SETON                           LR
0080 CSR               *PSSR      BEGSR
0090 C                 STATUS     IFEQ 0102
0110 C                 'DivByZer'DUMP
0110 C                            ENDIF
0120 CSR               ENDPSR     ENDSR
```

This example will produce a formatted dump listing with 'DivByZer' as its identifier. The fields TOTAL, ORDQTY UNIT and STATUS, and the indicator LR, are included in the formatted dump listing, along with several compiler-generated fields.

ELSE (Else Clause)

The ELSE operation is used with the IFxx operation. The ELSE operation follows the IFxx group and precedes the corresponding ENDIF statement. The group of statements between the ELSE operation and the corresponding ENDIF statement is performed when the condition specified for the IFxx is false.

Conditioning indicators are not valid for this operation.

Factor 1	OpCode	Factor 2	Result	Length	Dec	Ext	Resulting Ind.		
	ELSE								

Example 40 — ELSE used for conditioning.

```
SeqNoCLOnO1nO2nO3Factor1+++<28  to  32>Factor2+++ResultLenDXHiLoEq
0010 C           DAYS      IFLE        30
0020 C                     | MOVEL     '0-30'    AGING
0030 C                     +ELSE
0040 C           DAYS      | IFLE      60
0050 C                     | | MOVEL   '31-60'   AGING
0060 C                     | +ELSE
0070 C                     | | MOVEL   'Over-Due'AGING
0080 C                     | ENDIF
0090 C                     ENDIF
```

In this example, the field DAYS is compared to 30 and 60 days. When the IFLE operation is true, the MOVEL operation that immediately follows the IFLE operation is performed. Control then passes to the END statement associated with the IFLE operation. When the IFLE operation tests false, control passes to the ELSE statement within the IFLE group. In our example, this performs a subsequent IFLE operation.

ENDxx (End Do Group, Select Group, CASxx and IFxx)

The ENDxx operation closes a DO, DOUxx, DOWxx, CASxx, IFxx or SELEC group.

Factor 1	OpCode	Factor 2	Result	Length	Dec	Ext	Resulting Ind.		
	ENDxx	*[increment]*							

The *xx* of the ENDxx operation is optional and can be specified to document the type of END operation.

END	End an IFxx, DOxxx, SELEC, or CAS operation.
ENDCS	End a CASxx operation.
ENDDO	End a DO, DOWxx or DOUxx operation.
ENDIF	End an IFxx operation.
ENDSL	End a SELEC operation.

Factor 2 (allowed only when closing a DO...ENDDO group) is optional and may contain the increment value for a Do loop counter.

Conditioning indicators are optional when closing a DO, DOWxx or DOUxx group. If the conditioning indicator test is true, the ENDDO statement is performed and control passes back to the top of the loop. If the conditioning indicator test is false, control passes to the operation following the ENDDO statement.

Example 41 — End a DOUEQ loop and an IFEQ.

```
SeqNoCLOn01n02n03Factor1+++<28  to  32>Factor2+++ResultLenDXHiLoEq
0010 C           CSTNBR    CHAIN     CUSTMAST                  54
0020 C                     MOVE      *IN54     EOF
0030 C           EOF       IFEQ      *OFF
0040 C           EOF       | DOUEQ   *ON
0050 C           RELNO     | ORGE    20
0060 C                     | | ADD   1         RELNO
0070 C                     | | WRITE SUBFILE
0080 C                     | | READ  CUSTMAST                      58
0090 C                     | | MOVE  *IN58     EOF
0100 C                     | ENDDO
0110 C                     ENDIF
```

ENDSR (End Subroutine)

The ENDSR operation marks the end of a subroutine. It must be the last statement of a subroutine. Factor 1 is optional and may contain a label that will be used as the target of a GOTO or CABxx operation.

Factor 1	OpCode	Factor 2	Result	Length	Dec	Ext	Resulting Ind.		
[label]	**ENDSR**	*[return point]*							

Controlling level indicators, conditioning indicators and resulting indicators are not valid for this operation. Columns 7-8 must contain either the constant SR or blanks. Normally, SR is used in columns 7-8 to provide a visual indication of the end of a subroutine.

Example 42 — End subroutine with a label.

```
SeqNoCLOn01n02n03Factor1+++OpCodFactor2+++ResultLenDXHiLoEq
0010 C                     EXSR COUNT
0020 C           ENDPGM    TAG
0030 C                     MOVE *ON       *INLR

0040 CSR         COUNT     BEGSR
0050 C                     ADD  1         C
0060 C                     MOVE 'MIDRANGE'NEW,C
0070 CSR         ENDCNT    ENDSR
```

More about ENDSR

Example 43 — Exception/Error subroutine with program cancel.

```
SeqNoCLOn01n02n03Factor1+++OpCodFactor2+++ResultLenDXHiLoEq
0010 C                     READ CUSTMAST                 5658
0020 C           *IN56     CASEQ*ON       *PSSR
0030 C                     END

0040 CSR         *PSSR     BEGSR
0050 C           STATUS    IFEQ TIMOUT
0060 C                     MOVE *ON       *INLR
0070 C                     ENDIF
0080 CSR         ENDERR    ENDSR'*CANCL'
```

Factor 2 may contain a six-position field, constant or named constant when the subroutine is an exception/error handling subroutine. Factor 2 can contain a field name or a constant that identifies the returning point after the subroutine is performed. If the exception/error handling routine is called with either the EXSR or CASxx operations and Factor 2 is blank, control returns to the statement following the EXSR or CASxx operation.

The valid exception/error returns points that can be specified in Factor 2 for the ENDSR operation are listed in Figure 4-51.

Routine	Description
*DETC	Beginning of detail-time calculations.
*DETL	Beginning of detail-time output.
*GETIN	Get input routine (read next record).
*TOTC	Beginning of total-time calculations.
*TOTL	Beginning of total-time calculations.
*OFL	Beginning of overflow lines.
*CANCL	Abnormal end-of-program.
blanks	Return to statement following interruption.

Figure 4-51: Exception/Error Return Points (Factor 2 of ENDSR)

EXCPT (Exception Output)

The EXCPT operation performs an immediate write to either a program defined output file or an externally described file's record format.

Factor 1	OpCode	Factor 2	Result	Length	Dec	Ext	Resulting Ind.		
	EXCPT	*[except label]*							

Factor 2 can contain the name of an except label. Except labels are used to control the output to the output record. When an except label is present, only those output specifications that contain the except label are written. More than one output specification can contain the same except label.

When an except label is not used, only those exception output records without an except label are written, provided that the output format conditioning indicators are true.

The EXCPT operation can be used to release records of a database file that have been locked by another operation.

When an EXCPT operation is performed on an externally described file and database fields are specified on the output specification, only those fields specified are written to the database record. Other fields within the record go unchanged.

To write out all fields in the record format, the figurative constant *ALL must be the first and only field specified for the exception output.

When updating a record, fields not specified for output go unchanged. When writing a new record, fields not specified for output are set to zero or blanks depending on their attribute.

The examples on the following pages illustrate four uses of the EXCPT operation:

1. EXCPT output to a program defined printer file.
2. EXCPT output with an except label to a program defined printer file.
3. EXCPT output to an externally described database file format.
4. EXCPT output to release a locked record.

More about EXCPT

Example 44 — Exception output to a program defined printer file.

```
SeqNoCLOn01n02n03Factor1+++OpCodFactor2+++ResultLenDXHiLoEq
0010 C           INDEX     CHAINCUSTMAST                54
0020 C                     MOVE *IN54     NF
0030 C           NF        DOWEQ*OFF

0040 C                     EXCPT

0050 C           INDEX     READECUSTMAST                    58
0060 C                     MOVE *IN58     NF
0070 C                     ENDDO
```

```
SeqNoOFilenameEFBASBSAn01n02n03Field+EBEnd+POutputconstant++++++++++
0080 OQPRINT  E  1
0090 O                         CUST# Z   10
0100 O                         CSTNAM  +  2
0110 O        E  1             DETAIL
0120 O                         BALDUE3   10
```

In Example 44, the first record matching the key value in the field INDEX is retrieved from the customer master file CUSTMAST. Then an exception output line is printed, printing the customer number and customer name. Since the EXCPT operation on line 40 contains no except name, the output specifications on lines 80 to 100 will be output and lines 110 to 120 will not.

Example 45 — Exception output with an except label to a program described file.

```
SeqNoCLOn01n02n03Factor1+++OpCodFactor2+++ResultLenDXHiLoEq
0010 C           INDEX     CHAINCUSTMAST                54
0020 C                     MOVE *IN54     NF
0030 C           NF        DOWEQ*OFF

0040 C                     EXCPTDETAIL

0050 C           INDEX     READECUSTMAST                    58
0060 C                     MOVE *IN58     NF
0070 C                     ENDDO
```

continued on the following page

More about EXCPT

continued from the preceding page

```
SeqNoOFileNameEFBASBSAn01n02n03Field+EBEnd+POutputconstant+++++++++++
0080 OQPRINT  E  1
0090 O                             CUST# Z   10
0100 O                             CSTNAM  +  2
0110 O        E  1                 DETAIL
0120 O                             BALDUE3   10
```

In Example 45, the exception label DETAIL is used to control the output of the printer file. The output specifications on lines 110 and 120 will print the balance due. The output specifications on lines 80 to 100 will not be output because they are not conditioned by the DETAIL exception name.

Example 46 — Exception output to an externally described database file format.

```
SeqNoFFileNameIPE.E....RLEN...K.OV....EDevice+RecNbrKOptionEntry+
0010 FCUSTINV IF  E           K        DISK

SeqNoCLOn01n02n03Factor1+++OpCodFactor2+++ResultLenDXHiLoEq
0020 C                INDEX     CHAINCUSTINV                 54
0030 C                          MOVE *IN54     NF
0040 C                NF        DOWEQ*OFF
0050 C                          Z-ADD0         BALDUE
0060 C                          EXCPTNEWBAL
0070 C                INDEX     READECUSTINV                     58
0080 C                          MOVE *IN58     NF
0090 C                          ENDDO

SeqNoOFilenameEFBASBSAn01n02n03Field+EBEnd+POutputconstant+++++++++++
0100 OCSTMST  E                    NEWBAL
0110 O                             BALDUE
```

In Example 46, the first record matching the key value in the field INDEX is retrieved from the customer orders file CUSTINV. Then, the balance due field BALDUE is zeroed, giving the customer a zero balance-due account. To update only that field, an exception label is used on line 60 to rewrite the customer record with a zero balance.

More about EXCPT

Example 47 — Exception output to release a locked record.

```
SeqNoCLOn01n02n03Factor1+++OpCodFactor2+++ResultLenDXHiLoEq
0010 C           INDEX     CHAINCUSTMAST                 54
0020 C                     MOVE *IN54     NF
0030 C           NF        IFEQ *OFF

0040 C                     EXCPTRELEAS

0050 C                     EXFMTDISPLAY
0060 C                     ENDIF

SeqNoOFilenameEFBASBSAn01n02n03Field+EBEnd+POutputconstant+++++++++++
0070 OCSTMST  E                 RELEAS
```

In Example 47, the record matching the key value in the field INDEX is retrieved from the customer master file CUSTMAST. Since CUSTMAST is opened for update, the record will be locked by data management. The information in that record will be displayed by the EXFMT operation on line 50.

To release the record lock, line 40 uses the EXCPT operation with an except label containing no fields. This releases the record lock. Note: The exception label RELEAS is used for easy identification of the release function.

This technique works with program defined and externally described database files and is functionally equivalent to the UNLCK operation.

When an except name is used on a file that has been opened for OUTPUT-only, and no output fields have been specified for the exception output—as described in Example 47—a record containing blank and zero fields (depending on the field attribute) will be written to the database file.

EXFMT (Write/Read a Workstation File Format)

The EXFMT operation performs a WRITE followed by a READ to the same WORKSTN file record format. The EXFMT operation is a combined and optimized form of WRITE followed by READ.

Factor 1	OpCode	Factor 2	Result	Length	Dec	Ext	Resulting Ind.		
	EXFMT	*workstn format*						[error]	

Factor 2 must contain the name of a WORKSTN file record format. Resulting indicator 2 is optional and, if specified, it will signal when a workstation error has occurred. EXFMT, however, cannot be used for workstation time-out. See the READ operation on page 252 for information on workstation time-out.

Resulting Indicator Legend			
Columns	**Ind.**	**Usage**	**Set On Condition**
54 - 55	1	N/A	Not used by this operation.
56 - 57	2	[error]	An error occurred during the operation.
58 - 59	3	N/A	Not used by this operation.

Example 48 — Retrieve and display a data file record.

```
SeqNoFFileNameIPE.E....RLEN...K.OV.....Device+RecNbrKOptionEntry+
0010 FCUSTINQ CF  E                    WORKSTN
0020 FCUSTMASTIF  E           K        DISK

SeqNoCLOn01n02n03Factor1+++OpCodFactor2+++ResultLenDXHiLoEq
0030 C           INDEX     CHAINCSTMST                 56
0040 C                     MOVE *IN56     NF
0050 C           NF        IFEQ *OFF
0060 C                     EXFMTCUSTFMT                56
0070 C                     ENDIF
```

In this example, the database fields in the file CUSTMAST are the same as those used in the workstation file format CUSTFMT. Consequently, no MOVE operations need to be performed to get the database information into the workstation record format.

The EXFMT operation is widely used with interactive programming. It provides the easiest method of displaying information contained in a display file at a WORKSTN device.

EXSR (Perform Subroutine)

The EXSR operation calls an internal subroutine (known as a procedure in some languages.) After the subroutine has completed, control normally returns to the statement following the EXSR operation.

If a GOTO operation within the subroutine caused branching outside of the domain of the subroutine, or an exception/error handling subroutine caused branching to a different part of the program cycle, control will not return to the statement following the EXSR operation.

Factor 1	OpCode	Factor 2	Result	Length	Dec	Ext	Resulting Ind.		
	EXSR	*subroutine name*							

Factor 2 can contain a user-written subroutine name, or the name of the exception/error subroutine (*PSSR) or the initialization subroutine (*INZSR). It can also contain a file exception/error subroutine (INFSR) name. The name of that subroutine must can be up to six characters in length and must appear in Factor 1 of a BEGSR operation.

Example 49 — Perform a subroutine to compute profit.

```
SeqNoCLOn01n02n03Factor1+++OpCodFactor2+++ResultLenDXHiLoEq
0010 C           INDEX     CHAINITEMMAST                 54
0020 C                     MOVE *IN54     NF
0030 C           NF        IFEQ *OFF
0040 C                     MOVE 'FOUND'   MSG

0050 C                     EXSR PROFIT

0060 C                     ENDIF
0070 C                     MOVE *ON       *INLR

0080 CSR         PROFIT    BEGSR
0090 C           PRICE     MULT QTYORD    EXTEND
0100 C           ITMCST    MULT QTYORD    EXTCST
0110 C           EXTPRC    SUB  EXTCST    GRSPFT
0120 CSR                   ENDSR
```

More about EXSR

In Example 49, the database file ITEMMAST (item master) is accessed on line 10. The subroutine PROFIT is then performed on line 50 to compute the gross profit of the item retrieved by the CHAIN operation on line 10. The subroutine PROFIT begins on line 80 with the BEGSR operation. The gross profit is calculated. The subroutine ends with the ENDSR operation (line 120). Control returns to line 60.

Subroutine Considerations

RPG will supports up to 256 subroutines per program. Each subroutine must be outside the domain of other subroutines; that is, a subroutine cannot contain another subroutine—although a subroutine can call another subroutine.

Any RPG operation may be specified with a subroutine, including the EXSR and CASxx operations. Therefore, a subroutine can call another subroutine. However, recursive calls to the same subroutine can cause the program to loop.

Control level-break indicators are not allowed. The constant SR can be specified in the control level-break indicator columns (7-8), to indicate that this is a subroutine. Most programs contain the SR only on the BEGSR and ENDSR statements. This visually identifies the beginning and end of the subroutine.

The GOTO operation can be used to branch within the subroutine or to branch to a location outside of the subroutine's domain. It cannot, however, branch to a label contained within another subroutine.

Example 50 — Diagram of mainline flow with EXSR.

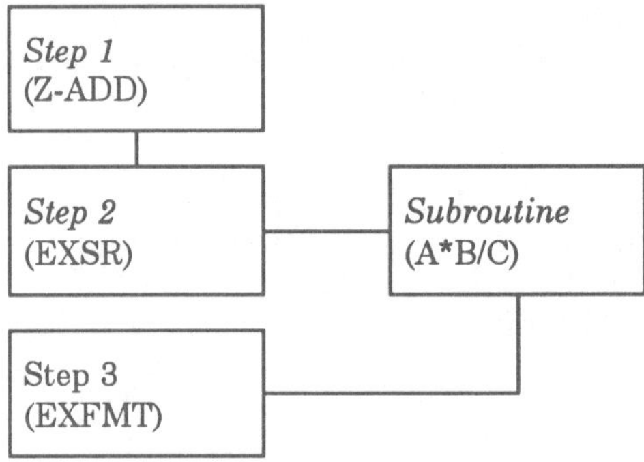

FEOD (Force End of Data)

The FEOD operation positions a file's "cursor" to the end of file, releases any record locks that exist, and forces any buffered data to be written to the device. For example, the last few lines of a printed report are normally not sent to the printer until after the print file is closed. The FEOD operation forces those last few printed lines to the printer without closing the printer file.

Factor 1	OpCode	Factor 2	Result	Length	Dec	Ext	Resulting Ind.		
	FEOD	*file name*						[error]	

Factor 2 must contain the name of the file for the FEOD operation. If the FEOD fails, resulting indicator 2 is set on.

Resulting Indicator Legend			
Columns	**Ind.**	**Usage**	**Set On Condition**
54 - 55	1	N/A	Not used by this operation.
56 - 57	2	[error]	An error occurred during the operation.
58 - 59	3	N/A	Not used by this operation.

This operation differs from the CLOSE operation in that acquired device files (see ACQ operation on page 145) are not released (i.e., disconnected) from the program. The file must be repositioned before any subsequent read operation can access the file's data.

Example 51 — Force the End-of-Data of a data file.

```
SeqNoCLOn01n02n03Factor1+++OpCodFactor2+++ResultLenDXHiLoEq
0010 C                     FEOD CUSTMAST                 56
```

In this example, the file CUSTMAST is forced to end-of-data. Any CUSTMAST records locked by the program are released. Resulting indicator 2 (indicator 56 in our example) is set on if the FEOD fails.

FORCE (Force Input Priority)

The FORCE operation controls the sequence in which records are read by the RPG cycle. Only primary and secondary files are read by the RPG cycle.

This operation is valid at *Detail Time* calculations only.

Factor 1	OpCode	Factor 2	Result	Length	Dec	Ext	Resulting Ind.		
	FORCE	*file name*							

Factor 2 must contain the name of the primary or secondary file that will be read on the next RPG cycle. If the file specified in Factor 2 is at end of file, the FORCE operation is ignored, and the RPG cycle will select the next file to be read.

When more that one FORCE operation occurs during the same RPG cycle, the final FORCE operation has priority over all other FORCE operations.

Example 52 — Force input from a secondary file.

```
SeqNoFFileNameIPE.E....RLEN...K.OV.....Device+RecNbrKOptionEntry+
0010 FCUSTMASTIPE E                    DISK
0020 FITEMMASTISE E                    DISK
0030 FORDERS  ISE E                    DISK

SeqNoCLOn01n02n03Factor1+++OpCodFactor2+++ResultLenDXHiLoEq
0040 C           COUNT     IFEQ 0
0050 C                     ADD  1         COUNT   30
0060 C                     FORCEORDERS
0070 C                     ENDIF
0080   *** user code
```

In this example, the file ORDERS will be read on the next input cycle, bypassing the normal Primary/Secondary selection priority.

FREE (Deactivate an Active Program)

The FREE operation deactivates an active program. A program remains active if it completes with the LR (last record) indicator set off. Normally this is accomplished by one of the following: (1) performing the RETRN operation with the LR indicator off; or (2) by setting on the RT indicator and completing the current RPG cycle or performing a RETRN operation.

Essentially, the FREE operation clears the target program from memory, destroying the value of its fields, arrays and data structures. Files that are opened in the program being freed are not closed, and data areas that have been locked are not unlocked.

Factor 1	OpCode	Factor 2	Result	Length	Dec	Ext	Resulting Ind.		
	FREE	*program name*						[error]	

Factor 2 is required and must contain either a field or a constant that contains the name of the program that will be deactivated by the FREE operation.

Resulting indicator 2 is set on by the FREE operation when the program is not FREEd. For example, if the program named in Factor 2 is not active when the FREE operation is performed or if the program does not support the FREE operation, resulting indicator 2 is set on.

Resulting Indicator Legend			
Columns	**Ind.**	**Usage**	**Set On Condition**
54 - 55	1	N/A	Not used by this operation.
56 - 57	2	[error]	An error occurred during the operation.
58 - 59	3	N/A	Not used by this operation.

Example 53 — Free a program by naming the program as a constant.

```
SeqNoCL0n01n02n03Factor1+++OpCodFactor2+++ResultLenDXHiLoEq
0010 C                     FREE 'PRICEORD'               56
```

In this example, Factor 2 contains the literal value 'PRICEORD', which is the name of the program that will be freed. Resulting indicator 2 (indicator 56 in our example) is set on if the FREE operation fails.

GOTO (Go To)

The GOTO operation allows branching to different areas of the program. A label, called a TAG in RPG, is the target of the GOTO operation. Labels are declared with the TAG and ENDSR operation.

Factor 1	OpCode	Factor 2	Result	Length	Dec	Ext	Resulting Ind.		
	GOTO	*label*							

The GOTO operation performs a permanent branch to the label specified in Factor 2. Control never returns to the GOTO statement.

For the most part, the GOTO can branch anywhere in the program, from anywhere in the program. However, a subroutine cannot be branched into from outside of that subroutine. Also, detail calculations cannot be branched to from total time calculations.

Example 54 — GOTO controlled looping.

```
SeqNoCLOn01n02n03Factor1+++OpCodFactor2+++ResultLenDXHiLoEq
0010 C           READ      TAG
0020 C                     READ CUSTMAST                 LR
0030 C           *INLR     CABEQ*ON       ENDPGM
     C*... user code .........
0500 C                     GOTO READ
     C*... more user code.....
0900 C           ENDPGM    TAG
```

In this example, the GOTO operation on line 500 performs an unconditional branch to the label READ on line 10.

IFxx (If Conditional Comparison)

The IFxx operation compares the value in Factor 1 to the value in Factor 2. If the comparison is true, the group of calculations between the IFxx and its associated END operation (or ELSE operation) are performed.

The IFxx operation can be extended through the use of one or more ANDxx or ORxx operations. In this case, the group of calculations between the final ANDxx or ORxx operation and the associated END operation (or ELSE operation) is performed when the compound conditioning is true.

Conditioning indicators are valid for the IFxx operation. However, conditioning indicators cannot be used on ANDxx and ORxx operations.

Factor 1	OpCode	Factor 2	Result	Length	Dec	Ext	Resulting Ind.		
compare value 1	`IFxx`	*compare value 2*							

Factor 1 and Factor 2 are required and must be of like attributes (e.g., both must be numeric or alphanumeric.)

If a conditioning indicator is used, it is tested before the IFxx operation. When the indicator condition is false, the IFxx operation is not performed. Control passes to the associated END operation for this IFxx operation, even if an ELSE operation is specified. When the indicator condition is true, the IFxx operation, along with any ANDxx and ORxx conditioning, is performed.

The IFxx operation can be used to conditionally perform a group of operations by testing a range, a list of values, a single value or a compound set of values. See examples that follow for details.

The IFxx operation requires a relationship test xx, where xx may be any of the Boolean operators (EQ, GE, GT, LE, LT, or NE). See page 135 for details.

More about IFxx

Example 55 — Condition a group of operations on a single comparison.

```
SeqNoCL0n01n02n03Factor1+++OpCodFactor2+++ResultLenDXHiLoEq
0010 C           INDEX     CHAINCUSTMAST                54
0020 C           *IN54     IFEQ *OFF
0030 C                     EXFMTDISPLAY
0040 C                     ENDIF
```

In Example 55, the CHAIN operation on line 10 accesses the database file CUSTMAST. If a record is found, resulting indicator 1 (indicator 54 in our example) will be set off. The IFEQ (if equal) operation on line 20 tests indicator 54 for the off condition and performs an EXFMT operation if the condition is true (i.e., indicator 54 is off).

Example 56 — Use the IFxx and the ORxx to test for a list of values.

```
SeqNoCL0n01n02n03Factor1+++OpCodFactor2+++ResultLenDXHiLoEq
0010 C                     EXFMTDISPLAY
0020 C           OPTION    IFEQ 'A1'
0030 C           OPTION    OREQ 'B1'
0040 C           OPTION    OREQ 'C1'
0050 C                     MOVE 'OK'      STATUS
0060 C                     ENDIF
```

In Example 56, the EXFMT operation prompts the user. The format DISPLAY is written to and read from the display device. After the format is read, the compound IFxx operation on lines 20 to 40 compare the field OPTION to 'A1', 'B1' or 'C1'. If the field OPTION is equal to any of these values, the MOVE operation on line 50 is performed.

More about IFxx

Example 57 — Use the IFxx and the ANDxx to test for a range.

```
SeqNoCLOn01n02n03Factor1+++OpCodFactor2+++ResultLenDXHiLoEq
0010 C                     EXFMTDISPLAY
0020 C           OPTION    IFGE '1'
0030 C           OPTION    ANDLE'9'
0040 C                     MOVE 'OK'      STATUS
0050 C                     ENDIF
```

In Example 57, the workstation format DISPLAY is sent to and read from the display via the EXFMT operation. When the workstation file is read, the compound IFxx operation on lines 20 and 30 compare the field OPTION to be greater than or equal to '1' and less than or equal to '9'. If the field OPTION satisfies that condition, the MOVE operation on line 40 will be performed.

Example 58 — Use the compound form of IFxx to control entry into a subroutine.

```
SeqNoCLOn01n02n03Factor1+++<28  to  32>Factor2+++ResultLenDXHiLoEq
0010 C                     EXFMT      DISPLAY
0020 C           OPTION    IFEQ       '9'
0030 C           FILE      ANDNE      *BLANKS
0040 C           LIBR      ANDNE      *BLANKS
0050 C           FILE      ANDNE      '*DELETED'
0060 C           USERID    | IFEQ     'SECURITY'
0070 C           USERID    | OREQ     'MANAGER'
0080 C           AUT       | ANDEQ    'DELRGHT'
0090 C                     | | EXSR   DELETE
0100 C                     | ENDIF
0110 C                     ENDIF
```

More about IFxx

In Example 58, the workstation format DISPLAY is written to and read from the workstation via the EXFMT operation. When the workstation file is read, the compound IFxx operation that begins on line 20 is tested. When the compound condition is met, the nested compound IFxx operation that begins on line 60 is tested.

If the IFxx condition (lines 60 to 80) is met, the EXSR operation is performed.

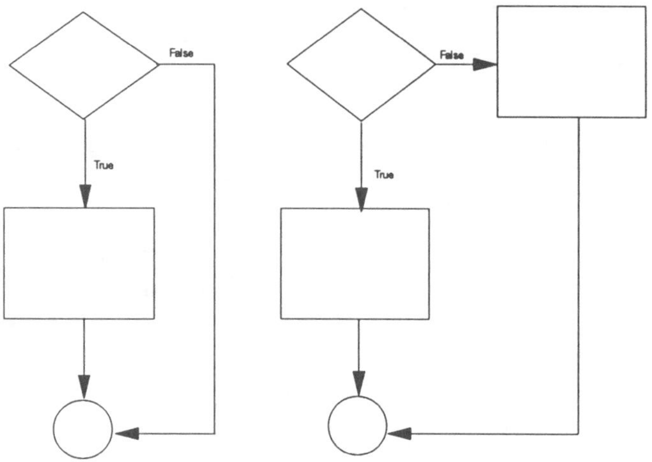

Figure 4-52: Two Forms of IF-THEN-ELSE

The leftmost flowchart in Figure 4-52 illustrates a tradition IF-THEN operation. If the test is true, the process is performed, if the test is false, the process is bypassed.

The rightmost flowchart illustrates the IF-THEN-ELSE operation. If the test is true, the process is performed, if the test is false, an alternate process is performed.

IN (Read in a Data Area)

The IN operation retrieves one or all of the data areas defined in the program; it also optionally allows the data area to be locked. When a data area is locked, no other program can access that data area until an UNLCK (unlock data area) operation is performed. Before a IN operation can be used on a data area, the *NAMVAR DEFN operation; must have been used to assign the data area to a field.

Factor 1	OpCode	Factor 2	Result	Length	Dec	Ext	Resulting Ind.		
[*LOCK]	**IN**	*data area variable*						[error]	
[*LOCK]	**IN**	*NAMVAR						[error]	

Factor 1 can contain the constant *LOCK which will cause the data area specified in Factor 2 to be locked. Factor 1 can be left blank, which causes the data area specified in Factor 2 to be retrieved without being locked.

Factor 2 can contain a data area name or the constant *NAMVAR. When a data area name is specified, the data area is retrieved and optionally locked by the program. When *NAMVAR is specified, all data areas declared to the program are retrieved and optionally locked by the program.

Resulting Indicator Legend			
Columns	**Ind.**	**Usage**	**Set On Condition**
54 - 55	1	N/A	Not used by this operation.
56 - 57	2	[error]	An error occurred during the operation.
58 - 59	3	N/A	Not used by this operation.

If Factor 1 is blank for an IN operation code, the previous IN operation dictates the lock/no-lock status. That is, the first IN operation of a succession of IN operations controls the object lock placed on the data area.

Example 59 — Define then retrieve a data area.

```
SeqNoCLOn01n02n03Factor1+++OpCodFactor2+++ResultLenDXHiLoEq
0010 C           *NAMVAR   DEFN ACCTCTL   CTLNBR
0020 C           *LOCK     IN   CTLNBR
```

In this example, the data area ACCTCTL is defined to the program on line 10. The field CTLNBR is the field that will be assigned to the data area. Line 20 retrieves the data area ACCTCTL into the field CTLNBR. The data area will be locked.

ITER (Iterate a Loop)

The ITER operation can be used within a DO, DOWxx and DOUxx to cause the iteration of the loop being processed. Iteration is accomplished by transferring control to the logical "top" of the Do loop. Typically, however, the RPG compiler generates code that transfers control to the ENDxx operation associated with the Do group. Any conditioning that controls the Do group will be performed after the transfer.

Factor 1	OpCode	Factor 2	Result	Length	Dec	Ext	Resulting Ind.		
	ITER								

The ITER operation is used within a Do loop, typically in conjunction with the LEAVE operation, to enhance control of the Do loop.

To control performing the ITER operation, conditioning indicators or, more properly, an IFxx operation can be used.

Example 60 — Use ITER to bypass unnecessary code.

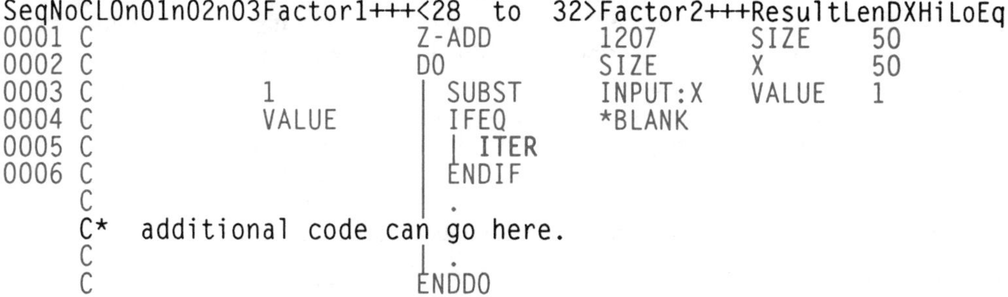

```
SeqNoCLOn01n02n03Factor1+++<28  to  32>Factor2+++ResultLenDXHiLoEq
0001 C                     Z-ADD      1207      SIZE    50
0002 C                     DO         SIZE      X       50
0003 C           1         | SUBST    INPUT:X   VALUE   1
0004 C           VALUE     | IFEQ     *BLANK
0005 C                     | | ITER
0006 C                     | ENDIF
     C                     | .
     C*  additional code can go here.
     C                     | .
     C                     ENDDO
```

In Example 60, the field SIZE is initialized to the length of the field INPUT (a data structure name). Then, each character of INPUT is compared to a blank. Any position of INPUT that is blank is bypassed by the ITER operation (lines 4, 5, 6). All other characters are processed by the remaining operations of the Do group.

KFLD (Key List Key Field)

The KFLD operation is a non executable operation that defines an element of a key list. Multiple successive KFLD operation codes are used to define a key list, which is used in accessing keyed database files. The KFLD operation may appear anywhere in the calculation specifications, but it must follow a KLIST operation (see page 215) or another KFLD operation code.

Conditioning indicators are not valid for this operation.

Factor 1	OpCode	Factor 2	Result	Length	Dec	Ext	Resulting Ind.		
	KFLD		*key field*	[size]	[dec]				

The Result field must contain the name of the field that defines the key field. This field will be used with other key fields (if specified) to form a key list (KLIST). The key list is used to access a database file.

One or more KFLD operation codes are needed to define a key list. The attributes of each key field must match those of the database file that will be accessed via the key list. The number of KFLD operation codes that are permitted per key list depends on the index (i.e., access path) of the database file that is being accessed. The key list may contain as many KFLD operation codes as there are fields defined in the database file's index. If fewer KFLD operation codes appear on the key list than are actually contained in the database file's index, then that subset will be used to access the file.

Example 61 — Key field used for access by warehouse and part number.

```
SeqNoCLOn01n02n03Factor1+++OpCodFactor2+++ResultLenDXHiLoEQ
0010 C           PART      KLIST
0020 C                     KFLD           WHSNBR
0030 C                     KFLD           PRTNBR
0040 C           PART      CHAINPARTMAST                 54
```

KLIST (Key List)

The KLIST operation defines a composite key or "key list" made up of one or more KFLD operation codes. The key list is used to access a database file by an index.

Conditioning indicators are not valid for this operation.

Factor 1	OpCode	Factor 2	Result	Length	Dec	Ext	Resulting Ind.		
key list name	**KLIST**								

Factor 1 must contain the name of the key list that is being defined.

The KLIST operation must be followed by one or more KFLD operation codes (see page 214. The KLIST operation defines the key list name; the KFLD operation code(s) defines the key field(s). It can appear in Factor 1 of the CHAIN, DELET, READE SETGT and SETLL operation codes, for externally described files only.

Example 62 — Access a part master file via a key list.

```
SeqNoCL0n01n02n03Factor1+++OpCodFactor2+++ResultLenDXHiLoEQ
0010 C           WHSE      KLIST
0020 C                     KFLD           WHSNBR

0030 C           PART      KLIST
0040 C                     KFLD           WHSNBR
0050 C                     KFLD           PRTNBR

0060 C           PART      CHAINPARTMAST              54
0070 C           WHSE      CHAINPARTMAST              54
```

In this example, line 10 defines the key list WHSE, consisting of the field WHSNBR. Line 30 defines the key list PART, consisting of the fields WHSNBR and PRTNBR.

LEAVE (Leave a Do Group)

The LEAVE operation can be used to exit a DO, DOWxx and DOUxx group. The LEAVE operation transfers control to the statement following the Do groups ENDxx operation.

Factor 1	OpCode	Factor 2	Result	Length	Dec	Ext	Resulting Ind.		
	LEAVE								

The LEAVE operation is used within a Do loop, typically in conjunction with the ITER operation, to enhance control of the Do loop.

To control performing the LEAVE operation, conditioning indicators or, more properly, an IFxx operation can be used.

Example 63 — Use LEAVE to exit a DOUEQ loop.

```
SeqNoCLOn01n02n03Factor1+++<28  to  32>Factor2+++ResultLenDXHiLoEq
0001 C                    Z-ADD      1207      CUST#   70
0002 C                    DO         20        SFLRRN
0003 C          CUST#      | READE   ORDERS                  58
0004 C          *IN58      | IFEQ    *ON
0005 C                     | | LEAVE
0006 C                     | ENDIF
0007 C                     | WRITE   SUBFILE
0008 C                    ENDDO
0009 C                    EXFMT      ORDPANEL
```

In Example 63, the Do group fills a subfile with up to 20 orders for a given customer. If the end of orders indicator is detected (line 4), the LEAVE operation (line 5) is performed and control is transferred to the statement following the ENDDO operation. That is, control is transferred to line 9.

LOKUP (Lookup Array or Table)

The LOKUP operation searches an array or table for a search argument. At least one resulting indictor is required with this operation.

Factor 1	OpCode	Factor 2	Result	Length	Dec	Ext	Resulting Ind.		
search argument	LOKUP	*array[,start elem]*					[HI]	[LO]	[EQ]
search argument	LOKUP	*table to search*	*alt table*				[HI]	[LO]	[EQ]

Factor 1 must contain a search argument. The search argument must be the same attribute as the array or table elements.

When a lookup is performed on an array, an optional starting element can be specified. If a starting element is specified, the lookup begins with that array element. If the lookup is successful, and the starting element is a numeric variable, the variable is set to the element where the search was satisfied.

When a lookup is performed on a table, the Result field can contain an alternate table name. If the lookup operation is successful, the table in the Result field is set to the corresponding element where the search argument is located.

Resulting indicators control the type of search that is performed by LOKUP. Up to two resulting indicator can be specified for a single LOKUP operation.

Resulting Indicator Legend			
Columns	**Ind.**	**Usage**	**Set On Condition**
54 - 55	1	[HI]	Causes LOKUP to search for the first element greater than Factor 1.
56 - 57	2	[LO]	Causes LOKUP to search for the first element less than Factor 1.
58 - 59	3	[EQ]	Causes LOKUP to search for the first element equal to Factor 1.

Resulting indicators 1 and 3 can both be specified to cause the LOKUP to search for the first element that is greater than or equal to Factor 1.

Resulting indicators 2 and 3 can both be specified to cause the LOKUP to search for the first element that is less than or equal to Factor 1.

More about LOKUP

The LOKUP operation is widely used in RPG. Although more flexible string handling operation codes have been added to the language in recent years, LOKUP still proves value. In the following example, a typical use of the LOKUP operation is illustrated.

Example 64 — Search an array for a valid code.

```
SeqNoE....FromfileTofile..ArrnamEPRDim+LenPDAAltnamLenPDA
0010 E                    VLDCOD  4   4  1
0020 E                    CODTXT  1   4 20

SeqNoCL0n01n02n03Factor1+++OpCodFactor2+++ResultLenDXHiLoEQ
0030 C                     Z-ADD1         X
0040 C           CODE      LOKUPVLDCOD,X                  58
0050 C           *IN58     IFEQ *ON
0060 C                     MOVELCODTXT,X  MSGLIN
0070 C                     ENDIF
**
ABCD
**
Advanced lesson
Beginners lesson
Change answers
Delete test results
```

In Example 64, line 10 defines the 4-element array named VLDCOD. Line 20 defines the 4-element array named CODTXT. The array VLDCOD is a valid code array, and CODTXT is the code's text description. A description of each code stored in the VLDCOD array is located in the corresponding element in the CODTXT array.

When the LOKUP operation on line 40 is successful, the variable X contains the array element of the code being processed. By simply using that variable as the array element of the CODTXT array, the code's description is retrieved.

MxxZO (Move Zone to Zone)

The four MxxZO operations copy the specified zone of either the left or rightmost character of Factor 2 to the left or rightmost character of the Result field. This operation is rarely used, except when the program is processing data from a system other than the host computer.

Factor 1	OpCode	Factor 2	Result	Length	Dec	Ext	Resulting Ind.		
	MxxZO	*source*	*target*	[size]					

The four Move Zone to Zone operations are as follows:

1. The MHHZO (Move High to High Zone) operation copies the zone portion (i.e., bits 0, 1, 2 and 3) of the leftmost character in Factor 2 to the zone portion of the leftmost character of the Result field. Factor 2 must contain a character field. The Result field must contain a character field.
2. The MHLZO (Move High to Low Zone) operation copies the zone portion (i.e., bits 0, 1, 2 and 3) of the leftmost character in Factor 2 to the zone portion of the rightmost character of the Result field. Factor 2 must contain a character field. The Result field can contain either a character or numeric field.
3. The MLHZO (Move Low to High Zone) operation copies the zone portion (i.e., bits 0, 1, 2 and 3) of the rightmost character in Factor 2 to the zone portion of the leftmost character of the Result field. Factor 2 can contain either a character or numeric field. The Result field must contain a numeric field.
4. The MLLZO (Move Low to Low Zone) operation copies the zone portion (i.e., bits 0, 1, 2 and 3) of the rightmost character in Factor 2 to the zone portion of the rightmost character of the Result field. Factor 2 can contain either a character or numeric field. The Result field can also contain a character or numeric field.

MOVE (Copy Data Right-Adjusted)

The MOVE operation copies the data from Factor 2, right justified to the Result field. When the Result field is an array, resulting indicators are not valid.

Factor 1	OpCode	Factor 2	Result	Length	Dec	Ext	Resulting Ind.		
	MOVE	*source*	*target*	[size]	[dec]	[P]	[+]	[−]	[0 or b̸]

Factor 2 can be any data type—literal value or variable.

The Result field can be any variable data type. When the Result field is an array, Factor 2 is moved into each element of the array. (See line 30 of Example 65.) Factor 2 and the Result field cannot be overlapping data structure subfields.

When the length of Factor 2 is less than the length of the Result field, the number of characters replaced in the Result field is equal to the length of Factor 2, unless the operation extender P is used. If the operation extender P is used, the Result field is cleared before the MOVE operation is performed.

When the length of Factor 2 is greater than or equal to the length of the Result field, a complete replacement of the Result field with Factor 2 is performed. Any additional data in Factor 2 is not moved.

Resulting Indicator Legend			
Columns	Ind.	Usage	Set On Condition
54 - 55	1	[+]	The Result field is greater than zero.
56 - 57	2	[−]	The Result field is less than zero.
58 - 59	3	[0 or b̸]	The Result field is equal to zero or, if the Result field is character-based, the Result field contains blanks.

The MOVE operation has traditionally be used to clear the contents of the character Result field by **MOVEing *BLANKS** to the Result field. The CLEAR operation, added recently to RPGIII, accomplishes the same task, and is data type independent. So character or numeric fields, data structures, record formats, arrays, and array elements can be cleared with a single CLEAR operation code.

More about MOVE

The examples that follow illustrate the MOVE operation. The following field names, type and lengths are assumed by these examples.

```
ARR(5)    DEC    7  (An array containing five, 7-digit elements)
ERRMSG    CHAR  30
MSGLIN    CHAR  10
MSGCON    CHAR   4
CSTNBR    DEC    7
```

The field ERRMSG is initialized as follows:

```
          *... ... 1 ... ... 2 ... ... 3
ERRMSG = 'The customer number is 1234567'
```

Example 65 — Various MOVE operations.

```
SeqNoCLOn01n02n03Factor1+++OpCodFactor2+++ResultLenDXHiLoEQ
0010 C                     MOVE ERRMSG    MSGLIN
0020 C                     MOVE ERRMSG    CSTNBR
0030 C                     MOVE CSTNBR    ARR
```

After line 10 in Example 65 is performed, the field MSGLIN contains the following:

```
MSGLIN = ' is 1234567'
```

After line 20 in Example 65 is performed, the field CSTNBR contains the following:

```
CSTNBR = 1234567
```

After line 30 in Example 65 is performed, each element in the array named ARR contains the value 1234567. The value of CSTNBR is moved to each array element—as though independent MOVE operations to each ARR,X were performed (with X being the array index).

```
ARR    = 1234567,1234567,1234567,1234567,1234567
```

More about MOVE

Example 66 — Move with length of Factor 2 greater than the Result field.

```
SeqNoCLOn01n02n03Factor1+++OpCodFactor2+++ResultLenDXHiLoEQ
0010 C                     MOVE MSGLIN    MSGCON
```

In Example 66, after the MOVE operation is performed, the Result field would contain the following:

```
MSGCON = '4567'
```

Example 67 — Move with length of Factor 2 shorter than the Result field.

```
SeqNoCLOn01n02n03Factor1+++OpCodFactor2+++ResultLenDXHiLoEQ
0010 C                     MOVE 'XXXX'    MSGCON
0020 C                     MOVE MSGCON    ERRMSG
```

In Example 67, after the MOVE operation on line 20 is performed, the Result field will contain the following:

```
          *... ... 1 ... ... 2 ... ... 3
ERRMSG = 'The customer number is 123XXXX'
```

MOVEA (Move Array)

The MOVEA operation is a string manipulation operation code. It copies the contents of Factor 2, left justified, to the Result field. Factor 2 and/or the Result field must be an array.

Factor 1	OpCode	Factor 2	Result	Length	Dec	Ext	Resulting Ind.		
	MOVEA	*source*	*target*	[size]	[dec]	[P]	[+]	[-]	[0 or ƀ]

Factor 2 can contain a field, data structure, data structure subfield, array, array element, constant or named constant.

The Result field can contain a field, data structure, data structure subfield, array or array subscript. however, it cannot contain the same array name as Factor 2.

Resulting Indicator Legend			
Columns	**Ind.**	**Usage**	**Set On Condition**
54 - 55	1	[+]	The Result field is greater than zero.
56 - 57	2	[–]	The Result field is less than zero.
58 - 59	3	[0 or ƀ]	The Result field is equal to zero or, if the Result field is character-based, the Result field contains blanks.

An array or array subscript must be specified in Factor 2 and/or the Result field. If an array subscript is specified, the *move* operation begins with the specified array element. For example, if the array subscript ARR,3 is used with the MOVEA operation, the move would begin with the third element of the array name ARR.

The MOVEA operation will operate with either character or zoned numeric arrays. It will not operate on array whose elements are defined as binary or packed numeric.

The MOVEA operation operates on a byte-by-byte basis. It aligns Factor 2 and the Result field based on any array index, then performs the equivalent of the MOVEL (move left) operation code. The length of array elements is meaningless, except when an array index is used as a starting point for the MOVEA operation code.

More about MOVEA

The length of the string that is moved is determined by the shorter length of Factor 2 and the Result field. The length of the string can be calculated with the following formula:

```
E = The number of elements in the array.
L = Length of a single array element.
I = The index of the array.

Length = E * L - ((I - 1) * L)
```

For example, if an array consists of 10 elements of 5 characters each and the array index is 4, then the length of the string moved will be 35.

```
10 * 5 - ((4 - 1) * 5) = 35
```

There is no way to control the ending element for the move. If the field in Factor 2 is longer than the total length of the array specified in the Result field, the move will continue through the last element in the array.

Example 68 — Move a field to an array. No indexing.

```
SeqNoE....FromfileTofile..ArrnamEPRDim+LenPDAAltnamLenPDA
0010 E                    STG        256  1

SeqNoCLOn01n02n03Factor1+++OpCodFactor2+++ResultLenDXHiLoEQ
0020 C                     MOVEAMSG       STG
```

In Example 68, the field MSG is moved into the array STG. Since the array STG contains 256 single-character elements, each position of the field MSG occupies a single array element. If the defined length of the field MSG is less than 256, the balance of the array remains as it was before the MOVEA operation was performed. If the defined length of the field MSG is greater than 256, every array element will be replaced; the data in positions beyond 256 in the field MSG will not be moved.

More about MOVEA

Example 69 — Move a field to an array with indexing in the Result field.

```
SeqNoE....FromfileTofile..ArrnamEPRDim+LenPDAAltnamLenPDA
0010 E                    STG       256  1

SeqNoCLOn01n02n03Factor1+++OpCodFactor2+++ResultLenDXHiLoEQ
0020 C                     Z-ADD45        X
0030 C                     MOVEAMSG       STG,X
```

In Example 69, the field MSG is moved into the array STG starting with array element X. Since X was set to 45 on line 20, the move will replace data in the array STG beginning with the 45th element.

Example 70 — Move an array to a field with indexing in Factor 2.

```
SeqNoE....FromfileTofile..ArrnamEPRDim+LenPDAAltnamLenPDA
0010 E                    STG       256  1

SeqNoCLOn01n02n03Factor1+++OpCodFactor2+++ResultLenDXHiLoEQ
0020 C                     Z-ADD128       X
0030 C                     MOVEASTG,X     MSG
```

In Example 70, the array STG is moved beginning with its 128th element, to the field MSG. Since we are starting with the 128th array element, 127 array elements are not eligible to be moved, therefore, the length of the move will not exceed 129 characters.

Example 71 — Move an array to an array with indexing in Factor 2 and the Result field.

```
SeqNoE....FromfileTofile..ArrnamEPRDim+LenPDAAltnamLenPDA
0010 E                    STG       256  1
0020 E                    SUBSTG    256  1

SeqNoCLOn01n02n03Factor1+++OpCodFactor2+++ResultLenDXHiLoEQ
0030 C                     Z-ADD128       X
0040 C                     Z-ADD207       Y
0050 C                     MOVEASUBSTG,X  STG,Y
```

More about MOVEA

In Example 71, the array SUBSTG is moved to the array STG. The move begins with the 128th element of the array SUBSTG, which is moved into the 207th element of the array STG. The length of this move will be 50 characters.

MOVEA with Figurative Constants

It is often useful to move a repeating string to an array. This enables all zeros, blanks or other characters to be moved to each element of an array. The MOVEA operation used in conjunction with figurative constants provides this function.

Example 72 — Move a value repeatedly to an array.

```
SeqNoE....FromfileTofile..ArrnamEPRDim+LenPDAAltnamLenPDA
0010 E                    ARR1      50  3
0020 E                    ARR2       8  5

SeqNoCLOn01n02n03Factor1+++OpCodFactor2+++ResultLenDXHiLoEQ
0030 C                      MOVEA*ZEROS    ARR1
0040 C                      MOVEA*ALL'XYZ' ARR1
0050 C                      MOVEA*ALL'XYZ' ARR2
```

In Example 72, the figurative constant *ZEROS is used on line 30 to move zeros into all locations of each element of the array ARR1. After the MOVEA operation on line 30 is performed, each array element of the array ARR1 will contain '000'.

The figurative constant *ALL is used with XYZ on line 40 to move a literal value of 'XYZ' to each element of the array ARR1. After this MOVEA operation is performed, each array element of the array ARR1 will contain 'XYZ'.

The figurative constant *ALL is used with XYZ on line 50 to move a repeating literal value to the array ARR2. After the MOVEA operation is performed, each element of the array ARR2 will contain the pattern that follows:

ARR2 Element Values							
1	**2**	**3**	**4**	**5**	**6**	**7**	**8**
XYZXY	ZXYZX	YZXYZ	XYZXY	ZXYZX	YZXYZ	XYZXY	ZXYZX

MOVEL (Copy Data Left-Adjusted)

The MOVEL operation copies the data from Factor 2, left justified, to the Result field. When the Result field is an array, resulting indicators are not valid for this operation.

Factor 1	OpCode	Factor 2	Result	Length	Dec	Ext	Resulting Ind.		
	MOVEL	*source*	*target*	[size]	[dec]	[P]	[+]	[-]	[0 or ƀ]

When the length of Factor 2 is greater than or equal to the length of the Result field, a complete replacement of the Result field with Factor 2 is performed, regardless of the presence of the operation extender. The data in Factor 2 extending beyond the length of the Result field is not copied. This is known as low-order truncation.

When the length of Factor 2 is less than the length of the Result field and the operation extender is not specified, the number of characters replaced in the Result field is equal to the length of Factor 2 unless the operation extender P is specified.

If the operation extender P is specified, the addition positions in the Result field are padded with blanks. When the operation extender is used, the content of the Result field is replaced with the content of Factor 2, left justified and padded with blanks.

Factor 2 can be a data structure, data structure subfield, literal value, named constant, figurative literal value, array or array element. Factor 2 and the Result field cannot be overlapping data structure subfields.

The Result field can be any variable data type. When the Result field is an array, Factor 2 is moved into each element of the array.

Resulting Indicator Legend			
Columns	**Ind.**	**Usage**	**Set On Condition**
54 - 55	1	[+]	The Result field is greater than zero.
56 - 57	2	[–]	The Result field is less than zero.
58 - 59	3	[0 or ƀ]	The Result field is equal to zero or, if the Result field is character-based, the Result field contains blanks.

The MOVEL operation has traditionally be used to clear the contents of the character Result field by **MOVELing *BLANKS** to the Result field. The CLEAR operation, added recently to RPGIII, accomplishes the same task, and is data type independent. So character or numeric fields, data structures, record formats, arrays, and array elements can be cleared with a single CLEAR operation code.

More about MOVEL

The MOVEL operation differs from the MOVE operation in that the data in Factor 2 is moved, left justified, to the Result field. For more information on MOVE, see the MOVE operation on page 220 in this chapter.

When data is moved to a numeric field, if the length of Factor 2 is greater than or equal to the Result field, the sign of Factor 2 is used as the sign for the Result field. If the length of Factor 2 is less than the Result field, the sign of the Result field is retained.

Example 73 — Move a nine-digit phone number to an area code field.

```
SeqNoCLOn01n02n03Factor1+++OpCodFactor2+++ResultLenDXHiLoEQ
0010 C                         MOVELPHONE     AREACD
```

The field names, types and lengths used by the following examples are:

```
TEXT           CHAR  30
MEDIUM         CHAR  12
```

The field TEXT is initialized as follows:

```
          *... ... 1 ... ... 2 ... ... 3
  TEXT = 'The customer number is 1234567'
```

Example 74 — Move Left with Factor 2 longer than the Result field.

```
SeqNoCLOn01n02n03Factor1+++OpCodFactor2+++ResultLenDXHiLoEQ
0010 C                         MOVELTEXT      MEDIUM
```

In Example 74, after the MOVEL operation is performed, the Result field would contain the following:

```
MEDIUM = 'The customer'
```

More about MOVEL

Example 75 — Move Left with Factor 2 shorter than the Result field.

```
SeqNoCLOn01n02n03Factor1+++OpCodFactor2+++ResultLenDXHiLoEQ
0010 C                      MOVEL'XXXX'    TEXT
```

In Example 75, after the MOVEL operation is performed, the Result field will contain the following:

```
          *... ... 1 ... ... 2 ... ... 3
  TEXT = 'XXXXcustomer number is 1234567'
```

Example 76 — Move Left with Factor 2 shorter than the Result field with Pad.

```
SeqNoCLOn01n02n03Factor1+++OpCodFactor2+++ResultLenDXHiLoEQ
0010 C                      MOVEL'ZZZZZ'   TEXT      P
```

In Example 76, after the MOVEL operation with the operation extender is performed, the Result field will contain the following:

```
          *... ... 1 ... ... 2 ... ... 3
  TEXT = 'ZZZZZ                         '
```

MULT (Multiply)

The MULT operation is used to calculate the product (result) of the multiplication of two operands.

Factor 1	OpCode	Factor 2	Result	Length	Dec	Ext	Resulting Ind.		
[value 1]	MULT	*value 2*	*product*	[size]	[dec]	[H]	[+]	[-]	[0]

Factor 1 is optional and, if specified, is multiplied by the value specified for Factor 2. The product is stored in the Result field. If Factor 1 is not specified, the Result field is used in place of Factor 1 and is multiplied by Factor 2. The product is returned to the Result field.

The operation extender H can be specified to cause the result to be half adjusted, that is, rounded up based-on the absolute (i.e., positive) value of the Result field.

Resulting Indicator Legend			
Columns	**Ind.**	**Usage**	**Set On Condition**
54 - 55	1	[+]	The Result field is greater than zero.
56 - 57	2	[−]	The Result field is less than zero.
58 - 59	3	[0]	The Result field is equal to zero.

Example 77 — Long and short forms of multiply.

```
SeqNoCLOn01n02n03Factor1+++OpCodFactor2+++ResultLenDXHiLoEq
0010 C                 A         MULT B          C
0020 C                           MULT B          C
```

The above example, if written in traditional mathematical expressions, and using the asterisk as the multiplication symbol, would read as follows:

```
A * B = C

C * B = C
```

More about MULT

In Example 77, the MULT operation on line 10 multiplies field A by field B, and the product is placed in field C. In the MULT operation on line 20, field C is multiplied by field B and the product replaces the value in field C. Also, if the product is greater than zero (i.e., a positive number), resulting indicator 1 is set on. If the product is less than zero (i.e., a negative number), resulting indicator 2 is set on. If the product is equal to zero, resulting indicator 3 is set on.

Example 78 — Multiplication with rounding.

```
SeqNoCLOn01n02n03Factor1+++OpCodFactor2+++ResultLenDXHiLoEq
0010 C              A          MULT B         C         H
```

In Example 78, the H that appears in the Half Adjust column (column 53) causes the product (Result field) to be rounded.

The product will vary based on the decimal positions of the Result field. For example:

```
If A = 3 and B = 4.25, then A * B = 12.75
```

With half adjust in effect, the product would be C = 13.

If the product is defined with 1 decimal position, the result would be:

```
C = 12.8 (rounding to the tenths position).
```

MVR (Move Remainder of Division)

The MVR operation moves the remainder of a division operation to the Result field. The MVR operation must immediately follow a DIV operation code (see page 181. If it does not, the RPG run-time exception/error handling routine will be called.

The half adjust option cannot be specified for this operation. Nor can it be specified for the DIV operation for which the MVR operation is being used.

Factor 1	OpCode	Factor 2	Result	Length	Dec	Ext	Resulting Ind.		
	MVR		*remainder*	[size]	[dec]		[+]	[–]	[0]

Factor 1 and Factor 2 must not contain an entry. The remainder of the previous DIV operation is stored in the Result field.

Resulting Indicator Legend			
Columns	**Ind.**	**Usage**	**Set On Condition**
54 - 55	1	[+]	The Result field is greater than zero.
56 - 57	2	[–]	The Result field is less than zero.
58 - 59	3	[0]	The Result field is equal to zero.

Example 79 — Integer division with remainder.

```
SeqNoCLOn01n02n03Factor1+++OpCodFactor2+++ResultLenDXHiLoEq
0010 C                 A         DIV  B         C      30
0020 C                           MVR            REMDR  30
```

In this example suppose A = 10; and B = 4. If A, B and C are defined as 3-digit numeric fields with no decimal positions, the result of the MVR operation would store a value of 2 in the field REMDR.

NEXT (Force Next Input From a Specific Device File)

The NEXT operation forces input from a specific device file. For example, if a single program is communicating with multiple workstations, the NEXT operation can be used to force a READ operation to read from a specific workstation.

Factor 1	OpCode	Factor 2	Result	Length	Dec	Ext	Resulting Ind.		
workstn device ID	**NEXT**	*workstn file*						[error]	

Factor 1 must contain the name of the device that will be read from by the next explicit READ operation or cycle read. Factor 1 must be either a quoted constant or a 10-position character field name containing the name of the device.

Factor 2 must contain the name of the device file from which the READ operation will be requested.

Resulting Indicator Legend			
Columns	**Ind.**	**Usage**	**Set On Condition**
54 - 55	1	N/A	Not used by this operation.
56 - 57	2	[error]	An error occurred during the operation.
58 - 59	3	N/A	Not used by this operation.

After the NEXT operation is issued, a READ operation or a cycle read to the file specified in Factor 2 of the NEXT operation will read from the program device specified in Factor 1.

The NEXT operation is often used in conjunction with the ACQ operation. The ACQ operation acquires the devices for the program; the NEXT operation is used to control the input sequence.

A file continuation specification keyword—NUM, ID or SAVDS—is required to define a workstation file as a multiple device file.

More about NEXT

In the example that follows, lines 30 and 40 acquire the workstation devices named DSP01 and DSP02. Line 50 and 60 send the workstation file record format named PROMPT to the device named DSP01. Lines 70 and 80 do the same for the device named DSP02.

Example 80 — Control input sequence with the NEXT operation.

```
SeqNoFFileNameIPE.E....................Device.RcdNbrKOptionEntry+
0010 FGLENTRY CF  E                    WORKSTN       KNUM       3
0020 F                                               KID    WSID
SeqNoCLOn01n02n03Factor1+++OpCodFactor2+++ResultLenDXHiLoEq
0030 C            'DSP01'    ACQ  GLENTRY                56
0040 C            'DSP02'    ACQ  GLENTRY                56

0050 C                       MOVEL'DSP01'   WSID
0060 C                       WRITEPROMPT
0070 C                       MOVEL'DSP02'   WSID
0080 C                       WRITEPROMPT

0090 C            'DSP01'    NEXT GLENTRY                56
0100 C                       READ PROMPT
0110 C                       EXSR DOWORK

0120 C            'DSP02'    NEXT GLENTRY                56
0130 C                       READ PROMPT
0140 C                       EXSR DOWORK
```

Line 90 issues the NEXT operation code. Factor 1 contains the constant 'DSP01' which conditions the program to access the DSP01 device. When line 100 is performed, the READ operation issues its read to the device named DSP01. Line 110 processes the data received on that read operation. Lines 120 to 140 do the same for the device named DSP02.

OCUR (Set/Retrieve Data Structure Occurrence)

The OCUR operation code performs one of two functions: (1) It sets the occurrence or index of the multiple occurrence data structure specified in Factor 2. Once the occurrence is set, all subsequent RPG operations performed against data in that data structure affect that occurrence until another OCUR operation changes the occurrence. (2) It retrieves the occurrence of the multiple occurrence data structure specified in Factor 2.

The OCUR operation can be used within the *INZSR subroutine to assign unique values to each data structure occurrence.

Factor 1	OpCode	Factor 2	Result	Length	Dec	Ext	Resulting Ind.		
[occurrence to set]	OCUR	*data structure*	*[occurrence]*	[size]	[dec]			[error]	

Factor 1 is optional; if specified it will cause the OCUR operation to set the occurrence of the data structure specified in Factor 2 to the occurrence specified by Factor 1. Factor 1 can be a numeric field (with zero decimal positions), a numeric constant (e.g., 15), or another multiple occurrence data structure.

If Factor 1 contains a constant or a numeric field, the value of Factor 1 is used to set the occurrence of the data structure specified in Factor 2. For example, if Factor 1 contains the number 12, the occurrence of the data structure specified in Factor 2 is set to its 12th occurrence.

If Factor 1 contains another data structure name, that data structure's occurrence is used to set the occurrence of the data structure specified in Factor 2. For example, if the data structure in Factor 1 is set to its 14th occurrence, the occurrence of the data structure in Factor 2 is set to 14.

Factor 2 must contain the name of a multiple occurrence data structure, the occurrence of which, is set or retrieved by the OCUR operation.

The Result field is optional unless Factor 1 is omitted. It can contain a numeric field name (with zero decimal positions) that will receive the value of the occurrence of the data structure specified in Factor 2.

More about OCUR

Resulting Indicator Legend			
Columns	**Ind.**	**Usage**	**Set On Condition**
54 - 55	1	N/A	Not used by this operation.
56 - 57	2	[error]	An error occurred during the operation.
58 - 59	3	N/A	Not used by this operation.

Resulting indicator 2 can be specified to signal when the value specified in Factor 1 is less than or equal to zero, or greater than the maximum number of occurrences for the data structure.

The OCUR operation; provides a high-level of function. For example, since arrays can be specified as a data structure subfield, two dimensional array can be created. See the examples that follow.

Example 81 — Illustrate the use of the OCUR operation.

```
SeqNoE....FromfileTofile++ArrnamEPRDim+LenPDAAltnamLenPDA
0010 E                    ARR          10 10

SeqNoIDSName....EUDSExternalname..........OcurLen+DField+
0020 TWODIM       DS                         10
0030 I                                        1 100 ARR
0040 IDATA2       DS                         10
0050 I                                        1   6 FIELDD
0060 I                                        7  12 FIELDE

SeqNoCLOn01n02n03Factor1+++OpCodFactor2+++ResultLenDXHiLoEq
0070 C            3         OCUR TWODIM

0080 C                      Z-ADD4         INDEX   30
0090 C            INDEX     OCUR DATA2

0100 C                      OCUR TWODIM    OCCURS  30

0110 C            DATA2     OCUR TWODIM    NEWOCR  30    56
0120 C            *IN56     CASEQ*ON       ERRDS
0130 C                      END
```

More about OCUR

In Example 81, line 70 sets the occurrence of the data structure TWODIM to its third occurrence. Line 80 initializes the field INDEX to 4, then line 90 sets the occurrence of the data structure DATA2 to the value contained in the field INDEX. Line 100 contains no value for Factor 1; therefore, the occurrence of the data structure TWODIM is unchanged, and its occurrence is placed into the Result field OCCURS.

Line 110 sets the occurrence of the data structure TWODIM to the same occurrence as the data structure DATA2, specified in Factor 1. Line 110 also stores the occurrence set by the operation in the Result field NEWOCR. If the occurrence set on line 110 is outside the range of the data structure TWODIM, resulting indicator 2 (indicator 56, in our example) is set on, and subroutine ERRDS is called.

A multiple occurrence data structure is a form of array. Each occurrence of a data structure can be compared to an element of an array. Unlike array elements, however, data structure occurrences are referenced by the OCUR operation and are defined with the input specifications.

Normal data structures do not have to be named. If a data structure is a multiple occurrence data structure, it must be named.

For example, a multiple occurrence data structure consisting of four occurrences, each containing two fields, is described below.

Example 82 — A multiple occurrence data structure.

```
SeqNoIDSName....EUDSExternalname..........OcurLen+DField+
0010 ICOMPNY      DS                      4
0020 I                                    1    50ACTNBR
0030 I                                    6   25 CSTNAM
```

Line 10 defines the data structure name as COMPNY. Column 47 contains an entry of 4, indicating that this data structure consists of 4 occurrences. Lines 20 and 30 define the two fields that make up the data structure format.

If this data structure is filled with data, it could look like this.

Occurrence	ACTNBR	CSTNAM
1	05320	Perlman-Rocque
2	05340	Champion Parts
3	01207	Maui Pineapple
4	09406	Cozzi Research

OPEN (Open a File)

The OPEN operation opens the full-procedural or combined file specified in Factor 2. The file be close in order to avoid an error. The User Control open option (UC) can be specified in columns 71-72 of the File Description specification for the file, in this case an OPEN operation is normally required to open the file. Also see CLOSE operation on page 171.

Factor 1	OpCode	Factor 2	Result	Length	Dec	Ext	Resulting Ind.		
	OPEN	*file name*						[error]	

Factor 2 must contain the name of the file being opened. If columns 71 and 72 of the File Description specification are blank, the file is initially opened by RPG and an initial OPEN operation may fail. If the File Description specification contains UC (user controlled file open) in columns 71 and 72, the file can be opened for the first time in the program by the OPEN operation.

When a workstation device file is opened (i.e., the device WORKSTN is specified in columns 40 to 47 of the specification) and a workstation ID (WSID) file continuation specification is present, the WSID field is set to blanks. For more information on workstation file ID, see the ACQ operation code in this chapter on page 145.

Resulting Indicator Legend			
Columns	**Ind.**	**Usage**	**Set On Condition**
54 - 55	1	N/A	Not used by this operation.
56 - 57	2	[error]	An error occurred during the operation.
58 - 59	3	N/A	Not used by this operation.

In the example that follows, the file CUSTMAST is opened. If the OPEN operation (line 50) does not complete successfully, resulting indicator 2 (indicator 56 in our example) will be set on, signaling that the open attempt failed.

More about OPEN

The remainder of the program reads and prints each record in the file CUSTMAST. The file is then closed, and a line of totals is printed.

This example uses the DOWEQ loop and READ operation to set on and test the condition of indicator LR, which controls the ending of the Do loop—and the program.

Example 83 — Open a file, print it, then close the file.

```
SeqNoFFileNameIPE.E....RLEN...K.OV....EDevice+RecNbrKOptionEntry+.....UC
0010 FCUSTMASTIF  E                     DISK
0020 FPRINTER O   E                     PRINTER

SeqNoCLOn01n02n03Factor1+++OpCodFactor2+++ResultLenDXHiLoEq
0050 C                     OPENCUSTMAST                56

0060 C           *IN56     IFEQ *OFF
0070 C                     READ CUSTMAST                 LR
0080 C           *INLR     DOWEQ*OFF
0090 C                     ADD  AMOUNT    TOTAL
0100 C                     WRITEDETAIL
0110 C                     READ CUSTMAST                 LR
0120 C                     ENDDO
0130 C                     CLOSECUSTMAST
0140 C                     WRITETOTALS
0150 C                     ENDIF
```

ORxx (Or Condition)

The ORxx operation is used in conjunction with the IFxx, DOUxx and DOWxx operations. The ORxx operation complements these other operation codes in that their conditioning is extended through the use of the ORxx operation.

Conditioning indicators are not allowed for this operation.

Factor 1	OpCode	Factor 2	Result	Length	Dec	Ext	Resulting Ind.		
compare value 1	ORxx	*compare value 2*							

Factor 1 and Factor 2 are required and must contain a variable, literal value, array element or figurative constant. Factor 1 is compared to Factor 2 using the ORxx operation Boolean operator. For information on the Boolean operators (GE, GT, LE, LT, EQ and NE) see page 135.

Factor 1 and Factor 2 must be the same type.

Example 84 — OREQ used to extend the DOUxx operation.

```
SeqNoCLOn01n02n03Factor1+++OpCodFactor2+++ResultLenDXHiLoEq
0010 C              *IN58     DOUEQ*ON
0020 C              C         OREQ 10
0030 C                        ADD  1         C      30
0040 C                        READ CUSTMAST                58
0050 C                        ENDDO
```

In this example, the Do until loop will be performed until indicator 58 is set on or field C equals 10.

OUT (Output an external data area)

The OUT operation code sends data to the data area named in Factor 2. The data sent to the data area replaces all data in the data area. Before an OUT operation can be used on a data area, the *NAMVAR DEFN operation must have been used to assign the data area to a field.

Factor 1	OpCode	Factor 2	Result	Length	Dec	Ext	Resulting Ind.		
[*LOCK]	OUT	*data area field*						[error]	
[*LOCK]	OUT	*NAMVAR						[error]	

Factor 1 can contain the reserved word *LOCK to retain the lock on the data area.

Factor 2 is required and must contain the name of the field assigned to the data area being output. Optionally, all data areas can be output with a single OUT operation by specifying *NAMVAR in Factor 2.

Resulting Indicator Legend			
Columns	**Ind.**	**Usage**	**Set On Condition**
54 - 55	1	N/A	Not used by this operation.
56 - 57	2	[error]	An error occurred during the operation.
58 - 59	3	N/A	Not used by this operation.

Example 85 — Use a data area to store a control number.

```
SeqNoIDSName....EUDSExternalname..........PFromTo++DField+
0010 ICONTRL      DS
0020 I                                       1    50NXTNBR

SeqNoCLOn01n02n03Factor1+++OpCodFactor2+++ResultLenDXHiLoEq
0030 C           *NAMVAR   DEFN CTRLDATA  CONTRL
0040 C           *LOCK     IN   CONTRL
0050 C                     ADD  1         NXTNBR
0060 C                     Z-ADDNXTNBR    ACTNBR
0070 C                     OUT  CONTRL
```

In Example 85, lines 10 and 20 define the data structure CONTRL. Line 30 defines the data area CTRLDATA and assigns it to the data structure CONTRL. The data area is input to the program on line 40. The contents of the data area is altered (line 50) and output with the OUT operation (line 70).

OTHER (Otherwise)

The OTHER operation is used to perform a default or "catch all" routine within an inline case group delimited with the SELEC/ENDSL operations.

Conditioning indicators are not valid for this operation.

Factor 1	OpCode	Factor 2	Result	Length	Dec	Ext	Resulting Ind.		
	OTHER								

The OTHER operation identifies one or more operations that will be run when no WHxx (When) condition within the case group has been satisfied. Only one OTHER operation can be specified per inline case group. An inline case group is defined by SELEC/WHxx/OTHER/ENDSL operations.

The OTHER operation of the SELEC/WHxx/OTHER/ENDSL case group and the ELSE operation of an IFxx/ELSE/ENDIF case group are functionally equivalent.

Most operation codes can appear within an inline case group, including another inline case group. The BEGSR and ENDSR operations cannot appear within an inline case group.

Example 86 — Test input and perform a routine

```
SeqNoCLOn01n02n03Factor1+++<28  to  32>Factor2+++ResultLenDXHiLoEq
     *   Stay in loop until exit is requested
     C          FUNCT     DOUEQ     EXIT
     C                     | EXFMT     INQUIRY                   58
     C                     | EXSR      RTVMAC
     C                     | SELEC
     *   If the exit key was pressed, then leave the Do loop
     C          FUNCT      | WHEQ      EXIT
     C                     | | MOVE    *ON       *INLR
     C                     | | LEAVE
     *   If the OPTION is B to Z, then send an error
     C          OPTION     | WHGE      'B'
     C          OPTION     | ANDLE     'Z'
     C                     | | MOVEL   'ERROR'   MSG
     *   Otherwise, ask the user to confirm their choice
     C                     | OTHER
     C                     | | EXFMT   CONFIRM
     C                     | ENDSL
     C                    ENDDO
```

PARM (Parameter Declaration)

The PARM operation is used to define a parameter. A parameter is a method used to pass data between programs. Parameters are passed between programs via the CALL operation code. A parameter can be defined on a parameter list with the PLIST operation, or directly following a CALL operation. If the PARM operation follows a CALL operation, that PARM operation is associated with the CALL operation. If the PARM operation follows a PLIST operation, the parameter is associated with the PLIST. To use the parameter list, the name of the PLIST must appear in the Result field of the CALL operation.

Parameters are used extensively in the modern RPG language. Modular program design, structured programming and flexible systems design all contribute to the need for the program-to-program call operation. The parameter is a useful part of this operation.

Factor 1	OpCode	Factor 2	Result	Length	Dec	Ext	Resulting Ind.		
input from parm	PARM	*output to parm*	*parameter*	[size	[dec]				

Factor 1 and Factor 2 are optional, and if present, must be the same type of field as the Result field. Factor 1, if present, must be a field, (i.e., it cannot be a constant). Factor 2 can be a field or a constant.

Factor 1 can be used to receive the value of the parameter. If Factor 1 is specified, data passed to the program by a CALL operation from another program is moved to the field in Factor 1 from the Result field. This technique is often used to move data into a data structure subfield, indicator variable, or array element.

Factor 2 can be used to place data into the parameter when a program ends or calls another program. The data in Factor 2 is moved into the Result field when the program ends or calls another program. This technique is often used to move a data structure subfield, indicator variable, constants, or array elements into the Result field before calling another program and upon program completion.

The effect on the Result field when using Factor 2 with the PARM operation is equivalent to using a MOVEL or Z-ADD operation. Character fields are moved to the Result field left justified, padded with blanks. Numeric data is moved to the Result field right justified and padded with zeros.

More about PARM

The Result field is required and must conform to the following criteria.

If Factor 1 is specified, the Result field must match its type and length. It must match the type and length of Factor 2 when Factor 2 contains a field name, and it must match the type of Factor 2 when Factor 2 is a literal value, figurative constant or reserved word.

When used as an *ENTRY PLIST parameter, the Result field can be a field name, array name, or data structure name, but cannot be a data structure subfield name or an array element.

When used as a parameter of the CALL operation, the Result field can be a field name, data structure name, data structure subfield name, array name, or an array element.

Parameters are passed by reference, not value. That is, the address or *pointer* of the parameter is passed to the program being called. The called program references the parameter by defining a parameter of its own. Both parameters address the same memory location. Therefore, if the value of a parameter in one program is changed, the value in the second program is also changed.

The program status data structure is used to determine the number of parameters passed to a program. A pre-defined subfield location referred to as *PARMS provides a value for the number of parameters passed to the RPG program. If no parameters are passed, *PARMS will equal zero.

In Example 86, the *ENTRY PLIST operation on line 30, 40 and 50 define the entry parameter list and two parameters that can be passed to the program. Line 20 declares the *PARMS reserved word. Its associated field PARMS will represent the number of parameters actually passed to the program.

Most programs that accept parameters use this convention to avoid errors that can arise when too few or too many parameters are passed to a program.

Note: Numeric fields that are defined within the scope of a calculation specification default to packed numeric in RPGIII and later, and to zoned numeric in RPGII and earlier. This can cause problems when passing parameters between programs. To avoid these problems, insure that numeric parameters are of the same type (zoned, packed or binary) and length.

More about PARM

Example 87 — Pass parameters to a called program.

```
SeqNoIDSName....EUDSExternalname..........PFromTo++DField+
0010 I            SDS
0020 I                                        *PARMS    PARMS

SeqNoCLOn01n02n03Factor1+++OpCodFactor2+++ResultLenDXHiLoEq
0030 C            *ENTRY    PLIST
0040 C                      PARM           PACCT
0050 C                      PARM           PMODE
      *   If two parms are passed in, then use parm 2,
      *   else, use a default value for MODE.
0060 C            PARMS     IFGE 2
0070 C                      MOVE PMODE     MODE
0080 C                      ELSE
0090 C                      MOVE 'INQUIRY' MODE
0100 C                      ENDIF
0110 C            FUNCT     DOUEQ'EXIT'
0120 C            MODE      IFEQ 'INQUIRY'
0130 C                      CALL 'CUSTINQ'
0140 C                      PARM           ACTNBR
0150 C                      PARM           SEARCH
0160 C                      ELSE
0170 C            MODE      IFEQ 'UPDATE'
0180 C                      CALL 'CSTUPD'  PLIST1             Call w/PLIST
0190 C                      ELSE
0200 C            MODE      IFEQ 'DELETE'
0210 C                      CALL 'CSTDEL'  PLIST1             Call w/PLIST
0220 C                      ENDIF
0230 C                      ENDIF
0240 C                      ENDIF
0250 C                      ENDDO
0260 C            PLIST1    PLIST                            PLIST define
0270 C                      PARM           ACTNBR
0280 C                      PARM MODE      FUNCT
0290 C            RETURN    PARM           RTNCOD
```

More about PARM

In Example 87, lines 60 to 100 move the parameters into fields that are used in the program. If the number of parameters passed to a program is different from the number of parameters defined on the *ENTRY PLIST parameter list, *PARMS can be used to avoid errors. For example, if only one parameter (the field PACCT) is received by the program, and the field PMODE (the second parameter) is addressed in any way by the RPG code, a run-time error will be generated.

Note that in Example 87, the comparison for the number of parameters (line 60) uses the IFGE (if greater than or equal to) operation. This is used instead of the IFEQ operation to insure that the program will continue to function without changing line 60, should additional parameters be added in the future.

Parameters are a part of a parameter list. See the PLIST operation on page 247 for more information on parameters lists. A named parameter list is produced with the PLIST operation. An unnamed parameter list is produced by placing the PARM operations immediately after the CALL operation.

Example 88 — Define a parameter list.

```
SeqNoCLOn01n02n03Factor1+++OpCodFactor2+++ResultLenDXHiLoEq
0010 C           GETPRT    PLIST
0020 C                     PARM           PRTNBR            Part No.
0030 C                     PARM           CMPNTS            Components
     ... program code can go here.
xxxx C                     CALL 'PARTINQ' GETPRT        56
```

Example 89 — Specifying parameters with no parameter list.

```
SeqNoCLOn01n02n03Factor1+++OpCodFactor2+++ResultLenDXHiLoEq
0010 C                     CALL 'PARTINQ'               56
0020 C                     PARM           PRTNBR            Part No.
0030 C                     PARM           CMPNTS            Components
```

PLIST (Parameter List Declaration)

The PLIST operation defines a list of parameters (PARM) that will be used when the program is called, when a program calls another program and when an I/O operation to a SPECIAL device is performed. At least one PARM operation must appear immediately following the PLIST operation.

A parameter list can be specified (a) as the Result field of a program-to-program call operation; or (b) in columns 60 to 65 of the File Description specification of SPECIAL device files.

Factor 1	OpCode	Factor 2	Result	Length	Dec	Ext	Resulting Ind.		
parm list name	PLIST								

Factor 1 must contain a unique name of the parameter list being defined. Optionally, the reserved word *ENTRY can be specified in Factor 1. *ENTRY is a special parameter list. It defines the parameters that are received by the program when it is called.

There are two kinds of parameter lists: named parameter lists and unnamed parameter lists. Named parameter lists are defined with the PLIST operation. The name of the parameter list is specified in Factor 1 of the calculation specification. A named parameter list can be used by more than one CALL operation, or as the parameter list of a SPECIAL device file.

An unnamed parameter list is produced by placing the PARM operations immediately after a CALL operation. Unnamed parameter lists do not use the PLIST operation.

The following examples illustrate the three areas in which a PLIST can be used.

Example 90 — Define a program-entry parameter list.

```
SeqNoCLOn01n02n03Factor1+++OpCodFactor2+++ResultLenDXHiLoEq
0010 C            *ENTRY    PLIST
0020 C                      PARM           ACCT#
```

Example 90 contains an entry parameter list. When this program is called, a single parameter, ACCT#, will be received by the program.

More about PLIST

Example 91 — Define a parameter list for a program call.

```
SeqNoCLOn01n02n03Factor1+++OpCodFactor2+++ResultLenDXHiLoEq
0010 C           GETPRT    PLIST
0020 C                     PARM           PRTNBR             Part No.
0030 C                     PARM           CMPNTS             Components
xxxx  *     ... additional program code goes here.
0256 C                     CALL 'RTVPART' GETPRT          56 Rtv part
```

Example 91 contains a named parameter list, GETPRT. The parameter list can be used by any number of CALL operations. Line 256 uses the parameter list in the Result field. All parameters of the parameter list GETPRT will be passed to the called program RTVPART.

Example 92 — Additional parameters of a SPECIAL device file.

```
SeqNoFFileNameIPE.E....RLEN...K.OV....EDevice+RecNbrKOptionEntry+
0010 FTAPEDRV IF  E                    SPECIAL       TAPEIO
0020 F                                              KPLIST TAPDRV

SeqNoCLOn01n02n03Factor1+++OpCodFactor2+++ResultLenDXHiLoEq
0030 C           TAPDRV    PLIST
0040 C                     PARM           TIMDTE
0050 C                     PARM           USERID
0060 C                     READ TAPEDRV                     58
```

Example 92 illustrates the SPECIAL device file use of the PLIST. When a SPECIAL device is used, RPG automatically constructs a parameter list. When additional parameters are required for the SPECIAL device routine, a user-written PLIST has to be created.

These additional parameters are appended to the parameter list that RPG will automatically generate. Example 92 illustrates the appending of a date/time stamp and user ID to the SPECIAL device parameter list.

More about SPECIAL PLIST

A parameter list consisting of the following parameters, is automatically created by RPG for SPECIAL device files.

1. *Operation Code.* A single-character that identifies the operation that is being requested. The following table contains a list of possible operations.

Operation Code	Description
O	Open the file.
C	Close the file.
R	Read the file and move the contents of the next record read into the *data area* parameter (parameter 4).
W	Write to the file, using the *data area* parameter (parameter 4) as the output data.
D	Delete the current record from the file.
U	Replace (update) the current record's data with the data from the *data area* parameter (parameter 4).

2. *Return Code.* A single-character parameter that contains the status of the operation request. The following table contains a list of return codes.

Return Code	Description
0	Normal completion of requested operation.
1	End-of-file detected.
2	The operation did not run—an error has occurred.

3. *Error Code.* A five-digit zoned numeric field that contains an error code. When parameter 2, the return code, equals '2', the error code (parameter 3) is moved into the field specified for *RECORD in the file information data structure.

4. *Data Area.* A character field that contains the data that will be transferred between the program and the SPECIAL device routine. The length of this parameter is equal to the record length of the SPECIAL file.

POST (Post Device Information)

The POST operation places status or input/output information into the file information data structure.

Factor 1	OpCode	Factor 2	Result	Length	Dec	Ext	Resulting Ind.		
workstn device ID	`POST`	*workstn dev file*	*[infds]*					[error]	

Factor 1 is optional and can contain a field name or quoted constant containing a program device name. Specifying Factor 1 causes the POST operation to place status information into the information data structure. If Factor 1 is omitted, the POST operation will place input/output information into the information data structure.

Factor 2 and the Result field are mutually optional; that is, one or the other or both must be specified. Factor 2 can contain the name of the workstation file about which the POST operation will place information into the information data structure. If the Result field is blank, the information data structure associated with the file specified in Factor 2 is used as the target of the POST operation.

The Result field can contain the name of an information data structure into which the POST operation will place the status or input/output information. If both Factor 2 and the Result field are specified, the Result field must contain the name of the information data structure associated with the file specified in Factor 2. If Factor 2 is blank, the Result field is required and the information data structure's associated file name will be used as the file for the POST operation.

Resulting Indicator Legend			
Columns	**Ind.**	**Usage**	**Set On Condition**
54 - 55	1	N/A	Not used by this operation.
56 - 57	2	[error]	An error occurred during the operation.
58 - 59	3	N/A	Not used by this operation.

More about POST

Example 93 — POST status information to an information data structure.

```
SeqNoFFileNameIPE.E....RLEN...K.OV....EDevice+RecNbrKOptionEntry+++
0010 FGLENTRY CF  E                     WORKSTN      KINFDS INFDS

SeqNoIDSName....EUDSExternalname..........PFromTo++DField+
0020 IPSDS        SDS
0030 I                                       244 253 WSID
0040 IINFDS        DS
0050 I                                      *STATUS  STATUS
0060 I                                       272 275 DEVICE
0070 I                                       276 277 MODEL

SeqNoCL0n01n02n03Factor1+++OpCodFactor2+++ResultLenDXHiLoEq
0080 C                WSID      POST GLENTRY                56

0090 C                DEVICE    IFEQ '3180'
0100 C                DEVICE    OREQ '3477'
0110 C                          MOVE *ON      DS4     1              Dev=3180?
0120 C                          ELSE
0130 C                          MOVE *ON      DS3     1              Dev=5250
0140 C                          ENDIF

0150 C                DS4       IFEQ *ON
0160 C                          EXFMTPANEL4
0170 C                          ELSE
0180 C                          EXFMTPANEL3
0190 C                          ENDIF
```

In Example 93, the workstation file GLENTRY is the target of the POST operation.

Note: The information data structure for WORKSTN device files differs from system to system. The file information data structure positions in this example are for RPGIII on the IBM AS/400 and may differ on other systems.

READ (Read From a File)

The READ operation reads a record from a full procedural file (i.e., the letter F appears in column 16 of the File Description specification for the file). For data files, the record that is read will be the next record in the file; for workstation file formats, the record format specified in Factor 2 will be the record that is read; for workstation files, the record format that was sent to the workstation last will be read.

Factor 1	OpCode	Factor 2	Result	Length	Dec	Ext	Resulting Ind.		
	READ	*format*						[error]	eof
	READ	*file name*	*[data struct]*					[error]	eof

Factor 2 is required and can contain the name of the file or file record format that will be read. If a record format name is specified, the file must be an externally described file (i.e., an E must be specified in column 19 of the File Description specification for the file).

The Result field can contain the name of a data structure when Factor 2 contains a program described file name. When the READ operation completes successfully, the content of the record is copied to the data structure specified in the Result field. This technique provides support of external file definitions for program described files, through the use of an externally described data structure.

The operation extender N can be used when a file is opened for update. This causes the record to be retrieved but avoids locking the record.

Resulting Indicator Legend			
Columns	**Ind.**	**Usage**	**Set On Condition**
54 - 55	1	N/A	Not used by this operation.
56 - 57	2	[error]	Record allocation (time-out) error.
58 - 59	3	eof	End of file is reached.

The following characteristics apply when a record is accessed with the READ operation.

- For INPUT files, the record is retrieved, but no record-locking occurs.
- For OUTPUT-only files, this operation is not valid.
- For UPDATE files, if no operation extender is specified, the record is retrieved and locked until it is released via one of the following:

More about READ

1. Another READ, READE, READP, REDPE or CHAIN operation.
2. The record is updated by an UPDAT or EXCPT operation.
3. The record is deleted by a DELET or EXCPT with DEL operation.
4. The record is implicitly released by one of the following operations:
   - Except to an empty output format: EXCPT
   - Unlock the record: UNLCK
   - Set lower limit: SETLL
   - Set greater than: SETGT
   - Force end of data: FEOD
   - Close file: CLOSE

Example 94 — Read a file until end-of-file is detected.

```
SeqNoCLOn01n02n03Factor1+++OpCodFactor2+++ResultLenDXHiLoEq
     *  Read the first record in the file.
0010 C                     READ CUSTMAST                 LR
     *  If records exist, then enter the read/print loop
     *  and print the first record.
0020 C           *INLR     DOWEQ*OFF
     *  Print the record's data.
0030 C                     EXCPTREPORT
     *  Read the next record in the file.
0040 C                     READ CUSTMAST                 LR
0050 C                     ENDDO
```

In this example, the READ operation on line 10 reads the first record in the file CUSTMAST. The DOWEQ operation (line 20) begins the Do while group that processes each record in the file. Resulting indicator 3 (LR in our example) will be set on if the file is at end-of-file when the READ operation is performed (line 40).

More about READ

When a workstation device file record format is specified in Factor 2 and the record format has not been written to the workstation, the following occurs: (1) if the write-before-read keyword exists in the file definition, the record format is written to the workstation, then the READ option is performed; or (2) if the write-before-read keyword is not specified, resulting indicator 2, if specified, is set on. If resulting indicator 2 is not specified, control is passed to the RPG exception/error routine.

If Factor 2 contains a workstation file name, the last workstation file record format written to the device will be read. When Factor 2 contains a workstation file name, workstation time-out can be detected.

Workstation time-out occurs after a period of inactivity at the workstation. For example, if the workstation operator hasn't pressed <Enter> for a period of time (say 5 minutes), the workstation will time-out, resulting indicator 2 will be set on. After a workstation record format is written, workstation time-out can be detected by issuing a READ to the workstation file. See Example 95.

To support the workstation time-out feature, the INVITE (invite from device) keyword must exist in the device file. Also, a File Description Continuation specification NUM keyword must be specified. Normally, the number of devices equals 1.

Example 95 — Read a workstation file with time-out support.

```
SeqNoFFileNameIPE.E...........K........Device+RcdNbrKOptionEntry+
0010 FCUSTINQ CF  E                    WORKSTN      KNUM        01
0020 FCUSTMASTIF  E           K        DISK

SeqNoCLOn01n02n03Factor1+++OpCodFactor2+++ResultLenDXHiLoEq
0030 C           ACTNBR    CHAINCUSTMAST                 54
0040 C           *IN54     IFEQ *OFF
0050 C                     WRITEINQUIRY
0060 C                     READ CUSTINQ                    5658
0070 C           *IN56     IFEQ *ON
0080 C           STATUS    CASEQ'1331'    TIMOUT
0090 C                     END
0100 C                     ENDIF
0110 C                     ENDIF
      *... the program continues.
```

READC (Read Next Changed Workstation Record)

The READC operation reads the changed records from a subfile. A record is read only if its data has been changed.

Factor 1	OpCode	Factor 2	Result	Length	Dec	Ext	Resulting Ind.		
	READC	*subfile format*						[error]	eof

Factor 2 is required and must contain the name of a WORKSTN device file record format that is defined as a subfile. A WORKSTN record format is declared a subfile by specifying the SFILE keyword on the File Continuation specification.

Resulting Indicator Legend			
Columns	**Ind.**	**Usage**	**Set On Condition**
54 - 55	1	N/A	Not used by this operation.
56 - 57	2	[error]	Error occurred during this operation.
58 - 59	3	eof	End of subfile changes—no more changed records exist in the subfile.

Example 96 — Display a subfile then read all changed records.

```
SeqNoFFileNameIPE.E...................EDevice+RcdNbrKOptionEntry+++
0010 FCUSTINQ CF   E                    WORKSTN
0020 F                                            RRN    KSFILE CUSTLIST

SeqNoCLOn01n02n03Factor1+++OpCodFactor2+++ResultLenDXHiLoEq
0030 C                     EXFMTLISTCTL
0040 C                     READCCUSTLIST                     58
0050 C           *IN58     DOWEQ*OFF
0060 C* additional code would go here.
0070 C                     READCCUSTLIST                     58
0080 C                     ENDDO
```

In this example, line 20 defines the record format CUSTLIST as a subfile. Line 30 issues an EXFMT operation that displays the subfile. The READC operation on line 40 reads the first changed record in the subfile. The Do While loop on lines 50 to 80 processes each changed subfile record.

READE (Read Next Record with an Equal Key)

The READE operation uses the full or partial key value specified in Factor 1 to sequentially retrieve a record from the keyed file specified in Factor 2.

Factor 1	OpCode	Factor 2	Result	Length	Dec	Ext	Resulting Ind.		
[key value]	**READE**	*format*				[N]		[error]	eof
[key value]	**READE**	*file name*	*[data struct]*			[N]		[error]	eof

Factor 1 is optional and can contain the key value for the READE operation. If Factor 1 is blank, the next record with a key equal to the current record is retrieved. If a record with an equal key does not exist, resulting indicator 3 is set on.

Factor 2 is required and must contain a database file or format name to be read.

The Result field can contain the name of a data structure into which the data from the file is copied. This option is valid only for program defined database files.

The operation extender N can be specified for a file that is opened for update. This causes the record to be retrieved, but avoids locking the record.

Resulting Indicator Legend			
Columns	**Ind.**	**Usage**	**Set On Condition**
54 - 55	1	N/A	Not used by this operation.
56 - 57	2	[error]	An error occurred during the operation.
58 - 59	3	N/A	Not used by this operation.

The following characteristics apply when a record is accessed by the READE operation.

- For INPUT files, the record is retrieved, but no record-locking occurs.
- For OUTPUT-only files, this operation is not valid.
- For UPDATE files, if no operation extender is specified, the record is retrieved and locked until it is released via one of the following:
  1. Another READ, READE, READP, REDPE or CHAIN operation.
  2. The record is updated by an UPDAT or EXCPT operation.

More about READE

3. The record is deleted by a DELET or EXCPT with DEL operation.
4. The record is implicitly released by one of the following operations:
   - Except to an empty output format: EXCPT
   - Unlock the record: UNLCK
   - Set lower limit: SETLL
   - Set greater than: SETGT
   - Force end of data: FEOD
   - Close file: CLOSE

The READE operation is used when a data file contains non-unique full or partial keys. The READE operation provides sequential access to those non-unique keys. When the READE operation is the first input/output operation after an OPEN operation, the first record that matches the key value specified in Factor 1 is retrieved.

For example, if a part master file contains division number, part number and quantity on hand, and if the part number exists in more than one division, the READE operation can be used to read the quantity on hand of a part number for all divisions (assuming the access path is by part number).

Example 97 — Add up the quantity on hand for a specific part number.

```
SeqNoFFileNameIPE.E....RLEN...K.OV....EDevice+RecNbrKOptionEntry+
     FPARTMASTIF  E           K        DISK

SeqNoCLOn01n02n03Factor1+++OpCodFactor2+++ResultLenDXHiLoEq
     C                PART#     KLIST
     C                          KFLD           PART    10
      * Establish the part number to total.
     C                          MOVEL'CEC01'   PART       P
      * Retrieve the first record for the part number
      * (this example uses an index of part number/division)
     C                PART#     CHAINPARTMAST             54
     C                          MOVE *IN54     NF
     C                NF        DOWEQ*OFF
     C                          ADD  QTYOH     PARTOH
      * Retrieve the next record contain the same part number.
     C                PART#     READEPARTMAST                58
     C                          MOVE *IN58     NF
     C                          ENDDO
```

READP (Read Prior Record From a Data File)

The READP reads the previous record from the database file specified in Factor 2.

Factor 1	OpCode	Factor 2	Result	Length	Dec	Ext	Resulting Ind.		
	READP	*format*				[N]		[error]	bof
	READP	*file name*	*[data struct]*			[N]		[error]	bof

Factor 2 is required and must contain the name of a database file or an externally described database file format name.

The Result field can be specified for a program described file only. The Result field can contain the name of a data structure into which the retrieved record's data is placed. When the record is retrieved, the data is copied into the data structure.

The operation extender N can be used when a file is opened for update. This causes the record to be retrieved but avoids locking the record.

Resulting Indicator Legend			
Columns	**Ind.**	**Usage**	**Set On Condition**
54 - 55	1	N/A	Not used by this operation.
56 - 57	2	[error]	Record allocation (time-out) error or some other error.
58 - 59	3	bof	Beginning of file has been reached.

After an unsuccessful READP operation, resulting indicator 3 is set on. The file must be repositioned by a CHAIN, SETLL or SETGT operation before any other input operation can be performed on the file.

The following characteristics apply when a record is accessed with the READP operation.

More about READP

- For INPUT files, the record is retrieved, but no record-locking occurs.
- For OUTPUT-only files, this operation is not valid.
- For UPDATE files, if no operation extender is specified, the record is retrieved and locked until it is released via one of the following:
    1. Another READ, READE, READP, REDPE or CHAIN operation.
    2. The record is updated by an UPDAT or EXCPT operation.
    3. The record is deleted by a DELET or EXCPT with DEL operation.
    4. The record is implicitly released by one of the following operations:
        - Except to an empty output format: EXCPT
        - Unlock the record: UNLCK
        - Set lower limit: SETLL
        - Set greater than: SETGT
        - Force end of data: FEOD
        - Close file: CLOSE

Example 98 — Read a data file backwards and fill a subfile with the data.

```
SeqNoFFileNameIPE.E....RLEN...K.OV....EDevice+RecNbrKOptionEntry+EX
0010 FCUSTMASTIF  E            K        DISK
0020 FCUSTINQ CF  E                     WORKSTN
0030 F                                           RRN   KSFILE CUSTLIST
SeqNoCLOn01n02n03Factor1+++<28  to  32>Factor2+++ResultLenDXHiLoEq
0040 C             *HIVAL    SETGT     CUSTMAST
0050 C                       READP     CUSTMAST                  58
0060 C                       MOVE      *IN58     BOF      1
0070 C             BOF       DOWEQ     *OFF
0080 C                       | ADD     1         RRN      50
0090 C                       | WRITE   CUSTLIST
0100 C                       | READP   CUSTMAST                  58
0110 C                       | MOVE    *IN58     BOF
0120 C                       ENDDO
0130 C                       EXFMT     CUSTPANL
0140 C                       EXSR      RTVMAC
```

More about READP

In Example 98, the workstation file defined on line 20 is used to display a customer master file. Line 40 positions the file to end-of-file, with the *HIVAL figurative constant. Line 50, therefore, reads the last record in the file CUSTMAST.

The Do while loop (lines 70 to 120) writes to the subfile CUSTLIST, then reads the next previous record in the file CUSTMAST (line 10).

The subfile CUSTLIST uses the relative record number field RRN to control the records that are written. Line 80 increments the subfile relative record. Line 90 writes the data retrieved by the previous READP operation to the subfile. This technique assumes that the subfile record contains the same field names as the data file CUSTMAST and that the subfile should be filled completely before presenting the information to the user.

To improve performance, the subfile could be filled with a few records—a page at a time—then displayed to the user. The following code would replace the Do while loop in the previous example.

Example 99 — Read a data file backwards and fill a subfile one page at a time.

```
SeqNoCL0n01n02n03Factor1+++<28  to  32>Factor2+++ResultLenDXHiLoEq
0065 C                       MOVEL     'ROLLDOWN'FUNCT
0066 C           FUNCT       DOWEQ     'ROLLDOWN'
0067 C                        | Z-ADD  0          RRN
0070 C           BOF          | DOWEQ  *OFF
0075 C           RRN          | ANDLE  20
0080 C                        |  | ADD    1          RRN
0090 C                        |  | WRITE  CUSTLIST
0100 C                        |  | READP  CUSTMAST             58
0110 C                        |  | MOVE   *IN58      BOF
0120 C                        | ENDDO
0130 C                        | EXFMT  CUSTPANL
0140 C                        | EXSR   RTVMAC
0145 C                       ENDDO
```

In Example 99, the Do while loop (line 66) is added to cause the looping processes to occur each time the user presses the ROLLDOWN function key. In addition, only 20 subfile records are written each time this process is performed. (The subroutine RTVMAC on line 140 sets the value of the field FUNCT.)

REDPE (Read Prior Record with an Equal Key)

The REDPE operation uses the key value specified in Factor 1 to sequentially retrieve the prior record from the keyed file specified in Factor 2. The REDPE operation provides sequential access to records with non-unique keys, in descending order ("up" through the file). The full or partial index of the record will be equal to the key value specified in Factor 1.

Factor 1	OpCode	Factor 2	Result	Length	Dec	Ext	Resulting Ind.		
[key value]	**REDPE**	*format*				[N]		[error]	bof
[key value]	**REDPE**	*file name*	*[data struct]*			[N]		[error]	bof

Factor 1 is optional and can contain the key value for the REDPE operation. If Factor 1 is blank, the previous record with a key equal to the current record is retrieved. Resulting indicator 3 is set on when a record with an equal key does not exist in the file

Factor 2 is required and must contain the name of a file or a format of an externally described file. If Factor 2 contains a file name, the Result field can contain the name of a data structure into which the input data from the file is copied. This option is valid only for program defined database files.

The operation extender N can be used for a file that is opened for update. This causes the record to be retrieved, but avoids locking the record.

Resulting Indicator Legend			
Columns	**Ind.**	**Usage**	**Set On Condition**
54 - 55	1	N/A	Not used by this operation.
56 - 57	2	[error]	Record allocation (time-out) error or some other error.
58 - 59	3	bof	Beginning of file is reached, or the prior record is outside the scope of the key value specified in Factor 1, or the operation was performed immediately following the open of the file specified in Factor 2.

The following characteristics apply when a record is accessed with the REDPE operation.

More about REDPE

- For INPUT files, the record is retrieved, but no record-locking occurs.
- For OUTPUT-only files, this operation is not valid.
- For UPDATE files, if no operation extender is specified, the record is retrieved and locked until it is released via one of the following:
    1. Another READ, READE, READP, REDPE or CHAIN operation.
    2. The record is updated by an UPDAT or EXCPT operation.
    3. The record is deleted by a DELET or EXCPT with DEL operation.
    4. The record is implicitly released by one of the following operations:
        - Except to an empty output format: EXCPT
        - Unlock the record: UNLCK
        - Set lower limit: SETLL.
        - Set greater than: SETGT.
        - Force end of data: FEOD.
        - Close file: CLOSE.

Example 100 — Add the quantity on hand for a specific item number.

```
SeqNoFFileNameIPE.E....RLEN...K.OV....EDevice+
0010 FITEMMASTIF  E           K        DISK

SeqNoCLOn01n02n03Factor1+++OpCodFactor2+++ResultLenDXHiLoEq
0020 C           ITEM#     KLIST
0030 C                     KFLD           ITEM
     * Establish the item number to total.
0040 C                     MOVEL'CEC01'   ITEM
     * Retrieve the last record for the item number
0050 C           ITEM#     REDPEITEMMAST                  58
0060 C                     MOVE *IN58     NF      1
0070 C           NF        DOWEQ*OFF
0080 C                     ADD  QTYOH     ITEMOH
     * Retrieve previous record containing same item number
0090 C           ITEM#     REDPEITEMMAST                  58
0100 C                     MOVE *IN58     NF
0110 C                     ENDDO
```

REL (Release an Acquired Device File)

The REL operation releases the WORKSTN device ID specified in Factor 1. The device ID can be one acquired by the ACQ operation (see page 145) or it can be the WORKSTN device running the program.

Factor 1	OpCode	Factor 2	Result	Length	Dec	Ext	Resulting Ind.		
workstn device ID	**REL**	*workstn file name*						[error]	

Factor 1 is required and must contain the name of the program device that will be released—for example 'DSP01'. Factor 1 can be a 10-character field or a constant enclosed in apostrophes. If a constant is specified, the device name can not exceed 8 characters.

Factor 2 is required and must contain the name of the WORKSTN device file that has previously acquired the WORKSTN device ID.

Resulting Indicator Legend			
Columns	**Ind.**	**Usage**	**Set On Condition**
54 - 55	1	N/A	Not used by this operation.
56 - 57	2	[error]	An error occurred during the operation.
58 - 59	3	N/A	Not used by this operation.

Example 101 — Release an acquired workstation device.

```
SeqNoFFileNameIPE.E....RLEN...K.OV....EDevice+RecNbrKOptionEntry+
0010 FGLENTRY CF  E                    WORKSTN      KNUM        3
0020 F                                              KID    WSID

SeqNoCLOn01n02n03Factor1+++OpCodFactor2+++ResultLenDXHiLoEq
0030 C                'DSP01'   ACQ  GLENTRY               56
0040 C                *IN56     CASEQ*ON       *PSSR
0050 C                          END
0060 C                          MOVEL'DSP01'   WSID   10 P
0070 C                          EXFMTPROMPT
0080 C                WSID      REL  GLENTRY               56
```

In this example, the acquired program device DSP01 is released from the program on line 80. The field WSID contains the name of the previously acquired device.

RESET (Reset Variable to it's Initial Value)

The RESET operation changes the value of the variable specified in Factor 2, to its initial value. For example, a numeric field named COUNT can be reset to an initial value of 1. The RESET operation can be run anywhere in the RPG program except within the *INZSR subroutine or any subroutine that is called by *INZSR.

Factor 1	OpCode	Factor 2	Result	Length	Dec	Ext	Resulting Ind.		
[*NOKEY]	**RESET**	*variable to reset*						[error]	

Factor 1 is optional and can be specified only when Factor 2 is a record format for a keyed database file. When a keyed database file is specified, Factor 1 can contain the constant *NOKEY. This indicates that the key field values for the record are to be preserved (i.e., not reset) when the record format is reset.

Factor 2 is required and can contain any variable, including a field name, data structure, data structure subfield, record format, array, array element, table or named indicator.

If Factor 2 contains a record format, the corresponding file must be opened for update, output-only, or combined (input/output) processing. The RESET operation cannot be used on a record format for a file that is opened for input-only. Only fields defined as output or input/output are reset. Input-only fields are not reset in the record format.

If Factor 2 contains a multiple occurrence data structure, only the current occurrence of the data structure is reset. If an array is specified, the entire array (every element) is reset. If an array element is specified (e.g., ARR,3) only that element is reset. When the RESET operation is performed on a data structure, each subfield is reset in order of its appearance in the data structure. See the example that follows.

Resulting Indicator Legend			
Columns	**Ind.**	**Usage**	**Set On Condition**
54 - 55	1	N/A	Not used by this operation.
56 - 57	2	[error]	Operation run from within *INZSR subroutine.
58 - 59	3	N/A	Not used by this operation.

RESET and Initial Values

The RESET operation is intended for use with initial values—it moves the initial value of a variable into the variable.

More about RESET

When the RESET operation is specified, storage containing a copy of the variable's initial value is allocated by the compiler. Whenever the RESET operation is performed, that copy of the variable's initial value is copied to the variable.

It should be pointed out, however, that the default initial value for data structure subfields (regardless of type) is blanks. Therefore, unlike the CLEAR operation, the RESET operation will typically move blanks into data structure subfields unless those subfields have some other initial value.

The initial value for all of the subfields of a data structure can be set to reflect the subfield's attribute by specifying the letter I in column 18 of the data structure specification. This causes an initial value to be set for each subfield, based on the subfield's attribute (i.e., character fields are initialized with blanks and numeric fields are initialized to zeros). When this option is used, the RESET and CLEAR operations will perform similar functions.

In addition, individual subfields can be initialized by specifying the letter I in column 8 of the subfield specification. A specific initial value can be specified in columns 21 to 42 of the subfield specification, or within the *INZSR subroutine. If the letter I is specified in column 8 and no specific initial value is specified in columns 21 to 42, an initial value of blanks or zeros (based on the subfield's attribute) will be defined by the compiler.

Example 102 — Reset a Data Structure.

```
SeqNoIDSname....EIDSExt-File++.............OcurLen+
     IITEMS      IDS

SeqNoI.I............Initialvalue+++++++++++PFromTo++DSubFld
     I                                     P   1   42PRICE
     I                                     P   5   82COST
     I                                         9  120ITMNBR
     I I             '0100'                    9  12 ITMCHR
     I                                        13  62 ITMDSC

SeqNoCLOn01n02n03Factor1+++OpCodFactor2+++ResultLenDXHILOEQ
     C                     RESETITEMS
     C                     Z-ADD9402      ITMNBR
     C                     RESETITEMS
```

More about RESET

In this example, the data structure ITEMS is the target of the RESET operation. The following illustrates the sequence of events that occur in this example.

1. The compiler initializes each data structure subfield (the letter I is specified in column 18 of the data structure specification) to blanks or zeros, except for the subfield ITMCHR, which is initialized to '0100'.
2. Additional storage is allocated containing a copy of the initialized data structure, its subfields and their initial values.
3. The first RESET operation moves the initial values of each data structure subfield to the data structure subfields.
4. The MOVE operation places 9402 into the ITMNBR subfield.
5. The second RESET operation resets the ITMCHR subfield to '0100'.

The data structure subfield ITMCHR appears after ITMNBR in the data structure, but occupies the same location. When the RESET operation is performed on the data structure ITEMS, the subfield ITMNBR and ITMCHR (which occupy the same positions within the data structure,) are set to the initial value '0100'.

The subfield ITMCHR was selected to be initialized and appears after ITMNBR in the data structure input specifications. Therefore, its initial value is used as the initial value for the data structure positions specified for ITMNBR and ITMCHR.

Under this scenario, even if ITMNBR had some other explicit initial value, the initial value for ITMCHR would supersede it.

The initial value for a data structure subfield (e.g., ITMNBR) can be overridden by moving a value into the subfield during the *INZSR subroutine.

The initial value for any field, data structure, data structure subfield, array, array element or indicator is established after the *INZSR subroutine is performed for the first time.

Since data structure subfield initialization occurs before the *INZSR subroutine is performed, the initial value of a data structure subfield can be overridden by altering the data structure subfield's value during the *INZSR subroutine.

RETRN (Return to Calling Program)

The RETRN operation returns control to the caller of the program. If the halt and LR indicators are off when the RETRN is performed, the program will be suspended, but remain resident.

Factor 1	OpCode	Factor 2	Result	Length	Dec	Ext	Resulting Ind.		
	RETRN								

The RETRN operation has no parameters and does not support resulting indicators. The RETRN operation works as follows:

1. If any halt indicator (H1 to H9) is on, the program ends abnormally.
2. If indicator LR is on and the halt indicators are off, the program ends normally and returns to the calling program.
3. If indicator LR is off and the halt indicators are off, the program remains active in memory, but control returns to the calling program. When this condition occurs, open files remain open; fields, data structures, arrays, and indicators retain their value and the program remains active, but suspended. The next time the program is called, control is transferred to the program much faster than to an inactive program.

Example 103 — Retrieve the system time and return to caller.

```
SeqNoCLOn01n02n03Factor1+++OpCodFactor2+++ResultLenDXHiLoEq
0010 C           *ENTRY    PLIST
0020 C                     PARM           TIME    60
0030 C                     TIME           TIME
0040 C                     RETRN
```

In this example, the RPG program retrieves the system time and returns it to the caller via the parameter TIME. The RETRN operation (line 40) returns control to the caller (which can be, for example, a COBOL, PL/I, RPG, CL or Pascal program) but leaves this program active (indicator LR is off). This improves performance on subsequent calls to the program.

ROLBK (Roll Back)

The ROLBK operation is a relational database management function. It performs the roll-back function of the Relation Model by abandoning all changes made to files since the prior commit or roll-back operation.

Factor 1	OpCode	Factor 2	Result	Length	Dec	Ext	Resulting Ind.		
	ROLBK							[error]	

The roll-back and commit operations are performed on all files that are currently under commitment control for a process (i.e., job), regardless of whether they are actually defined in the program performing the ROLBK and COMIT operations.

When the ROLBK operation is performed, all records that have been locked during the commit process are released (including records that have been committed outside of the domain of the current program).

Resulting Indicator Legend			
Columns	Ind.	Usage	Set On Condition
54 - 55	1	N/A	Not used by this operation.
56 - 57	2	[error]	An error occurred during the operation.
58 - 59	3	N/A	Not used by this operation.

Example 104 — Roll back a file under commitment control.

```
SeqNoFFileNameIPE.E....RLEN...K.OV....EDevice+RecNbrKOptionEntry+
0010 FCUSTMASTUF  E                        DISK          KCOMIT

SeqNoCLOn01n02n03Factor1+++OpCodFactor2+++ResultLenDXHiLoEq
0020 C              'HUNGER'  DELETCUSTMAST             54
0020 C                        ROLBK                       56
```

In this example, the file continuation specification (line 10) specifies that the file CUSTMAST is under commitment control. Line 20 issues the ROLBK operation, causing all changes made to the file CUSTMAST since the previous commit or roll-back operation to be abandoned.

SCAN (Scan String or Array)

The SCAN operation scans the character variable or array specified in Factor 2 for the argument specified in Factor 1. If the argument is found, the position of the first character of the argument is returned to the Result field. If a numeric array is specified as the Result field, each occurrence of the argument found in Factor 2 is returned in a corresponding array element.

Factor 1	OpCode	Factor 2	Result	Length	Dec	Ext	Resulting Ind.		
argument[:length]	SCAN	*search variable[:start]*	*[position(s)]*	[size]	[dec]			[error]	[found]

Factor 1 is required and must contain a field, data structure, data structure subfield, array element, constant or named constant that contains the search argument.

Factor 1 has one optional parameter: ARGUMENT-LENGTH. This parameter is separated from the *argument* in Factor 1 by a colon (:). This parameter indicates how many characters of the search argument can be used for the scan. The ARGUMENT-LENGTH parameter can be any valid numeric value. The ARGUMENT-LENGTH must be greater than 0 and less than or equal to the length of the search argument. If the ARGUMENT-LENGTH parameter is omitted, the entire search argument is used.

Factor 2 is required and must contain the value to be scanned. Factor 2 can be any valid data type except a figurative constant.

Factor 2 has one optional parameter: START-POSITION. This parameter is separated from the entry in Factor 2 by a colon (:). This parameter indicates the starting position of the scan within the scan data. If the START-POSITION parameter is omitted, the starting position for the scan is 1.

The Result field is optional and can contain a numeric variable that will receive the position of the left most character of the search argument within the scan data. If a numeric array is specified, each occurrence of the search argument within the scan data is stored in a corresponding array element.

Resulting Indicator Legend			
Columns	**Ind.**	**Usage**	**Set On Condition**
54 - 55	1	N/A	Not used by this operation.
56 - 57	2	[error]	An error occurred during the operation.
58 - 59	3	[found]	The search argument is found in Factor 2.

More about SCAN

If the search argument is not found, the Result field is set to zero. If the Result field contains an array, each array element is set to zero.

If the Result field is not specified, resulting indicator 3 is required and will be set on if the search argument is found.

Example 105 — Find a search argument in a character variable.

```
SeqNoFFileNameIPE.E....RLEN...K.OV.....Device.RcdNbrKOptionEntry+
     FQRPGSRC IF  F      92               DISK

SeqNoIFilenameNS..IN.....................PFromTo++DField+
     IQRPGSRC NS
     I                                        13  92 SRCDTA

SeqNoCLOn01n02n03Factor1+++OpCodFactor2+++ResultLenDXHILOEQ
      *  Argument length.
     C                     Z-ADD4         LEN     50
      *  Scan data starting position.
     C                     Z-ADD1         ST      50
      *  Scan argument.
     C                     MOVEL'DISK'    PATRN  45
      *  Let's scan RPG source for DISK files.
     C                     READ QRPGSRC                  58
     C                     MOVE *IN58     EOF
     C           EOF       DOWEQ*OFF

      * Scan the source record for the argument 'DISK'.
     C           PATRN:LEN SCAN SRCDTA:ST POS     50

      *  Count how many times DISK files are used in the program.
     C           POS       IFGT 0
     C                     Z-ADDPOS       ST
     C                     ADD  1         FNDCNT  50
     C                     ENDIF
     C                     READ QRPGSRC                  58
     C                     MOVE *IN58     EOF
     C                     ENDDO
```

SELEC (Start Inline CASE Group)

The SELEC operation is used to begin an inline case group. Inline case groups contain one or more WHxx (When) operations and an optional OTHER operation. The SELEC and ENDSL operations define the scope of the inline case group.

Factor 1	OpCode	Factor 2	Result	Length	Dec	Ext	Resulting Ind.		
	SELEC								

The SELEC operation must be immediately followed by one or more WHxx (When) operations.

An inline case group can be defined by either the SELEC/WHxx/OTHER/ENDSL operations or IFxx/ELSE/ENDIF operations. The differences between these two forms follows.

Differences between SELEC/WHxx and IFxx/ELSE

The SELEC/WHxx/OTHER/ENDSL require only one ENDxx operation for the entire case group. The IFxx operation requires one ENDxx for each IFxx operation.

The WHxx (When) operation includes an implicit ELSE operation. A sequential ELSE and IFxx sequence can provide function similar to the WHxx operation.

The OTHER operation is the functionally equivalent of the "catch all" or "final" ELSE operation of an IFxx/ELSE/ENDIF group.

Any RPG operation, except BEGSR and ENDSR, can be specified within an inline case group, including another inline case group. For more information see the IFxx operation on page 208.

More about SELEC

Example 106 — Use SELEC statement to delimit an inline case group.

```
SeqNoCLOn01n02n03Factor1+++OpCodFactor2+++ResultLenDXHiLoEq
0001 C                     READ ORDERS                   58
0002 C                     SELEC
0003 C           *IN58     WHEQ *ON
0004 C                     EXSR ALLDON
0005 C           REGION    WHEQ MIDWST
0006 C                     ADD  AMOUNT    MWSALE
0007 C           REGION    WHEQ CENTRL
0008 C                     ADD  AMOUNT    CTSALE
0009 C           REGION    WHEQ WESTRN
0010 C                     ADD  AMOUNT    WCSALE
0011 C                     OTHER
0012 C                     ADD  AMOUNT    HQSALE
0013 C                     ENDSL
```

In Example 106, the READ operation on line 1 reads a record from the orders file. Then, the select group is entered. The WHxx operation (line 3) checks for end-of-file. If the end of file indicator is on, subroutine ALLDON is performed then control transfers to the ENDSL operation (line 13).

If the test performed by the WHxx operation on line 3 is false, control passes to the next WHxx operation and performs its test. This continues until a WHxx test is true. Then the statements associated with the WHxx operation are performed. If none of the tests of the WHxx operations are true, control passes to the default routine associated with the OTHER operation.

SETLL (Set Lower Limit)

The SETLL operation positions the full procedural file specified in Factor 2 to the record that is greater than or equal to the index or relative record number specified in Factor 1. A subsequent READ operation will retrieve the next record in the file; a subsequent READP operation will retrieve the previous record in the file. The file's data is not returned to the program with this operation.

Factor 1	OpCode	Factor 2	Result	Length	Dec	Ext	Resulting Ind.		
key value	**SETLL**	*file name*					[n/f]	[error]	[found]
key value	**SETLL**	*format name*					[n/f]	[error]	[found]

Factor 1 is required and must contain an index value (field, literal value, figurative constant or key list) or a relative record number. The value of the index or relative record number is used to position the file so that a subsequent READ operation will retrieve the record whose index value or relative record number is greater than or equal to Factor 1.

Factor 2 is required and must contain the name of a full procedural file or externally described file record format.

Resulting Indicator Legend			
Columns	**Ind.**	**Usage**	**Set On Condition**
54 - 55	1	[n/f]	The key value in Factor 1 is greater than the highest corresponding key value in the file. The file cursor is positioned to end-of-file.
56 - 57	2	[error]	An error occurred during the operation.
58 - 59	3	[found]	A key exists in the file that equals the key value specified in Factor 1.

Example 107 — Position a file with SETLL.

```
SeqNoFFileNameIPE.E....RLEN...K.OV....EDevice+RecNbrKOptionEntry+
0010 FCUSTMASTIF  E                    DISK

SeqNoCLOn01n02n03Factor1+++OpCodFactor2+++ResultLenDXHiLoEq
0020 C            22        SETLLCUSTMAST                 58
0030 C            *IN58     CASEQ*ON       GETREC
0040 C                      END
0050 C*... the program continues...
```

More about SETLL

In Example 107, the file CUSTMAST is positioned to the 22nd relative record number (line 20). If relative record number 22 exists in the file CUSTMAST, resulting indicator 3 (indicator 58) is set on and subroutine GETREC (get record) is performed (line 30).

If relative record number 22 does not exist, but relative record number 23 does, the file would be positioned to relative record 23 and resulting indicator 3 (indicator 58) would not be set on.

Graphically, if the file is positioned to relative record number 22 using SETLL, the file cursor would be positioned between records 21 and 22. See Figure 4-53.

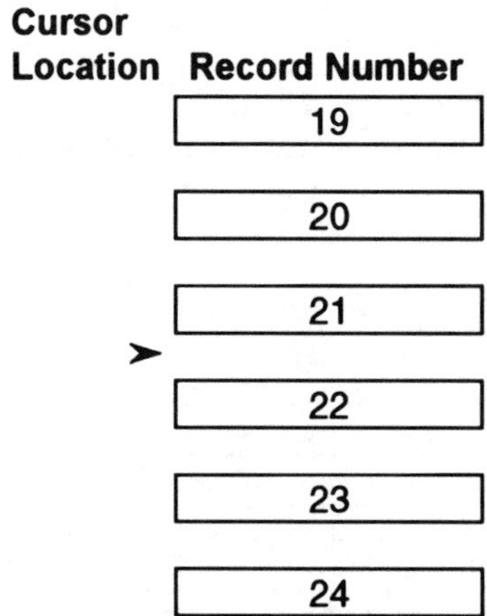

Figure 4-53: SETLL Operation by Relative Record Number

As is illustrated in Figure 4-53, the SETLL operation from Example 107 positions the file cursor before record 22. A subsequent READ operation will retrieve record 22; a READP operation will retrieve record 21.

SETGT (Set Greater Than)

The SETGT operation positions the file specified in Factor 2 to the record that is greater than the index or relative record number specified in Factor 1. The file's data is not returned to the program by this operation.

Factor 1	OpCode	Factor 2	Result	Length	Dec	Ext	Resulting Ind.		
key value	**SETGT**	*file name*					[n/f]	[error]	
key value	**SETGT**	*format name*					[n/f]	[error]	

Factor 1 is required and must contain a key value or a record number. The key value or record number is used to position the file so that a subsequent READ operation will retrieve the record whose key value or relative record number is greater than Factor 1. A subsequent READP operation will retrieve the previous record in the file.

Factor 2 is required and must contain a full procedural file name or an externally described file's format name.

Resulting Indicator Legend			
Columns	**Ind.**	**Usage**	**Set On Condition**
54 - 55	1	[n/f]	The key value in Factor 1 is greater than the highest corresponding key value in the file. The file cursor is positioned to end-of-file.
56 - 57	2	[error]	An error occurred during the operation.
58 - 59	3	N/A	Not used by this operation.

Example 108 — Position a file with SETGT.

```
SeqNoFFileNameIPE.E....RLEN...K.OV....EDevice+RecNbrKOptionEntry+
0010 FCUSTMASTIF  E           K        DISK
SeqNoCLOn01n02n03Factor1+++OpCodFactor2+++ResultLenDXHiLoEq
0020 C           'C999999' SETGTCUSTMAST                 54
0030 C           *IN54     IFEQ *ON
0040 C           *LOVAL    SETLLCUSTMAST
0050 C                     ENDIF
```

In this example, the file CUSTMAST is positioned to the index value that is greater than 'C999999'. If the end-of-file indicator is set on, the file is repositioned by the SETLL operation to beginning-of-file.

SETOF (Set Off an Indicator)

The SETOF operation sets off the indicators specified in the resulting indicators. At least one resulting indicator must be specified.

Factor 1	OpCode	Factor 2	Result	Length	Dec	Ext	Resulting Ind.		
	SETOF						[ind1]	[ind2]	[ind3]

Resulting indicators 1, 2 and 3 are optional, but at least one must be specified. The resulting indicator(s) specified will be set off.

The SETOF operation performs the equivalent of a MOVE '0' or MOVE *OFF operation to a named indicator variable. When indicators are set to zero, they are off. When they are set to one, they are on.

Example 109 — Set off various indicators.

```
SeqNoCLOn01n02n03Factor1+++OpCodFactor2+++ResultLenDXHiLoEq
0010 C                     SETOF                     545658
0020 C                     SETOF                     01  02
0030 C                     MOVE '0'       *IN54
0040 C                     MOVE *OFF      *IN56
0050 C                     MOVE '0'       *IN,58
0060 C                     MOVEA'00'      *IN,01
```

In this example, line 10 sets off indicators 54, 56 and 58. Line 20 sets off indicators 01 and 02. Since the SETOF operation is functionally equivalent to a MOVE operation to a named indicator variable, lines 30, 40 and 50 perform the same function as line 10. Line 60 uses the MOVEA operation with the indicator array to set off indicators 01 and 02; this is the equivalent of line 20.

SETON (Set On an Indicator)

The SETON operation sets on the indicators specified in the resulting indicators. At least one resulting indicators must be specified.

Factor 1	OpCode	Factor 2	Result	Length	Dec	Ext	Resulting Ind.		
	SETON						[ind1]	[ind2]	[ind3]

Resulting indicators 1, 2 and 3 are optional, but at least one must be specified. The resulting indicator(s) specified will be set on.

The SETON operation performs the equivalent of a MOVE '1' or MOVE *ON operation to a named indicator variable. When indicators are set to one, they are on. When they are set to zero, they are off.

Example 110 — Set on various indicators.

```
SeqNoCLOn01n02n03Factor1+++OpCodFactor2+++ResultLenDXHiLoEq
0010 C                     SETON                       545658
0020 C                     SETON                       01  02
0030 C                     MOVE '1'       *IN54
0040 C                     MOVE *ON       *IN56
0050 C                     MOVE '1'       *IN,58
0060 C                     MOVEA'11'      *IN,01
```

In this example, line 10 sets on indicators 54, 56 and 58. Line 20 sets on indicators 01 and 02. Since the SETON operation is functionally equivalent to a MOVE operation to a named indicator, lines 30, 40 and 50 perform the same function as line 10. Line 60 uses the MOVEA operation to the indicator array to set on indicators 01 and 02; this is the equivalent of line 20.

SHTDN (Test for Shut Down Request)

The SHTDN operation tests for a system shut down request. This can be any function that requests the program to end, including, but not limited to system power down and an end-session request.

Factor 1	OpCode	Factor 2	Result	Length	Dec	Ext	Resulting Ind.		
	SHTDN						true		

Resulting indicator 1 is required and will be set on if the shut down test is successful—that is, it is set on when session shut down has been requested.

Resulting Indicator Legend			
Columns	**Ind.**	**Usage**	**Set On Condition**
54 - 55	1	TRUE	Shut down in progress; program should be ended.
56 - 57	2	N/A	Note used by this operation.
58 - 59	3	N/A	Not used by this operation.

Example 111 — Test for session shut down request.

```
SeqNoCLOnO1nO2nO3Factor1+++OpCodFactor2+++ResultLenDXHiLoEq
0010 C           *ENTRY    PLIST
0020 C                     PARM           TIME    60
0030 C                     TIME           TIME
0040 C           ENDPGM    TAG
0050 C                     SHTDN                      LR
0060 C                     RETRN
```

In this example, the program normally ends with the LR indicator off. This would leave the program suspended, but resident. However, when session shut down has been requested, indicator LR is set on (line 50), causing the program to be removed from memory when it returns to its caller (line 60).

SORTA (Sort Array)

The SORTA operation arranges an array in the order specified (ascending or descending) in position 45 of the Extension specification for the array.

Factor 1	OpCode	Factor 2	Result	Length	Dec	Ext	Resulting Ind.		
	SORTA	*array name*							

Factor 1 is required and must contain the name of the array that will be sorted. The indicator array, *IN cannot be sorted. If the array being sorted has an associated *alternate array,* the alternate array is not sorted.

Example 112 — Sort the array ALPHA in ascending order.

```
SeqNoE....FromfileTofile..ArrnamEPRDim+LenPDAAltnamLenPDA
0010 E                    LETTER  4   4  1

SeqNoCLOn01n02n03Factor1+++OpCodFactor2+++ResultLenDXHiLoEq
0020 C                     SORTALETTER
0030 C                     MOVE *ON       *INLR
**
DCAB
```

In this example, the 4-element compile-time array LETTER (line 10) is initialized to DCAB when the program is started. The SORTA operation (line 20) sorts the array LETTER in ascending order.

Before SORTA	After SORTA
D,C,A,B	A,B,C,D

SQRT (Square Root)

The SQRT operation calculates the square root of the value specified in Factor 2 and places the result into the Result field.

Factor 1	OpCode	Factor 2	Result	Length	Dec	Ext	Resulting Ind.		
	SQRT	*numeric value*	*square root*	[size]	[dec]	[H]			

Factor 2 is required and must contain a numeric field, literal value, array or array element. The square root of the value in Factor 2 will be placed in the Result field. The value specified in Factor 2 must be greater than or equal to zero. If Factor 2 is less than zero, the exception/error routine is called.

If Factor 2 is an array, the Result field must also be an array—as the square root of each element will be placed into the corresponding element in the array specified in the Result field.

The Result field is required and must contain the name of a numeric field, array or array element that will receive the square root of the value specified in Factor 2.

The operation extender H can be specified to cause the result to be half adjusted, that is, rounded up.

Example 113 — Calculate the square root of a value.

```
SeqNoCLOn01n02n03Factor1+++OpCodFactor2+++ResultLenDXHiLoEq
0010 C                     Z-ADD16        VALUE   30
0020 C                     SQRT VALUE     ANSWER  75
```

In this example, the field VALUE is initialized to 16 (line 10). On line 20, the square root of the field VALUE is calculated (4) and placed into the Result field ANSWER.

SUB (Subtract)

The SUB operation is used to produce the difference of two values. Factor 2 is subtracted from Factor 1 (long form); the difference is placed into the Result field.

Factor 1	OpCode	Factor 2	Result	Length	Dec	Ext	Resulting Ind.		
[numeric value 1]	SUB	*numeric value 2*	*difference*	[size]	[dec]	[H]	[+]	[-]	[0]

Factor 1 is optional and, if specified, will be used as the basis for the subtraction—that is, Factor 2 will be subtracted from Factor 1.

If Factor 1 is omitted, Factor 2 is subtracted from the current value of the Result field. The difference replaces the value of the Result field.

Factor 2 is required and will be subtracted from Factor 1, if specified, or from the current value of the Result field, if Factor 1 is omitted.

The Result field is required. The result of the SUB operation will be placed into the Result field.

The operation extender H can be specified to cause the result to be half adjusted, that is, rounded up.

Resulting Indicator Legend			
Columns	**Ind.**	**Usage**	**Set On Condition**
54 - 55	1	[+]	The Result field is greater than zero.
56 - 57	2	[-]	The Result field is less than zero.
58 - 59	3	[0]	The Result field is equal to zero.

Example 114 — Subtract Factor 2 from Factor 1, then decrement the result.

```
SeqNoCLOnO1nO2nO3Factor1+++OpCodFactor2+++ResultLenDXHiLoEq
0010 C             A        SUB  B         C
0020 C                      SUB  1         C          545658
```

More about SUB

Example 114, if written in traditional mathematical expressions, would read as follows:

```
A - B = C

C - 1 = C
```

In Example 114, field B is subtracted from field A (line 10); the difference is stored in field C. Then field C is decremented by 1 (line 20).

After the second SUB operation (line 20) is performed, if field C is greater than zero (i.e., a positive number), resulting indicator 1 (indicator 54) is set on; if field C is less than zero (i.e., negative), resulting indicator 2 (indicator 56) is set on; and if field C equals zero, resulting indicator 3 (indicator 58) is set on.

Example 115 — Illustrate array handling by the SUB operation.

```
SeqNoE....FromfileTofile..ArrnamEPRDim+LenPDAAltnamLenPDA
0010 E                    ARR1          5  3 0
0020 E                    ARR2          5  3 0
0030 E                    DIFF          5  3 0

SeqNoCLOn01n02n03Factor1+++OpCodFactor2+++ResultLenDXHiLoEq
0040 C           ARR1      SUB  3          DIFF
0050 C           ARR1      SUB  ARR2       DIFF
0060 C                     SUB  5          DIFF
0070 C           ARR1,4    SUB  ARR2,5     ANSWER  30
```

In Example 115, each element of the array ARR1 has 3 subtracted from it (line 40), and it is placed into the corresponding element in the array DIFF. On line 50, each element of array ARR2 is subtracted from the corresponding element of array ARR1, and the difference is placed into the corresponding elements of array DIFF. On line 60, the constant 5 is subtracted from each element of the array DIFF. On line 70, the fifth element of the array ARR2 is subtracted from the fourth element of the array ARR1; the difference is placed into the field ANSWER.

SUBST (Substring then Move Left)

The SUBST operation copies a portion of the value in Factor 2 to the Result field.

Factor 1	OpCode	Factor 2	Result	Length	Dec	Ext	Resulting Ind.		
[length of source]	SUBST	*source [:start]*	*target*	[size]		[P]		[error]	

Factor 1 is optional and can contain the length for the substring. Factor 1 can be a numeric field, data structure subfield, array element, or constant. If Factor 1 is omitted, the length is automatically calculated by the operation; the length is calculated through the end of the variable specified in Factor 2.

Factor 2 is required and must contain a character field, data structure, data structure subfield, array, array element, or constant that will be copied.

Factor 2 has one optional parameter: START-POSITION. This parameter is separated from the entry in Factor 2 by a colon (:). START-POSITION indicates the starting position for the substring. If the START-POSITION parameter is omitted, the starting position for the substring is 1. START-POSITION can be a literal value, named constant, numeric field or numeric data structure subfield.

The Result field is required and must contain a character field, data structure, data structure subfield, array element or table name. If no operation extender is specified and the substring length is less than that of the Result field, the field is moved, left justified, into the result. Any data in the Result field that is not overlaid by the substring is unchanged.

The operation extender P can be specified to cause the result to be cleared before the SUBST operation is performed.

Resulting Indicator Legend			
Columns	**Ind.**	**Usage**	**Set On Condition**
54 - 55	1	N/A	Not used by this operation.
56 - 57	2	[error]	An error occurred during the operation.
58 - 59	3	N/A	Not used by this operation.

More about SUBST

The SUBST operation is useful when a value needs to be separated from within a field. Traditional RPG programming would dictate moving a value into an array, then using that array to select the substring value for the field. The SUBST operation eliminates the need for most array handling techniques for non-array fields, array elements, data structures and data structure subfields.

Example 116 — Use SUBST with SCAN to split a name into first and last names.

```
SeqNoCLOnO1nO2nO3Factor1+++OpCodFactor2+++ResultLenDXHiLoEq
     *    Find the first blank following the first name
0010 C            *BLANK:1  SCAN NAME      POS     30
0020 C            POS       IFGT 1
     *    Subtract 1 from the position to compute its length
0030 C            POS       SUB  1         LEN     30
     *    Pull out the first name
0040 C            LEN       SUBSTNAME:1    FIRST  25 P
0060 C                      CLEARPOS
     *    Locate the first non-blank character of the last name
0070 C            *BLANK    CHECKNAME      POS
0080 C            POS       IFGT 0
     *    Compute the remaining length as 30 - POS
0050 C            30        SUB  POS       LEN
     *    Pull out the last name
0090 C            LEN       SUBSTNAME:POS  LAST   25 P
0100 C                      ENDIF
0110 C                      ENDIF
```

In this example, the field NAME is assumed to contain a proper name. For example:

```
          *...v ... 1 ... v ... 2 ... v ... 3
NAME  =   'Robert Kennedy               '
```

In this example, the SCAN operation locates the first blank after the first name (line 10). That value is used to calculate the length of the first name (line 30). The SUBST operation is used to extract the first name from NAME (line 40). Finally, first character of the last name is located (lines 50 to 110), and the last name is extracted. The result of this process is the following:

```
          *...v ... 1 ... v ... 2 ... v ... 3
FIRST  =  'Robert                       '
LAST   =  'Kennedy                      '
```

TAG (Label)

The TAG operation defines a label. A label can be used as the target of a GOTO or CABxx operation. A TAG can be specified anywhere in the program.

Conditioning indicators are not valid for this operation. Resulting indicators are not valid for this operation.

Factor 1	OpCode	Factor 2	Result	Length	Dec	Ext	Resulting Ind.		
label	**TAG**								

Factor 1 is required and must contain a label name of up to six characters. The label must be unique—that is no other field, array, data structure, data structure subfield or subroutine can be named the same as a TAG label.

The label is specified in Factor 2 of the GOTO operation and in the Result field of the CABxx operation. More than one GOTO and CABxx operation can branch to the same label.

Factor 1 of an ENDSR operation also functions as a target of a GOTO or CABxx operation, and has restrictions similar to the TAG operation.

Example 117 — Branch to a label when end-of-file is detected.

```
SeqNoCLOn01n02n03Factor1+++OpCodFactor2+++ResultLenDXHiLoEq
0010 C                     READ CUSTMAST                 LR
0020 C            *INLR    CABEQ*ON       ENDPGM
xxxx C*.... additonal user-code goes here.
0501 C            ENDPGM   TAG
0502 C                     RETRN
```

In this example, the CABEQ (compare and branch equal) operation (line 20) branches to the label ENDPGM (line 501) when end-of-file is detected (i.e., the READ operation on line 10 sets on the LR indicator).

TESTB (Test Bit Pattern)

The TESTB operation compares the bits specified in Factor 2 to the Result field. Bits that are not referenced in Factor 2 go untested in the Result field. At least one resulting indicator must be specified with this operation.

Factor 1	OpCode	Factor 2	Result	Length	Dec	Ext	Resulting Ind.		
	TESTB	*'bit nums to test'*	*char variable*	[size]			[XOR]	[mix]	[equal]

Factor 2 is required and must contain "bit numbers" (see example) or a 1-position character field. If a field is specified for Factor 2, then the bit configuration of Factor 2 is compared to the bit configuration of the Result field. If Factor 2 contains a field with no bits on, no resulting indicators are set on.

The Result field is required and must contain a 1-byte character variable.

At least one resulting indicator must be specified for this operation. If Factor 2 contains only one bit, then resulting indicator 2 can not be specified.

Resulting Indicator Legend			
Columns	**Ind.**	**Usage**	**Set On Condition**
54 - 55	1	[XOR]	All the bits specified in Factor 2 are off in the Result field.
56 - 57	2	[mixed]	Mixed bit matching between Factor 2 and the Result field.
58 - 59	3	[equal]	All the bits specified in Factor 2 are on in the Result field.

There are 8 bits in a byte in EBCDIC. When addressing a bit with the TESTB operation, the bits are numbered from the top, down beginning with 0. Graphically, the bits are identified as follows:

Bit Number	Binary Value If set to '1'	
0	8	Top half of byte
1	4	
2	2	
3	1	
4	8	Bottom half of byte
5	4	
6	2	
7	1	

More about TESTB

Since RPG is written horizontally, addressing bits vertically would be awkward. Therefore, RPG uses a horizontal method of addressing bits, as follows:

```
Bit Number ☞    0123  4567
Bit Value ☞     8421  8421
```

Remember, bits can be either on or off; that is, they will be equal to '1' or '0'. When a bit is on, it is equal to '1' and represents the value for its bit number. When a bit is off it is equal to '0' and represents a value of zero. For example, if bits 5 and 7 are on and all the other bits are off, the byte will represent a hex value of X'05', a binary value of B'00000101' and a numeric value of 5.

Example 118 — Test various field bit values.

```
SeqNoCLOn01n02n03Factor1+++OpCodFactor2+++ResultLenDXHiLoEq
0010 C                     TESTB'127'     FIELDA     545658
0020 C                     TESTBFIELDA    FIELDB     545658
0030 C                     TESTB'026'     FIELDA     54  58
```

```
Bit Number ☞                0123 4567
Bit pattern for FIELDA =    0100 0001
Bit pattern for FIELDB =    0101 1101
```

In this example, the bit pattern in Factor 2 is different than the Result field (line 10) so only resulting indicator 2 (indicator 56) is set on. On line 20, bits 1, 2 and 7 are tested, and the bits that are on in FIELDA are on in field FIELDB so only resulting indicator 3 (indicator 58) is set on. On line 30, all of the bits specified in Factor 2 are off in the Result field so resulting indicator 1 (indicator 54) is set on.

TESTN (Test Character Field for Numeric Data)

The TESTN operation tests the value of the Result field for zoned numeric data. At least one resulting indicator must be specified for this operation.

Factor 1	OpCode	Factor 2	Result	Length	Dec	Ext	Resulting Ind.		
	TESTN		*char variable*	[size]			[num]	[mix]	[blank]

The Result field is required and must be a character variable. The contents of the Result field will be tested for numeric data. Resulting indicators are set on accordingly. No resulting indicators are set on when the Result field contains invalid numeric data; except when the Result field is blank.

Resulting Indicator Legend			
Columns	**Ind.**	**Usage**	**Set On Condition**
54 - 55	1	[num]	All the characters in the Result field are numeric.
56 - 57	2	[mixed]	The Result field is numeric with one or more leading blanks.
58 - 59	3	[blank]	The result field contains blanks.

Numeric data in the Result field can be positive or negative. If the data is negative, the rightmost character of the Result field would contain the letters J to R.

Example 119 — Illustrate the TESTN operation.

```
SeqNoCLOn01n02n03Factor1+++OpCodFactor2+++ResultLenDXHiLoEq
0010 C                     MOVE '12345'   FLDA      5
0020 C                     MOVE '  345'   FLDB      5
0030 C                     MOVE '     '   FLDC      5
0040 C                     MOVE '400 Q38' FLDD      7
0050 C                     TESTN          FLDA         545658
0060 C                     TESTN          FLDB         545658
0070 C                     TESTN          FLDC         545658
0080 C                     TESTN          FLDD         545658
```

In this example, the TESTN operation on line 50 will set on resulting indicator 1. The TESTN operation on line 60 will set on resulting indicator 2. The TESTN operation on line 70 will set on resulting indicator 3. The TESTN operation on line 80 will set on no resulting indicators because FLDD does not contain valid numeric data.

TESTZ (Test the Zone of a Field)

The TESTZ operation tests the zone of the leftmost character of the Result field. At least one resulting indicator must be specified with this operation.

Factor 1	OpCode	Factor 2	Result	Length	Dec	Ext	Resulting Ind.		
	TESTZ		*char variable*	[size]			[+]	[−]	[other]

The Result field is required and must contain a character variable. The zone of the leftmost character of the Result field is tested.

Resulting Indicator Legend			
Columns	**Ind.**	**Usage**	**Set On Condition**
54 - 55	1	[+]	The rightmost character of the Result field contains an ampersand (&), the letter A to I, or any character with the same zone as the letter A.
56 - 57	2	[−]	The rightmost character of the Result field contains a minus sign (−), the letters J to R, or any character with the same zone as the letter J.
58 - 59	3	[other]	The rightmost character contains a value that is not represented by either Resulting indicator 1 or 2.

Example 120 — Illustrate the TESTZ operation.

```
SeqNoCLOn01n02n03Factor1+++OpCodFactor2+++ResultLenDXHiLoEq
0010 C                     TESTZ          FIELDA     545658
0020 C                     TESTZ          FIELDB     545658
0030 C                     TESTZ          FIELDC     545658

FIELDA = 'ABCD'
FIELDB = 'J200'
FIELDC = '    '
```

In this example, the TESTZ operation on line 10 will set on resulting indicator 1 (indicator 54). The TESTZ operation on line 20 will set on resulting indicator 2 (indicator 56). The TESTZ operation on line 30 will set on resulting indicator 3 (indicator 58).

TIME (Retrieve System Time and Date)

The TIME operation retrieves the system time and, optionally, the system date. The retrieved time is stored in the Result field. The length of the Result field determines whether TIME will return only the system time or the system time and system date.

Factor 1	OpCode	Factor 2	Result	Length	Dec	Ext	Resulting Ind.		
	TIME		*num variable*	[size]	[dec]				

The Result field is required and must contain either a 6, 12 or 14-position numeric field. If a 6-position field is specified, the system time is retrieved. If a 12-position numeric field is specified, the system time and system date are retrieved. If a 14-position numeric field is specified, the system time and system date (including the century) are retrieved.

When both time and date are retrieved, the time is returned in positions 1 to 6, and the date is returned in positions 7 to 12 or 7 to 14.

The time is returned in the format: HHMMSS and is based on a 24-hour clock. That is, 1:45 p.m. is returned as 134500.

If the system date is also retrieved, the date is returned in the format specified in column 19 of the header specification. For example, if position 19 of the header specification contains a Y, the TIME operation will return the time and date in the following format: HHMMSSYYMMDD

When the Result field is 14 positions in length, the century is returned. The 2-digit century will prefix the year. For example, if position 19 of the Header specification contains the letter Y, the TIME operation will return the time and date in the following format: HHMMSSCCYYMMDD

Example 121 — Retrieve the system time; and the system time and date.

```
SeqNoCLOn01n02n03Factor1+++OpCodFactor2+++ResultLenDXHiLoEq
0010 C                     TIME           TM        60
0020 C                     TIME           TMDT     120
0030 C                     TIME           TMDTCN   140
```

In this example, line 10 retrieves the system time and places it into the field TM. Line 20 retrieves both time and date and places them into the field TMDT. Line 30 retrieves the time, date and century and places them into the field TMDTCN.

UNLCK (Unlock Data Area/Release Record Lock)

The UNLCK operation releases a lock applied to one or all data areas that are locked by the program. In addition, the UNLCK operation unlocks a locked database file record. For the UNLCK operation to be used on a data area, the *NAMVAR DEFN operation must have been used to assign the data area to a variable within the program. For the UNLCK operation to be used on a file, the file must have been opened for update processing and a record must be locked.

Factor 1	OpCode	Factor 2	Result	Length	Dec	Ext	Resulting Ind.		
	UNLCK	*data area name*						[error]	
	UNLCK	*NAMVAR						[error]	
	UNLCK	*database file name*						[error]	

For data areas, Factor 2 is required and must contain the name of the data area that will be released. The reserved word *NAMVAR can be specified to indicate that all data areas locked by the program are to be released. The local data area (*LDA) cannot be unlocked by this operation.

For database files, Factor 2 is required and must contain the name of the file whose record will be unlocked. The file must have been opened for update processing and a record must be locked.

Resulting indicator 2 is optional and, if specified, will indicate when an error occurs during the UNLCK operation—for example, "Data area not used by this program." Or, "Record not previously locked."

Resulting Indicator Legend			
Columns	**Ind.**	**Usage**	**Set On Condition**
54 - 55	1	N/A	Not used by this operation.
56 - 57	2	[error]	An error occurred during the operation.
58 - 59	3	N/A	Not used by this operation.

More about UNLCK

Example 122 — Release all data area locks for a program.

```
SeqNoCLOn01n02n03Factor1+++OpCodFactor2+++ResultLenDXHiLoEq
0010 C             *NAMVAR   DEFN CTRLDATA  CONTRL  90
0020 C             *NAMVAR   DEFN NEXTCUST  NXTCST  90
0030 C             *LOCK     IN   *NAMVAR
0040 C                       ADD  1         NXTCST
0050 C                       OUT  NXTCST
0060 C                       Z-ADDNXTCST    CONTRL
0070 C                       OUT  CONTRL
0080 C                       UNLCK*NAMVAR
```

In Example 122, two data areas (CTRLDTA and NEXTCUST) are defined to the program (lines 10 and 20), then retrieved and locked (line 30). After some data manipulation, the data areas are rewritten (lines 50 and 70). Finally, the data areas are unlocked with the UNLCK operation (line 80).

Example 123 — Unlock a record previously locked.

```
SeqNoFFileNameIPE.E....RLEN...K.OV.....Device+RcdNbrKOptionEntry+
     FCUSTMASTUF  E             K        DISK          KINFDS INFDS

SeqNoCLOn01n02n03Factor1+++OpCodFactor2+++ResultLenDXHiLoEq
     C             EOF       DOUEQ*ON
     C                       READ CUSTOMER                 58
     C                       MOVE *IN58     EOF     1
     * If at EOF, then leave the DO loop
     C             EOF       IFEQ *OFF
     C                       LEAVE
     C                       ENDIF
     * Print an invoice based on the region
     C                       SELEC
     C             REGION    WHEQ MIDWST
     C             REGION    OREQ PACIFC
     C                       EXSR INVBLU
     C             REGION    WHEQ CENTRL
     C                       EXSR INVRED
     C                       OTHER
     * If we're not printing invoices for this customer's region,
     * then unlock the customer file record.
     C                       UNLCKCUSTMAST
     C                       ENDSL
     * additional code could go here.
     C                       ENDDO
```

UPDAT (Update a file)

The UPDAT operation rewrites the data file record currently retrieved and locked by the program. The file specified in Factor 2 must be opened for update (i.e., the letter U must be specified in position 15 of the file's File Description specification). In addition, the record must have been previously read and locked by a CHAIN, READ, READE, READP or REDPE operation.

Factor 1	OpCode	Factor 2	Result	Length	Dec	Ext	Resulting Ind.		
	UPDAT	*record format*						[error]	
	UPDAT	*file name*	*[data struct]*					[error]	

Factor 2 is required and must conform to the following rules:

1. For an externally described file, a record format name must be specified.
2. For program described files, a file name is required. (The Result field is required.)
3. For workstation files, only the name of a subfile record format can be specified.

The Result field is optional for externally described files and is required for program described files. When the Result field is specified, it must contain the name of a data structure from which the file will be updated.

Resulting indicator 2 is optional and can be used to signal when the UPDAT operation does not complete successfully—for example, when the record being rewritten is not the last record retrieved from the file.

Resulting Indicator Legend			
Columns	**Ind.**	**Usage**	**Set On Condition**
54 - 55	1	N/A	Not used by this operation.
56 - 57	2	[error]	An error occurred during the operation.
58 - 59	3	N/A	Not used by this operation.

Before an UPDAT operation can be issued, a record must have been retrieved for update by the program. The READ, READC, READE, READP and CHAIN operations can be used to retrieve the record for update.

More about UPDAT

The UPDAT operation can be used on primary and secondary files; however, unpredictable results can occur if the operation is issued at ***total-time*** calculations.

Example 124 — Update a master data file and a subfile.

```
SeqNoFFileNameIPE.E....RLEN...K.OV....EDevice+RecNbrKOptionEntry+++
0010 FCODETBL IF  E           K         DISK
0020 FCUSTMASTUF  E           K         DISK
0030 FDISPLAY CF  E                     WORKSTN
0040 F                                         RRN   KSFILE PANEL02

SeqNoCLOn01n02n03Factor1+++OpCodFactor2+++ResultLenDXHiLoEq
0050 C           123       CHAINCSTMST               54
0060 C                     MOVE *IN54     NF
0070 C           NF        IFEQ *OFF
0080 C                     EXSR FILSFL
0090 C                     EXFMTPANEL01
0100 C                     EXSR RTVFCT
0110 C           FUNCT     IFEQ 'UPDATE'

0120 C                     UPDATCSTMST

0130 C                     EXSR UPDSFL
0140 C                     ENDIF
0150 C                     ENDIF
```

In this example, line 20 defines the data file CUSTMAST as an UPDATE file and line 30 defines the workstation file DISPLAY as a COMBINED file. This allows the subfile records in the subfile PANEL02 (line 40) to be written to and updated.

Line 50 retrieves the record whose index value is 123 and, if it is found, performs the routine to fill the subfile PANEL02 (line 80).

The record's data and the subfile is displayed at the workstation by the EXFMT operation on line 90. If the user modifies the data, the file CUSTMAST is rewritten (line 120) and the subfile is updated through a subroutine (line 130).

WHxx (Inline CASE Selection/When True then Select)

The WHxx operation is used to perform the selection within an inline case group of the SELEC/WHEN/ENDSL operations.

Conditioning indicators are not valid for this operation. Resulting indicators are not valid for this operation.

Factor 1	OpCode	Factor 2	Result	Length	Dec	Ext	Resulting Ind.		
compare value 1	WHxx	*compare value 2*							

Factor 1 is required and can contain any data item. Factor 2 is also required and must contain a data item with attributes similar to those of Factor 1.

The WHxx, OTHER and SELEC operations define an inline case group. The SELEC operation is used to identify the case group. The WHxx (When) operation is used to conditionally perform specific blocks of code. An OTHER operation identifies the block of code to be performed when all of the conditions for the WHxx operations are false. The OTHER operation can be thought of as a "catch all" routine.

Factor 1 is compared with Factor 2 using the *xx* Boolean operator specified for the WHxx operation code. When a WHxx condition is satisfied, the operations that follow the WHxx operation are performed until the OTHER, ENDSL or another WHxx operation is encountered. Then control passes the ENDSL statement that closes the case group.

The WHxx condition can be extended by the ANDxx and ORxx operations.

In Example 125, that follows, the WHxx (When) operation is used to conditional various program statements. Also, several levels of nested IF, SELEC/WHxx and DOxx loops are featured.

More about WHxx

Example 125 — Inline case group with SELEC/WHxx/OTHER statements.

```
SeqNoCLOn01n02n03Factor1+++<28  to  32>Factor2+++ResultLenDXHiLoEq
0001 C           FUNCT     DOUEQ     EXIT
0002 C                     | EXFMT   PANEL01                   56
0003 C                     | EXSR    RTVMAC
0004 C                     | SELEC
0005 C           FUNCT     | WHEQ    EXIT
0006 C                     | | MOVE  *ON       *INLR
0007 C                     | | LEAVE
0010 C           CODE      | WHEQ    '2'
0009 C                     | | MOVEL 'ADD'     OPTION
0011 C                     | | ADD   5000      AMOUNT
0014 C           CODE      | WHEQ    '9'
0015 C           OBMNAM    | ANDNE   '*DELETED'
0016 C                     | | MOVEL 'DELETE'  OPTION
0017 C                     | | SELEC
0018 C           TYPE      | | WHEQ  '*PGM'
0019 C                     | | | EXFMT CFMPGM
0022 C           TYPE      | | WHEQ  '*LIB'
0023 C                     | | | EXFMT CFMLIB
0024 C                     | | ENDSL
0025 C           CONFRM    | | IFEQ  'Y'
0026 C                     | | | CALL 'DLTOBJ'               56
0027 C                     | | | PARM            OBJNAM
0028 C                     | | +ELSE
0029 C                     | | | CLEAR OPTION
0030 C                     | | ENDIF
0031 C                     | OTHER
0032 C                     | | MOVEL 'UNKNOWN' FUNCT
0033 C                     | ENDSL
0034 C                     ENDDO
```

WRITE (Write to a file)

The WRITE operation outputs a record to a file. If the file is a data file then a new record is created in the file, if the file is a device file; the record is sent to the device.

Factor 1	OpCode	Factor 2	Result	Length	Dec	Ext	Resulting Ind.		
	WRITE	*record format*						[error]	[full]
	WRITE	*file name*	*[data struct]*					[error]	

Factor 2 is required and must conform to the following rules:

1. For an externally described file, a record format name must be specified.
2. For program described files, a file name is required. The Result field is also required and must contain the name of a data structure, from which the file's data will be retrieved and written to the file.

Resulting indicator 3 is optional and can be specified when Factor 2 contains a subfile record format name. The indicator signals when the subfile is full. (Subfiles have a specific size and can be filled when records are written to them.)

Resulting Indicator Legend			
Columns	**Ind.**	**Usage**	**Set On Condition**
54 - 55	1	N/A	Not used by this operation.
56 - 57	2	[error]	An error occurred during the operation.
58 - 59	3	[full]	The WRITE operation to a subfile detail record did not complete because the subfile is full.

If resulting indicator 3 is omitted for subfile record formats, the following applies:

1. For extendible subfiles—those where the subfile page is less than the subfile size—the subfile is automatically extended.
2. For fixed-size subfiles—those where the subfile page equals the subfile size—the program's exception/error routine is called.

The write operation adds records to database files and outputs formats to WORKSTN device files. Device file formats are sent to the device depending on the external attributes of the WORKSTN file.

More about WRITE

Example 126 — Write to a master data file and a subfile.

```
SeqNoFFileNameIPE.E....RLEN...K.OV....EDevice+RecNbrKOptionEntry+++
0010 FCODETBL IF  E           K        DISK
0020 FCUSTMASTUF  E           K        DISK                      A
0030 FDISPLAY CF  E                    WORKSTN
0040 F                                        RRN   KSFILE PANEL02

SeqNoCL0n01n02n03Factor1+++OpCodFactor2+++ResultLenDXHiLoEq
0050 C           123       CHAINCSTMST               54
0060 C                     MOVE *IN54     NF
0070 C           NF        IFEQ *OFF
0080 C                     EXSR FILSFL
0090 C                     EXFMTPANEL01
0100 C                     EXSR RTVFCT
0110 C           FUNCT     IFEQ 'WRITE'

0120 C                     WRITECSTMST

0130 C                     ENDIF
0140 C                     ENDIF
0150 CSR         FILSFL    BEGSR
0160 C           EOF       DOUEQ*ON
0170 C                     ADD  1         RRN

0180 C                     WRITEPANEL02

0190 C                     READ CODETBL                  58
0200 C                     MOVE *IN58     EOF
0210 C                     ENDDO
0220 CSR         ENDFIL    ENDSR
```

In this example, a new record is added to the file CUSTMAST (line 120). The subfile PANEL02 is filled in the subroutine FILSFL (line 180). The subfile relative record number is incremented. It contains the number of the record to be added (line 170) to the subfile.

XFOOT (Cross Foot an Array)

The XFOOT operation adds all the elements of the numeric array specified in Factor 2 and places the sum into the Result field.

Factor 1	OpCode	Factor 2	Result	Length	Dec	Ext	Resulting Ind.		
	XFOOT	*numeric array*	*sum of array*	[size]	[dec]	[H]	[+]	[–]	[0]

Factor 2 is required and must contain a numeric array name whose elements will be added together.

The Result field is required and must contain a numeric field or array element. An element of the array specified in Factor 2 can be used as the Result field. The sum of all the elements of the array specified in Factor 2 is placed into the Result field.

The operation extender H can be specified to cause the result to be half adjusted, that is, rounded up.

Resulting Indicator Legend			
Columns	**Ind.**	**Usage**	**Set On Condition**
54 - 55	1	[+]	The Result field is greater than zero.
56 - 57	2	[–]	The Result field is less than zero.
58 - 59	3	[0]	The Result field is equal to zero.

Example 127 — Illustrate XFOOT with a numeric array.

```
SeqNoE....FromfileTofile..ArrnamEPRDim+LenPDAAltnamLenPDA
0010 E                          MONTHS      12  7 2
```

```
SeqNoCLOn01n02n03Factor1+++OpCodFactor2+++ResultLenDXHiLoEq
0020 C                          XFOOTMONTHS    YRSLS   92
```

In this example, the numeric array MONTHS (line 10) contains the monthly sales figures; the XFOOT operation (line 20) sums the monthly sales figures and places the result into the Result field YRSLS (yearly sales total).

XLATE (Translate a Character String)

The XLATE operation translates each character of Factor 2 based on the *from* and *to* translation values specified in Factor 1. The resulting translated value is placed in the Result field.

Factor 1	OpCode	Factor 2	Result	Length	Dec	Ext	Resulting Ind.		
from value : to value	XLATE	*source[:start]*	*target*	[size]		[P]		[error]	

Factor 1 is required and must contain the *from* and *to* values that will be used to translate the value specified in Factor 2. The *from* and *to* values can be a literal value, named constant, field, array element, data structure or data structure subfield.

Factor 2 is required and must contain a literal value, named constant, field, array element, data structure or data structure subfield that will be used as the source of the translation. The translated value is placed in the Result field.

Factor 2 accepts one optional parameter: START-POSITION. This parameter is used to specify the starting position in Factor 2 where translation will begin. If the START-POSITION parameter is omitted, translation begins in position one of Factor 2. START-POSITION can be a literal value, named constant, numeric field or numeric data structure subfield.

Translation occurs by substituting each character of Factor 2 (beginning with the START-POSITION) that matches a character of the *from* value with the corresponding character of the *to* value. The result of the translation, including any positions of Factor 2 that are bypassed (i.e., via the START-POSITION), are moved left adjusted to the Result field.

Resulting Indicator Legend			
Columns	Ind.	Usage	Set On Condition
54 - 55	1	N/A	Not used by this operation.
56 - 57	2	[error]	An error occurred during the operation.
58 - 59	3	N/A	Not used by this operation.

More about XLATE

Example 128 — Translate lower case characters to upper case characters.

```
SeqNoI..............NamedConstant+++++++++C.........Const+
0001 I               'abcdefghijklmnopqrst-C         LOWER
0002 I               'uvwxyz'
0003 I               'ABCDEFGHIJKLMNOPQRST-C         CAP
0004 I               'UVWXYZ'

SeqNoCLOn01n02n03Factor1+++OpCodFactor2+++ResultLenDXHiLoEq
0005 C           LOWER:CAP XLATENAME       NAME
```

In Example 128, the named constants LOWER and CAP are used to translate lower case letters in the field NAME to upper case. Note that any characters of Factor 2 that are not represented in the *from* value go unchanged when moved to the Result field. An example of the results from this routine follows:

Before:

```
          *...v... 1 ...v... 2 ...v... 3
NAME  =  'Robert F. Kennedy              '
```

After:

```
          *...v... 1 ...v... 2 ...v... 3
NAME  =  'ROBERT F. KENNEDY              '
```

In the previous example, lower case characters are translated to upper case. These same named constants, however, can be reversed in Factor 1. This would cause upper case characters to be translated to lower case.

Example 129 — Translate blanks to periods.

```
SeqNoCLOn01n02n03Factor1+++OpCodFactor2+++ResultLenDXHiLoEq
     C           ' ':'.'   XLATEPROMPT    PROMPT
```

More about XLATE

In Example 129, blank characters in the field PROMPT are translated to periods. A before and after example of the data used by this routine follows:

Before:

```
              *...v... 1 ...v... 2 ...v... 3
PROMPT   =   'Customer name                  '
```

After:

```
              *...v... 1 ...v... 2 ...v... 3
PROMPT   =   'Customer.name..................'
```

In the previous example, a period appears between the words "Customer" and "name". If the desired result is to begin substitution after the two words, "Customer name", the START-POSITION parameter can be used. See examples that follow.

Example 130 — Translate with starting position.

```
SeqNoCLOn01n02n03Factor1+++OpCodFactor2+++ResultLenDXHiLoEq
     C              ' '       CHEKRPROMPT    S        50        Find last
     C                        ADD  1         S                  Goto end
     C              ' ':'.'   XLATEPROMPT:S  PROMPT             Translate
```

The results of this routine would be as follows:

Before:

```
              *...v... 1 ...v... 2 ...v... 3
PROMPT   =   'Customer name                  '
```

After:

```
              *...v... 1 ...v... 2 ...v... 3
PROMPT   =   'Customer name..................'
```

Z-ADD (Zero and Add)

The Z-ADD operation moves the value specified in Factor 2 to the Result field. Any data in the Result field, including the sign, is replaced with the new value.

Factor 1	OpCode	Factor 2	Result	Length	Dec	Ext	Resulting Ind.		
	Z-ADD	*numeric value*	*num variable*	[size]	[dec]	[H]	[+]	[-]	[0]

Factor 2 is required and must contain the name of a numeric field, array element or constant whose data will replace the data in the Result field.

The Result field is required and must contain the name of a numeric field or numeric array element that will receive the value specified in Factor 2.

The operation extender H can be specified to cause the result to be half adjusted, that is, rounded up.

Resulting Indicator Legend			
Columns	**Ind.**	**Usage**	**Set On Condition**
54 - 55	1	[+]	The Result field is greater than zero.
56 - 57	2	[-]	The Result field is less than zero.
58 - 59	3	[0]	The Result field is equal to zero.

The Z-ADD operation has traditionally be used to clear the contents of the numeric Result field, by **Z-ADD 0** to the Result field. The CLEAR operation, added recently to RPGIII, accomplishes the same task, and is data type independent. So numeric fields, character fields, data structures, record formats, arrays, and array elements can be cleared with a single operation code.

Example 131 — Illustrate the Z-ADD operation.

```
SeqNoCLOn01n02n03Factor1+++OpCodFactor2+++ResultLenDXHiLoEq
0010 C                     Z-ADD3         FIELDA
0020 C                     Z-ADDFIELDA    FIELDB
0030 C                     Z-ADD0         TOTAL
```

In this example, the value 3 replaces the contents of the field FIELDA (line 10). The value of field FIELDA replaces the value of the Result field FIELDB (line 20). The value 0 replaces the value of the Result field TOTAL (line 30).

Z-SUB (Zero and Subtract)

The Z-SUB operation subtracts the value of Factor 2 from zero, then moves the result into the Result field. Any data in the Result field, including the sign, is replaced with the new value.

Factor 1	OpCode	Factor 2	Result	Length	Dec	Ext	Resulting Ind.		
	Z-SUB	*numeric value*	*num variable*	[size]	[dec]	[H]	[+]	[-]	[0]

Factor 2 is required and must contain the name of a numeric field, array element or constant whose data will be subtracted from zero then placed into the Result field.

The Result field is required and must contain the name of a numeric field or numeric array element that will receive the result of the subtraction operation.

The operation extender H can be specified to cause the result to be half adjusted, that is, rounded up.

Resulting Indicator Legend			
Columns	**Ind.**	**Usage**	**Set On Condition**
54 - 55	1	[+]	The Result field is greater than zero.
56 - 57	2	[-]	The Result field is less than zero.
58 - 59	3	[0]	The Result field is equal to zero.

Example 132 — Illustrate the Z-SUB operation.

```
SeqNoCLOn01n02n03Factor1+++OpCodFactor2+++ResultLenDXHiLoEq
0010 C                     Z-SUB3         FIELDA
0020 C                     Z-SUB-2        FIELDB
0030 C                     Z-SUB0         TOTAL
0040 C                     Z-SUBFIELDC    FIELDC
```

In this example, the Result field FIELDA after the Z-SUB operation on line 10 will equal -3. The Result field FIELDB after the Z-SUB operation on line 20 will equal 2. The Result field TOTAL after the Z-ADD operation on line 30 will equal 0.

Line 40 illustrates a primary use of the Z-SUB operation. The result of line 40 is that the sign of FIELDC is reversed.

Chapter 5

Modern Operation Code Usage

Structured programming is a way of life for many programmers. New structured-based and object oriented languages such as ADA, C++ and Modula-2 are becoming increasingly popular. PL/I, which is probably the most structured programming language, was developed by IBM during the early '60s and introduced to the data processing community in 1966. PL/I supports more structured programming constructs than any other popular language. PL/I never made a strong stand in the data processing community, however. The exact reasons for this are a matter of controversy, but the most common speculation is that it was just too big. PL/I tried to do too much—to be all things to all people. At the time, magnetic media was new and not very dense, so a "big" language just wasn't practical.

RPG was also developed in the early '60s. It, too, contains most—but certainly not all—structured programming constructs. However, there are major differences between PL/I and RPG. One primary difference is size: RPG is a small language. Its code can be considered "tight." It was designed for small diskless machines like the 1400 and 360 model 20.

This chapter illustrates the use of RPG operation codes in the modern RPG language. The structured constructs such as IF-THEN-ELSE, CASE, DO, DO WHILE and DO UNTIL are covered in addition to the other operation codes. The structured operations, covered in more detail in Chapter 6, support the top-down approach to structured program design and development. Additionally, a comparison of the modern RPG language to traditional RPG coding is provided for experienced RPG programmers who are learning the modern RPG language.

Each example in this chapter can be considered a task within a larger program or system. Some may be fully functional; others illustrate the use of specific operations.

Optimizing

Optimizing application code is a popular topic today. Ironically, most of the optimizing has focused more on the performance of the compiler and not on application programs. Application programmers should, of course, be concerned with the application's performance, not the compiler's.

With RPG, using indicators can lead to poor application performance. An entry in columns 9 to 17 (conditioning indicators) of the calculation specification will generate one "compare" instruction for each indicator used. Therefore, if three indicators condition an operation, three separate compare instructions will be performed.

One could deduce from this that the use of RPG indicators is not good for performance. This, is in fact, true. The modern RPG programmer avoids the use of indicators and in their place, uses the IFxx, DOWxx, DO, DOUxx, CABxx, CASxx, SELEC and WHxx operations to control program flow.

Most operation codes generate a corresponding machine instruction. A MOVE generates a copy instruction; an ADD generates an add numeric instruction; a COMP generates a compare instruction; an IFEQ generates a compare instruction; and so on.

Subscript fields (i.e., arrays and multiple occurring data structures) generate additional overhead. Therefore, when the same array element is used throughout a routine, moving the array element to a field then performing the operations on the field will improve performance.

Some operations generate entire routines containing dozens of machine instructions. The SQRT, LOKUP, and CALL operations, for example, generate many machine instructions. Since it is impractical to avoid these operations, if program size becomes a concern, they can be placed into subroutines, then, those subroutine can be called when the function is needed.

For example, if a program calls an external (subprogram) error-handling routine at eight different locations, the CALL operation is inserted into the program at each of those eight locations. The compiler generates the same CALL-related instructions eight times. This would lead to a larger program that is difficult to maintain.

The call to the subprogram can be placed into a subroutine and performed through the EXSR (perform subroutine) or CASxx (compare and perform subroutine) operations. The subroutine would then be called each time the subprogram is needed. In addition, since the code needed to call the subprogram is not used in multiple locations, the program will be smaller and provide fewer chances for programming errors.

Other considerations for program speed are the use of MULT (multiply) and DIV (divide) operations. On most computers, these instructions are transients; that is, they cause the machine to "burp" slightly whenever they are performed. For example, the MOVE, ADD and SUB operations run several times faster than the MULT, DIV and SQRT operations. However, the number of times an operation code is performed per transaction must also be considered. If the code is only performed once or twice per transaction, there is little need to worry about how fast it runs.

Indicator-Controlled Logic

RPGII programmers have traditionally used indicators to control program logic; read a record, turn on an indicator; compare two values, turn on an indicator; search an array, turn on an indicator; terminate the program, turn on an indicator.

Indicators were the most consistent way to control program logic. An indicator takes up only two positions on a coding specifications, and since the fixed-format column design of RPG severely limited the amount of space per line of code, indicators were a logical solution.

Today, however, RPG has been enhanced to support structure operations similar to those found in PL/I. New operations such as IF-THEN-ELSE-END, Do, Do While, Do until, CASE, Read Equal, Read Prior, Write and Update have turned RPG into a modern language.

When an indicator is used, RPG generates a compare-and-branch instruction. If multiple indicators control an operation code, multiple compare-and-branch instructions are generated. This effect was minimized in RPGII by reversing the indicators and using them to control a GOTO operation that jumps around the program code. See Figure 5-54.

```
SeqNoCLOn01N02n03Factor1+++OpCodFactor2+++ResultLenDXHiLoEq
     C            FIELDA    COMP '01'                   22
     C   N22                GOTO NOTOT1
     C                      ADD  QTY       TQTY
     C                      ADD  QTY       GQTY
     C                      MOVE '**'      FLAG2
     C                      MOVE '***'     FLAG3
     C            NOTOT1    TAG
```

Figure 5-54a: Indicator-controlled Branching

```
SeqNoCLOn01N02n03Factor1+++OpCodFactor2+++ResultLenDXHiLoEq
     C            FIELDA    COMP '01'                   22
     C    22                ADD  QTY       TQTY
     C    22                ADD  QTY       GQTY
     C    22                MOVE '**'      FLAG2
     C    22                MOVE '***'     FLAG3
```

Figure 5-54b: Traditional Indicator Usage

Figure 5-54a illustrates the preferred method of controlling the program logic before modern operation codes became available. Figure 5-54b illustrates the older, or traditional method of controlling program logic. *Neither technique, however, is viable in today's world of advanced application programming.*

When multiple indicators are needed to condition the same section of a program, the OR condition (columns 7 and 8) can be used. See Figure 5-55.

```
SeqNoCLOn01N02n03Factor1+++OpCodFactor2+++ResultLenDXHiLoEq
     C           FLDA      COMP 'A'                    21
     C           FLDB      COMP 'B'                    22
     C  N21
     CORN22                GOTO NOTOT2
     C                     ADD  QTY       TQTY
     C                     ADD  QTY       GQTY
     C                     MOVE '**'      FLAG2
     C                     MOVE '***'     FLAG3
     C           NOTOT2    TAG
```

Figure 5-55a: Multi-Indicator-controlled Branching

```
SeqNoCLOn01N02n03Factor1+++OpCodFactor2+++ResultLenDXHiLoEq
     C           FLDA      COMP 'A'                    21
     C           FLDB      COMP 'B'                    22
     C   21 22             ADD  QTY       TQTY
     C   21 22             ADD  QTY       GQTY
     C   21 22             MOVE '**'      FLAG2
     C   21 22             MOVE '***'     FLAG3
```

Figure 5-55b: Traditional Multi-Indicator-controlled Usage

Figure 5-55a illustrates the preferred method of controlling program logic with multiple indicators before modern operation codes became available. The technique illustrated in Figure 5-55b, unfortunately, is used more often. Once again, neither of these techniques are useful for today's advanced application programming needs.

Indicator-less Controlled Logic

There are two inherent problems with using traditional methods for controlling operations and branching:

1. It can lead to "spaghetti code", unreadable programs that are harder to debug and modify. Is indicator 37 used for the same thing in every program?
2. It isn't long before meaningful names for labels give way to less useful names. What function is performed at the SKIP2 or SKIP3 tags?

To follow a more structured approach, the IFxx or DO operation codes are used to produce more readable programs. The IFxx operation allows two or more fields or values to be tested before performing a section of program code. This along with their modern operation codes, removes the need for any indicator-controlled logic and most "GOTO — TAG" operations. For example, the RPG code in Figures 5-55a and 5-55b should be written with modern operation codes. See Figures 5-56a and 5-56b.

```
SeqNoCLOn01N02n03Factor1+++OpCodFactor2+++ResultLenDXHiLoEq
     C            FLDA      IFEQ 'A'
     C            FLDB      ANDEQ'B'
     C                      ADD  QTY       TQTY
     C                      ADD  QTY       GQTY
     C                      MOVE '**'      FLAG2
     C                      MOVE '***'     FLAG3
     C                      ENDIF
```

Figure 5-56a: IFxx Controlled Operations

```
SeqNoCLOn01N02n03Factor1+++OpCodFactor2+++ResultLenDXHiLoEq
     C            FLDA      COMP 'A'                    21
     C            FLDB      COMP 'B'                    22
     C   21 22              DO
     C                      ADD  QTY       TQTY
     C                      ADD  QTY       GQTY
     C                      MOVE '**'      FLAG2
     C                      MOVE '***'     FLAG3
     C                      ENDDO
```

Figure 5-56b: Combined Indicator/DO Controlled Operations

Figure 5-56a illustrates the preferred method of controlling program logic. Although Figure 5-56b is more popular with some RPG programmers, Figure 5-56a is preferred for the following reasons:

1. It provides immediate identification of conditions that control the code.
2. It removes indicators from the section of code.

If performance is a concern, Figure 5-56a contains the most optimized code, while Figure 5-56b performs redundant comparisons: (1) the COMP operations that will set on the indicators, and (2) testing the indicator condition before entering the Do loop.

Do Loops

Do loops make it much easier to write routines that are performed more than once. For example, to count the occurrences of a character in a character string, the DO and IFEQ operations can be used to process the array. See Figure 5-57.

```
SeqNoE....FromfileTofile..ArrnamEPRDim+LenPDAAltnamLenPDA
0001 E                    TEXT   80  80  1

SeqNoCLOn01N02n03Factor1+++OpCodFactor2+++ResultLenDXHiLoEq
0002 C                     DO    80          X
0003 C            TEXT,X   IFEQ 'Q'
0004 C                     ADD   1           COUNT
0005 C                     ENDIF
0006 C                     ENDDO
**
Quality Programmers write Quality code, not Quantity.
```

Figure 5-57: Combining DO and IFxx Operations

Figure 5-57 illustrates a typical programming task: counting the occurrences of a letter contained in an array. The array TEXT defined on line 1 is an 80-element array. Each element is one character in length.

The Do loop started on line 2 is performed eighty times. The field X is used as the counter index of the Do loop and is used for the index of the array TEXT (line 3).

The array element X is compared to the letter Q on line 3. If the array element equals the letter Q, the value 1 is added to the field COUNT (line 4). When the Do loop completes its eightieth pass, the field COUNT will be set to the number of occurrences of the letter Q that are found in the array TEXT.

DO Loops with Level-Break Processing

Do loops can be used in several areas. For example, if an older program using level-break processing is in need of maintenance, the DO operation can be used to improve performance.

As mentioned earlier, one compare instruction is generated for each conditioning and level-break indicator. Therefore, programs using level-break processing—which uses the same level-break indicator on several consecutive program lines—will perform poorly.

The DO operation can be used to condition level-break processing. By conditioning only the DO operation on the level-break indicator and the subsequent operations on indicator L0, the program's performance will improve. See Figure 5-58.

```
SeqNoCLOn01N02n03Factor1+++OpCodFactor2+++ResultLenDXHiLoEq
     CL1                    DO
     CLO                    MOVE FLDA      FLDB
     CLO                    ADD  AMT       TOTAL
     CLO                    MOVE '**'      FLAG2
     CLO                    MOVE '***'     FLAG3
     CLO                    EXCPTSUBTOT
     CLO                    Z-ADDO         TQTY
     CLO                    Z-ADDO         GQTY
     CLO                    ENDDO
```

Figure 5-58a: Do Loop Controlled Level-Break Processing

```
SeqNoCLOn01N02n03Factor1+++OpCodFactor2+++ResultLenDXHiLoEq
     CL1                    MOVE FLDA      FLDB
     CL1                    ADD  AMT       TOTAL
     CL1                    MOVE '**'      FLAG2
     CL1                    MOVE '***'     FLAG3
     CL1                    EXCPTSUBTOT
     CL1                    Z-ADDO         TQTY
     CL1                    Z-ADDO         GQTY
```

Figure 5-58b: Traditional Level-Break Processing

Figure 5-58a is the preferred technique because only one indicator test is performed. Since L0 (an indicator that is, by definition, always on) is used in place of redundant L1 indicators, the compiler avoids generating code that tests the status of the indicator on each line of code.

In Figure 5-58b, one compare instruction is generated for each occurrence of indicator L1. Thus, since seven indicators are present, seven compare operations are generated.

Do While and Do Until Operations

The Do while and Do until operations provide a high level of flexibility for application development. Do while is used to perform a routine repetitively, while a condition is true. Do until is used to perform a routine repetitively, *until* a condition is true.

For example, the DOUxx operation can be used with the READ operation to read a file until a field contains a specific value. See Figure 5-59.

```
SeqNoCLOn01N02n03Factor1+++OpCodFactor2+++ResultLenDXHiLoEq
     C           DEPT      DOUEQ'Q38'
     C           EOF       OREQ *ON
     C                     READ EMPLOYEE                 58
     C                     MOVE *IN58     EOF
     C                     ENDDO
```

Figure 5-59: Combining DOUxx and ORxx Operations

In Figure 5-59, the DOUEQ operation is used to find the first occurrence of the department 'Q38' in the file EMPLOYEE. The OREQ operation extends the Do until to include a test for an end-of-file condition.

The same function can be performed using the DOWxx operation. The condition test must be reversed, however, since the loop is performed *while* the condition is true. See Figure 5-60.

```
SeqNoCLOn01N02n03Factor1+++OpCodFactor2+++ResultLenDXHiLoEq
     C           DEPT      DOWNE'Q38'
     C           EOF       ANDEQ*OFF
     C                     READ EMPLOYEE                 58
     C                     MOVE *IN58     EOF
     C                     ENDDO
```

Figure 5-60: Combining DOWxx and ANDxx Operations

When using these techniques, be certain to specify each condition that controls the looping process. Poorly coded Do while and Do until loops are major causes of never-ending loops. For example, in Figure 5-60, if the EOF condition is not tested and department Q38 does not exist, the Do while loop would loop endlessly.

Compare and Branch

The compare operation evaluates the relationship between two items. The branch operation performs a transfer to another part of the program.

The COMP and GOTO operations in conjunction with conditioning indicators have a significant number of alternatives in the modern RPG language. See Figure 5-61.

Opcode	Description
ANDxx	Extend IFxx, DOWxx, and DOUxx conditioning.
CABxx	Compare two values then branch to a label.
CASxx	Compare two values then calls a subroutine.
COMP	Compare two values and set resulting indicators on/off.
DO	Begin Do loop with an optional counter.
DOUxx	Begin Do-until loop.
DOWxx	Begin Do-while loop.
ELSE	Else clause, used in conjunction with the IFxx operation.
ENDxx	Ends a Do, Do while, Do until, Case, Select and If/then/else group.
GOTO	Performs an unconditional branch to a label.
IFxx	Compares two values and performs a block of code.
ITER	Branch to the top of the DO loop.
LEAVE	Exit a DO loop.
ORxx	Extend IFxx, DOWxx, and DOUxx conditioning.
OTHER	Otherwise clause of the SELECT/WHEN group.
WHxx	Compares two values and performs a block of code.

Figure 5-61: Comparing and Branch Operations

Figure 5-62 contains examples of the various compare and branch operations.

```
SeqNoCLOn01N02n03Factor1+++OpCodFactor2+++ResultLenDXHiLoEq
     C            FLDA      CABEQ'A'        LABEL       21
```

Figure 5-62a: Compare and Branch Operation

```
SeqNoCLOn01n02n03Factor1+++OpCodFactor2+++ResultLenDXHiLoEq
     C            FLDA      COMP 'A'                    21
     C   21                 GOTO LABEL
```

Figure 5-62b: Compare and GOTO Operations

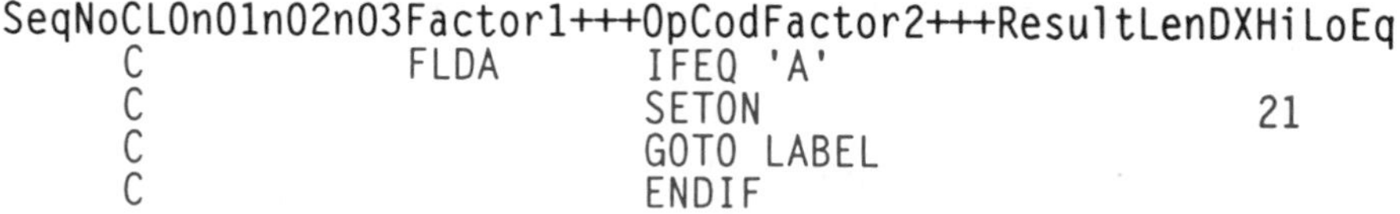

```
SeqNoCLOn01n02n03Factor1+++OpCodFactor2+++ResultLenDXHiLoEq
     C            FLDA      IFEQ 'A'
     C                      SETON                       21
     C                      GOTO LABEL
     C                      ENDIF
```

Figure 5-62c: IFxx and GOTO Operations

All three of these examples perform an identical task. Figure 5-62a is the preferred technique for several reasons:

1. It is a single RPG operation code.
2. It generates the least number of instructions.
3. The technique featured in Figure 5-62b is what the CABxx operation replaces.

When the technique featured in Figure 5-62a is used, resulting indicators are not normally used unless the program is communicating with an externally described file. For example, the indicator may control the attributes of a field in a workstation device file.

Compare Operation

As illustrated in Figure 5-62, the COMP operation is not used often in the modern RPG language. It is, however, often overlooked when communicating with an externally described workstation or printer file.

When an indicator is needed to communicate with an external file, the COMP operation is used to test the condition and set on a resulting indicator. The resulting indicator can be used by the externally described file to issue an error message, change the color of a field or cause additional fields to be written to the display or printer. See Figure 5-63.

```
SeqNoCLOn01n02n03Factor1+++OpCodFactor2+++ResultLenDXHiLoEq
     C           FLDA      COMP 'A'                      21
     C                     EXFMTERRORMSG
```

Figure 5-63a: COMP to Signal an Error

```
SeqNoCLOn01n02n03Factor1+++OpCodFactor2+++ResultLenDXHiLoEq
     C           FLDA      IFEQ 'A'
     C                     SETON                         21
     C                     ENDIF
     C                     EXFMTDSPERROR
```

Figure 5-63b: IFEQ and SETON to Signal an Error

Figure 5-63a illustrates the preferred technique. The COMP operation compares Factor 1 to Factor 2 and sets on the appropriate resulting indicators. Figure 5-63b illustrates what happens when a traditional RPG programmer gets carried away with the IFxx operation.

Ranges, Lists, and Select and Omit

Testing for a range, a list or specific select/omit values is a tradition in programming. The modern RPG language provides support for these operations with the IFxx, ANDxx and ORxx operation.

For a simple range, traditional RPG programs have used the COMP operation as illustrated in Figure 5-64b. The modern RPG language programmer, however, avoids using indicators whenever possible; and uses the preferred technique illustrated in Figure 5-64a.

```
SeqNoCLOnO1nO2nO3Factor1+++OpCodFactor2+++ResultLenDXHiLoEq
     C                      DO   35         X       30
     C                      MOVE NAME,X     CHAR    1
     C            CHAR      IFGE 'a'
     C            CHAR      ANDLE'z'
     C                      BITON'1'        NAME,X
     C                      ENDIF
     C                      ENDDO
```

Figure 5-64a: IFxx and ANDxx to Test for a Range

Figure 5-64a states that:

```
If CHAR is Greater than or Equal to 'a'
       AND Less than or Equal to 'z', then. . .
```

```
SeqNoCLOnO1nO2nO3Factor1+++OpCodFactor2+++ResultLenDXHiLoEq
     C            LOOP      TAG
     C                      ADD  1          X       30
     C                      MOVE NAME,X     CHAR    1
     C            CHAR      COMP 'a'                   21  21
     C    21      CHAR      COMP 'z'                     2323
     C    21 23             BITON'1'        NAME,X
     C            X         COMP 35                      56
     C    56                GOTO LOOP
```

Figure 5-64b: Traditional RPG COMP to Test for a Range

Figure 5-64a is the preferred technique because it says exactly what it does. The technique illustrated in Figure 5-64b performs exactly the same function, but is so convoluted and inflexible that maintenance will be difficult.

Testing a list of values is a simple operation with the ORxx operation. For example, to test for the occurrence of the letters R, P, G or the number 3 in the array NAME, the IFEQ in conjunction with the OREQ operation can be used. See Figure 5-65.

```
SeqNoCLOn01n02n03Factor1+++OpCodFactor2+++ResultLenDXHiLoEq
     C                     DO   35        X       30
     C                     MOVE NAME,X    CHAR     1
     C           CHAR      IFEQ 'R'
     C           CHAR      OREQ 'P'
     C           CHAR      OREQ 'G'
     C           CHAR      OREQ '3'
     C                     EXSR RPG3
     C                     ENDIF
     C                     ENDDO
```

Figure 5-65a: IFxx and ORxx to Test for a List of Values

```
SeqNoCLOn01n02n03Factor1+++OpCodFactor2+++ResultLenDXHiLoEq
     C           LOOP      TAG
     C                     ADD  1         X       30
     C                     MOVE NAME,X    CHAR     1
     C           CHAR      COMP 'R'                         61
     C   N61     CHAR      COMP 'P'                         61
     C   N61     CHAR      COMP 'G'                         61
     C   N61     CHAR      COMP '3'                         61
     C    61               EXSR RPG3
     C           X         COMP 35                        61
     C    61               GOTO LOOP
```

Figure 5-65b: Traditional RPG COMP to Test for a List of Values

Figure 5-65a is the preferred technique. Its straightforward approach is concise and can be easily modified. Figure 5-65b, on the other hand, is complex and cumbersome. Care should be taken when modifications are made.

Note in Figure 5-65, that element X of the array NAME is moved to the field CHAR. Then the field CHAR is compared via the IFxx and ORxx operations. This technique can improve processing time.

File Processing

In the past RPG was a language of very few calculation specifications and several input and output specifications. This was primarily due to the way cycle was used in programming applications. The RPG cycle did most of the work. See Figure 5-66.

```
SeqNoFFileNameIPE.E....RLEN...K.OV....EDevice+RecNbrKOptionEntry+
0001 FSALES   IPE F       35             DISK
0002 FREPORT  O   F      132      OV     PRINTER

SeqNoIRecdnameNSNOINPos.NCCPos.NCCPos.NCCSPFromTo++DField+LB
0003 ISALES   NS  10    1 CD   2 C1
0004 I            20    1 CD   2 C2
0005 I                                        1   2 DEPT
0006 I                                        3  10 ITEM
0007 I                                       11  152PRICE
0008 I                                       16  35 SLSPRSL1
0009 I        NS  99

SeqNoCLOn01n02n03Factor1+++OpCodFactor2+++ResultLenDXHiLoEq
0010 C   99                 GOTO ENDTOT
0011 C   20                 GOTO DEPT2
0012 C                      ADD  PRICE     SOLD1   72
0013 C                      ADD  PRICE     TOT1    72
0014 C                      GOTO ENDTOT
0015 C            DEPT2     TAG
0016 C                      ADD  PRICE     SOLD2   72
0017 C                      ADD  PRICE     TOT2    72
0018 C            ENDTOT    TAG
```

continued on the following page

Figure 5-66: Sales Report Using RPG Cycle (1 of 2)

continued from preceding page

```
SeqNoOFilenameEFBASBSAn01n02n03Field+EBEnd+POutputconstant++++++++++++
0019 OREPORT  H  101   1P
0020 O       OR        OV
0021 O                                   10 'Dept-1'
0022 O                                   20 'Dept-2'
0023 O                                   35 'Sales Person'
0024 OREPORT  H  1     1P
0025 O       OR        OV
0026 O                                   10 '------'
0027 O                                   20 '------'
0028 O                                   35 '------------'
0029 OREPORT  T  1     L1
0030 O                    10   SOLD1 JB  10
0031 O                    20   SOLD2 JB  20
0032 O                         SLSPRS    40
0033 OREPORT  T  1     LR
0034 O                                   22 '------------------'
0035 OREPORT  T  1     LR
0036 O                         TOT1  JB  10
0037 O                                   12 '**'
0038 O                         TOT2  JB  20
0039 O                                   22 '**'
```

Figure 5-66: Example Sales Report Using RPG Cycle (2 of 2)

Figure 5-66 illustrates a typical report listing that takes advantage of the RPG cycle. Level-break processing is used to control printing (lines 8 and 32). Record identifying indicators 10 and 20 are used to control the program logic and the location of the output fields (lines 3, 4, 11, 30 and 31). Last record processing is used to output the report totals (lines 33 and 35).

Although the modern RPG language, supports the RPG cycle, it is primarily a language of calculation specifications. Externally described files have all but replaced input/output specifications. See Figure 5-67.

```
SeqNoFFileNameIPE.E....RLEN...K.OV....EDevice+.............
0001 FSALES   IF  E            K        DISK
0002 FREPORT  O   F     132      OV     PRINTER

SeqNoCLOn01n02n03Factor1+++OpCodFactor2+++ResultLenDXHiLoEq
0005 C           *LIKE     DEFN PRICE     SOLD1 + 2
0006 C           *LIKE     DEFN PRICE     SOLD2 + 2
0007 C           *LIKE     DEFN PRICE     TOT2  + 2
0008 C           *LIKE     DEFN PRICE     TOT2  + 2
0009 C           *LIKE     DEFN SLSPRS    SAVSLS
0010 C                     MOVE *ON       *INOV
0011 C                     READ SALESREC                 LRLR
0012 C                     MOVE SLSPRS    SAVSLS
0014 C           *INLR     DOWEQ*OFF
0015 C           *INOV     IFEQ *ON
0016 C                     EXCPTHEADER
0017 C                     MOVE *OFF      *INOV
0018 C                     ENDIF
0019 C           SLSPRS    IFNE SAVSLS
0020 C                     EXCPTSUBTOT
0021 C                     MOVE SLSPRS    SAVSLS
0022 C                     ENDIF
0023 C           DEPT      IFEQ 'D1'
0024 C                     ADD  PRICE     SOLD1
0025 C                     ADD  PRICE     TOT1
0026 C                     ELSE
0027 C           DEPT      IFEQ 'D2'
0028 C                     ADD  PRICE     SOLD2
0029 C                     ADD  PRICE     TOT2
0030 C                     ENDIF
0031 C                     ENDIF
0032 C                     READ SALESREC                 LRLR
0033 C                     ENDDO
0034 C                     EXCPTTOTALS
```

continued on the following page

Figure 5-67: Example Sales Report Using Modern RPG (1 of 2)

continued from preceding page

```
SeqNoOFilenameEFBASBSAn01n02n03Field+EBEnd+POutputconstant+++++++++++
0035 OREPORT  E  101           HEADER
0036 O                                   10 'Dept-1'
0037 O                                   20 'Dept-2'
0038 O                                   35 'Sales Person'
0039 OREPORT  H  1             HEADER            HEADER
0040 O                                   10 '------'
0041 O                                   20 '------'
0042 O                                   35 '------------'
0043 OREPORT  E  1             SUBTOL
0044 O                         SOLD1 JB  10
0045 O                         SOLD2 JB  20
0046 O                         SLSPRS    40
0047 OREPORT  T  1             TOTALS
0048 O                                   22 '-----------------'
0049 OREPORT  T  1             TOTALS
0050 O                         TOT1  JB  10
0051 O                                   12 '**'
0052 O                         TOT2  JB  20
0053 O                                   22 '**'
```

Figure 5-67: Sales Report Using Modern RPG (2 of 2)

The program listed in Figure 5-67 is definitely more lengthy than the program listed in Figure 5-66, but it avoids using indicators and the RPG cycle. It will run faster. If performance isn't a concern, either program will get the job done, and in fact, Figure 5-66 may be a better choice.

Figure 5-67 illustrates a technique that simulates level-break processing. The changing fields are saved and compared after each record is retrieved. If the contents of the saved field do not equal the value just retrieved, a level-break condition is simulated.

Figure 5-68 illustrates an alternate technique that can be used when the file has an access path built over the fields that are changing.

The technique utilizes nested Do while loops and the READE (read equal key) operation to read records with like keys. Since the control fields are the same as the key fields, resulting indicator 3 (end-of-group) of the READE operation is used to detect a change in the control field(s).

```
SeqNoFFileNameIPE.E....RLEN...K.OV....EDevice+
0001 FSALES   IF  E           K       DISK
0002 FREPORT  O   F     132     OV    PRINTER

SeqNoCLOn01n02n03Factor1+++OpCodFactor2+++ResultLenDXHiLoEq
0005 C                     MOVE *OFF      ENDGRP  1
     *   Define total fields like the PRICE field
0006 C              *LIKE     DEFN PRICE     SOLD1 + 2
0007 C              *LIKE     DEFN PRICE     SOLD2 + 2
0008 C              *LIKE     DEFN PRICE     TOT2  + 2
0009 C              *LIKE     DEFN PRICE     TOT2  + 2
     *   Define the key list to access the data file.
0010 C              KEYLST    KLIST
0011 C                        KFLD SLSPRS
     *   Set ON the overflow indicator so that the
     *   headings will print on the first pass.
0012 C                        MOVE *ON       *INOV
     *   Retrieve the first record in the file.
0013 C                        READ SALES               LRLR
     *   Stay in the Do loop until end-of-file is ON.
0014 C              *INLR     DOWEQ*OFF
     *   Initialize the ENDGRP field.
0015 C                        MOVE *OFF      ENDGRP
     *   Stay in the Do loop while the salesperson
     *   name is the same. Simulate level-break.
0016 C              ENDGRP    DOWEQ*OFF
     *   If overflow detected, print the headings on
     *   the top of the next page and reset overflow.
0017 C              *INOV     IFEQ *ON
0018 C                        EXCPTHEADER
0019 C                        MOVE *OFF      *INOV
0020 C                        ENDIF
```

continued on the following page

Figure 5-68: Commented Sales Report Using Key Fields for Level-Break (1 of 3)

continued from preceding page

```
SeqNoCLOn01n02n03Factor1+++OpCodFactor2+++ResultLenDXHiLoEq
     *    Do the department D1 processing...
0021 C           DEPT      IFEQ 'D1'
0022 C                     ADD  PRICE     SOLD1
0023 C                     ADD  PRICE     TOT1
0024 C                     ELSE

     *    Do the department D2 processing...
0024 C           DEPT      IFEQ 'D2'
0025 C                     ADD  PRICE     SOLD2
0026 C                     ADD  PRICE     TOT2
0027 C                     ENDIF
0028 C                     ENDIF

     *    Retrieve the next sales record for this salesperson.
0029 C           KEYLST    READESALESREC                 5858
     *    If ENDGRP is signalled, no more sales records exist
     *    for this salesperson... Do the level-break routine.
0030 C                     MOVE *IN58     ENDGRP
0031 C                     ENDDO

     *    Print the salesperson totals and name.
0032 C                     EXCPTSUBTOT
     *    Reset the file cursor to the next salesperson.
0033 C           KEYLST    SETGTSALESREC
     *    Retrieve the first sales record for the sales person.
0034 C                     READ SALESREC                   LR
     *    If end-of-file is detected, then exit the do loop
0035 C                     ENDDO
     *    Print the sales totals for all departments
0036 C                     EXCPTTOTALS
     *    At this point, the program returns to its caller.
```

continued on the following page

Figure 5-68: Commented Sales Report Using Key Fields for Level-Break (2 of 3)

continued from preceding page

```
SeqNoOFilenameEFBASBSAn01n02n03Field+EBEnd+POutputconstant+++++++++++
0037 OREPORT  E  101           HEADER
0038 O                                   10 'Dept-1'
0039 O                                   20 'Dept-2'
0040 O                                   35 'Sales Person'
0041 OREPORT  H  1             HEADER
0042 O                                   10 '------'
0043 O                                   20 '------'
0044 O                                   35 '------------'
0045 OREPORT  E  1             SUBTOL
0046 O                         SOLD1 JB  10
0047 O                         SOLD2 JB  20
0048 O                         SLSPRS    40
0049 OREPORT  T  1             TOTALS
0050 O                                   22 '-------------------'
0051 OREPORT  T  1             TOTALS
0052 O                         TOT1  JB  10
0053 O                                   12 '**'
0054 O                         TOT2  JB  20
0055 O                                   22 '**'
```

Figure 5-68: Commented Sales Report Using Key Fields for Level-Break (3 of 3)

Figure 5-69 is an example of the output that will be produced by the programs listed in Figures 5-66, 5-67 and 5-68.

```
*... ... 1 ... ... 2 ... ... 3 ... ... 4 ... ... 5 ... ... 6 ... ... 7
    Dept-1    Dept-2   Sales Person
    ------    ------   ------------
     18.00             Neil Armstrong
               12.00   Alan Shephard
               42.50   Ben Wasman
     37.41             Han Solo
    -------------------
     55.41**   54.50**
```

Figure 5-69: Example Output

Chapter 6

Structured Programming

This chapter describes how to write structured programs. In dealing with this subject, the application of structured programming to the modern RPG language is presented.

The traditional approach to RPG programming has been to take advantage of the RPG cycle, indicators and branching (i.e., GOTO). This approach has led to a stockpile of RPG programs that, to the new RPG programmer, are difficult to understand and explain, and contain more comments than code. This has resulted in the inability of programmers to differentiate the logic portion of the program from the program processes.

Structured programming is not new. The concept has been around since the early 1970s. RPG, born in the early 1960s, is even older than structured programming. The Modern RPG Language, released in 1978, is a relatively new language that includes many features necessary to write structured programs.

Programming itself is both an art (creativity) and a science. Structured programming is a method of programming. Programming methods are bred from learning experiences and practice, not from trends.

Programming style is a highly personal matter. Programming problems are solved by programmers much like mathematicians solve an equations. Unlike mathematicians, however, few programmers agree on the best method for solving a problem. This is a primary cause for programming errors—programmers interjecting their own personality into the programs they're writing.

Like a general practitioner who must first go through internship and residency prior to becoming a family doctor, a programmer must first learn structured technologies and vocabulary then practice the art of structured programming before writing a major application using the structured approach.

The structured approach to program design consists of a set of related technologies for designing and writing application programs. These related technologies help reduce program errors through a series of formulas and guidelines, while providing for programmer creativity.

Some of the technology relating and contributing to structured programming includes:

Structured Analysis. The techniques used to separate a system into base components. This allows the most complex problem to be broken down into simple elements. Each item by itself becomes a simple programming task. When these tasks are properly combined, the complex problem is solved.

Structured Design. The methods used to take the results of the structured analysis (i.e., its components) and build program specifications. For example, a customer master inquiry application consists of a user-interface, a full-record display panel, a multi-record list panel and a method of querying the data.

Program Design. The methods used to translate a piece of structured design into a series of program or module definitions—for example, the logic behind a customer master inquiry. Most programming errors are actually created in this phase. Poorly thought-out logic, tasks that are too large, and inflexible communication with other program modules are major causes of programming errors.

Top-Down Program Development. The technique used for developing programs in an incremental manner. The modules of a program design are broken down into individual functions or tasks. The program developer simply assumes each task will function properly, leaving lower-level analysis for later.

Top-Down Programming

Top-down program design by definition, is performed before any programs are written. Currently, more than 40 billion lines of RPG code exist. Most of this code was written before the introduction of structured constructs into RPG. With so many lines of code already written, there must be several billion lines of unstructured code already in existence. Structured programming constructs should used to maintain this code. The changes made will be more readable, and the possibility of error will be reduced.

To begin top-down development, first define the major requirements of the module being created. The customer master inquiry example could be broken down into six primary elements, see Figure 6-70.

Naming Conventions

Naming conventions are important. Use clear and consistent names for fields, files and routines—for example, "Update an Order's Line Item".

As a by product, all names will depict their unique function. A routine named "Update an Order's Line Item", for example, performs the stated function.

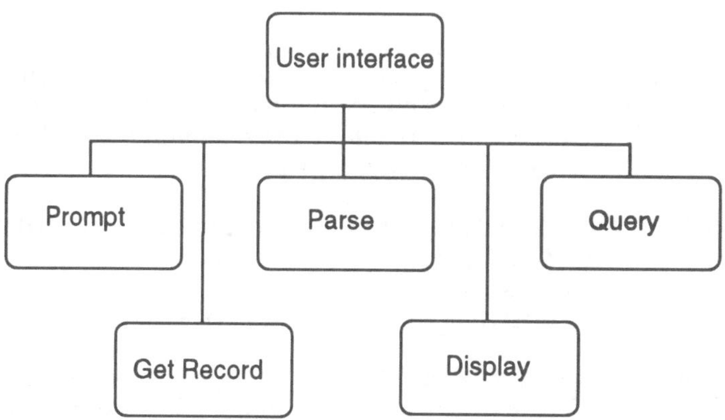

Figure 6-70: Hierarchy Chart for a Top-Down Design

The primary functions of the user-interface of the customer master inquiry have been outlined without concern for the detail behind it. Once the functions have been specified, each can be treated as an individual, less complex task. See Figure 6-71.

```
Step 1:
            Open the workstation device file.
Step 1A:
            Send the prompt panel to the workstation.
            Read the user's request from the workstation.
            If 'EXIT' requested, end the program.
Step 2:
            Parse the data the user has entered.
            Return the result to the main line.
Step 3:
            If the parser returns a customer number:
               Retrieve the customer record.
               Display the customer data.
Step 4:
            Else, if the parser returns search data:
               Query the customer file with the
            user's search criteria.
            GO TO Step 1A.
```

Figure 6-71: Outline for Top-Down Development

As seen in Figure 6-71, the outlining process can be used for top-down program development. The benefit of using an outline is that the programmer actually leads himself from the major functions of a structured program design to the low-level of the program code. For example, to further define step 1, the program code would be written. See Figure 6-72.

```
SeqNoCLOn01n02n03Factor1+++OpCodFactor2+++ResultLenDXHiLoEq
      *   Step 1
     C                      OPEN CUSTINQ
     C           FUNCT      DOUEQ'EXIT'
     C                      EXFMTPANEL1
     C                      EXSR RTVMAC
      *   Step 2
     C                      EXSR PARSE
     C                      TESTNRQSDTA               5456
     C                      MOVE *IN54     CSTRQS
     C                      MOVE *IN56     QRYRQS
      *   Step 3
     C           CSTRQS     CASEQ*ON       DSPCST
      *   Step 4
     C           QRTRQS     CASEQ*ON       QUERY
     C                      END
     C                      ENDDO
```

Figure 6-72: Program Code for Customer Inquiry

As mentioned earlier, Structured programming is a method of programming. Simply using structured operations such as IF-THEN-ELSE and DO does not constitute structured programming.

Structured programming is the linking of a set of single-function routines that perform to the design specification. These routines are the result of structured analysis, structured design and a top-down development specification.

Any properly structured routine will exhibit the following characteristics:

1. One and only one entry and exit point. An escape clause is permitted, however, provided that the escape function branches to the one and only exit point.
2. All program code in the routine is necessary. No unusable code exists.
3. Infinite loops are absent from the routine.
4. Redundant code does not exist in the routine.
5. Only structured constructs are used for logic control within the routine.

Remember, however, that these are the outward characteristics of a properly structured program. Using these characteristics as a guideline for programming routines does not mean properly structured programs are being written. In other words, don't confuse the results of hard work with the work itself.

The following rules should be known and respected when taking a structured approach to program development.

1. All modules must be broken down into single-function routines. These routines are broken down further to the lowest-level program code or program statements.
2. The function control routines (logic modules) contain conditional logical, testing, repetition and *flag* setting.
3. The low-level functions (function modules) are controlled (i.e., called upon) by higher-level logic modules.
4. Low-level functions are defined in one and only one location and called upon whenever and wherever needed.

To achieve cohesion between the low-level modules, each routine performs one and only one task. The bonding of the routines is controlled by high-level logic.

Remember, though, the mere use of structured operation codes does not mean well-formed structured programs are being written. They are only the tools used to write programs. The structure of those programs depends on the programmer.

According to the *Structured Programming Theorem*, only *sequence*, *choice* and *repetition* are needed to solve any logic problem. However, sometimes the efficiency of a program is achieved at the expense of structure. When a program has to conform to rigid size restrictions and still perform efficiently, non-structured techniques may be required (i.e., the branch operation).

Control Flow Constructs

Structured programming consists of three components or *constructs*:

Sequence — The processes or operations of an application.

Choice — The decision or conditioned logic of an application. This control structure is sometimes referred to as *selection*.

Repetition — The looping or consecutive rerunning of a sequence of operations. This construct is sometimes referred to as *iteration*.

The following is a description and example of each of these control flow constructs.

Sequence — One or more processes of an application. Flow passes from one process to another without concern. In the RPG language, a process can be a series of one or more successive operations, a subroutine, or an entire program.

For example, the following "Update an Order's Line Item" routine contains only *sequence* operations.

```
SeqNoCLOn01n02n03Factor1+++OpCodFactor2+++ResultLenDXHiLoEq
     C           PRCITM    BEGSR
      *  Price an Order's Line Item
     C           ORDQTY    MULT PRICE     EXTEND
     C           EXTEND    MULT DISPCT    DISCNT              Discount%
     C                     SUB  DISCNT    EXTEND              New price
     C           ENDPRC    ENDSR
```

All RPG operation codes could be considered *sequence* operations.

Choice — Control structures or decisions that control *sequence* operations. If the decision is true, one path is taken; if the decision is false, a different path is taken. These control structures are known as IF-THEN-ELSE and CASE structures. The CASE structure is a special form of IF-THEN-ELSE. It provides a more readable method of composing thick nests of *choice* constructs.

The RPG language supports both types of *choice* constructs with the IFxx-ELSE-END (IF-THEN-ELSE) and CASxx (CASE) operation codes.

For example, the IF-THEN-ELSE control structure could be used to condition a pricing routine based on the item ordered being available and the quantity ordered being greater than zero.

```
SeqNoCLOn01n02n03Factor1+++OpCodFactor2+++ResultLenDXHiLoEq
     C           ITEM      CHAINITEMMAST              54
     C                     MOVE *IN54     NOTFND              Not found?
     C           NOTFND    IFEQ *OFF
     C           QTYORD    ANDGTO
     C                     EXSR PRCITM
     C                     ENDIF
```

Figure 6-73 lists the RPG operation codes that support the *choice* construct.

OpCode	Description
IFxx	IF then ELSE... ENDIF
CASxx	Compare, then perform subroutine
COMP	Compare Factor 1 to Factor 2
CABxx	Compare Factor 1 to Factor 2, then branch.
SELEC	Select — Begin a case group
WHxx	Compare Factor 1 to Factor 2 in a case group

Figure 6-73: RPG Operation Codes for Choice

Repetition — Looping control of *sequence*. The routine is performed a specified number of times or as long as the condition is true.

The RPG language supports *repetition* with the DOWxx (DO WHILE), DOUxx (DO UNTIL) and DO (DO repeated) operation codes.

For example, the "Price an Ordered Item" routine could price all items of an order by using the DOWxx construct for *repetition*.

```
SeqNoCL0n01n02n03Factor1+++OpCodFactor2+++ResultLenDXHiLoEq
0001 C           ORDNBR    CHAINORDFILE              54
0002 C                     MOVE *IN54     EOF
0003 C           EOF       DOWEQ*OFF
0004 C           ORDQTY    CASGT0         PRCORD
0005 C                     END
0006 C           ORDNBR    READEORDFILE              58
0007 C                     MOVE *IN58     EOF
0008 C                     ENDDO
```

Figure 6-74 lists the RPG operation codes that support the *repetition* construct.

OpCode	Description
DO	Do...EndDo (Repeat process *n* times)
DOUxx	Do Until...EndDo (Repeat process until condition is true)
DOWxx	Do While...EndDO (Repeat process while condition is true)
ITER	Iteration Loop (Stop processing do loop at current step and branch up to the top of the do loop to perform the next iteration)
LEAVE	Leave Loop (Leave the do loop by branching to the statement following the corresponding ENDDO operation)

Figure 6-74: RPG Operation Codes for Repetition

Structured Operation Codes

A program of structure results when coherent logic and organizational skills are used in the analysis and design phases of program development.

Program language operation codes are used to build the low-level of a program. (For more information on all RPG operation codes see Chapter 4.) These operation codes are essential in structured programming. Already featured in Chapter 4, they are reviewed here under the context of top-down structured programming.

Boolean Operators

The IFxx, CASxx, DOUxx, DOWxx and WHxx operations all support boolean operators. Boolean operators are used to control the type of relationship test that is performed between Factor 1 and Factor 2. All of these operations can use the first six boolean operators listed in Figure 6-75 in place of the xx place holder. The CASxx operation can use blanks as an operator.

Operator	Relationship Test
EQ	Factor 1 is equal to Factor 2
NE	Factor 1 is not equal to Factor 2
GE	Factor 1 is greater than or equal to Factor 2
GT	Factor 1 is greater than Factor 2
LE	Factor 1 is less than or equal to Factor 2
LT	Factor 1 is less than Factor 2
blank	Relationship test result is used to set on resulting indicators.
CT	Factor 1 is contained in Factor 2[1]

Figure 6-75: Boolean Operation Descriptions

[1] The CT (contains) operator has not been implemented in RPGIII.

The IF-THEN-ELSE Structure

The IF-THEN-ELSE structure is used to control the process section of a program. In the IFxx operation code, xx is the boolean comparison operator used to control the relationship test between Factor 1 and Factor 2. The available IF-THEN-ELSE boolean operators are listed in Figure 6-75.

The IFxx operation can test only a relationship; it cannot evaluate an expression. For example, to test the relationship between two fields the following logic applies:

```
IF  A = B  THEN...
```

To evaluate an expression, however, the following logic applies:

```
IF A = (B + C) THEN...
```

To evaluate an expression, an RPG program must first calculate the result of the expression, then use the result with the IFxx operation. For example:

```
D = B + C

IF A = D THEN...
```

The following RPG code illustrates this technique.

```
SeqNoCLOnO1nO2nO3Factor1+++OpCodFactor2+++ResultLenDXHiLoEq
      *****************************
      *  If A = (B + C) then... *
      *****************************
0001 C           B         ADD  C         D
0002 C           A         IFEQ D
0003 C                     .
0004 C                     .
0005 C                     .
0006 C                     ENDIF
```

The IFxx operation works like this:

When the relationship test between Factor 1 and Factor 2 is true, the statements following the IFxx operation are performed until an associated ELSE or ENDIF operation is encountered. At this point, control passes to the statement following the associated ENDIF operation. If the relationship test is false, the program branches to (1) the associated ELSE operation if one exists, or (2) the associated ENDIF statement, if an ELSE operation does not exist.

In the examples on the next few pages, assume fields A, B, C and D are set as follows:

```
A = 100,  B = 20,  C = 30,  D = 40
```

Example 133 — A simple relationship test.

```
SeqNoCLOn01n02n03Factor1+++<28  to  32>Factor2+++ResultLenDXHiLoEq
0001 C             A         IFGT        5
0002 C                       | ADD       20       C
0003 C                       | MOVE      'Current' MSG
0004 C                       ENDIF
```

In Example 133, the relationship test between field A and the numeric constant 5 is true. Therefore, lines 2 and 3 are performed. If the relationship was false, control would pass to the associated ENDIF operation on line 4; lines 2 and 3 would not be performed.

Example 134 — A relationship test, with branching to an ELSE operation.

```
SeqNoCLOn01n02n03Factor1+++<28  to  32>Factor2+++ResultLenDXHiLoEq
0001 C             B         IFGT C
0002 C                       | ADD       10       C
0003 C                       | MOVE      'OVERDUE' MSG
0004 C                       +ELSE
0005 C                       | ADD       10       B
0006 C                       | MOVE      'Current' MSG
0007 C                       ENDIF
```

In Example 134, the relationship test between field B and field C is false. Since an ELSE operation exists for this IFxx operation, control passes to the ELSE operation on line 4; lines 5 and 6 will be performed.

If the relationship test between fields B and C were true, however, lines 2 and 3 would be performed; then control would pass to the ENDIF operation on line 7.

IFxx operations can be extended to form more complex conditioning. ANDxx and ORxx operations can be used with the IFxx operation to extend the relationship test.

Example 135 — Testing for a list of values.

```
SeqNoCLOn01n02n03Factor1+++<28  to  32>Factor2+++ResultLenDXHiLoEq
0001 C            A          IFGT B
0002 C            A          ANDGTD
0003 C            A          ANDGTC
0004 C                       | MOVEL      'A HIGH'  MSG
0005 C                       | Z-ADD      20        A
0006 C                       ENDIF
```

In Example 135, the IFxx and ANDxx operations on lines 1 to 3 state: If A is greater than B and D and C, then perform statements 4 and 5.

Relationship tests can be nested by using multiple IFxx operations. The outer-level IF-THEN-ELSE structure is tested first, and if it proves true, the next level IF-THEN-ELSE structure is tested. See Example 136.

Example 136 — Compound relationship test with nesting.

```
SeqNoCLOn01n02n03Factor1+++<28  to  32>Factor2+++ResultLenDXHiLoEq
0001 C            A          IFGT B
0002 C            A          ANDGTD
0003 C            A          ANDGTC
0004 C                       | MOVEL      'A HIGH'  MSG
0005 C            C          | IFLT       D
0006 C                       | | MOVEL    'C LOW'   TEXT
0007 C                       | | ADD      50        ACCT
0008 C                       | ENDIF
0009 C                       ENDIF
```

In Example 136, the same conditioning used in Example 135 is used to control the IF-THEN-ELSE structure. However, when line 5 is reached, if its relationship test is true, lines 6 and 7 are performed. If its relationship test is false, control would pass to the ENDIF statement on line 8, ending the inner IF-THEN-ELSE structure.

Additional operations can be specified between the ENDIF statements, for example:

Example 137 — Perform operations between ENDIF statements.

```
SeqNoCLOn01n02n03Factor1+++<28  to  32>Factor2+++ResultLenDXHiLoEq
0001 C              A          IFGT B
0002 C              A          ANDGTD
0003 C              A          ANDGTC
0004 C                         | SUB       10        C
0005 C              D          | IFLT      C
0006 C                         | | ADD     50        C
0007 C                         | | MOVEL   'D LOW'   TEXT
0008 C                         | ENDIF
0009 C                         | ADD       20        B
0010 C                         | ADD       30        C
0011 C                         | ADD       40        D
0012 C                         ENDIF
```

Example 137 contains three ADD operations on line 9 to 10. They will be performed when the outer IF-THEN-ELSE structure is entered and after the inner IF-THEN-ELSE structure has been performed or bypassed.

IF-THEN-ELSE structures can be nested to a high-level (at least 100 levels with most RPG compilers). While there is no hard and fast rule, readability tends to deteriorate when more than three levels of IF-THEN-ELSE structures are nested. If more than three levels of nesting is required, the CASE structure can be used to improve readability.

The CASE Structure

The CASE structure is used to control sections of the program. CASE offers greater readability than IF-THEN-ELSE when a high level of nesting is required or when the control structure is controlling several dozen lines of code. This is, in part, due to the inherent nature of CASE to separate the logic from the processes.

RPG supports both in-line and subroutine forms of CASE. The CASxx operation performs subroutines, while the SELEC/WHxx/OTHER operations perform in-line code. The boolean operators for CASxx and WHxx are listed in Figure 6-75 on page 335.

The CASE operations are considered *choice* constructs. Figure 6-76 illustrates the logic flow for the CASE structure.

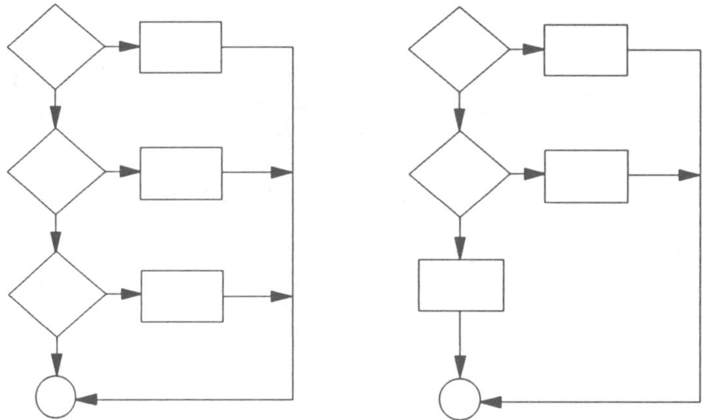

Figure 6-76: Two Forms of CASE

Example 138 — In-Line CASE using SELEC/WHxx/OTHER.

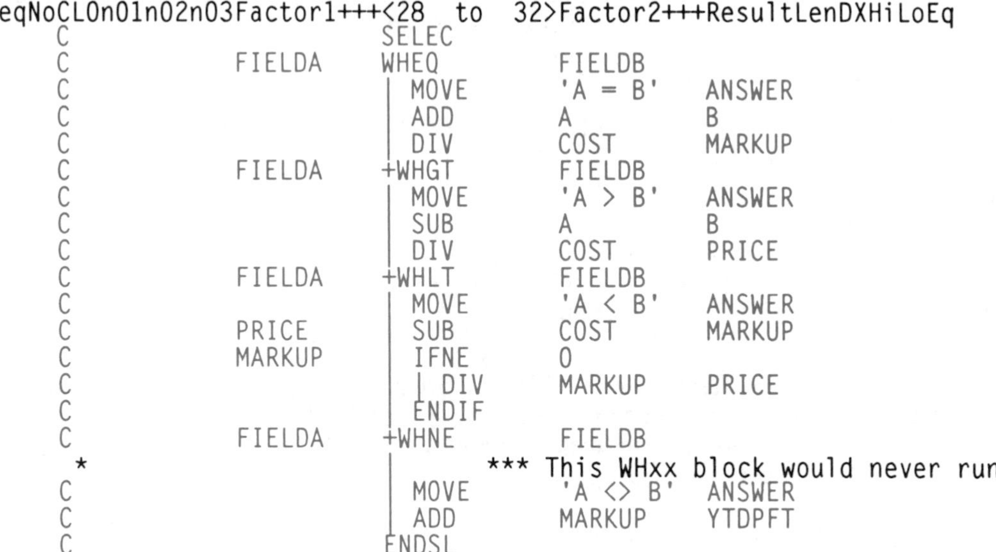

```
SeqNoCLOn01n02n03Factor1+++<28  to  32>Factor2+++ResultLenDXHiLoEq
     C                    SELEC
     C          FIELDA    WHEQ        FIELDB
     C                    | MOVE      'A = B'   ANSWER
     C                    | ADD       A         B
     C                    | DIV       COST      MARKUP
     C          FIELDA    +WHGT       FIELDB
     C                    | MOVE      'A > B'   ANSWER
     C                    | SUB       A         B
     C                    | DIV       COST      PRICE
     C          FIELDA    +WHLT       FIELDB
     C                    | MOVE      'A < B'   ANSWER
     C          PRICE     | SUB       COST      MARKUP
     C          MARKUP    | IFNE      0
     C                    | | DIV     MARKUP    PRICE
     C                    | ENDIF
     C          FIELDA    +WHNE       FIELDB
      *                   |      *** This WHxx block would never run
     C                    | MOVE      'A <> B'  ANSWER
     C                    | ADD       MARKUP    YTDPFT
     C                    ENDSL
```

In Example 138, the WHxx operations, like the IFxx/ELSE operations are very difficult to distinguish from the other operation codes. This causes the programmer to interpret the code being performed (i.e., the *process*), even if all that is needed is to check the logic (i.e., *choice*) of the program.

Complex or multiple conditions, such as those illustrated in Example 138, are necessary from time to time. In-line CASE statements can add power to the application. When the in-line CASE gets too complex, the power it provides is offset by the confusion created. At this point, it is important to consider using the CASxx operation.

Example 139 — Subroutine CASxx Operation.

```
SeqNoCLOn01n02n03Factor1+++OpCodFactor2+++ResultLenDXHiLoEq
     C          FIELDA    CASEQFIELDB    EQUAL
     C          FIELDA    CASGTFIELDB    GREATR
     C          FIELDA    CASLTFIELDB    LESSTH
     C          FIELDA    CASNEFIELDB    NOTEQ
     C                    END
```

Example 139 contains the much simpler CASxx structure. While the logic flow of the program is the same as in Example 138, Example 139 allows the programmer to concentrate on the logic (i.e., *choice*) of the program.

Example 140 — A basic CASE structure.

```
SeqNoCLOn01n02n03Factor1+++OpCodFactor2+++ResultLenDXHiLoEq
0001 C           FUNCT     CASEQ'DELETE'  DLTRCD
0002 C                     END
0003 C.....the program continues...
      /SPACE
0004 CSR         DLTRCD    BEGSR
0005 C           INDEX     DELETCUSTMAST                56
0006 CSR                   ENDSR
```

In Example 140, the field named FUNCT (function) is compared to the constant 'DELETE' on line 1. The xx of the CASxx is EQ (equal); therefore, a relationship test for equal is performed. If the test is true (i.e., FUNCT equals 'DELETE'), the subroutine DLTRCD (delete a record) is performed.

Upon completion of the subroutine DLTRCD, control returns to the END statement associated with the CASE structure, line 2 in our example. Then, the next successive operation, line 3 in our example, will be performed as the program continues.

Successive CASE Operations

As mentioned earlier, CASE is the preferred control structure for *choice* constructs. Successive CASE structures are easy to read and understand. They support top-down program design by allowing the programmer to concentrate on the logic of the program (i.e., the *Logic Modules*) until the detail (i.e., the *Function Modules)* must be written.

For example, if the design of a routine calls for the following:

```
PROMPT the workstation operator for the FUNCTION request.
READ the Operator's RESPONSE.
PARSE the Operator's RESPONSE.
BUILD the requested FUNCTION.
IF FUNCTION equals 'DELETE' then
     Perform the DELETE-RECORD routine.
ELSE, IF FUNCTION equals 'UPDATE' then
     Perform the UPDATE-RECORD routine.
ELSE, IF FUNCTION equals 'ADDNEW' then
     Perform the ADD-RECORD routine.
ELSE, IF FUNCTION equals 'SEARCH' then
     Perform the SEARCH routine.
ELSE, IF FUNCTION equals 'EXIT' then
     Perform the END-PROGRAM routine.
ELSE, perform the DEFAULT handler.
```

The RPG code that supports this design is featured in Figure 6-77.

```
SeqNoCL0n01n02n03Factor1+++OpCodFactor2+++ResultLenDXHiLoEq
0001 C            FUNCT     DOUEQ'EXIT'
     * Prompt the workstation operator for a response.
0002 C                      EXSR PROMPT
     * Parse (interpret) the Operator's response.
0003 C                      EXSR PARSE
     * Finish up the PARSE by converting the request to FUNCT.
0004 C                      EXSR BLDFCT
     * Select the subroutine when the relationship is met.
0005 C            FUNCT     CASEQ'DELETE'  DLTRCD
0006 C            FUNCT     CASEQ'UPDATE'  UPDRCD
0007 C            FUNCT     CASEQ'ADDNEW'  ADDRCD
0008 C            FUNCT     CASEQ'SEARCH'  SCHFIL
0009 C            FUNCT     CASEQ'EXIT'    ENDPGM
0010 C                      CAS            DFTRTN
0011 C                      END
0012 C                      ENDDO
```

Figure 6-77: CASE-controlled logic module

As can be seen in Figure 6-77, the CASE structure makes this logic control module easy to read and comprehend. On the other hand, if IF-THEN-ELSE structures were to be used, they would create a much more complex module.

Upon entry into the CASE structure, the relationship between the field FUNCT and the constant 'DELETE' is performed. If the relationship is true, the subroutine DLTRCD is performed. Upon completion of the subroutine DLTRCD, control passes to the END statement associated with the CASE structure.

If the relationship test on line 5 is false, control passes to the CASEQ operation on line 6. If that relationship test is true, the subroutine UPDRCD is performed. Upon completion of the subroutine, control passes to the CASE structure END statement on line 11.

This process is repeated for each CASE structure in the CASE-group. If none of the CASE comparisons are true, the "catch all" CAS operation on line 10 will perform the subroutine DFTRTN.

Compare and Branch Operations

The CABxx (compare and branch) operation is unique to the RPG language. It differs from the CASxx operation in that the CASxx operation performs a subroutine and returns to the same point in the program while the CABxx operation branches to a label and does not return.

The CABxx operation supports the complete set of boolean operators listed in Figure 6-75 on page 335. When the relationship test is true, a branch to the label specified in the Result field is performed. When the relationship test is false, the program continues with the next successive instruction following the CASxx operation. If resulting indicators are specified, they will be set on accordingly—regardless of the boolean operator used with the operation.

Other RPG operations are required to provide a target for the CABxx operation. The TAG and ENDSR operation provide this function. Figure 6-78 lists the RPG operations that support branching.

OpCode	Description
CABxx	Compare and branch.
GOTO	Go to, (i.e., branches to) a label identified by a TAG or ENDSR opcode.
ENDSR	End Subroutine. Factor 1 can contain a label that can be used as the target of a CABxx or GOTO operation.
TAG	Label. Factor 1 contains a label that can be used as the target of a CABxx or GOTO operation.

Figure 6-78: RPG Operation Codes for Choice

The CABxx operation should be used primarily as an escape clause, to branch to an exit routine, or the end of a subroutine or program; CABxx should never be used to branch out of a subroutine. See Figure 6-79.

In Figure 6-79, a Do until loop is used to retry access to a database record when a record-lock condition is detected. When a record is locked, the RPG exception/error handling routine passes control to the *PSSR subroutine. The *PSSR subroutine tests for the record-lock condition, then decrements the counter field RETRY.

```
SeqNoFFileNameIPE.E....RLEN...K.OV....EDevice+RecNbrKOptionEntry+
0010 FCUSTMASTIF  E           K        DISK
0020 F                                                KINFDS INFDS
0030 F                                                KINFSR *PSSR
SeqNoIDSName....EUDSExternalname..........PFromTo++DField+
0040 IINFDS       DS
0050 I                                          *STATUS   STATUS
SeqNoCLOn01n02n03Factor1+++OpCodFactor2+++ResultLenDXHiLoEq
0060 C                     Z-ADD3         RETRY
0070 C           RETRY     DOUEQ0
0080 C           LCKERR    OREQ *ON
0090 C           INDEX     CHAINCUSTMAST                54
0010 C           *IN54     CASEQ*ON       NOTFND
0011 C                     END
0012 C                     ENDDO
xxxx C*...user code goes here
0109 C           ENDPGM    TAG
0110 C                     MOVE *ON       *INLR
0111 C                     RETRN

0112 CSR         *PSSR     BEGSR
      *     If recursion of exception/error handler
      *     is detected, ESCAPE the subroutine.
0113 C                     ADD  1         RECURS
0114 C           RECURS    CABGT1         ESCAPE
0115 C           STATUS    IFEQ RCDLCK
0116 C           RETRY     IFGT 0
0117 C                     SUB  1         RETRY
0118 C                     ELSE
0119 C                     MOVE *ON       LCKERR
0120 C                     ENDIF
0121 C                     ENDIF
0122 C                     Z-ADD0         RECURS
0123 CSR         ESCAPE    ENDSR
```

Figure 6-79: CABxx to Exit an Error Routine

Chapter 7

Modular Programming

A primary characteristic of structured programming is that it comprises modular programs. Modular programs consist of a series of mainline routines, subroutines and subprograms known as modules.

With traditional programming, an application and all of its components are placed into a few large multi-function programs. With modular programming, an application is broken into multiple single-function modules. Whether a module is a subroutine or a subprogram depends on its complexity and the requirements of the application.

Modular programming provides several benefits that contribute to reduced cost and simplification of the programming task. For example:

1. Since applications are broken into multiple modules, the programming tasks required for different modules can be spread among several programmers. Thus, an application program can be completed more quickly.
2. Modules that consist of just a few functions are developed more reliably due to reduced opportunity for errors that normally occur during module development. Once the module functions properly, it can be "put away" without impact to the other modules in the application.
3. Individual modules can be maintained with little or no impact to the other modules. For example, if an invoice aging routine needs maintenance, it can be revised without impact to the rest of the application. In addition, if the module is used by more than one application, program maintenance need be performed only once.
4. Occasionally, modules can be reused by other applications. For example, a date routine that calculates the number of days between two dates may be of use in several different accounting applications.

Modular programs consist of two types of modules:

1. Logic control modules
2. Function modules

Logic control modules contain mostly *choice* and *repetition* constructs (see Chapter 6, *Structured Programming*, for more information on these constructs). The logic of a routine is driven by logic control modules. There is little or no *work*, in the traditional sense, performed in a logic control module. Only relationship testing (i.e., *choice*), looping (i.e., *repetition*) and conditional branching via structured operations is performed.

Function modules consist primarily of *sequence* constructs. (See Chapter 6, Structured Programming, for more information on these constructs.) The processes of the application are performed by function modules. A function module also contains choice and repetition constructs that control branching and looping within the function module. Function modules exist at the lowest level of the program design. They perform one and only one task, then return to the logic control module.

To guarantee the top-down (i.e., vertical) relationship between logic control modules and function modules, a hierarchy chart should be created that illustrates the module relationship. See Figure 7-80.

A proper program, and consequently, a proper module, will exhibit the following characteristics:

1. One entry and one exit point
2. No unusable program code
3. No infinite loops

In addition, to ensure correctness in the application module hierarchy, the following guidelines should be kept in mind when designing an application:

1. Logic control modules control access to all lower-level modules.
2. Module access is always vertical, never horizontal. A module can call only lower-level modules, not modules at the same or higher level. An exception is that any module may call itself when recursive programming is required.
3. Modules are reusable. That is, modules may be called by multiple modules.

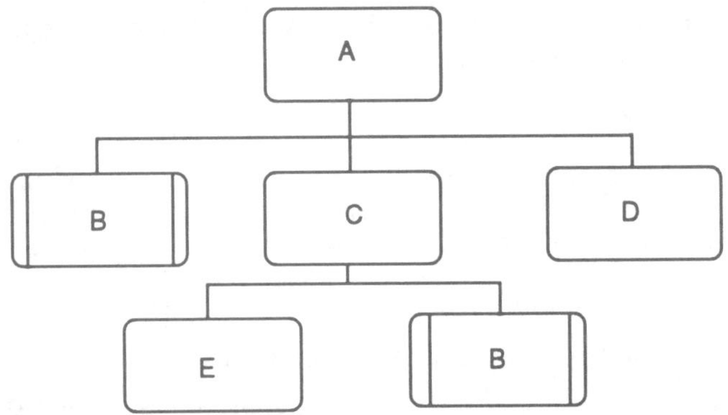

Figure 7-80: A Hierarchy Chart of a Modular Application

Figure 7-80 illustrates a hierarchy chart. Each module is represented by a rectangle.

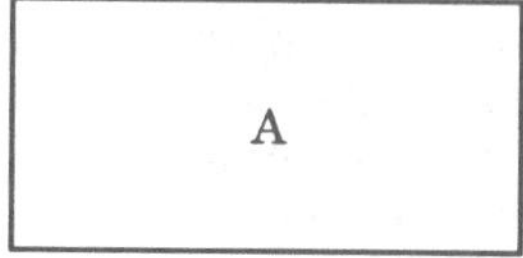

When a module is reused, additional vertical lines on the left and right edge of the rectangle identify the module as reusable.

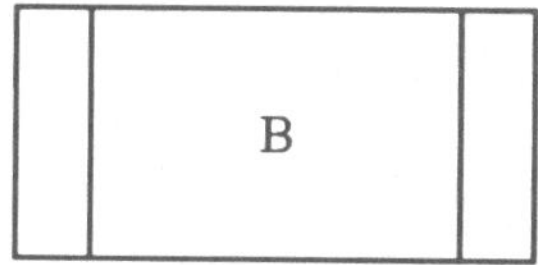

Each module can be a subroutine or a subprogram. When a module is a subprogram, it can be further defined by a *Program Hierarchy Chart.* The top-most box of the program's hierarchy is the core of the program. It exhibits the function of the module.

A program hierarchy chart is essentially the same as an application hierarchy chart. A program hierarchy chart, however, supports an additional symbol that identifies that module as being further defined by a flowchart.

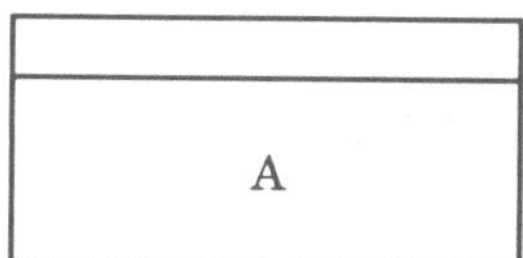

The additional horizontal line at the top of the rectangle identifies the module as one that is further defined by a flowchart.

Intermodule Communication

With so many modules making up an application, intermodule communication becomes an important issue. The most common techniques on the AS/400, for passing information between modules include the following:

1. Parameter passing.
2. Reading and writing to an external data area.

Other methods include system-dependent functions such as the following:

3. Data Queues.
4. Stacks.
5. Message sending.

Data queues are considered the fastest way to send large volumes of information between applications. This chapter, however, discusses only parameter passing and data area handling.

Parameter Passing

Parameter passing is perhaps the best method for communicating between program modules with RPG. Most operating systems, such as System/38 Control Program Facility (CPF) and AS/400 Operating System/400 (OS/400), support parameters in a consistent manner throughout all high-level languages. This makes it easy to send data from RPG programs to other programs regardless of the language in which they are written.

When a program transfers control to, or "calls" another program, it is referred to as the *calling program*. The program that receives control is referred to as the *called program*.

For example, if a program named PGMA (pronounced *program A*) calls a program named PGMB (pronounced *program B*), PGMA is the *calling program*, and PGMB is the *called program*. See Figure 7-81.

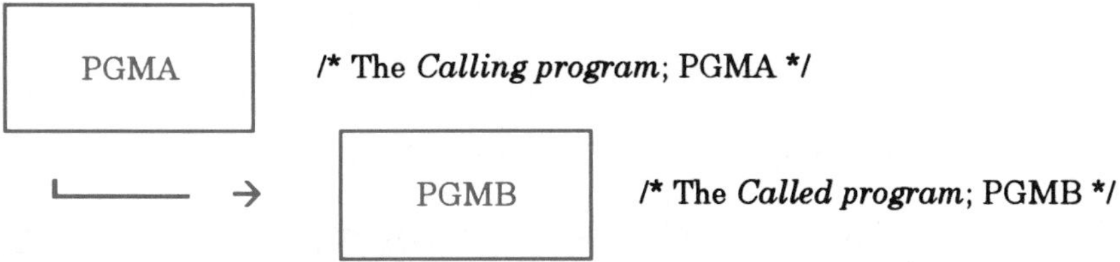
PGMA
/* The Calling program; PGMA */
PGMB
/* The Called program; PGMB */

Figure 7-81: Program to Program Call

Parameters are passed between program modules only. RPG cannot pass parameters to subroutines. The PLIST (parameter list) operation defines a parameter list name. Factor 1 of the Calculation specifications contains the name of the parameter list that is being defined.

```
SeqNoCLOn01n02n03Factor1+++OpCodFactor2+++ResultLenDXHiLoEq
     C           MATH      PLIST
     C                     PARM           RESULT  72
     C                     PARM           VALUE1  52
     C                     PARM           VALUE2  52
     C                     PARM           OPER    1
```

Figure 7-82: A simple parameter list named MATH

In Figure 7-82 the parameter list named MATH is defined. The individual fields that are passed between modules are called parameters and are defined by the PARM (parameter declaration) operation. In this example, four fields (RESULT, VALUE1, VALUE2 and OPER) are declared as parameters on the parameter list MATH. The number of parameters passed between programs is implied by the number of PARM operations.

A special purpose parameter list, known as the *Entry Parameter List*, is used to receive parameters into a called program and return them to the calling program. An entry parameter list (often referred to as the *entry plist*) is identified with *ENTRY in Factor 1 of the PLIST operation. For example, if the parameter list MATH is used to call a program named PGMB the entry parameter list for the program PGMB, would be written as follows:

```
SeqNoCLOn01n02n03Factor1+++OpCodFactor2+++ResultLenDXHiLoEq
     C           *ENTRY    PLIST
     C                     PARM           ANSWER  72
     C                     PARM           FACT1   52
     C                     PARM           FACT2   52
     C                     PARM           OPER    1
```

Figure 7-83: Entry Parameter List

Figure 7-83 illustrates a typical entry plist. The name implies that the entry plist is the entry-point into the program, it is not. The entry plist can appear anywhere in the program, however, RPG always starts processing at the beginning of the RPG cycle.

Each parameter of the parameter list MATH (Figure 7-82) has a corresponding parameter in the called program listed in Figure 7-83. Typically, identical parameter lists are defined in the calling and called program.

On the System/38 and AS/400, parameters are traditionally passed by reference, not value. That is, the parameter's address in memory (a type of pointer) is transferred between programs. The data itself is accessed through a field, array or data structure. Internally, RPG accesses the data through the address; however, this is entirely transparent to the application program.

When a program is called, the fields specified on the entry plist are assigned the address of the parameters being passed to the program. This means that fields on the entry plist in the called program actually point to the original data in the calling program. Any changes to the data by the called program automatically effect the field values in the calling program.

For example, assume a field named RESULT in the program PGMA has a memory address of X'00287DC0' and is a parameter used on a call operation to the program PGMB. Program PGMB uses the field ANSWER as its *ENTRY parameter list.

When program PGMA calls program PGMB, the address of the field RESULT (from PGMA) is assigned to the field ANSWER (in PGMB). In the illustration in Figure 7-84 the field ANSWER is assigned an address of X'00287DC0'. This is parameter passing by reference.

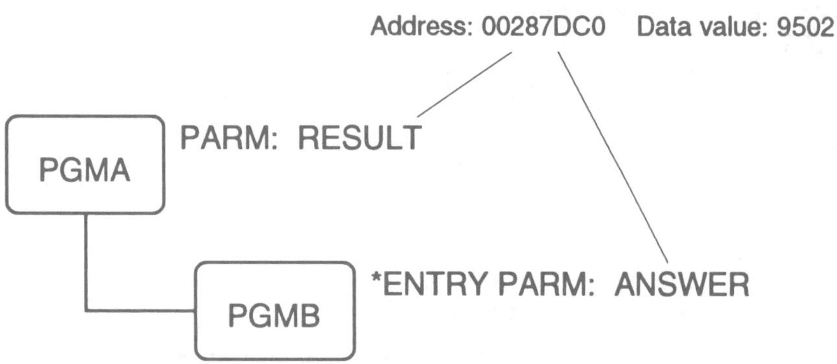

Figure 7-84: Parameter Passing by Memory Address

The called program should define a parameter list that can accommodate (i.e., receive) the parameter's address. The names and attributes (e.g., length, type, etc.) of the fields being used as parameters in the calling program do not have to match those defined in the called program. However, if the attribute of the parameters in the calling and called programs do not match, data integrity can be compromised—for example, a character field containing blanks could be passed to a numeric field, which would cause an error.

Assume the parameters of the parameter list MATH are assigned the following values:

```
RESULT= 0.0           /* This value is returned from the called program. */
VALUE1= 3.5
VALUE2= 6.0
OPER   = *
```

Both the calling program and the called program will reference these values. If the value of a field is changed by the called program, the field in the calling program is also changed because both fields reference the same memory location.

When a program is called and passed the parameter list MATH, a series of four parameter addresses are transferred to the called program. Those addresses represent the location in memory of the values assigned to the parameter fields.

In Figure 7-85 that follows, the memory address of each field used on the parameter list MATH (listed in Figure 7-82) and the data represented by those fields is illustrated. The memory address is to the left; the data is to the right and boxed.

Field Name on PLIST	Memory Address	Data
RESULT	X'003618'	X'0000000F'
VALUE1	X'0046C5'	X'00350F'
VALUE2	X'0046C8'	X'00600F'
OPER	X'0052D6'	*

Figure 7-85: Memory Location of Fields of a Parameter List

The following table illustrates the addresses for parameters passed by the PGMA program to the PGMB program via the MATH parameter list.

Program	Field	Address in memory
PGMA	RESULT	X'003618'
	VALUE1	X'0046C5'
	VALUE2	X'0046C8'
	OPER	X'0052D6'

The following table illustrates the address for parameters received by the PGMB program. These parameters a received via the *ENTRY parameter list.

Program	Field	Address in memory
PGMB	ANSWER	X'003618'
	FACT1	X'0046C5'
	FACT2	X'0046C8'
	OPER	X'0052D6'

The above table illustrates the relationship between fields and their address in memory. As stated earlier in this chapter, the name of the fields used for the called program's parameter list do not have to match those used in the calling program's parameter list. However, the sequence of the parameters is important. Corresponding parameters in different programs must be in the same relative location on the parameter list.

For example, if a program named PGMA uses the parameter list MATH (listed in Figure 7-82) to call the program named PGMB, the fields used on the entry parameter list in PGMB are assigned the same address as the corresponding parameter in PGMA. See Figure 7-86.

Field Name on PLIST	Memory Address	Data
ANSWER	X'003618'	X'0000000F'
FACT1	X'0046C5'	X'00350F'
FACT2	X'0046C8'	X'00600F'
OPER	X'0052D6'	*

Figure 7-86: Address Assignment of Fields Used in Called Program Parameter List

When program PGMA calls program PGMB, program PGMB will perform a task, then returns control to program PGMA. The memory locations of the parameters are not affected.

```
SeqNoCLOn01n02n03Factor1+++OpCodFactor2+++ResultLenDXHiLoEq
0001 C           MATH      PLIST
0002 C                     PARM           RESULT  72
0003 C                     PARM           VALUE1  52
0004 C                     PARM           VALUE2  52
0005 C                     PARM           OPER    1

0006 C                     Z-ADD0         RESULT
0007 C                     Z-ADD3.5       VALUE1
0008 C                     Z-ADD6         VALUE2
0009 C                     MOVE '*'       OPER

0010 C                     CALL 'PGMB'    MATH

0011 C                     MOVE *ON       *INLR
```

Figure 7-87: Program PGMA with a Named Parameter List

Figure 7-87 above contains the program listing for PGMA. It begins by assigning values to the fields that will be used as parameters (lines 6 to 9).

Then, on line 10, the program PGMB is called using the parameter list MATH. Lines 1 to 5 define the parameter list MATH. As stated in Chapter 4, parameter lists are declarations; therefore, they can be specified anywhere in the program.

The technique illustrated in Figure 7-87 uses a named parameter list. The parameter list MATH is defined independent of the CALL operation and, therefore, can be used by more than one CALL operation.

```
SeqNoCLOn01n02n03Factor1+++OpCodFactor2+++ResultLenDXHiLoEq
0002 C           *ENTRY    PLIST
0003 C                     PARM           ANSWER  72
0004 C                     PARM           FACT1   52
0005 C                     PARM           FACT2   52
0006 C                     PARM           OPER    1

0007 C           '+'       CASEQOPER      SUM
0008 C           '-'       CASEQOPER      SUBTR
0009 C           '*'       CASEQOPER      MULTI
0010 C           '/'       CASEQOPER      DIVIDE
0011 C                     END
0012 C                     MOVE *ON       *INLR

0013 CSR         SUM       BEGSR
0014 C           FACT1     ADD  FACT2     ANSWER
0015 CSR                   ENDSR

0016 CSR         SUBTR     BEGSR
0017 C           FACT1     SUB  FACT2     ANSWER
0018 CSR                   ENDSR

0019 CSR         MULTI     BEGSR
0020 C           FACT1     MULT FACT2     ANSWER
0021 CSR                   ENDSR

0022 CSR         DIVIDE    BEGSR
0023 C           0         IFNE FACT2
0024 C           FACT1     DIV  FACT2     ANSWER
0025 C                     ENDIF
0026 CSR                   ENDSR
```

Figure 7-88: Program PGMB—A Called Program

Figure 7-88 illustrates a called program. The entry parameter list (lines 2 to 6) contains four parameters. While this program uses all of the parameters passed to it, only the first parameter—the field ANSWER—is modified by the program.

A parameter list can be specified immediately following a CALL operation. In this situation, the parameter list is assigned exclusively to the CALL operation that precedes it. See Figure 7-89.

```
SeqNoCLOn01n02n03Factor1+++OpCodFactor2+++ResultLenDXHiLoEq
0002 C                          Z-ADD0         RESULT
0003 C                          Z-ADD3.5       VALUE1
0004 C                          Z-ADD6         VALUE2
0005 C                          MOVE '*'       OPER

0006 C                          CALL 'PGMB'
0007 C                          PARM           RESULT
0008 C                          PARM           VALUE1
0009 C                          PARM           VALUE2
0010 C                          PARM           OPER
0011 C                          MOVE *ON       *INLR
```

Figure 7-89: Program PGMA with Unnamed Parameter List

Factor 2 can be specified for a PARM operation. When a program calls another program, the content of Factor 2 of the PARM operation (if present) is copied into the Result field. This allows the program to avoid explicitly moving the parameter data into the parameter fields. See Figure 7-90.

```
SeqNoCLOn01n02n03Factor1+++OpCodFactor2+++ResultLenDXHiLoEq
0001 C                          CALL 'PGMB'
0002 C                ANSWER    PARM           RESULT  72
0003 C                          PARM 3.5       VALUE1  52
0004 C                          PARM 6         VALUE2  52
0005 C                          PARM '*'       OPER    1
```

Figure 7-90: Parameter Movement Upon Calling a Program

Factor 1 can be specified for a PARM operation. When a program is called the content of the Result fields of the entry parameter list is copied into Factor 1. See Figure 7-91.

```
SeqNoCLOn01n02n03Factor1+++OpCodFactor2+++ResultLenDXHiLoEq
0001 C                *ENTRY    PLIST
0002 C                ANSWER    PARM ANSWER    RESULT  72
0003 C                          PARM           VALUE1  52
0004 C                          PARM           VALUE2  52
0005 C                          PARM           OPER    1
```

Figure 7-91: Parameter Movement Upon Entering a Called Program

When a program returns to its caller, that is when it ends, the content of Factor 2 of its entry parameter list is copied into the Result field. See Figure 7-92.

```
SeqNoCLOn01n02n03Factor1+++OpCodFactor2+++ResultLenDXHiLoEq
0001 C             *ENTRY    PLIST
0002 C             ANSWER    PARM ANSWER    RESULT  72
0003 C                       PARM           VALUE1  52
0004 C                       PARM           VALUE2  52
0005 C                       PARM           OPER    1
```

Figure 7-92: Parameter Movement Upon Exiting a Called Program

This effect illustrated in Figure 7-92 is similar to that illustrated in Figure 7-90.

When a called program returns control to the calling program, the Result fields of the parameter list in the calling program are copied into Factor 1. See Figure 7-93.

```
SeqNoCLOn01n02n03Factor1+++OpCodFactor2+++ResultLenDXHiLoEq
0001 C                       CALL 'PGMB'
0002 C             ANSWER    PARM           RESULT  72
0003 C                       PARM 3.5       VALUE1  52
0004 C                       PARM 6         VALUE2  52
0005 C                       PARM '*'       OPER    1
```

Figure 7-93: Parameter Movement Upon Returning to the Calling Program

Figure 7-94 contains a cross-reference of the figures that illustrate program-to-program call operations with parameters being passed between the programs.

CALL/RETURN Action	Figure Illustrating Action in PGMA	Figure Illustrating Action in PGMB
PGMA call PGMB	7-90	7-91
PGMB ends, control returns to PGMA	7-93	7-92

Figure 7-94: Cross-Reference Call/Return Action to Figures

Parameters can be virtually any RPG field, data structure or array name. A technique often used to pass multiple fields as parameters involves using a data structure with the fields defined as data structure subfields. This avoids having to code a PARM operation for each parameter that will be passed.

For example, if the fields RESULT, VALUE1, VALUE2 and OPER need to be passed, a single parameter can be defined that passes a data structure that is made up of these fields. See Figure 7-95.

```
SeqNoIDSName....EUDSExternalname..........PFromTo++DField+
0001 IPDATA        DS
0002 I                                    P    1    42RESULT
0003 I                                    P    5    72VALUE1
0004 I                                    P    8   102VALUE2
0005 I                                        11   11 OPER

SeqNoCLOn01n02n03Factor1+++OpCodFactor2+++ResultLenDXHiLoEq
0006 C                         CALL 'PGMB'                56
0007 C                         PARM           PDATA
```

Figure 7-95: Data Structure as a Parameter

The data structure PDATA is made up of four data structure subfields: RESULT, VALUE1, VALUE2 and OPER (lines 2 to 5). When the program PGMB is called (line 6) and is passed the single parameter PDATA (line 7), all of the data of the data structure will be addressable. Consequently, all four subfields are addressable by the called program (program PGMB).

To address the four subfields of the data structure, the parameter can be received in the called program as a data structure. See Figure 7-96.

```
SeqNoIDSName....EUDSExternalname..........PFromTo++DField+
0001 IPDATA        DS
0002 I                                    P    1    42RESULT
0003 I                                    P    5    72VALUE1
0004 I                                    P    8   102VALUE2
0005 I                                        11   11 OPER

SeqNoCLOn01n02n03Factor1+++OpCodFactor2+++ResultLenDXHiLoEq
0006 C                 *ENTRY  PLIST
0007 C                         PARM           PDATA
```

Figure 7-96: Data Structure as a Parameter of an Entry Parameter List

Data Area

A data area is a location on the computer that is used to store information. A data area is separate from a program and can be used for communication between program modules. Data areas are global and can be accessed by any program module. This could be compared to a single record data file.

Data is communicated between modules through system functions and RPG operation codes. Unlike parameters, a copy of the actual data contained in the data area is passed between modules. Specifically, when a data area is retrieved, a copy of its data is placed into a field or data structure. Any manipulation of the data is performed on the program's copy of the data. The data area is updated with new information when the data is written to the data area.

Data areas can be implicitly or explicitly retrieved and written. A data area is implicitly retrieved and written at the beginning and end of a program by defining the data area as a *data area data structure.*

The letters DS in columns 19 and 20 identified the input specification as a data structure. The letter U specified in column 18 of the input specification identifies the data structure as a data area. Columns 7 to 12 contain the name of the data area and the data structure. See Figure 7-97.

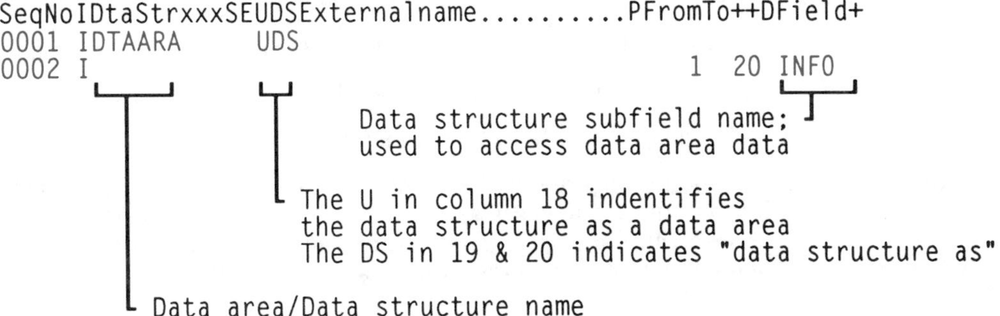

Figure 7-97: Data Area Data Structure Specification

When a data area is defined in this manner, RPG implicitly retrieves the data area into the data structure when the program is started and writes the data structure to the data area when the program ends. If the data area does not exist when the program is run, it will be created. On the AS/400, the data area will be created in the QTEMP library with the attributes of the data area data structure. The same name is assigned to both the data area and the data structure.

The data area data structure can be externally described, by specifying the letter 'E' in column 18 of the data structure specification and the database file name in columns 21 to 30. Data structure subfields can be specified to further define the data area. See Figure 7-98.

```
SeqNoIDSName....EUDSExternalname..........PFromTo++DField+
0001 IDTAARA     UDS
0002 I                                       1   70NEXTCN
0003 I                                       8  130LASTUS
0004 I                                      14  30 DESC
```

Figure 7-98: Data Area Data Structure

Figure 7-98 defines the data area data structure DTAARA. Positions 1 to 30 within the data area are sub-defined with three fields. The field NEXTCN (next customer number) might contain the next customer number to be assigned to a new customer; the field LASTUS (last date used) might contain the last date a customer was added to the customer file; the field DESC (description) might contain the name of the company or user that last added a customer to the customer file.

Data areas can be explicitly retrieved and written with the IN and OUT operation codes. Four RPG operation codes provide explicit access to data areas:

1. DEFN — Assigns a field to receive the data area data.
2. IN — Retrieves the data area data and places it into its assigned field.
3. OUT — Writes the contents of the assigned field to the data area.
4. UNLCK — Releases the data area from a lock state.

The DEFN operation names a data area and assigns a field in the RPG program to the data area. That field is where the data area's data will be stored when an IN operation is used to retrieve the data area. That field is also the source of the data that will be written when an OUT operation is used to write the data area.

A data area can be assigned to a variable field, data structure or data structure subfield. See Figure 7-99a to 7-99d.

```
SeqNoIDSName....EUDSExternalname..........PFromTo++DField+
0001 IACCT        DS
0002 I                                        1   70NEXTCN
0003 I                                        8  130LASTUS
0004 I                                       14  30 DESC

SeqNoCLOn01n02n03Factor1+++OpCodFactor2+++ResultLenDXHiLoEq
0005 C            *NAMVAR   DEFN ACCOUNTS  ACCT
```


Figure 7-99a: Assign a Data Area to a Data Structure

In Figure 7-99a, the data structure named ACCT (lines 1 to 4) is assigned to the data area named ACCOUNTS (line 5).

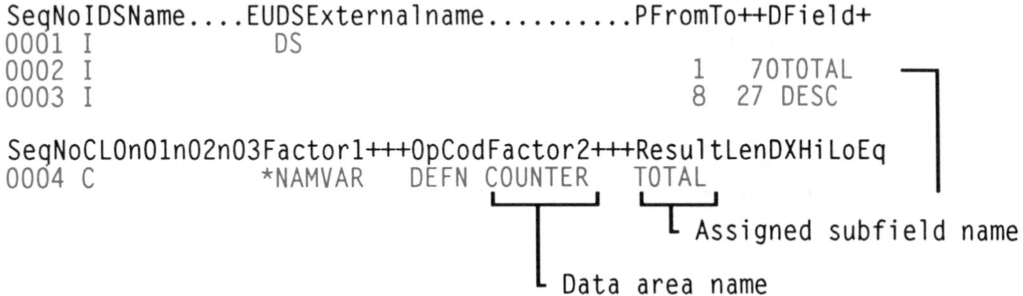

```
SeqNoIDSName....EUDSExternalname..........PFromTo++DField+
0001 I            DS
0002 I                                        1   70TOTAL
0003 I                                        8  27 DESC

SeqNoCLOn01n02n03Factor1+++OpCodFactor2+++ResultLenDXHiLoEq
0004 C            *NAMVAR   DEFN COUNTER   TOTAL
```


Figure 7-99b: Assign a Data Area to a Data Structure Subfield

In Figure 7-99b, the data structure subfield TOTAL (line 2) is assigned to the data area COUNTER (line 4).

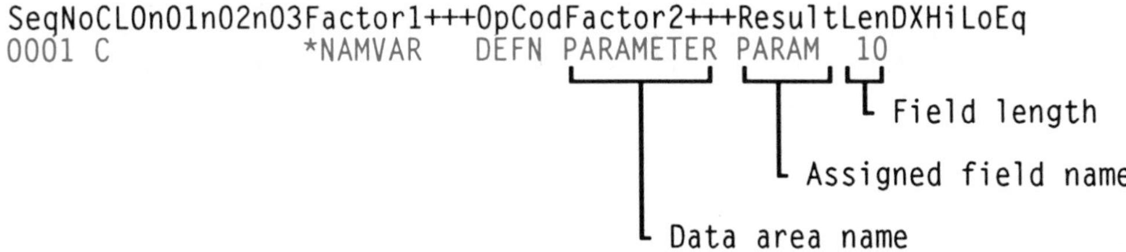

```
SeqNoCLOn01n02n03Factor1+++OpCodFactor2+++ResultLenDXHiLoEq
0001 C            *NAMVAR   DEFN PARAMETER PARAM   10
```


Figure 7-99c: Assign a Data Area to a Field

In Figure 7-99c, the field PARAM (line 1) is defined as a 10-character field and is assigned to the data area PARAMETER.

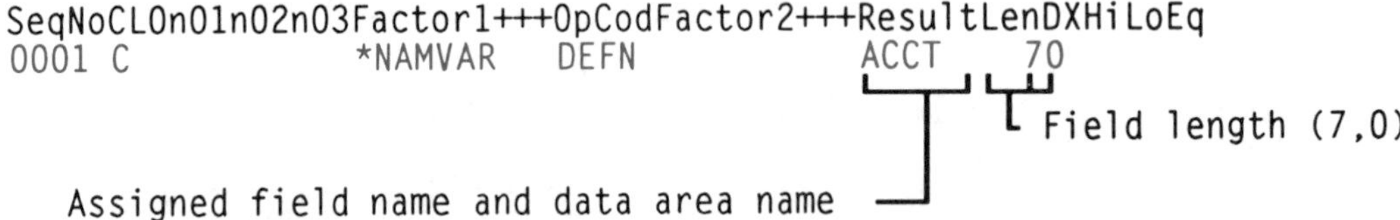

Figure 7-99d: Assign a Data Area to a Field of the Same Name

In Figure 7-99d, the field ACCT (line 1) is defined as a 7-digit numeric field and is assigned to the data area ACCT. When Factor 2 is omitted, the name of the data area is assumed to be the same as the Result field name.

The IN operation retrieves the data area named in Factor 2 and stores the data in the assigned field. See Figure 7-100. The Result field of the *NAMVAR DEFN operation is used as Factor 2 of the IN operation.

```
SeqNoCLOn01n02n03Factor1+++OpCodFactor2+++ResultLenDXHiLoEq
0001 C               *NAMVAR   DEFN PARAMETER PARAM  10
0002 C                         IN   PARAM
```

Figure 7-100: Retrieve the Data Area named PARAMETER

In Figure 7-100, the IN operation (line 2) retrieves the data area PARAMETER. The DEFN operation on line 1 assigns the field PARAM to the data area. When the IN operation is performed, the content of the data area PARAMETER is moved into the field PARAM.

The IN operation allows the data area to be locked for exclusive use by the program. Specifying *LOCK in Factor 1 of the IN operation causes the lock to occur. Once a data area is locked, no other user's application can retrieve or change the locked data area until the data area is written with the OUT operation or unlocked with the UNLCK operation. The Result field of the *NAMVAR DEFN operation is used as Factor 2 of the OUT operation. See Figure 7-101.

```
SeqNoIDSName....EUDSExternalname.........PFromTo++DField+
0001 IACCT         DS
0002 I                                        1   70NEXTCN
0003 I                                        8  130LASTUS

SeqNoCLOn01n02n03Factor1+++OpCodFactor2+++ResultLenDXHiLoEq
0004 C           *NAMVAR   DEFN ACCOUNTS  ACCT
0005 C           *LOCK     IN   ACCT
0006 C                     Z-ADDNEXTCN    CUST
0007 C                     ADD  1         NEXTCN
0008 C                     Z-ADDUDATE     LASTUS
0009 C                     OUT  ACCT
```

Figure 7-101: Retrieve, Lock and Update the Data Area ACCOUNTS

In Figure 7-101, the data area ACCOUNTS is assigned to the data structure ACCT (line 4). The *LOCK IN operation on line 5 retrieves and locks the data area. Lines 6, 7 and 8 manipulate the fields NEXTCN and LASTUS; then, the data area ACCOUNTS is written with the OUT operation on line 9.

The OUT operation writes the data area and releases the lock. The data area can remain locked after the OUT operation is performed by specifying *LOCK in Factor 1 of the OUT operation. The OUT operation can only be used on data areas that have been locked.

A second method for unlocking a locked data area is the UNLCK (unlock) operation. Factor 2 of the UNLCK operation can contain the name of the data area to be unlocked, or it can contain *NAMVAR, which unlocks all data areas locked by the program. Figure 7-102 illustrates the various types of access methods for data areas.

```
SeqNoIDSName....EUDSExternalname..........PFromTo++DField+
0001 IACCT         DS
0002 I                                       1   70NEXTCN
0003 I                                       8  130LASTUS
0004 I             DS
0005 I                                       1   70TOTAL
0006 I                                       8  27 DESC

SeqNoCLOn01n02n03Factor1+++OpCodFactor2+++ResultLenDXHiLoEq
0007 C           *NAMVAR   DEFN COUNTER   TOTAL
0008 C           *NAMVAR   DEFN ACCOUNTS  ACCT
0009 C           *NAMVAR   DEFN PARAM     PARAM  10
0010 C           *LOCK     IN   *NAMVAR
0011 C                     Z-ADDNEXTCN    CUST
0012 C                     Z-ADDUDATE     LASTUS
0013 C                     ADD  1         NEXTCN
0014 C                     ADD  1         TOTAL
0015 C                     MOVELPARAM     DESC
0016 C                     OUT  TOTAL
0017 C                     OUT  ACCT
0018 C                     UNLCKPARAM
```

Figure 7-102: Retrieve, Lock, Update and Unlock Several Data Areas

In Figure 7-102, all data areas defined in the program are retrieved and locked (line 10). Then the information stored in data areas COUNTER and ACCOUNTS is modified and the data areas are written and unlocked (line 16 and 17). Since, data area PARAMETER did not need to be updated (i.e., its information was only read), it is unlocked by the UNLCK operation on line 18.

Program Flexibility

Well-planned modular application programs will be very flexible. Program flexibility is the ability to adapt to changes in program requirements with little or no impact on the overall application.

Flexible programming techniques exhibit the following characteristics:

1. Structured programming constructs instead of indicators.
2. Soft coded constants, such as named constants or fields.
3. Function controlled logic instead of indicators.
4. Task processing in place of general purpose routines.

Structured programming constructs instead of indicators is a central part of modular programming. Structured operation codes provide a high level of readability and, therefore, greater flexibility than indicators. For example, it is much easier to control the logic of a program with an IF-THEN-ELSE operation than a series of indicators. See Figure 7-103a.

```
SeqNoCLOn01n02n03Factor1+++OpCodFactor2+++ResultLenDXHiLoEq
     C              AMOUNT    IFGT 0
     C              AMOUNT    ANDLE10000
     C                        Z-ADD30        TERM,1
     C                        Z-ADD60        TERM,2
     C                        Z-ADD90        TERM,3
     C                        MOVE 'PAST DUE'TERM,4
     C                        MOVE CSTNBR    BADEBT
     C                        WRITEPANEL01
     C                        ENDIF
```

Figure 7-103a: Structured construct controlled logic

```
SeqNoCLOn01n02n03Factor1+++OpCodFactor2+++ResultLenDXHiLoEq
     C                        SETOF                      56
     C              AMOUNT    COMP 0                   54
     C   54         AMOUNT    COMP 10000                 5656
     C      56                Z-ADD30        TERM,1
     C      56                Z-ADD60        TERM,2
     C      56                Z-ADD90        TERM,3
     C      56                MOVE 'PAST DUE'TERM,4
     C      56                MOVE CSTNBR    BADEBT
     C      56                WRITEPANEL01
```

Figure 7-103b: Indicator-controlled logic

Figure 7-104a illustrates the clarity of using structured operations. Figure 7-104b illustrates the inflexibility of using indicators. If the conditions change and additional testing is required, the number of indicators and, therefore, the complexity increases. However, if structured operations are used and additional testing is necessary, the clarity of the program module is maintained. For example, if an additional test for a due date is necessary, the logic would be altered.

```
SeqNoCLOn01n02n03Factor1+++OpCodFactor2+++ResultLenDXHiLoEq
     C                AMOUNT    IFGT 0
     C                AMOUNT    ANDLE10000
     C                DUEDAT    ANDLEPSTDUE
     C                          Z-ADD30        TERM,1
     C                          Z-ADD60        TERM,2
     C                          Z-ADD90        TERM,3
     C                          MOVE 'PAST DUE'TERM,4
     C                          MOVE CSTNBR    BADEBT
     C                          WRITEPANEL01
     C                          ENDIF
```

Figure 7-104a: Structured construct controlled logic

```
SeqNoCLOn01n02n03Factor1+++OpCodFactor2+++ResultLenDXHiLoEq
     C                          SETOF                     545658
     C                AMOUNT    COMP 0                    54
     C   54           AMOUNT    COMP 10000                  5858
     C             58DUEDAT     COMP PSTDUE                 5656
     C      56                  Z-ADD30        TERM,1
     C      56                  Z-ADD60        TERM,2
     C      56                  Z-ADD90        TERM,3
     C      56                  MOVE 'PAST DUE'TERM,4
     C      56                  MOVE CSTNBR    BADEBT
     C      56                  WRITEPANEL01
```

Figure 7-104b: Indicator-controlled logic

As can be seen in Figure 7-104a, only one line of code was added to the program listed in Figure 7-103. Figure 7-104b, however, required that one new line be added, two lines be changed and one new indicator added. These four modifications can increase complexity, reduce readability and flexibility.

Soft coded constants—the use of fields in place of literal values—solves a major problem in program maintenance. When a value that controls the program in some manner must be changed and a literal value is used, each and every occurrence of the literal has to be located and changed. If, instead, a field is initialized with the literal value, and used in place of the literal, when the value needs to be change, only the value in the field will have to be modified.

One example of this is a menu application in which the user is prompted for an option. The option typed into the system is interpreted by the program.

```
SeqNoCLOn01n02n03Factor1+++OpCodFactor2+++ResultLenDXHiLoEq
0001 C                     EXFMTMENU01
0002 C           1         CASEQOPTION    ORDERS
0003 C           2         CASEQOPTION    PRINT
0004 C           3         CASEQOPTION    INVOIC
0005 C           99        CASEQOPTION    ENDPGM
0006 C                     CAS            NOOPT
0007 C                     END
```

Figure 7-105: Programming with constants proves inflexible

In Figure 7-105, line 1 displays a prompt to the user, requesting a menu option. If the user types in the number 1, the subroutine ORDERS is called. If the user types in the number 2, the subroutine PRINT is called, and so on. While this is good structure and apparently modular, the program code is inflexible. Because the options are coded as constants, each time a new option is added or an existing option changes, the constant for the change will have to be located and changed.

By using a field in place of a literal value, new options are added more easily, and existing options can be enhanced without major program maintenance. This technique is illustrated in Figure 7-106.

```
SeqNoCLOn01n02n03Factor1+++OpCodFactor2+++ResultLenDXHiLoEq
0001 C                     EXFMTMENU01
0002 C           ORDENT    CASEQOPTION    ORDERS
0003 C           ORDPRT    CASEQOPTION    PRINT
0004 C           ORDINV    CASEQOPTION    INVOIC
0005 C           SIGNOF    CASEQOPTION    ENDPGM
0006 C                     CAS            NOOPT
0007 C                     END
      /SPACE
0008 CSR         *INZSR    BEGSR
0009 C                     Z-ADD1         ORDENT             Enter Orders
0010 C                     Z-ADD2         ORDPRT             Print Orders
0011 C                     Z-ADD3         ORDINV             Invoicing
0012 C                     Z-ADD99        SIGNOF             Sign Off
0013 CSR                   ENDSR
```

Figure 7-106: Soft coding constants proves flexible

In Figure 7-106, the *INZSR subroutine is used to initialize the fields that are used in place of literal values. Lines 1 to 5 test the options by comparing the value of the fields to what the user has typed.

If the value of an option needs to be changed, the initialization routine is the only area that needs to be changed. For example, to change the *Sign Off* option from 99 to 90 would require that only line 12 be modified.

Named Constants

Using named constants can provide similar flexibility in application control. The fields ORDENT, ORDPRT, ORDINV, and SIGNOF could easily be described as named constants (see Figure 7-107). Using named constants insures that all constant values are defined in one location in the program. However, named constants are somewhat more restrictive than fields in that their value cannot be changed after a program is compiled.

```
SeqNoI..............ConstantValue+++++++++C.........CONST+
     I              1                     C         ORDENT
     I              2                     C         ORDPRT
     I              3                     C         ORDINV
     I              99                    C         SIGNOF

SeqNoCL0n01n02n03Factor1+++OpCodFactor2+++ResultLenDXHiLoEq
     C                     EXFMTMENU01
     C           ORDENT    CASEQOPTION    ORDERS
     C           ORDPRT    CASEQOPTION    PRINT
     C           ORDINV    CASEQOPTION    INVOIC
     C           SIGNOF    CASEQOPTION    ENDPGM
     C                     CAS            NOOPT
     C                     END
```

Figure 7-107: Named Constants as Option Control Fields

Fields, on the other hand, allow their values to be modified at any time. This allows the value for the user-controlled options to be specified outside the program. They could be stored, for example, in a database file and retrieved when the program is started. This technique provides the ultimate flexibility.

Function Controlled Logic

Function controlled logic in place of indicators adds a high-level of readability and flexibility to program modules. Indicators are rigid, inflexible and hard to read.

Function controlled logic takes advantage of soft coded constants whenever possible to add a higher level of readability to the program module—for example, if a module must loop until a certain condition exists and perform selected tasks based on a user request. See Figure 7-108.

```
SeqNoCLOn01n02n03Factor1+++OpCodFactor2+++ResultLenDXHiLoEq
0001 C           *IN91     DOUEQ*ON
0002 C                     EXFMTPANEL01                    56
0003 C           *IN91     CASEQ*ON       ENDPGM
0004 C           *IN97     CASEQ*ON       SEARCH
0005 C           *IN98     CASEQ*ON       HELPTX
0006 C           *IN56     CASEQ*ON       TIMOUT
0007 C                     CAS            DFTRTN
0008 C                     END
0009 C                     ENDDO
```

Figure 7-108: Indicator-controlled logic with structured constructs

Figure 7-108 illustrates clear structure-based logic. Basically, the Do loop (lines 1 to 9) is performed until indicator 91 is on. A display file is sent to the workstation (line 2), and the program continues by calling sub-modules (subroutines) based on indicator settings.

While the function of a submodule is described by its name, the circumstance under which the submodule is performed is not. Although it is obvious that when indicator 97 is on, the sub-module SEARCH is called, how was indicator 97 set on? It was probably set on by the workstation operator pressing a function key. However, these type of guesswork often leads to errors and extended programming time.

Function controlled logic can improve programmer productivity by clarifying and simplifying the readability and flexibility of the program. See Figure 7-109.

```
SeqNoCLOn01n02n03Factor1+++OpCodFactor2+++ResultLenDXHiLoEq
     C           'EXIT'    DOUEQFUNCT
     C                     EXFMTPANEL01                    56
     C                     EXSR RTVFCT
     C           'EXIT'    CASEQFUNCT     ENDPGM
     C           'SEARCH'  CASEQFUNCT     SEARCH
     C           'HELP'    CASEQFUNCT     HELPTX
     C           'IOERR'   CASEQFUNCT     TIMOUT
     C                     CAS            DFTRTN
     C                     END
     C                     ENDDO
```

Figure 7-109: Function controlled logic

Taking this one step further, the module listed in Figure 7-109 could be easily converted to work with soft coded functions. The functions themselves would be stored in fields or named constants which would then be used in place of the literal values. See Figure 7-110.

```
SeqNoI..............ConstantValue+++++++++C.........CONST+
     I              'EXIT                 ' C         EXIT
     I              'SEARCH               ' C         SEARCH
     I              'HELP                 ' C         HELP
     I              'IOERR                ' C         IOERR

SeqNoCL0n01n02n03Factor1+++OpCodFactor2+++ResultLenDXHiLoEq
     C           EXIT      DOUEQFUNCT
     C                     EXFMTPANEL01
     C                     EXSR RTVFCT
     C           EXIT      CASEQFUNCT     ENDPGM
     C           SEARCH    CASEQFUNCT     SEARCH
     C           HELP      CASEQFUNCT     HELPTX
     C           IOERR     CASEQFUNCT     TIMOUT
     C                     CAS            DFTRTN
     C                     END
     C                     ENDDO
     C           ENDPGM    TAG
     C                     MOVE *ON       *INLR
     C                     RETRN
```

Figure 7-110: Soft coded function controlled logic

Function Key Programming

A predominant annoyance in flexible programming is interactive workstation device handling. Specifically, workstation function keys. Workstation function keys are keyboard keys that a workstation operator uses to request that a specific function be performed. Hence the name *Function Keys*.

There are three methods for detecting which function key was pressed:

1. Test a status code returned to the information data structure.
2. Test the status of an indicator assigned to the function key.
3. Test the status of the default RPG function key indicator.

The first method was the original method used when interactive workstation support was added to computer systems on which RPG was available. This technique is becoming more popular as it provides a way to move from indicators to function-based logic.

The second method, used in most RPGIII applications, sets on an indicator when the operator presses a function key. Indicators are assigned to function keys in the workstation device file. Normally, AS/400 *Data Description Specifications* (DDS) are used to build workstation display file formats. See Figure 7-111.

The third method was used in later implementations of RPGII with workstation support. RPG does not, however, assign default indicators to all function keys. This tends to create inconsistency and confusion in the program and, therefore, this technique is not often used in RPGIII applications

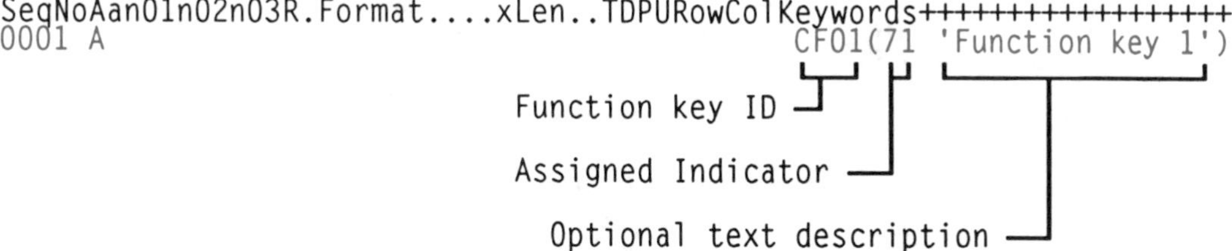

Figure 7-111: Indicator Assignment to Function Keys

Figure 7-111 illustrates how an indicator is assigned to a function key. The DDS keyword CF01 represents function key 1. The letters CF stand for *Command Function*. The 01 identifies the function key being defined. Indicator 71 is assigned to the function key. A text description is used to document the indicator usage. When the workstation operator presses function key 1, indicator 71 will be set on in the RPG program.

A workstation display file record format or *panel* is also defined using DDS. For example, in a customer inquiry application the following basic components are needed in a panel defined with DDS:

1. A customer number and its prompt text.
2. An EXIT function key.
3. A HELP function key.

These items are specified in the workstation file DDS illustrated in Figure 7-112.

```
SeqNoAan01n02n03R.Format....xLen..TDPURowColKeywords..................
     A                                      CF01(71 'Alternate Help')
     A                                      CF03(73 'Exit request')
     A                                      CF12(82 'Cancel')
     A                                      HELP(98 'Help key')
     A                                      VLDCMDKEY(70 'Enter')
     A          R PANEL1                    TEXT('Customer Inquiry')
     A                                      OVERLAY
     A                                  1  2'CUSTINQ'
     A                                  1 27'Customer Inquiry'
     A                                  3  5'Customer:'
     A            ACTNBR         5Y 0B   + 2TEXT('Account Number')
     A                                 22  3'F3=Exit  HELP=Help'
     A          R PANEL2                    TEXT('Customer Display')
     A                                  1  2'CUSTDISP'
     A                                  1 27'Customer Inquiry Display'
     A                                  3  5'Customer:'
     A            ACTNBR         5S 00   + 2
     A                                  4  5'Address:'
     A            CSTADR        30    0  + 2
     A                                  5  5'City:'
     A            CSTCTY        25       + 2
     A                                 20  2'F3=Exit  HELP=Help'
     A          R PANEL                     TEXT('Inquiry Error')
     A                                  4 12'************************'
     A                                  4 12'** Customer Not Found **'
     A                                  4 12'************************'
```

Figure 7-112: Customer Inquiry Display Panels

Figure 7-112 illustrates three indicators assigned to three function keys. Indicator 71 is assigned to function key 1 (line 1), indicator 73 is assigned to function key 3 (line 2), indicator 82 is assigned to function key 12 (line 3) and indicator 98 is assigned to the HELP key (line 4). Lines 6 to 12 define a prompt and an input field.

Function key 1 will be used as an alternative HELP key for workstation keyboards that do not have a HELP key.

Function key 3 will be used as the EXIT key. When the user presses F3, indicator 73 will be set on, and the program should react to it by exiting the program.

The HELP function key will be the normal HELP request key. When the HELP key is pressed, indicator 98 will be set on. The program should react to it by displaying the help text for the application.

When the workstation display panel listed in Figure 7-112 is created and written to the workstation device by an RPG program, it will appear as shown in Figure 7-113.

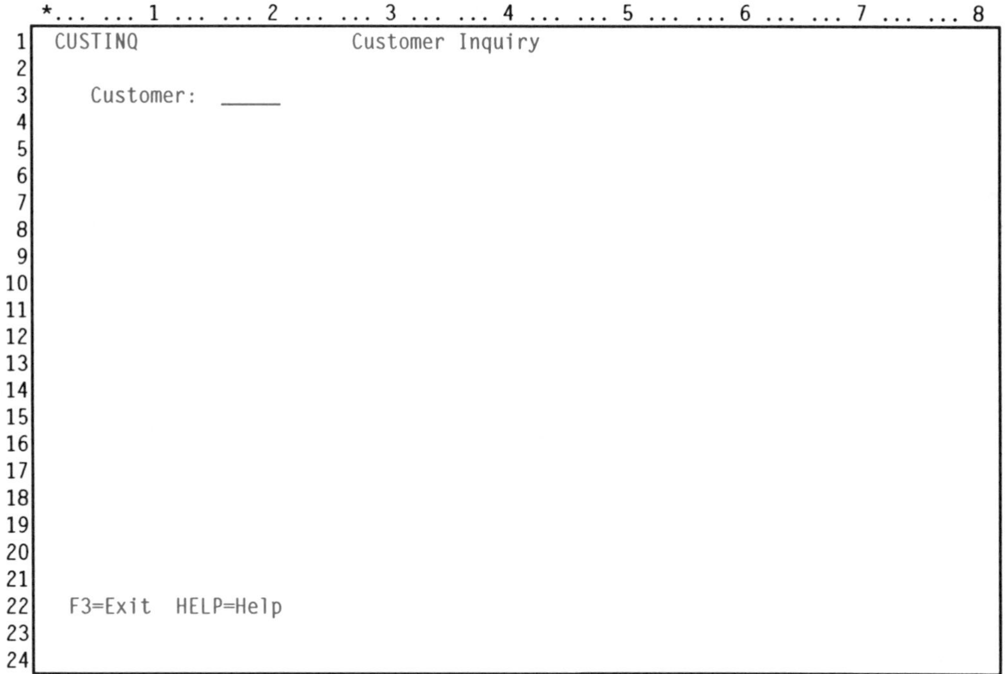

Figure 7-113: Workstation Display Panel

The RPG source code that will display this panel is listed in Figure 7-114.

```
SeqNoFFileNameIPE.E....RLEN...K.OV....EDevice+RecNbrKOptionEntry+
0001 FCUSTDISPCF  E                    WORKSTN
0002 FCUSTMASTIF  E           K        DISK

SeqNoI..............ConstantValue+++++++++C.........CONST+
0003 I              'EXIT               ' C         EXIT
0004 I              'SEARCH             ' C         SEARCH
0005 I              'HELP               ' C         HELP
0006 I              'ERROR              ' C         ERROR
0007 I              'ENTER              ' C         ENTER
0008 I              'DISPLAY CUST       ' C         DSPCST

SeqNoCL0n01n02n03Factor1+++OpCodFactor2+++ResultLenDXHiLoEq
0009  /COPY QRPGSRC,STDDCL
0010 C                     MOVEL*BLANKS   FUNCT  20
0011 C           EXIT      DOUEQFUNCT
0012 C                     EXFMTPANEL1
0013 C                     EXSR RTVFCT
0014 C           ENTER     CASEQFUNCT     INQRY
0015 C           HELP      CASEQFUNCT     HELPTX
0016 C                     END
0017 C           DSPCUST   IFEQ FUNCT
0018 C                     EXFMTPANEL2
0019 C                     EXSR RTVFCT
0020 C                     ENDIF
0021 C           ERROR     IFEQ FUNCT
0022 C                     WRITEPANEL3
0023 C                     ENDIF
0024 C                     ENDDO
0025 C           ENDPGM    TAG
0026 C                     MOVE *ON       *INLR
```

Continued on the following page

Figure 7-114: Example Customer Inquiry Program (1 of 2)

continued from the preceding page

```
SeqNoCLRN01N02N03Factor1+++OpCodFactor2+++ResultLenDXHILOEQ
0027 CSR           INQRY     BEGSR
0028 C             ACTNBR    CHAINCUSTREC              54
0029 C                       MOVE *IN54     NOTFND
0020 C             NOTFND    IFEQ *ON
0031 C                       MOVELERROR     FUNCT     P
0032 C                       ELSE
0033 C                       MOVELDSPCST    FUNCT     P
0034 C                       ENDIF
0035 CSR           ENDINQ    ENDSR

0036 CSR           RTVFCT    BEGSR
0037  /COPY QRPGSRC,RTVFCT
0038 CSR           ENDFCT    ENDSR
```

Figure 7-114: Example Customer Inquiry Program (2 of 2)

In Figure 7-114, the user is prompted for a customer number (line 12). The display format PANEL1 is written to the workstation file CUSTDISP by the EXFMT operation. When the user types a customer number, then presses ENTER or a function key, the display format PANEL1 will be read by the EXFMT operation.

Next, the subroutine RTVFCT is performed (line 13) to determine which function key, if any was pressed. Figure 7-117 on page 380 contains a list of the array FCT and subroutine RTVFCT.

If no function key was pressed, the ENTER key is assumed and the subroutine INQRY is performed. The subroutine INQRY validates and retrieves the customer master record. If the customer exists, display format PANEL2 is written to the workstation by the EXFMT operation on line 18. (See Figure 7-115.) If the customer does not exist, or is allocated to another program, display format PANEL3 is written to the workstation with the WRITE operation on line 22. This informs the user that there is a problem with the customer number. (See Figure 7-116.)

```
*... ... 1 ... ... 2 ... ... 3 ... ... 4 ... ... 5 ... ... 6 ... ... 7 ... ... 8
 PANEL2                          Customer Inquiry

     Customer:  5381
     Address:   12 Artemis Drive
     City:      Geneva
















   F3=Exit  HELP=Help


```

Figure 7-115: Found Customer Record

```
*... ... 1 ... ... 2 ... ... 3 ... ... 4 ... ... 5 ... ... 6 ... ... 7 ... ... 8
 PANEL3                       Customer Inquiry

    Customer:  _____
            ************************
            ** Customer Not Found **
            ************************















  F3=Exit  HELP=Help


```

Figure 7-116: Customer Not Found Error Display

Soft Coded Function Keys

A primary characteristic of modular programming is flexible program modules. Function keys can hinder flexible programming when the indicator assigned to the function key is interpreted as an action instead of a function key. This situation can be overcome by soft coding the function key action. See Figure 7-117.

```
SeqNoE....FromfileTofile..ArrnamEPRDim+LenPDAAltnamLenPDA
0001 E                    FCT     5  30 10

SeqNoCLOn01n02n03Factor1+++OpCodFactor2+++ResultLenDXHiLoEq
0002 CSR          RTVFCT    BEGSR
0003 C            *IN70     IFEQ *ON
0004 C                      MOVE *OFF      *IN70
0005 C                      ELSE
0006 C                      MOVE *ON       *IN70
0007 C                      ENDIF

0008 C                      Z-ADD70        X
0009 C            X         DOWLT99
0010 C            *IN,X     ANDEQ*OFF
0011 C                      ADD  1         X
0012 C                      ADD  1         Y
0013 C                      ENDDO

0014 C            *IN,X     IFEQ *ON
0015 C                      MOVELFCT,Y     FUNCT
0016 C                      ELSE
0017 C                      MOVEL*BLANK    FUNCT
0018 C                      ENDIF
0019 CSR          ENDFCT    ENDSR
**
ENTER     HELP                EXIT

                    PREVIOUS


                   HELP
```

Figure 7-117: Subroutine to Retrieve Function Key Action

Figure 7-117 illustrates the components of the RTVFCT (retrieve function key action) subroutine. The array FCT (line 1) contains the function key actions that will be returned when a function key is pressed. Lines 20 to 26 contain the array data for this compile-time array.

Lines 3 to 7 of the subroutine RTVFCT reverse the status of the indicator assigned to the ENTER key. This is necessary since DDS does not provide a direct method for detecting when ENTER is pressed.

Lines 8 to 13 search through the indicator array for the first indicator that is on. If indicator 70 is on, then the ENTER key was pressed, if indicator 71 is on then function key 1 was pressed, if indicator 73 is on then function key 3 was pressed, etc.

After determining which function key was pressed, the function key action is moved into the field FUNCT (line 15). The action is retrieved from the array FCT. The element of the array FCT corresponds to the function key.

By soft coding the function key action, that is, by storing the actions in an array, they can be easily modified without changing the program code or logic. Only the compile-time array will need to be changed. For example, to allow function key 24 to cause a program exit, the 25th element of the array FCT would be set to 'EXIT'.

The 25th element is used because the action for the <Enter> key action uses array element 1, so each function key is offset by 1.

Modular programming requires a complex thought process. However, modular programming can become easy with practice. Well thought out modular applications can result in flexible program modules that are easy to read and easy to maintain. Soft coding the actions of function keys simplifies the programming process by avoiding the reliance of bound or hard-coded actions to function keys.

Chapter 8

File Processing

The modern RPG language supports several types of file access:

1. Primary/secondary processing via the RPG cycle.
2. Demand file processing.
3. Record address file (ADDROUT) processing.
4. Special file processing.
5. Prerun time-table and array processing.
6. Full procedural processing.

This section discusses full procedural file processing.

Full Procedural File Processing

Full procedural files are files in which input and output operations to the file are controlled completely by RPG operation codes. Contrasted with cycle-bound files, where the RPG cycle controls most of the input and output processing.

Full procedural files are defined by placing the letter F into column 16 of the File Description specification. Figure 8-118 that follows illustrates a typical declaration for a full procedural file.

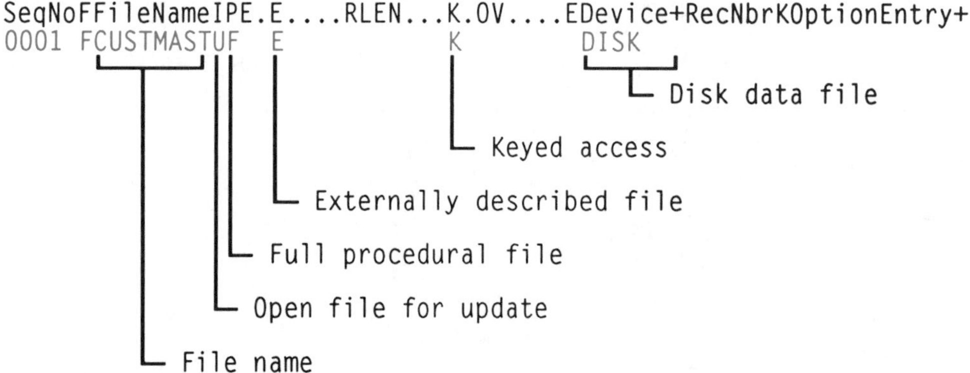

Figure 8-118: File Description Specification for a Full Procedural File

Both program described and externally described database files can be declared as full procedural. Full procedural file processing is performed by several RPG operation codes. For example, to read a record from a file, the READ operation is used; to write a new record to a file, the WRITE operation is used and so on. Figure 8-119 contains a list of RPG operation codes that can be used with full procedural files.

OpCode	Description
ACQ	Acquire program device.
CHAIN	Random file access by index.
COMIT	Commitment control, commit group.
DELET	Delete record of a file.
EXCPT	Write program defined or externally described record format.
EXFMT	Write then read workstation device.
FEOD	Reset the file "cursor," free locked records.
KFLD	Define key field of a key list.
KLIST	Define key list.
OPEN	Open file.
POST	Retrieve and post device-specific information to a data structure.
READ	Read record.
READC	Read next changed subfile record.
READE	Read next data file record with matching index.
READP	Read previous data file record.
REDPE	Read previous data file record with matching index.
REL	Release acquired program device.
ROLBK	Commitment control, roll back group.
SETGT	Set file cursor greater than the specified index.
SETLL	Set file cursor less than the specified index.
UPDAT	Update record.
WRITE	Write record.

Figure 8-119: File Operation Codes

In discussing file processing, several terms will be used. Figure 8-120 contains a brief glossary of file terminology.

AS/400 Database File Terminology

Access path: An object used to access data in a file in a specific sequence.

Cross-Reference: A set of files containing file/field where and how used information.

Library:: A directory of a group of related and unrelated objects that have been placed into a specific context.

Field: In a record, one or more bytes of information that make up a single fact.

File: A directory of members and formats. Typically referred to as *physical, logical or join-logical files*. *File* is a generic term for database file.

Member: The entity within a database file that contains the actual data. A set of fields and records.

Index: See access path.

Join-logical file: A subset of fields and records from two or more files.

Key: See access path.

Key field: A field in a physical or logical file used to determine the order of entries in an access path.

Logical file: A subset of fields and records from a file.

Physical file: A data file containing records of real data.

Record: A horizontal line of data in a physical or logical file.

Random access: A method of processing a file randomly by its access path through its key fields.

View: A subset of fields and records from a file.

Figure 8-120: AS/400 Database File Terminology

Physical Files

Full procedural file processing provides access to disk files and workstation files. Disk files contain data and are referred to as data files or database files.

Database files are files that have been defined to the operation systems by the data definition services of the operation system. This allows RPG programs to access the file with operating systems services.

Database files consist of a group of related data records. Data records consist of one or more fields. Database files are defined with a data definition language, such as SQL (which is available on most computer systems), and Data Description Specifications (DDS), which is available on the IBM System/38 and AS/400 for data definition. SQL will be covered later in this chapter.

To define a file using DDS, source code describing the file must be created. File definition source is created in much the same way as an RPG source program; a source code editor is used to create data definition source code. For example, a file named CUSTMAST consisting of five fields and a key field can be created with the DDS source code listed in Figure 8-121.

```
SeqNoAan01n02n03R.Format++++.Len++TDPURowColKeywords+++++++++++++++++
0001 A          R CUSTREC                   TEXT('Customer file')
0002 A            ACTNBR         5P 0       TEXT('Account Number')
0003 A            CSTNAM        30          TEXT('Customer Name')
0004 A            CSTADR        30          TEXT('Street Address')
0005 A            CSTCTY        20          TEXT('City')
0006 A            CSTSTE         2          TEXT('State')
0007 A          K ACTNBR
```

Figure 8-121: Physical File DDS Source Code to Define the File CUSTMAST

In Figure 8-121, line 1 specifies the name CUSTREC for the record format of the file. Lines 2 to 6 define each field of the file. Line 7 specifies that the field ACTNBR (account number) is used as a key field.

Similar to program source code, data definition source code must be processed by the operating systems before it can be used by RPG. On the IBM System/38 and AS/400, DDS is compiled to create what is called a *File* or *File Object*.

When the DDS listed in Figure 8-121 is processed, a file consisting of five fields will be created. Only the file description is created; data will be added later.

Assume that five records are added to the file and that the records are accessible by RPG or other high-level languages. Figure 8-122 illustrates the file CUSTMAST after five records have been added.

ACTNBR	CSTNBR	CSTADDR	CSTCTY	CSTSTE
01207	Maui Pineapple	Kauai Blvd.	Maui	HI
05320	Perlman-Rocque	103rd Street	Lemont	IL
05340	Champion Parts	22nd Street	Oak Brook	IL
05381	Luna Spacecraft	12 Artemis Drive	Geneva	IL

Key field

Figure 8-122: CUSTMAST Database File

Figure 8-122 illustrates the file CUSTMAST after five records have been added. The field ACTNBR (account number) is the key field for the file. Therefore, when a file is accessed, it is arranged by the account number. Additionally, a record can be randomly accessed by its key field value. For example, to retrieve the record for `Luna Spacecraft`, the key field ACTNBR would be set equal to 5381.

```
SeqNoFFileNameIPE.E....RLEN...K.OV....EDevice+RecNbrKOptionEntry+
0001 FCUSTMASTIF  E           K        DISK

SeqNoCLOn01n02n03Factor1+++OpCodFactor2+++ResultLenDXHiLoEq
0002 C           *LIKE     DEFN ACTNBR    ACTKEY
0003 C           ACCT      KLIST
0004 C                     KFLD           ACTKEY
0005 C                     Z-ADD5381      ACTKEY
0006 C           ACCT      CHAINCUSTREC                  54
0007 C                     MOVE *IN54     NOTFND
0008 C                     .
0009 C                     . (the program continues)
0010 C                     .
```

Figure 8-123: Random Access of CUSTMAST with One Key Field

Figure 8-123 illustrates random file access using a key list. Since the file CUSTMAST has only one key field, a key list is optional. The field ACTKEY could have been used in Factor 1 of line 6, producing the same results. When a file's index is made up of multiple key fields, however, a key list is the easiest method to access its records.

Line 1 defines CUSTMAST as an externally described, full procedural, keyed file.

Line 2 defines the ACTKEY field with the same attributes as the ACTNBR field. ACTNBR is defined in the CUSTMAST file.

Line 3 defines the ACCT keylist, which is used to access the file randomly by key.

Line 4 defines the sole key field ACTKEY.

Line 5 initializes the ACTKEY field with the value of the key to be retrieved.

Line 6 randomly accesses the CUSTMAST file using the key list ACCT. If a record exists with a key that matches the key list specified in Factor 1, processing continues. If a record with a matching key does not exist, indicator 54 will be set on.

Multiple Key Fields

Sometimes more than one key field is necessary for file access. For example, if the customer master file listed in Figure 8-121 required an access path by CSTSTE (state) and ACTNBR (account number), then two key fields are necessary. See Figure 8-124.

```
SeqNoAan01n02n03R.Format++++.Len++TDPURowColKeywords+++++++++++++++++
0001 A            R CUSTREC                 TEXT('Customer file')
0002 A              ACTNBR         5P 0     TEXT('Account Number')
0003 A              CSTNAM        30        TEXT('Customer Name')
0004 A              CSTADR        30        TEXT('Street Address')
0005 A              CSTCTY        20        TEXT('City')
0006 A              CSTSTE         2        TEXT('State')
0007 A            K CSTSTE
0008 A            K ACTNBR
```

Figure 8-124: CUSTMAST with Two Key Fields

Line 7 contains the primary key field, line 8 contains the secondary key field. When records from this file are retrieved, they will be ordered by state, then by account number within state. See Figure 8-125.

ACTNBR	CSTNBR	CSTADDR	CSTCTY	CSTSTE
01207	Maui Pineapple	Kauai Blvd.	Maui	HI
05320	Perlman-Rocque	103rd Street	Lemont	IL
05340	Champion Parts	22nd Street	Oak Brook	IL
05381	Luna Spacecraft	12 Artemis Drive	Geneva	IL

Secondary Keyfield　　Primary keyfield

Figure 8-125: CUSTMAST Arranged by Key Fields

When the file CUSTMAST is processed, both key fields can be used to access the file. For example, to retrieve the record for `Perlman-Rocque`, the primary key field must be set to `'IL'` and the secondary key field must be set to `05320`. See Figure 8-126

```
SeqNoFFileNameIPE.E....RLEN...K.OV....EDevice+RecNbrKOptionEntry+++
0001 FCUSTMASTIF  E           K        DISK

SeqNoF............ExternFmt+..................RecNbrKKeywrdEntry+EX
0002 F             CUSTMAST                              KRENAMECUSTOMER

SeqNoCLOn01n02n03Factor1+++OpCodFactor2+++ResultLenDXHiLoEq
0003 C              *LIKE     DEFN CSTSTE    ST
0004 C              *LIKE     DEFN ACTNBR    ACTKEY
0005 C              ACCT      KLIST
0006 C                        KFLD           ST
0007 C                        KFLD           ACTKEY
0008 C                        Z-ADD5320      ACTKEY
0009 C                        MOVEL'IL'      ST
0010 C              ACCT      CHAINCUSTMAST               54
0011 C                        MOVE *IN54     NOTFND
0012 C                        .
0013 C                        . (the program continues)
0014 C                        .
```

Figure 8-126: Random Access of CUSTMAST by Two Key Fields

The program listed in Figure 8-126 illustrates random file access using two key fields. A key list is the preferred method for accessing files by key when multiple key fields exist for a file.

When multiple key fields exist, the number of key fields on a key list can be less than or equal to the number of key fields that make up the access path. When the number of key fields of a key list is less than the number of key fields for the file, that key list is called a *partial key list*.

Partial key lists are useful when non-unique primary keys exist in the file. For example, in the file CUSTMAST, three records exist for the state of Illinois. If the RPG program needs to process all records for the state of Illinois, a partial key list can be used to position the file to the first record with CSTSTE equal to `'IL'`, then read all records where CSTSTE equals `'IL'`. See Figure 8-127.

```
SeqNoFFileNameIPE.E....RLEN...K.OV....EDevice+RecNbrKOptionEntry+
0001 FCUSTMASTIF  E           K        DISK

SeqNoCL0n01n02n03Factor1+++OpCodFactor2+++ResultLenDXHiLoEq
0004 C           *LIKE     DEFN CSTSTE    ST
0005 C           STATE     KLIST
0006 C                     KFLD           ST
0007 C                     MOVEL'IL'      ST
0008 C           STATE     CHAINCUSTREC              54
0009 C                     MOVE *IN54     NOTFND  1
0010 C           NOTFND    DOWEQ*OFF
0011 C                     EXSR PRINT
0012 C           STATE     READECUSTREC                  58
0013 C                     MOVE *IN58     NOTFND
0014 C                     ENDDO
0015 C*    the program continues...
```

Figure 8-127: Random Access of CUSTMAST by Partial Key List

In Figure 8-127, the partial key list STATE (line 5) is used to access records in the file CUSTMAST. The access path for CUSTMAST consists of two key fields; CSTSTE and ACTNBR. The key list STATE is made up of the single key field ST. This provides file access by only the CSTSTE key field.

Line 4 defines the field ST with the same attributes as the field CSTSTE (the primary key field for the file CUSTMAST). Line 5 defines the key list STATE with one key field ST (line 6). Since no other key fields are specified, the key list becomes a partial key list.

Line 7 sets the field ST equal to 'IL'. This sets the value of the key list, which is used later to access the file. Line 8 chains to the file using the key list STATE. Since a partial key list is used, if records with duplicate keys exist, the first record in the file whose key matches the key list is retrieved.

Lines 10 to 14 read all records in the file whose key equals that of the key list. Line 12 retrieves the next record whose key equals the value of the partial key list STATE. When no more records exist that match the key list, resulting indicator 3 (indicator 58) is set on.

Partial key file processing is common in the modern RPG language. For example, in a manufacturing application a product structure file typically contains two key fields; the item number and the sub-item number.

When an item is manufactured, it is assembled into a "finished good" using sub-items. A product structure file contains the finished goods assembly. Figure 8-128 contains an illustration of a typical product structure file.

ITMNBR	SUBITM
101	127
101	501
101	602
201	127
201	333
201	402
201	602
450	101
450	333

Figure 8-128: Example Product Structure File

The ITMNBR field is the primary key; the SUBITM field is the secondary key. In order to process an item, a partial key list is used. See Figure 8-129.

```
SeqNoFFileNameIPE.E....RLEN...K.OV....EDevice+RecNbrKOptionEntry+
0001 FPRODSTRCIF  E              K        DISK

SeqNoCLOn01n02n03Factor1+++OpCodFactor2+++ResultLenDXHiLoEq
0004 C            PRIMRY    KLIST
0005 C                      KFLD           ITEM
0006 C                      Z-ADD201       ITEM
0007 C            PRIMRY    CHAINPRODUCTS                54
0008 C                      MOVE *IN54     NOTFND  1
0009 C            NOTFND    DOWEQ*OFF
0010 C                      EXSR PRINT
0011 C            PRIMRY    READEPRODUCTS                  58
0012 C                      MOVE *IN58     NOTFND
0013 C                      ENDDO
0014 C                      .
0015 C                      . (the program continues)
0016 C                      .
```

Figure 8-129: Sequential Keyed Access of a Product Structure File

Figure 8-129 processes the file PRODSTRC. Item number 201 is moved into the key list PRIMRY (line 6). That key list is used to retrieve the first record (sub-item 127) in the product structure file for item 201 (line 7). The Do while loop (lines 9 to 13) processes the remainder of the product structure with the READE operation.

Logical Files

Sometimes it is necessary to process a portion or *subset* of a data file. A *logical file* can be used to create a subset of the file. A logical file is a view of a physical file. It can contain some or all of the fields and records of the physical file. Additionally, an access path can be specified for the logical file.

Logical files do not contain data; they are vehicles through which data from physical files is supplied to an application program. Application programs treat both physical and logical files exactly the same.

As mentioned, logical files represent a subset of a physical file. For example, if an application requires only two fields of a five-field physical file, a logical file can be created to present only those two fields to the program. See Figure 8-130.

ACTNBR	CSTNBR	CSTADDR	CSTCTY	CSTSTE
01207	Maui Pineapple	Kauai Blvd.	Maui	HI
05320	Perlman-Rocque	103rd Street	Lemont	IL
05340	Champion Parts	22nd Street	Oak Brook	IL
05381	Luna Spacecraft	12 Artemis Drive	Geneva	IL

ACTNBR	CSTCTY
05381	Geneva
01207	Maui
05320	Lemont
05340	Oak Brook

Figure 8-130: Mapping of a Physical File to a Logical File

Logical files are created with DDS source in the same manner as a physical file. Logical file DDS, however, contains only the fields it needs for its subset. For example, the DDS necessary to create the logical file illustrated in Figure 8-130 is featured in Figure 8-131.

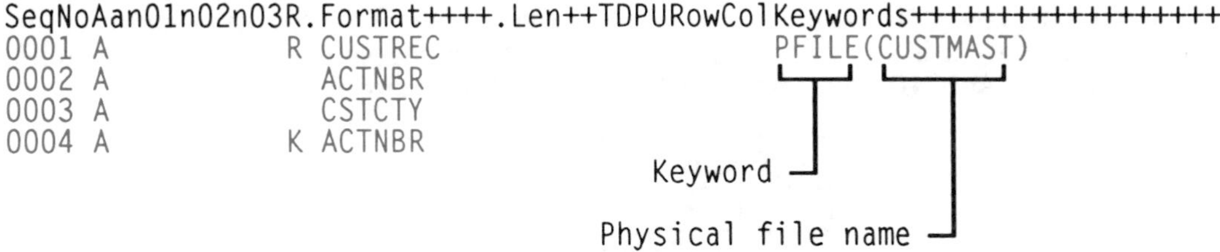

```
SeqNoAan01n02n03R.Format++++.Len++TDPURowColKeywords+++++++++++++++++
0001 A              R CUSTREC                        PFILE(CUSTMAST)
0002 A                ACTNBR
0003 A                CSTCTY
0004 A              K ACTNBR
```


Figure 8-131: Logical File DDS

Line 1, in Figure 8-131, defines the record format name for the logical file and the physical file on which the logical will be based; the keyword PFILE identifies this physical file.

Lines 2 and 3 identify the fields that will be included in the logical file. The field attributes (type, length, etc.) do not need to be specified; the attributes of the fields in the physical file are carried over to the logical file. The field attributes can, however, be overridden in the logical file.

Line 4 defines the key field that is used as the access path for the logical file. If the key field of the logical file is the same as that of the physical file, or some other logical file, the access path is shared. When an access path is shared, only one copy of the access path exists. This saves time when the access path is built and improves performance when records are added to the file.

The DDS listed in Figure 8-131 is for a logical file that contains a subset of fields of the physical file. If a subset of records is required, select/omit specifications can be added to the DDS for the logical file. Figure 8-132 contains a listing of DDS for a typical logical file with select/omit statements. Although both SELECT and OMIT operations are supported, traditionally only SELECT statements are used.

```
SeqNoAan01n02n03R.Format++++.Len++TDPURowColKeywords+++++++++++++++++
0001 A                                      DYNSLT
0002 A          R CUSTREC                   PFILE(CUSTMAST)
0003 A            ACTNBR
0004 A            CSTCTY
0005 A          K ACTNBR
0006 A          S ACTNBR                    COMP(GT 5000)
```

Figure 8-132: Logical File DDS with Select/Omit

Line 1 specifies that the select/omit specifications are dynamic—that is, the select/omit is not combined with the access path but is performed by the operating system as the records are read by a high-level language.

Line 6 contains the select/omit specification. The field ACTNBR must be greater than 5000 for the record to be included in this logical file. The resulting view of the physical file's data is shown in Figure 8-133. Note that account number 1207 is not included as its ACTNBR does not match the select/omit criteria.

ACTNBR	CSTCTY
05381	Geneva
05320	Lemont
05340	Oak Brook

Figure 8-133: Subset of Fields and Records for a Logical File

Join-Logical Files

AS/400 join-logical files are similar to logical files in that they provide a subset of a file. Join-logical files, however, can represent a subset of two or more physical files.

The topic of relational database and join-logical files has filled several volumes. In this section the equi-join file will be discussed.

An equi-join file is a join-logical file that joins two or more files by a common value. For example, an inventory file consisting of part number, quantity on-hand and part description, and a customer order history file consisting of customer number, part number and quantity ordered can be joined by part number forming a join-logical view of the two files.

When files are joined, a single join-record is created. The join-record can contain any or all of the fields from the files being joined. Figure 8-134 contains the DDS source necessary to perform a simple join over two physical files. Figure 8-135 illustrates sample data in the two physical files, as well the join view of the data.

```
SeqNoAAn01n02n03T.Name++++++RLen++TDcBRowColKeywords++++++++++++++++++
       *** Physical file: INVMAST
     A          R INVENTRY
     A            PARTNO         5P 0        COLHDG('Part' 'Number')
     A            QTYOH          7P 0        COLHDG('Qty' 'On' 'Hand')
     A            DESC          50A          COLHDG('Part' 'Desc.')
```

Figure 8-134a: DDS of Primary Physical File

```
SeqNoAAn01n02n03T.Name++++++RLen++TDcBRowColKeywords++++++++++++++++++
       *** Physical file: ORDHIST
     A          R HISTREC
     A            CUSTNO         5P 0        COLHDG('Part' 'Number')
     A            PARTNO    R                REFFLD(PARTNO INVMAST)
     A            QTYORD    R                REFFLD(QTYOH  INVMAST)
     A                                       COLHDG('Qty' 'Ordered')
```

Figure 8-134b: DDS of Second Physical File

```
SeqNoAAn01n02n03T.Name++++++RLen++TDcBRowColKeywords++++++++++++++++++
      *** Join-Logical file: INVORDHST
     A                                      JDFTVAL
     A          R INORHIST                  JFILE(INVMAST ORDHIST)
     A          J                           JOIN(1 2)
     A                                      JFLD(PART PART)
     A            PARTNO                    JREF(1)
     A            CUSTNO                    JREF(2)
     A            QTYORD                    JREF(2)
     A            DESC                      JREF(1)
     A          K PARTNO
```

Figure 8-134c: DDS of Join Logical View

Inventory File (INVMAST)

PART	QTYOH	DESC
100	5000	VGA Display
200	6	Hi-gain antennas
300	1	OS/2 Applications

Customer Order History (ORDHIST)

CUST	PART	QTYORD
1207	100	50
5340	100	1000
5381	200	1
5382	200	1

Resulting Join-Logical File: INVORDHST (File INVMAST Joined to ORDHIST)

PART	CUST	QTYORD	DESC
100	1207	50	VGA Display
100	5340	1000	VGA Display
200	5381	1	Hi-gain antennas
200	5382	1	Hi-gain antennas

Figure 8-135: Join-Logical View

File Access

File access within RPG programs is consistent with each type of file. All RPG data file operation codes function identically on physical, logical and join-logical files. The only exception to this is when a file has been defined to the operating system as read-only, in this situation, output operations are not allowed.

When a file is defined to a program as a keyed file (i.e., the letter K is specified in column 31 of the File Description specification), RPG processes the file by the file's access path. When a file is defined as a sequential file (i.e., column 31 contains a blank), RPG processes the file's records in the order in which they appear in the file.

When a file is defined as a keyed file to the RPG program, the operations that retrieve records from a file can access those records randomly through the access path. With some operations, the record's data is copied to the input (buffer) area for the file while others simply reposition the file cursor. The table featured in Figure 8-136 illustrates the effect of the file operation codes on a data file when the operation is successful.

Read Equal Key Anomaly

The READE (Read Next Record with Equal Key) and REDPE (Read Prior Record with Equal Key) operations can cause record-lock contention under the following conditions:

When the operation reads a record, the record is reviewed for the equal-key condition. If the key value for the record does not match the value in Factor 1, the record is released, and data is never copied to the input (buffer) area.

During the review of the key value for the record, the record is locked based on the conditions specified for the file on the File Description specification.

If the record is already locked by another application, the READE or REDPE operation will wait for the record to be released for a time specified by the file's description external to RPG.

When the wait-time expires, the RPG exception/error handling routine will receive control unless resulting indicator 2 is specified. If resulting indicator 2 is specified, it will be set on.

The READE and REDPE operations read a record and compare the key value of the record to Factor 1 in a manner similar to that of a READ or READP operation followed by a COMP or IFEQ operation. This can cause a long wait for the record that the READE or REDPE operation is attempting to retrieve.

File Operation Code Effects

OpCode	Data Returned	Record Status	Cursor Positioning
CHAIN	Yes	Locked	To record
DELET	No	Deleted	To no record
EXCPT	No	Released	To same record
FEOD	No	Released	To no record
OPEN	No	None	Beginning of file
READ	Yes	Locked	To record
READE	Yes	Locked	To record
READP	Yes	Locked	To record
REDPE	Yes	Locked	To record
SETGT	No	Released	After record
SETLL	No	Released	Before record
UNLCK	No	Released	To same record
UPDAT	No	Released	To same record
WRITE	No	Released	To same record

Figure 8-136: Cursor Positioning After Successful Operation

When any operation causes the file cursor to be positioned to the record, or before the record, a subsequent READ or READE operation will retrieve the next record in the file; a subsequent READP or REDPE will retrieve the prior record in the file. Additionally, if the N (no lock) operation extender is used with any of the input operations, no record lock is applied to the retrieved record.

The diagrams on the pages that follow illustrate the position of the file cursor after the specified operation code has been performed successfully.

The file PARTMAST is used in these examples. It contains the key field PART (part number). Only the key field is depicted in the figures. Prior to each operation, the record containing the part number '5738SS1' has been successfully retrieved with the CHAIN operation. What is illustrated in these diagrams is what happens to the file cursor and the part number record after the specified operation has been performed.

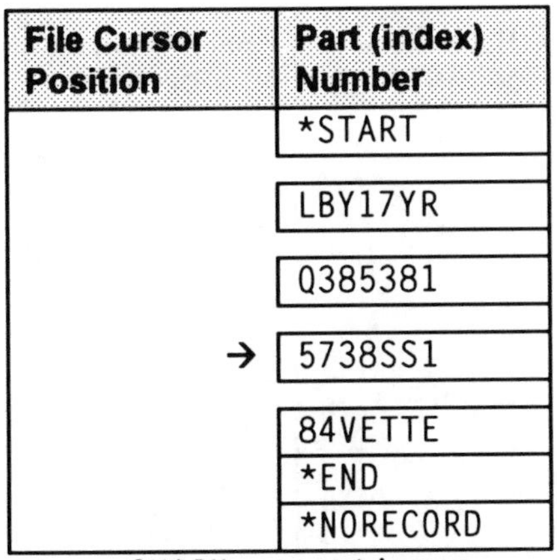

File Cursor Position	Part (index) Number
	*START
	LBY17YR
	Q385381
→	5738SS1
	84VETTE
	*END
	*NORECORD

CHAIN operation

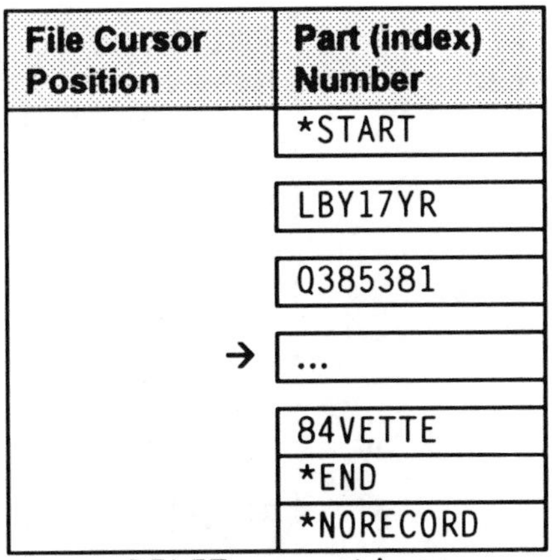

File Cursor Position	Part (index) Number
	*START
	LBY17YR
	Q385381
→	...
	84VETTE
	*END
	*NORECORD

DELET operation

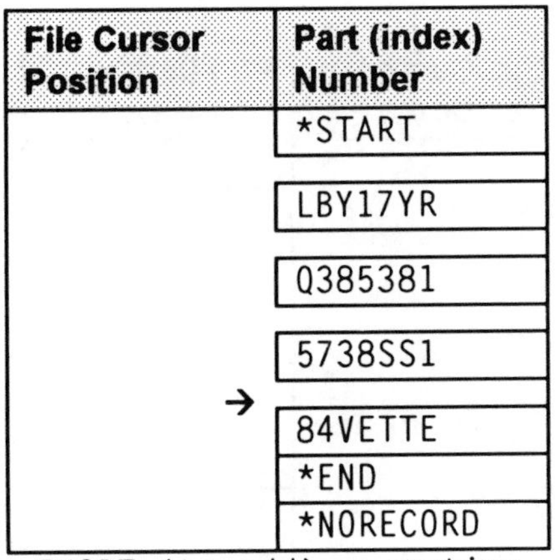

File Cursor Position	Part (index) Number
	*START
	LBY17YR
	Q385381
	5738SS1
→	
	84VETTE
	*END
	*NORECORD

EXCPT (to add) operation

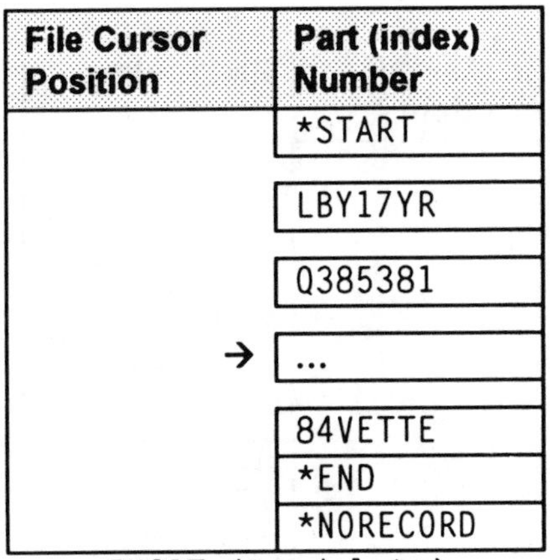

File Cursor Position	Part (index) Number
	*START
	LBY17YR
	Q385381
→	...
	84VETTE
	*END
	*NORECORD

EXCPT (to delete) operation

File Cursor Position	Part (index) Number
	*START
	LBY17YR
	Q385381
	5738SS1
→	
	84VETTE
	*END
	*NORECORD

EXCPT (to release) operation

File Cursor Position	Part (index) Number
	*START
	LBY17YR
	Q385381
	5738SS1
→	
	84VETTE
	*END
	*NORECORD

EXCPT (to update) operation

File Cursor Position	Part (index) Number
	*START
	LBY17YR
	Q385381
	5738SS1
	84VETTE
→	*END
	*NORECORD

FEOD operation[1]

File Cursor Position	Part (index) Number
→	*START
	LBY17YR
	Q385381
	...
	84VETTE
	*END
	*NORECORD

OPEN operation

---

[1] Although FEOD positions the file cursor to the end of the file, no input operations can be performed on the file until it is repositioned with another operation code. Specifically, the FEOD operation cannot be used to position the file to end of file for processing upward through the file.

File Cursor Position	Part (index) Number
	*START
	LBY17YR
	Q385381
	5738SS1
→	84VETTE
	*END
	*NORECORD

READ operation

File Cursor Position	Part (index) Number
	*START
	LBY17YR
	Q385381
	5738SS1
	84VETTE
	*END
→	*NORECORD

READE operation

File Cursor Position	Part (index) Number
	*START
	LBY17YR
→	Q385381
	5738SS1
	84VETTE
	*END
	*NORECORD

READP operation

File Cursor Position	Part (index) Number
	*START
	LBY17YR
	Q385381
	5738SS1
	84VETTE
	*END
→	*NORECORD

REDPE operation

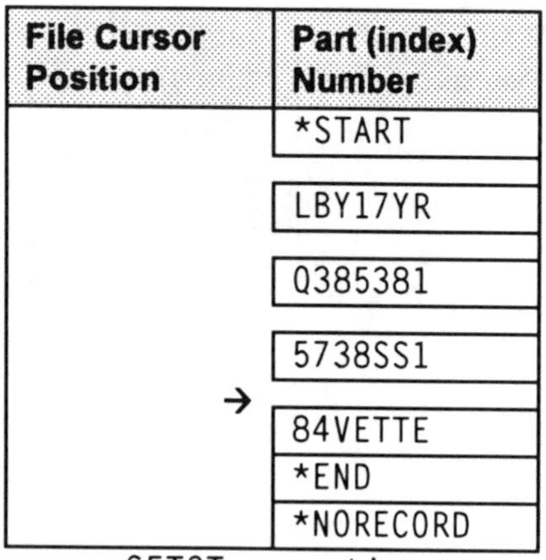

File Cursor Position	Part (index) Number
	*START
	LBY17YR
	Q385381
	5738SS1
→	
	84VETTE
	*END
	*NORECORD

SETGT operation

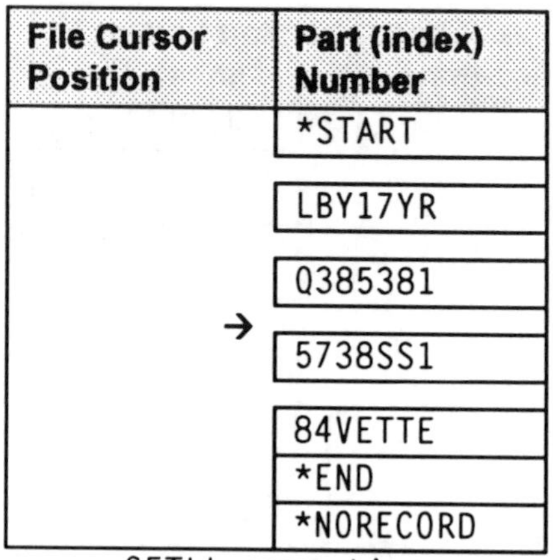

File Cursor Position	Part (index) Number
	*START
	LBY17YR
	Q385381
→	
	5738SS1
	84VETTE
	*END
	*NORECORD

SETLL operation

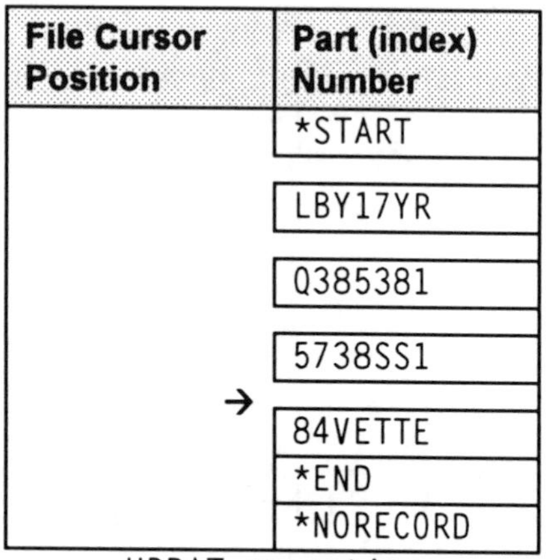

File Cursor Position	Part (index) Number
	*START
	LBY17YR
	Q385381
	5738SS1
→	
	84VETTE
	*END
	*NORECORD

UPDAT operation

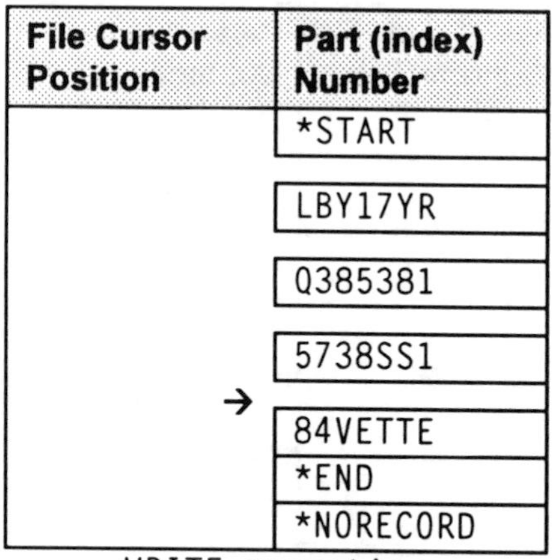

File Cursor Position	Part (index) Number
	*START
	LBY17YR
	Q385381
	5738SS1
→	
	84VETTE
	*END
	*NORECORD

WRITE operation

Access Path Processing

File access can be by record number, sequential or by access path. An index is used to process a file by its access path. An index can be a field, constant or key list.

When a field or constant is used as an index in Factor 1 of a file input, the entire composite key of the file is referenced. That is, all key fields for the file are treated as one large key field by RPG.

When a key list is used as the index by RPG, each key field of the file is referenced independently. Therefore, to reference the entire access path, a separate key field entry must exist in a key list for each key field that exists in the file's access path.

For example, an Order History file that consists of three fields, PART, CUST and QTYORD. The access path for the file consists of two key fields, PART and CUST. The DDS to create the file is listed in Figure 8-137.

```
SeqNoAan01n02n03R.Format++++.Len++TDPURowColKeywords+++++++++++++++++
0001 A            R ORDREC                  TEXT('Order History')
0002 A              PART           3P 0     TEXT('Part Number')
0003 A              CUST           5P 0     TEXT('Customer Number')
0004 A              QTYORD         7P 0     TEXT('Quantity Ordered')
0005 A            K PART
0006 A            K CUST
```

Figure 8-137: Order History File DDS (Keyed Physical File)

Assuming four records are written to the file; two for part number 100 and two for part number 200, the file would appear as illustrated in Figure 8-138.

PART	CUST	QTYORD
100	1207	50
100	5340	1000
200	5381	65
200	5382	30

Figure 8-138: Order History File Containing Four Records

RPG can process this file by its access path or sequentially, that is, in the order in which the records are physically arranged. A key list is used to process a file by its access path.

Figure 8-139 illustrates how the file ORDHIST would be defined in a program. The file is defined as an input, full procedural, externally described, keyed file.

```
SeqNoFFileNameIPE.E....RLEN...K.OV....EDevice+RecNbrKOptionEntry+
0001 FORDHIST IF E              K        DISK
0002 FREPORT  O                    OV    PRINTER

SeqNoCSRn01n02n03Factor1+++OpCodFactor2+++ResultLenDXHILOEQ
     ************************************
     *  Print each part number and the  *
     *  customers that have ordered it. *
     ************************************
0005 C            PART#     KLIST
0006 C                      KFLD           PART
0007 C            EOF       DOUEQ*ON
0008 C                      READ ORDHIST                   58
0009 C                      MOVE *IN58     EOK     1
0010 C            EOK       DOWEQ*OFF
0011 C                      EXCPTDETAIL
0012 C            PART#     READEORDHIST                   58
0013 C                      MOVE *IN58     EOK
0014 C                      ENDDO
0015 C            PART#     SETGTORDHIST                54
0016 C                      MOVE *IN54     EOF     1
0017 C                      ENDDO

SeqNoOFilenameEFBASBSAn01n02n03Field+EBEnd+POutputconstant+++++++++++
0017 OREPORT  E  1                 DETAIL
0018 O                             PART    +  1
0019 O                             CUST    +  1
0020 O                             QTYORDZ +  1
```

Figure 8-139: Access Path Processing by Key List

In Figure 8-139, the key list PART# is used to access the file ORDHIST. The key list consists of a single key field (PART). Since only one key field is specified for the key list PART#, only the first key field of the access path is referenced.

The READE operation (line 12) is used to access the file with the key list. Each time the READE operation is performed, the next record in the file whose key matches the value of the key list PART# is read. When no more keys match the key list value, resulting indicator 3 (indicator 58) is set on.

When a CHAIN operation is used with a partial key, key list, the first record in the file that matches the key list will be returned to the program. For example, if the key list key field PART was equal to 200, record 3 of the order history file would be retrieved.

Fields of a key list correspond to the key fields of an access path. For example, the order history file consists of two key fields, PART and CUST. A key list consisting of two key fields would correspond to those two access path key fields specified in the DDS for the file. Figure 8-140 contains the related DDS, RPG keylist and RPG File Description specifications.

Keyfield specification excerpt from DDS for ORDHIST File

```
0005 A               K PART
0006 A               K CUST
```

RPG keyfield statements used to access records in ORDHIST by key

```
     C          PRTCST    KLIST
     C                    KFLD           PART
     C                    KFLD           CUST
```

Use of PRTCST keylist to access ORDHIST

```
     FORDHIST IF E           K        DISK
     C          PRTCST    CHAINORDREC                 54
```

Figure 8-140: Related File Access Source Code

A key list can contain as many key fields as the access path. It can also contain fewer key fields than the access path. It cannot, however, contain more key fields than the access path.

Key lists and key fields can be used for all indexed file processing. They are flexible, clear, and provide a consistent method for specifying access path (index) structures.

Workstation Device File Processing

Workstations are display terminals, CRTs, video display stations, or personal computers and a keyboard through which a human interacts with a computer.

Workstations come in two varieties, *intelligent* and *dumb*. Dumb workstations are the most common for RPG programmers. Intelligent workstations, such as personal computers are widely used in information processing. When RPG programs are run from intelligent workstations, they are normally PCs emulating a dumb workstation; with the job running on a System/36 or AS/400. Hence, the intelligence isn't being utilized.

RPG supports workstations display devices through the WORKSTN device file type. Workstation device files can be defined to the RPG program as an input, output or combined file (I, O or C in column 15 of the File Description specification).

Figure 8-141 lists the RPG operation codes that can be used with workstation files.

OpCode	Description
ACQ	Acquire a device.
CHAIN	Random access of subfile records.
CLOSE	Close file.
EXFMT	Writes and then reads a workstation device.
OPEN	Open file.
POST	retrieve workstation device information into a data structure.
READC	Read next changed subfile record.
REL	Release an acquired device.
UPDAT	Update subfile record.
WRITE	Write workstation file format, (including a subfile record format).

Figure 8-141: Workstation File Operation Codes

On the pages that follow, each workstation operation code is illustrated as it relates to workstation device files. The RPG source code listed in the figures contains only that which is necessary to illustrate the operation code; complete and fully functional programs are not featured.

The ACQ and REL operations are seldom used and are not included in this section. For information on the ACQ and REL operations see "RPG Operation Codes" in Chapter 4.

CHAIN (Random File Access)

```
SeqNoFFileNameIPE.E....RLEN...K.OV....EDevice+RecNbrKOptionEntry+++
0001 FCUSTINQ CF  E                    WORKSTN
0002 F                                        RRN   KSFILE DISPLIST

SeqNoCLOn01n02n03Factor1+++OpCodFactor2+++ResultLenDXHiLoEq
     C                     .
     C                     .
     C                     .
0003 C           EOF       DOWEQ*OFF
0004 C           COUNT     ANDLT6
0005 C                     ADD  1         RRN     30
0006 C                     WRITEDISPLIST                Write SFL
0007 C                     READ CUSTMAST              58
0008 C                     MOVE *IN58     EOF
0009 C                     ENDDO
     C                     .
     C                     .
     C                     .
0010 C           5         CHAINDISPLIST            54
```

Figure 8-142: Random Access of Subfile Records

The file CUSTINQ is defined on line 1 as a combined, full procedural, workstation file. The file continuation line (line 2), defines the subfile DISPLIST and assigns the field RRN as the relative record number field used when processing this subfile.

Lines 4 to 9 fill the subfile with information from a data file.

Line 10 uses the CHAIN operation to randomly access subfile record number five. If the record exists, data will be returned to the program, if the record does not exist, resulting indicator 3 (indicator 58) will be set on.

OPEN and CLOSE (Open and Close a File)

```
SeqNoFFileNameIPE.E....RLEN...K.OV....EDevice+RecNbrKOptionEntry+A....UC
0001 FHELPTEXTCF E                     WORKSTN                          UC

SeqNoCLOn01n02n03Factor1+++OpCodFactor2+++ResultLenDXHiLoEq
0002 C                     OPEN HELPTEXT                56
0003 C                     MOVE *IN56     IOERR     1
0004 C           IOERR     IFEQ *OFF
0005 C                     EXFMTHELPRECD
     C                     .
     C                     .
     C                     .
0006 C                     CLOSEHELPTEXT
0007 C                     ENDIF
```

Figure 8-143: Open and Close a Workstation File

The file HELPTEXT is defined on line 1 as a combined, full procedural, workstation file. Also, the file HELPTEXT is a user-control file (columns 71 and 72 contain the letters UC). This is required in order for the OPEN operation to work the first time a file is opened. However, the user-control option is not required for the OPEN or CLOSE operations to be used on a file after the file is opened by RPG. That is, when a file is opened by RPG (columns 71 and 72 do not contain UC) and then closed with the CLOSE operation, the OPEN operation will reopen the file.

Line 2 opens the file HELPTEXT.

Line 6 closes the file HELPTEXT.

Remember, if the OPEN operation attempts to open a file; that has already been opened, an error occurs; resulting indicator 2, if it is specified, will be set on. If the CLOSE operation attempts to close a file that is already closed, an error occurs; resulting indicator 2, if it is specified, will be set on.

When *ALL is specified for Factor 2 of the CLOSE operation, all files that are currently opened, will be closed.

EXFMT (Write then Read Workstation Device)

```
SeqNoFFileNameIPE.E...........K.OV.....Device+RecNbrKOptionEntry+
0001 FCUSTINQ CF  E                    WORKSTN
0002 FCUSTMASTIF  E           K        DISK

SeqNoCLOn01n02n03Factor1+++OpCodFactor2+++ResultLenDXHiLoEq
0003 C              INDEX     CHAINCSTMST              54
0004 C                        MOVE *IN56     NOTFND
0005 C              NOTFND    IFEQ *OFF

0006 C                        EXFMTDSPCUST               56

0007 C                        ENDIF
```

Figure 8-144: Retrieve and Display a Data Record Using EXFMT

In Figure 8-144, a record from the data file CUSTMAST (line 2) is retrieved (line 3). The workstation file CUSTINQ (line 1) is written to and read from with the EXFMT (line 6). The workstation file format DSPCUST is used in Factor 2 of the EXFMT operation.

If many workstation file formats are needed on the display, then the additional format must be written with the WRITE operation. The final format, (the one after which a READ operation should be performed) should be written to the workstation file with the EXFMT operation.

POST (Post Device Specific Information)

In Figure 8-145 the program status data structure (PSDS) defined on lines 2 and 3 is used by the POST operation (line 9) to post device dependent feedback information to the information data structure (INFDS) for the workstation file CUSTINQ.

The field WSID (lines 3 and 9) will contain the name of the device that is being used to run the RPG program.

The information data structure for device files differs from system to system. The location of the DSPMOD subfield (position 252) is for the IBM System/38. The information data structure for the IBM System/36, AS/400 RPG compilers is different. For those systems, the POST operation may not return the same information featured in this example.

```
SeqNoFFileNameIPE.E....RLEN...K.OV....EDevice+RcdNbrKOptionEntry+
0001 FCUSTINQ CF  E                    WORKSTN      KINFDS WSDS

SeqNoIDSName....ESDSExternalname..........PFromTo++DField+
0002 IPSDS  SDS
0003 I                                       244 253 WSID
0004 IWSDS    DS
0005 I                                       *STATUS STATUS
0006 I                                       252 252 DSPMOD

SeqNoCLOn01n02n03Factor1+++OpCodFactor2+++ResultLenDXHiLoEq
     *  POST the workstation device information to the DS
0009 C            WSID      POST CUSTINQ              56

     *  Test for a device that supports 132-columns
0010 C            DSPMOD    IFEQ X'17'
0011 C                      Z-ADD132       SIZE    30         3180 Device?
0012 C                      ELSE
0013 C                      Z-ADD80        SIZE               5250 Device?
0014 C                      ENDIF

0015 C            SIZE      IFEQ 132
0016 C                      EXFMTPANEL4
0017 C                      ELSE
0018 C            SIZE      IFEQ 80
0019 C                      EXFMTPANEL3
0020 C                      ENDIF
0021 C                      ENDIF
```

Figure 8-145: POST Status Information to the INFDS

READ (Read a Record from a File)

```
SeqNoFFileNameIPE.E....RLEN...K.OV....EDevice+RcdNbrKOptionEntry+
0001 FCUSTINQ CF  E                     WORKSTN      KNUM        01

SeqNoCLOn01n02n03Factor1+++OpCodFactor2+++ResultLenDXHiLoEq
0002 C                        WRITEPANEL1
0003 C                        READ PANEL1                 58
      *   This routine writes, then reads four
      *   workstation file formats.
0004 C                        WRITEPANEL1
0005 C                        WRITEPANEL2
0006 C                        EXFMTPANEL3
0007 C                        READ PANEL1                 58
0008 C                        READ PANEL2                 58
      *   This routine writes the PANEL3 format,
      *   then reads the workstation file. If the
      *   workstation time-out threshold is reached,
      *   resulting indicator 2 is set on.
0009 C                        WRITEPANEL3
0010 C                        READ CUSTINQ              5658
```

Figure 8-146: Read Workstation Device File

The workstation file format, or panel, PANEL1 is written to the workstation file (line 2). The READ operation on line 3 reads the format PANEL1. The READ operation will wait for the user to respond to the panel, by pressing the <Enter> key or a function key.

Two workstation file formats, are written to the workstation file on lines 4 and 5. Line 6 uses the EXFMT operation to write and then read a third panel, PANEL3. Since these read operations wait for a user response (i.e., to press <Enter> or a function key), the EXFMT operation waits for the user to respond. When a response is detected, PANLE3's input is returned to the program. However, subsequent READ operations are required to return the input data from the other panels.

After the user response, the other panels currently active in the workstation file are read (lines 7 and 8). These READ operations do not wait for a user response since the read operation (i.e., the EXFMT operation on line 6) releases all workstation formats.

Line 9 writes the format PANEL3. Then, the CUSTINQ file (not one of its record formats) is read by the READ operation on line 10. This technique causes the workstation file to "time-out" after an inactivity threshold has been reached. The file continuation specification (line 1) indicates that the device can be "invited" thus allowing the time-out function to operate.

READC (Read Next Changed Subfile Record)

```
SeqNoFFileNameIPE.E....RLEN...K.OV....EDevice+RecNbrKOptionEntry+++
0001 FCUSTINQ CF  E                    WORKSTN
0002 F                                        RRN    KSFILE DISPLIST

SeqNoCLOn01n02n03Factor1+++OpCodFactor2+++ResultLenDXHiLoEq
0003 C                     EXFMTSFLCTL

0004 C           EOSFL     DOUEQ*ON
0005 C                     READCDISPLIST                 58
0006 C                     MOVE *IN58     EOSFL
0007 C           OPTION    CASEQ'1'       SELECT
0008 C           OPTION    CASEQ'9'       DELETE
0009 C                     END
0010 C                     ENDDO
```

Figure 8-147: Read Next Changed Subfile Record

Line 3 uses the EXFMT operation to write and then read the subfile control record SFLCTL. When the subfile control record is written to the workstation file, the subfile detail records are also written.

The READC operation (line 5) reads each record of the subfile that has been modified. Technically, each record that has the *modify data tag* set on will be returned with the READC operation. The modify data tag is a 5250 data stream flag that is switched on when the workstation user types data into a field that is displayed on the workstation.

The subfile relative record number field RRN is updated with the relative record number of the subfile record just processed by the READC operation.

UPDATE (Update a Record)

```
SeqNoFFileNameIPE.E....RLEN...K.OV....EDevice+RcdNbrKOptionEntry+++
0001 FCUSTINQ CF  E                    WORKSTN
0002 F                                        RRN    KSFILE DISPLIST

SeqNoCLOn01n02n03Factor1+++OpCodFactor2+++ResultLenDXHiLoEq
0003 C                     EXFMTSFLCTL

0004 C                     READCDISPLIST                 58
0005 C                     MOVE *IN58     EOSFL
0006 C           EOSFL     DOWEQ*OFF
0007 C           OPTION    CASEQ'1'       SELECT
0008 C           OPTION    CASEQ'9'       DELETE
0009 C                     END

0010 C                     UPDATDISPLIST

0011 C                     READCDISPLIST                 58
0012 C                     MOVE *IN58     EOSFL
0013 C                     ENDDO
```

Figure 8-148: Update Workstation Subfile Record

The subfile DISPLIST is read with the READC operation (lines 4 and 11). The subfile records are processed (lines 7 and 8), then the subfile record is updated with the UPDAT operation (line 10).

The logic of this example is as follows:

- Display the subfile control record and the subfile
- Read the first changed subfile record
- If there are changed records, process the first record
- Update the record (line 10)
- Read the next changed subfile record (line 11)
- Branch to the top of the do loop (line 13 branch to line 6)

WRITE (Write a Record)

```
SeqNoFFileNameIPE.E....RLEN...K.OV....EDevice+RcdNbrKOptionEntry+++
0001 FCUSTINQ CF  E                     WORKSTN
0002 F                                         RRN    KSFILE DISPLIST
0003 FCUSTMASTIF  E           K         DISK

SeqNoCLOn01n02n03Factor1+++OpCodFactor2+++ResultLenDXHiLoEq
0004 C           ACCT      KLIST
0005 C                     KFLD           CSTNBR
0006 C                     WRITESFLCTL                        Activate SFL
0007 C           ACCT      CHAINCSTMST              54        Retrieve REC
0008 C                     MOVE *IN56     EOF     1
   *                                                          Do While...
0009 C           EOF       DOWEQ*OFF                          EOF=off
0010 C                     ADD  1         RRN     50          Inc SFL RRN

0011 C                     WRITEDISPLIST                       Write SFL
0012 C           ACCT      READECSTMST                      58 Get Next Rec
0013 C                     MOVE *IN56     EOF
0014 C                     ENDDO

0015 C           RRN       IFGT 0
0016 C                     MOVE *ON       *IN21               DSPSFL
0017 C                     WRITEHEADING                       Display HDR
0018 C                     EXFTMSFLCTL
0019 C                     ENDIF
```

Figure 8-149: Write Workstation Formats and Subfile Records

The subfile DISPLIST is activated and initialized when the subfile control record is written (line 6). The data file CUSTMAST is read (line 12). The data from the file CUSTMAST is written to the subfile DISPLIST (line 11) after the subfile record number (RRN) is incremented (line 10).

The workstation format HEADING is written (line 17), then the subfile control record and subfile are sent to the workstation (line 18).

Interpreting the Cursor Position

When control returns to an application program after a workstation display input/output operation, it is sometimes necessary to interpret the location of the cursor. The cursor location can be used to assist in any of the following routines:

- Returning the cursor to the same location on the workstation
- Determining helptext requests for area and field-level helptext
- Determining the line number for item selection

Each routine is a simple process consisting of a few short steps.

To retain the cursor location:

- Retrieve the cursor location from the INFDS
- Convert it to usable values (i.e., 3-byte packed field)
- Place the values into the fields used with the DDS keyword CSRLOC
- Write out the workstation record

To retrieve line numbers for selection:

- Retrieve the cursor location from the INFDS
- Convert it to usable values (i.e., 3-byte packed or zoned decimal data)
- Using the line number as an array index, interpret which "record" was selected
- Process the selection

To determine the cursor location for use with helptext:

- Retrieve the cursor location from the INFDS
- Using the row and column number, determine what helptext is requested
- Display the helptext
- Issue a READ operation to the same workstation format

When the user presses <Enter> or a function key, workstation management returns the cursor location in the information data structure for the workstation file. Position 370 of the information data structure is set to the line number of the cursor. Position 371 of the information data structure is set to the column number of the cursor.

The cursor position is returned in "half binary," that is, one position is used to store the row and another to store the column. These values are in binary notation. RPG, however, does not support 1-byte binary fields, therefore the values need to be manipulated—moved to 2-byte binary fields—before they can be used.

The cursor location returned to the program is the position of the cursor on the workstation display when the user presses <Enter>. Figure 8-150 illustrates an example workstation display panel with the cursor positioned on row 5, column 15. That is, the cursor is positioned under the first number in the address line.

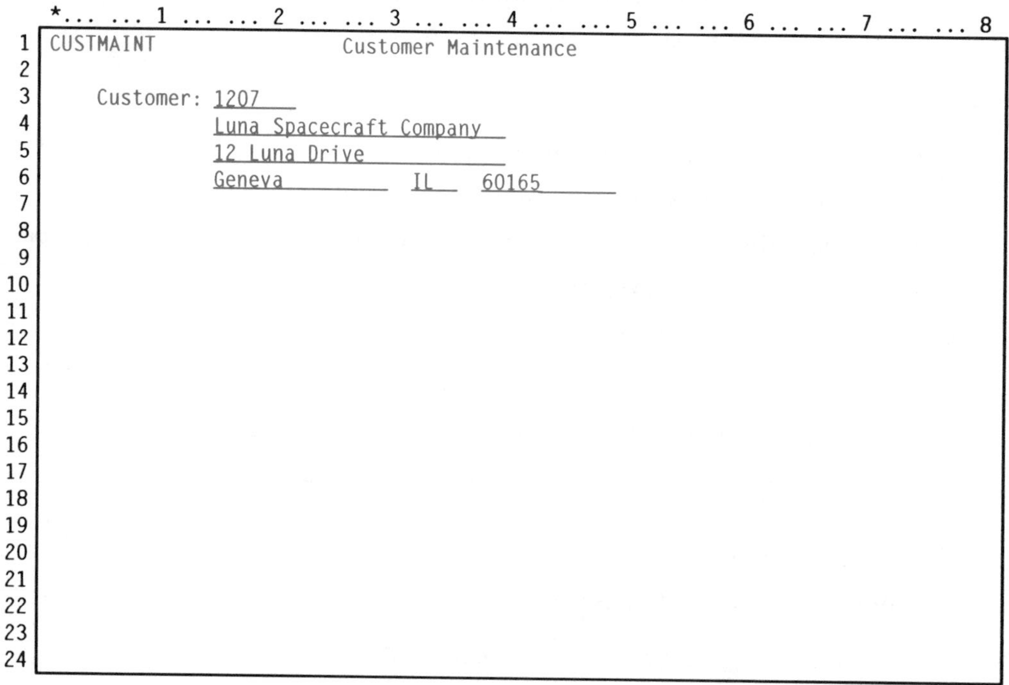

Figure 8-150: Example Workstation Panel used to Detect Cursor Location

Figure 8-151 illustrates a technique to retrieve the cursor location.

```
SeqNoFFileNameIPE.E....RLEN...K.OV....EDevice+RcdNbrKOptionEntry+
     FCUSTMANTCF  E                      WORKSTN      KINFDS WSDS

SeqNoIDSName....ESDSExternalname..........PFromTo++DField+
     IWSDS        DS
     I                                        370 370 XROW
     I                                        371 371  XCOL

     IWRKSTG DS
     I                                      B  01   020ZROW
     I                                         02   02 YROW
     I                                      B  03   040ZCOL
     I                                         04   04 YCOL

SeqNoCLOn01n02n03Factor1+++OpCodFactor2+++ResultLenDXHiLoEq
                              .
                              .
                              .
     C                        EXFMTCUSTMAINT
     C                        EXSR GETCSR
                              .
                              .
                              .
     CSR          GETCSR      BEGSR
      *   Convert 1-character Row/Col location to binary,
      *   then move them to decimal fields.
     C                        Z-ADD0         ZROW                InzDataStruc
     C                        MOVE XROW      YROW                Put Row->ROW
     C                        Z-ADDZROW      ROW    30           Move to *DEC

     C                        Z-ADD0         ZCOL                InzDataStruc
     C                        MOVE XCOL      YCOL                Put Col->COL
     C                        Z-ADDZCOL      COL    30           Move to *DEC
     CSR          ENDCUR      ENDSR
```

Figure 8-151: Retrieve Workstation Cursor Location

Chapter 9

Using Embedded SQL

Embedded SQL

This chapter illustrates how to use Structured Query Language (SQL) within the RPG language. It is not the intent of this chapter to teach SQL or SQL syntax.

SQL is available today on most computer systems. It provides a somewhat consistent language for database manipulation regardless of the computer system being used. The RPG language supports *SQL Host Language Coupling*, more commonly referred to as "embedded SQL," via an SQL preprocessor.

RPG supports embedded SQL similar to most other languages. The syntax of the SQL statements can be specified free-form in both upper and lower case letters—regardless of the rigid structure of RPG. Most ANSI standard SQL functions and many AS/400 extensions are supported, including, but not limited to AVG, COUNT, MAX, MIN, SUM, DECIMAL, DIGITS, FLOAT, INTEGER, LENGTH and SUBSTR. Mathematical expressions such as +, –, *, and / (addition, subtraction, multiplication, and division) can be used in the SQL statements.

When SQL is used to access a database file, the traditional RPG File Description specifications are not required. In fact, if one is specified, a second file "handle" or Open Data Path (ODP) is created. SQL supplies its own file data management and declaration routines.

SQL can be embedded in RPG programs in calculation specifications only. To begin an SQL statement, the /EXEC SQL directive is used. This directive must be specified in columns 7 to 15 of the calculation specification. Column 16 must contain a blank. The SQL statement can begin on the same line as the /EXEC SQL directive, or it can start on a subsequent line.

SQL statements can be continued onto succeeding lines by specifying a plus sign (+) in column 7 of the calculation specification. Column 8 must contain a blank. The continued SQL statement can appear in columns 9 to 74 of these continued calculation specification.

To end the SQL statement, a /END-EXEC directive is used. This directive must appear in columns 7 to 15 of the calculation specification. Columns 16 to 74 must contain blanks. No SQL statement can appear on the same line as the /END-EXEC delimiter.

Comments can be inserted between SQL statements (source code lines) using normal RPG comment notation (i.e., an asterisk in column 7).

SQL Preprocessor

SQL statements embedded in an RPG program are processed by an *SQL Preprocessor*. The preprocessor syntax checks SQL statements and prepares them for processing by the RPG program. The way the preprocessor prepares the statements may differ depending on the operating system and high-level language being used. The SQL preprocessor for OS/400 RPG stores the SQL statements intact, in the program's associated space[1].

Since the SQL preprocessor is separate from the RPG compiler, SQL statements must be specified within the main RPG source program—that is, they cannot be contained in an include member via the /COPY compiler directive.

The SQL preprocessor adds two steps to the compilation process. See Figure 9-152.

Without SQL	**With SQL**
Source Code	Source Code
RPG Compiler	SQL Preprocessor
Compiled Program	Generated (Modified) RPG Source
	RPG Compiler
	Compiled Program

Figure 9-152: RPG vs. SQL Compilation Steps

There are several reserved words that are used by the SQL preprocessor. All SQL reserved words begin with the letters SQL. Therefore, field names beginning with the letters "SQL" should be avoided. See Figure 9-156, *SQL Communications Area* on page 427 and Figure 9-155 on page 426 for a description of SQL reserved field names.

Relational Database Terminology

The terminology used in this chapter is that of *Relational Database*. Before using SQL it may be helpful to learn this terminology. Figure 9-153 contains a glossary of some common terms used in relational database. The glossary also provides a Cross-Reference between relational database and traditional terminology.

---

1 Under OS/400, an "associated space" is a string of bytes associated with an object such as a program. The RPG compiler creates and then links an associated space to the compiled program. An associated space is, essentially, a non-executable code, that is, it is a data area used to store information.

AS/400 Term	Relational Database Term
Library: A directory of a group of related and unrelated objects that have been placed into a specific context.	**Collection**: A library containing a journal, a journal receiver, and the SQL catalog. Sometimes referred to as a DATABASE.
Physical file: A data file of members that contain records of real data.	**Table**: An association of columns and rows that contain actual data.
Cross-Reference: A set of files containing file/field where and how used information.	**Catalog**: A repository of information on and about the collection.
Record: A horizontal line of data in a physical or logical file.	**Row**: A horizontal line in a table, made up of one or more columns.
Field in a format: One or more bytes of information in a record that make up a single fact.	**Column**: A vertical element of a table, representing a single data type.
Logical file: A subset of fields and records from a physical file.	**View**: A subset of columns and rows from a table.
Join-logical file: A subset view of fields and records from two or more physical file members.	**Join view**: A subset of columns and rows from two or more tables.
Access path: An object used to access data in a file in a specific sequence.	**Index**: A series of pointers according to the index key. An index provides fast access to specific rows in a table.
Key field: A field in a physical, logical or join-logical file used to determine the order of the entries in an access path.	**Index key**: The set of columns in a table used to determine the order of the index pointers.
Field: A data element of a specific type.	**Host variable**: A variable used by SQL to pass data between SQL and the HLL.
Data structure: A data element that is further defined by subfields.	**Host structure**: A structure containing one or more columns. Used by SQL to pass data between SQL and the HLL.

Figure 9-153: Relational Database Terminology

Tables, Rows and Columns

SQL Tables consist of rows and columns. Each row contains one or more columns. Each column defines the attributes of series of successive bytes (characters) of a row.

The following SQL statement creates a table named CUSTMAST in the CUSTDB collection. A collection is also referred to as a databaes. On the AS/400, a collection is a special type of OS/400 library.

```
CREATE TABLE custdb.custmast
            (account     DEC(5,0),
             customer    CHAR(30),
             address     CHAR(30),
             city        CHAR(20),
             state       CHAR(2)
            )
```

The CUSTMAST table contains five columns: ACCOUNT, CUSTOMER, ADDRESS, CITY, and STATE. When the table is created, only a description of the table exists. Data must be added to the table.

The SQL INSERT statement is used to add rows to a table. The following SQL statements add four rows of data to the table CUSTMAST.

```
INSERT INTO  custmast     (account, customer, address, city, state)
          VALUES(5320,'Perlman-Rocque','103rd Street','Lemont','IL')

INSERT INTO  custmast     (account, customer, address, city, state)
          VALUES(5340,'Champion Parts','22nd Street','Oak Brook','IL')

INSERT INTO  custmast     (account, customer, address, city, state)
          VALUES(1207,'Maui Pineapple','Kawai Blvd.','Maui','HI')

INSERT INTO  custmast     (account, customer, address, city, state)
          VALUES(5381,'Luna Spacecraft','12 Artemis Drive','Geneva','IL')
```

Figure 9-154 illustrates the contents of the CUSTMAST table after these four INSERT operations are performed.

Account	Customer	Address	City	State
05320	Perlman-Rocque	103rd Street	Lemont	IL
05340	Champion Parts	22nd Street	Oak Brook	IL
01207	Maui Pineapple	Kauai Blvd.	Maui	HI
05381	Luna Spacecraft	12 Artemis Drive	Geneva	IL

Figure 9-154: CUSTMAST Relational Database Table

Figure 9-154 contains an example database table. This table consists of four rows, each with five columns. The columns are the vertical columns of data, for example, the ACCOUNT column. The rows are the horizontal lines of data in the table. For example, the third row of this table contains:

```
01207 Maui Pineapple Kawai Blvd. Maui HI
```

SQL Views

A *view* is a subset of columns and rows. For example, if only the CUSTOMER and STATE columns of the CUSTMAST table are needed, the following SQL statement will create a view named CUSTSTATE that contains only those two columns:

```
CREATE VIEW custstate AS
           SELECT customer, state
           FROM custmast
```

This SQL statement would create an SQL *view* named CUSTSTATE. The resulting view would represent the subset that appears in Figure 9-155.

Customer	State
Perlman-Rocque	IL
Champion Parts	IL
Maui Pineapple	HI
Luna Spacecraft	IL

Figure 9-155: CUSTSTATE View of Table CUSTMAST

Note: The data presented by the view exists only in the original table. Views contain no data themselves. The *view's* view of the data is illustrated in Figure 9-155 for clarity.

There are several components that are used to embed SQL within a high-level language. The first is the SQL preprocessor, mentioned on page 421. The preprocessor translates embedded SQL statements into a form usable by the SQL runtime support library. When AS/400 RPGIII source containing embedded SQL statements are processed by the CRTSQLRPG (create SQL RPG program) command, the preprocessor stores the SQL statements in the *associated space* for the program being created. SQL statements in the RPG source are converted into comments and a CALL operation to the SQL runtime support program (QSQROUTE) is inserted into the RPG source.

SQL Communications Area

Embedding SQL into any high-level language program requires the SQL communications area (SQLCA). The SQL communications area is a data structure containing a set of fields used by the SQL runtime support to communicate with the high-level language program. This data structure is automatically inserted into RPG programs by the SQL preprocessor. Figure 9-155 contains descriptions of the SQL communications area subfields that are compatible with the AS/400's operating system, OS/400 as of Version 2, Release 2.

When the SQL communications area is inserted into RPG by the SQL preprocessor, a 136-byte data structure named SQLCA is created. The data structure should be treated as a "read only" item. The RPG program should only reference (i.e., READ) the data structure subfields, never change them.

Field	Attribute	Description
SQLAID	Char(8)	Contains the literal 'SQLCA' for debugging purposes.
SQLABC	Bin(4)	Length of the SQLCA structure.
SQLCOD	Bin(4)	SQL return code. 0 = Successful process. > 0 = Warning messages < 0 = Errors occurred.
SQLERL	Bin(2)	Length of SQLERM error message field.
SQLERM	Char(70)	Message text associated with the SQLCOD code.
SQLERP	Char(8)	Diagnostic information.
SQLERR	Char(24)	Six Bin(4) variables that contain diagnostic information: SQLER1 = Last four digits of an escape message ID. SQLER2 = Last four digits of a diagnostic message ID. SQLER3 = Number of rows (records) affected by an INSERT, UPDATE, DELETE SQL operation. SQLER4...SQLER6 reserved
SQLWN0	Char(1)	W = An error exists in one of the other error flags. b̸ = Indicates that there are no error/warning flags set.
SQLWN1	Char(1)	W = Value retrieved from the row (record) was truncated.
SQLWN2	Char(1)	Reserved
SQLWN3	Char(1)	W= The variable list does not equal the number of columns in the table.
SQLWN4	Char(1)	W = UPDATE or DELETE does not contain a WHERE clause.
SQLWN5	Char(1)	Reserved.
SQLWN6	Char(1)	Reserved.
SQLWN7	Char(1)	Reserved.
SQLWN8	Char(1)	Reserved.
SQLWN9	Char(1)	Reserved.
SQLWNA	Char(1)	Reserved.
SQLSTT	Char(5)	Status code for SQL run.

Figure 9-155: SQLCA Field Definitions

Figure 9-156 contains an example of the SQL communications area data structure that is automatically inserted into an RPG program by the SQL preprocessor. This format applies to OS/400 Version 2, Release 2.

```
SeqNoIDSName....EUDSExternalname..........PFromTo++DField+
     ISQLCA       DS
     I                                        1   8 SQLAID
     I                                   B    9  120SQLABC
     I                                   B   13  160SQLCOD
     I                                   B   17  180SQLERL
     I                                       19  88 SQLERM
     I                                       89  96 SQLERP
     I                                       97 120 SQLERR
     I                                   B   97 1000SQLER1
     I                                   B  101 1040SQLER2
     I                                   B  105 1080SQLER3
     I                                   B  109 1120SQLER4
     I                                   B  113 1160SQLER5
     I                                   B  117 1200SQLER6
     I                                      121 128 SQLWRN
     I                                      121 121 SQLWN0
     I                                      122 122 SQLWN1
     I                                      123 123 SQLWN2
     I                                      124 124 SQLWN3
     I                                      125 125 SQLWN4
     I                                      126 126 SQLWN5
     I                                      127 127 SQLWN6
     I                                      128 128 SQLWN7
     I                                      129 129 SQLWN8
     I                                      130 130 SQLWN9
     I                                      131 131 SQLWNA
     I                                      132 136 SQLSTT
     I
```

Figure 9-156: SQLCA Data Structure in RPG

SQL Data Types

SQL supports multiple data types including CHAR, SMALLINT, INTEGER, DECIMAL and NUMERIC. The FLOAT (floating point) and DBCS SQL data types are not supported by RPG. Figure 9-157 contains a list of SQL data types along with their equivalent RPG data type.

SQL Data Type	Equivalent or similar RPG Data Type
CHAR	Character. RPG char scalars can be up to 9,999 bytes in length SQL scalars can be up to 32,767 bytes in length
SMALLINT	2-byte binary. RPG bin(2) values range from –9,999 to +9,999 SQL SMALLINT values range from –32767 to +32767
INTEGER	4-byte binary RPG bin(4) values range from –999,999,999 to +999,999,999 SQL INTEGER values range from -2,147,483,648 to +2,147,483,648
DECIMAL	Packed decimal. RPG packed decimal fields can be up to 30,9 positions SQL DECIMAL fields can be up to 30,30 positions
NUMERIC	Zoned decimal. RPG zoned decimal fields can be up to 30,9 positions SQL NUMERIC fields can be up to 30,30 positions
DBCS	Double-byte character set (Graphic data type)
FLOAT	Floating point is not support by RPGIII

Figure 9-157: SQL Data Types vs. RPG

The SQL runtime support will convert any SQL data types to the RPG equivalent. Where differences, such as in the handling of INTEGER to BIN(4), imported data is truncated.

SQL Host Variables

Host variables are fields within an RPG program. SQL uses host variables to pass table data to the RPG program. The columns within the table are moved into the RPG program host variables by SQL run-time support. To specify host variables within the embedded SQL statement, prefix the RPG field name with a colon (:).

Figure 9-158 contains an example of an embedded SQL statement using host variables. The SQL statements and keywords used here and through this section are in upper case. Tables, views, columns, and host variables are in lowercase for clarity. Upper/lower case characters used in SQL statements are ignored, except for string constants.

```
SeqNoCLOn01n02n03Factor1+++OpCodFactor2+++ResultLenDXHiLoEq
0010 C           OPTION    IFEQ 'INQUIRY'
0020 C                     Z-ADD1207      CSTNBR
0030  *
0040 C/EXEC SQL  SELECT customer,address,city,state
0050 C+          INTO :cstnam,:cstadr,:cstcty,:cstste
0060 C+          FROM  orders.custmast
0070 C+          WHERE account = :cstnbr
0080 C/END-EXEC
0090 C                     ENDIF
```

Figure 9-158: Embedded SQL Using Host Variables

The SQL statement in Figure 9-158 selects all columns from the table CUSTMAST and reads them into the variable list specified with the INTO clause (line 50). Line 60 contains the FROM clause; it defines the table from which the data is selected. The table name in this example is CUSTMAST, which resides in the collection named ORDERS.

ANSI SQL uses the convention **userid.table** for qualifying a table to a collection. This is also the IBM Systems Application Architecture (SAA) SQL standard used in OS/2. The OS/400 SQL/400 supports two conventions, the ANSI standard and a proprietary convention **collection/table** (the collection[2] name is optional and will default to the OS/400 library list).

The example listed in Figure 9-158 is functionally equivalent to an RPG CHAIN operation. The value 1207 is moved into the field CSTNBR on line 20. The field CSTNBR is used as a host variable on line 70 to retrieve the desired row of the CUSTMAST table.

Note: When the SELECT clause is used in this manner, one and only one row can be returned to the program. If more than one row is returned, the SQLCOD field contains an error code.

SQL Host Structures

Host structures are RPG data structures that contain one or more subfields. A host structure is used to reduce the coding required when several host variables are needed. For example, a data structure can be defined using the format of an externally described table (i.e., file). That data structure can be used as a parameter of the INTO clause. This avoids coding extensive lists of field names on the INTO clause.

---

2 A COLLECTION is the AS/400 term for what is traditionally referred to as a DATABASE.

To specify host structures within the embedded SQL statement, prefix the structure name with a colon. Figure 9-159 is an example of the use of a host structure.

```
SeqNoIDSName....ESDSExternalname..........PFromTo++DField+
0001 IHCUST     E DSCUSTMAST
0002 I              ACCOUNT                         CSTNBR
0003 I              CUSTOMER                        CSTNAM
0004 I              ADDRESS                         CSTADR
0005 I              CITY                            CSTCTY
0006 I              STATE                           CSTSTE

SeqNoCLOn01n02n03Factor1+++OpCodFactor2+++ResultLenDXHiLoEq
0007 C          OPTION    IFEQ 'INQUIRY'
0008 C                    Z-ADD1207      CSTNBR
0009  *
0010 C/EXEC SQL SELECT *
0011 C+         INTO :hcust
0012 C+         FROM  orders.custmast
0013 C+         WHERE account = :cstnbr
0014 C/END-EXEC
0015 C                    ENDIF
```

Figure 9-159: Using a Host Structure With Embedded SQL

The SQL statement in Figure 9-159, (lines 10 to 13) selects all of the columns from the database table CUSTMAST and copies the data into the host structure HCUST. The 'SELECT *' convention causes all columns to be selected.

The format of the host structure HCUST (line 1) is based on the external definition of the file CUSTMAST, which is also the table used by the SELECT statement. Therefore, each column of the table CUSTMAST will also be a host variable (subfield) of the host structure HCUST, providing a one-to-one relationship between the SQL statement and the host structure.

SQL SELECT

As mentioned earlier, no File Description specifications can be used for tables (files) processed by embedded SQL. SQL provides its own database management functions. Both SQL and RPG File Description specifications, however, can be used in the same program on different file handles (open data paths). See Figure 9-160. Files declared with File Description specifications must be processed with standard RPG input/output operation codes. Tables declared with SQL must be processed with SQL statements.

The SQL SELECT verb, when used by itself, must result in the retrieval of one and only one row (record). If the SELECT statement results in more than one row, an error will be generated and no data will be retrieved.

SQL CURSOR

The SQL CURSOR is used when more than one row of data is needed. The cursor is a structure that *points* at one row of a set of rows. The SELECT statement appears as a parameter of the DECLARE CURSOR statement.

A cursor is a control structure. It is the "pointer" within the set of rows selected by the WHERE clause of the DECLARE CURSOR FOR SELECT. . . statement. The cursor is moved forward through the set of rows with the FETCH statement.

A cursor must be defined, opened and closed. Between the open and close, the selected rows are accessed with the following verbs: FETCH, to read the rows; UPDATE, to replace the data in the columns of a row; and DELETE, to destroy a row.

When the UPDATE and DELETE verbs are used, use the WHERE CURRENT OF CURSOR parameter. This directs the update or delete operation to the current row.

The following steps are used when using SQL to access multiple rows of a table:

1. Declare a cursor.
2. Open the cursor.
3. Fetch a row into a variable list.
4. If necessary, update or delete the row.
5. If more rows need to be processed, GOTO step 3.
6. Close the cursor.

```
SeqNoFFileNameIPE.E....RLEN...K.OV.....Device+RecNbrKOptionEntry+
0010 FACCTBAL IF  E           K        DISK

SeqNoF............ExternFmt+..................RecNbrKKeywrdEntry+EX
0020 F            ACCTBAL                            KRENAMEBALANCE

SeqNoIFormat..NSEUDSExternalname..........PFromTo++DField+
0030 IHCUST     E DSCUSTMAST
0031 I              ACCOUNT                         CSTNBR
0032 I              CUSTOMER                        CSTNAM
0033 I              ADDRESS                         CSTADR
0034 I              CITY                            CSTCTY
0035 I              STATE                           CSTSTE

SeqNoCL0n01n02n03Factor1+++OpCodFactor2+++ResultLenDXHiLoEq
0040 C/EXEC SQL DECLARE customer CURSOR FOR
0050 C+          SELECT *
0060 C+          FROM orders.custmast
0070 C+          WHERE state = 'IL'
0080 C+          ORDER BY account
0090 C/END-EXEC
0100 C/EXEC SQL
0110 C+          OPEN customer
0120 C/END-EXEC
0130 C/EXEC SQL
0140 C+          WHENEVER NOT FOUND go to EOF
0150 C/END-EXEC
0160 C           SQLCOD    DOWEQ0
0170 C/EXEC SQL
0180 C+          FETCH customer
0190 C+          INTO :HCUST
0200 C/END-EXEC
0210 C           CSTNBR    CHAINBALANCE              54
0220 C           *IN54     IFEQ *OFF
0230 C                     ADD  BALDUE    TOTAL
0240 C                     ENDIF
0250 C                     ENDDO
0260 C           EOF       TAG
0270 C                     SETON                        LR
0280 C/EXEC SQL
0290 C+          CLOSE customer
0300 C/END-EXEC
```

Figure 9-160: RPG Using Both SQL and Normal Input/Output Routines

Figure 9-160 illustrates both SQL and normal RPG file processing. Line 10 defines the file ACCTBAL. Since the record format of the file is the same as the file name, it has to be renamed. Line 20 renames the record format ACCTBAL to BALANCE. This is required because RPG does not allow record format names to be the same as file names. (See *Naming Conventions* in Chapter 1.)

Lines 40 to 80 define the SQL cursor. The cursor is named CUSTOMER.

Line 110 opens the cursor CUSTOMER. A cursor must be opened before it is processed.

Line 140 sets up the WHENEVER statement to branch to the label EOF at end of file.

Line 160 begins a Do while loop that will loop as long as the SQLCOD subfield of the SQLCA data structure is equal to zero. This means the DO-WHILE loop will continue to loop while no warning or error conditions occur.

Lines 180 and 190 FETCH the next available row from the file represented by the SQL cursor specified on line 40. This is similar to a READ operation in RPG.

The FETCH operation requires a variable list that corresponds exactly with the columns specified on the SELECT verb of the DECLARE CURSOR statement. Since a host structure is being used (line 190), the variable list needs to contain only the host structure name.

Lines 210 to 240 CHAIN to the record format named BALANCE, using the field CSTNBR. The value contained in CSTNBR is set in the FETCH statement.

Line 250 contains the closing END statement for the DO-WHILE loop.

Line 260 is the target label for the WHENEVER statement. SQL will cause a branch to the EOF label when the FETCH statements results in a not-found condition.

Line 260 sets on indicator LR, and line 290 closes the SQL cursor CUSTOMER.

RPG File OpCodes vs. SQL Statements

SQL is rich in its ability to manipulate data of a table or view. RPG is rich in its simple design and provides fast and efficient methods for retrieving, updating, writing, and deleting database records.

SQL embedded in a free-form procedure language like PL/I, C or Pascal is a real boon. Traditionally, these languages have had inferior record input/output routines.

RPG, however, has traditionally offered a rich set of instructions for database record input/output. The same instructions are used to access data files, communications files and workstation device files. The RPG programmer need not worry if the program is running on an IBM 370 under MVS, or an IBM AS/400®. The READ operation performs a read, and the WRITE operation performs a write. No extensive libraries containing run-time input/output routines are needed to support the language. The compilers have the support built-in.

Embedded SQL has several uses within RPG, among them are the following:

1. It provides a method of dynamically querying the database.
2. It provides a database join facility.
3. It provides a cross-system method of retrieving data into a program.

SQL can be used outside of RPG to create tables, views and indexes. Embedded SQL can query existing tables, views and non-SQL physical and logical files.

The use of SQL outside of RPG can lead to more stable RPG programs than embedded SQL. By embedding SQL within RPG, each time the SQL statement has to be modified, the RPG program has to change. This can lead to frequent program maintenance, and thus increases the possibility of errors.

Using SQL outside of the RPG program provides as much flexibility as embedded SQL, plus the additional flexibility of using the advanced RPG operation codes for input/output. Tables and views defined with SQL (outside of the RPG program) can be processed like any normal data file using the advanced RPG data file operation codes such as CHAIN, SETLL, READE and READP.

As illustrated in Figure 9-160, SQL can require several programming statements. While the number of lines of code has nothing to do with performance, it can complicate things. Figure 9-161 contains the same program written without embedded SQL. Which one is more readable to an application programmer?

```
SeqNoFFileNameIPE.E....RLEN...K.OV.....Device+RecNbrKOptionEntry+
0010 FCUSTMASTIF  E           K        DISK

SeqNoF............ExternFmt+..................RecNbrKKeywrdEntry+EX
0020 F            CUSTMAST                          KRENAMECUSTRECD
0030 FACCTBAL IF  E           K        DISK
0040 F            ACCTBAL                           KRENAMEBALANCE

SeqNoIRecdnameNSEUDSExternalname..........PFromTo++DField+
0050 ICUSTRECD
0060 I              ACCOUNT                         CSTNBR
0070 I              CUSTOMER                        CSTNAM
0080 I              ADDRESS                         CSTADR
0090 I              CITY                            CSTCTY
0100 I              STATE                           CSTSTE

SeqNoCLOn01n02n03Factor1+++OpCodFactor2+++ResultLenDXHiLoEq
0130 C           'IL'      SETLLCUSTMAST                LR
0140 C                     READ CUSTMAST                    LR
0150 C           *INLR     DOWEQ*OFF
0160 C           CSTNBR    CHAINBALANCE                 54
0170 C           *IN54     IFEQ *OFF
0180 C                     ADD  BALDUE    TOTAL
0190 C                     ENDIF
0200 C                     READ CUSTMAST                    LR
0210 C                     ENDDO
```

Figure 9-161: RPG Code Equivalent to Figure 9-160

The program listed in Figure 9-161 assumes that an access path exists (permanent or temporary) over the field STATE of the file CUSTMAST.

The program listed in Figure 9-161 would run several times faster than the program listed in Figure 9-160, depending on the method the operating system uses for retrieving database records. This is because the SQL method listed in Figure 9-160 is usually processed dynamically (such as when the program is run on an AS/400), while RPG input/output routines listed in Figure 9-161 are compiled into the program.

Figure 9-162 contains a chart that provides the RPG programmer with a frame of reference of RPG-to-SQL input/output routines. While there is no one-to-one correspondence between SQL verbs and RPG operations, the chart identifies close relationships.

RPG	SQL Verb	SQL Action
File Spec	DECLARE	Defines an SQL cursor to the RPG program.
OPEN	OPEN	Opens a previously declared cursor.
READ	FETCH	Reads a record into a variable list.
CHAIN	SELECT	Selects a record with the WHERE clause; reads it into a variable list.
READE	FELTCH	Retrieves then next record in the file that matches the WHERE and ORDER BY clauses of a DECLARE statement.
UPDAT	UPDATE	Rewrites the current record to the file using a variable list.
WRITE	INSERT	Writes a new record to a file using a variable list.
DELET	DELETE	Deletes one or more records (including all records) from a file.

Figure 9-162: RPG Function with Corresponding SQL Verb

SQL is not a substitute for RPG high-level language input/output operations. It is merely a method, developed in the late '60s, to manipulate a relational database.

RPG input/output operation codes provide better performance and more methods of retrieving individual records (e.g., the Read Prior operation). SQL provides flexibility for searching, joining and performing mathematical expressions not otherwise available in the modern RPG language.

There are other solutions that provide more flexibility than embedded SQL. The Open Query File (OPNQRYF) command supplied with CPF on the System/38 and OS/400 on the AS/400 is one solution. Other third party software products provide a superset of SQL that can be run external to RPG on both the System/38 and AS/400.

Chapter 10

Exception/Error Handling

File Information Data Structure

A large portion of application development is devoted to error detection, error handling, and exception analysis; commonly referred to as exception/error handling.

Exception analysis is the method used to study various error conditions, both expected and unexpected. Error handling is the method used to detect, recover and correct error conditions—unexpected problems that are a result of programming errors, human error and system failures.

File Status Error Codes

In addition to program status error codes, most operation codes also support file exception/error status codes. A file status error code appears when an error condition has been encountered after a file-specific operation is performed—for example, the CHAIN operation, where a record time-out error could occur.

Most of the operation codes set on resulting indicator 2 when an exception error is detected. If the programmer has specified this error indicator, the indicator is set on and control passes to the next RPG operation. If resulting indicator 2 is not specified and a file exception/error subroutine is specified in the program and on the INFSR file continuation keyword, control automatically transfers to that subroutine. At that point, the *STATUS code can be interrogated. See Figure 10-163. If resulting indicator 2 is not specified and a file exception/error subroutine is not specified, the RPG general exception/error handling subroutine receives control. The user or work station operator will usually receive an error message at this point.

Example 141 — Detect a record lock/time-out condition.

```
SeqNoFFileNameIPE.E....RLEN...K.OV.....Device+RecNbrKOptionEntry+
0001 FCUSTMASTIF  E            K       DISK          KINFDS INFDS
0002 F                                               KINFSR INFSR

SeqNoIDSName....ESDSExternalname..........PFromTo++DField+
0003 IINFDS       DS
0004 I                                      *STATUS  STATUS

SeqNoCLOn01n02n03Factor1+++OpCodFactor2+++ResultLenDXHiLoEq
0070 C                 1234567   CHAINCUSTMAST              54
0080 C                           MOVE *ON       *INLR
0090 CSR               INFSR     BEGSR
0100 C                 STATUS    IFEQ 1218
0110 C                           MOVE 'TIME-OUT'MSG
0120 C                           ENDIF
0130 CSR               ENDFSR    ENDSR
```

Status	Description
00000	No exception/error occurred.
00002	Function key used to return input from the display device.
00011	End of file detected on a READ operation.
00012	CHAIN operation resulting in no record found.
00013	WRITE operation to a subfile record resulted in subfile full; record not added.
01011	Undefined record type (record does not match the record identifying indicators).
01021	Attempted to write to an existing record or duplicate index not allowed.
01031	Matching record's match field's data out of sequence.
01041	Array/table loading sequence error.
01051	Too many array/table entries.
01052	Clearing of table prior to dump of data failed.
01071	Numeric sequence error.
01121	PRINT key pressed with no resulting indicator.
01122	ROLLUP (PAGEDOWN) key pressed with no resulting indicator.
01123	ROLLDOWN (PAGEUP) key pressed with no resulting indicator.
01124	CLEAR key pressed with no resulting indicator.
01125	HELP key pressed with no resulting indicator.
01126	HOME key pressed with no resulting indicator.
01127	reserved.
01201	Workstation record mismatch detected on input operation.
01211	Input or Output operation attempted on a closed file.
01215	OPEN operation issued to a file that was already opened.
01216	Error on an implicit (RPG cycle-based) OPEN or CLOSE operation.
01217	Error on an explicit OPEN or CLOSE operation code.
01218	Unable to allocate record (record locked by another program).

Figure 10-163: RPG Runtime File Status Error Codes (1 of 2)

Status	Description
01221	Update operation without a prior successful read operation.
01231	Error on SPECIAL file.
01235	Error in PRTCTL data structure spacing or skipping entries.
01241	ADDROUT record not found.
01251	Permanent workstation input/output error detected.
01244	Workstation session or device error occurred (recovery is possible).
01261	Attempted to exceed maximum number of acquired devices.
01281	Operation to an already acquired device.
01282	Session being canceled with controlled option.
01285	Attempted to acquire a device that is already acquired.
01286	Attempted to perform a shared file open on a file described with SAVDS or IND file continuation keywords.
01287	Response indicators overlap IND continuation keyword indicators.
01299	Miscellaneous input/output error detected.
01331	Wait-for-record time exceeded for READ or EXFMT operation.

Figure 10-163: Runtime File Status Error Codes (2 of 2)

File Information Data Structure

The file information data structure (INFDS) is a data structure that the RPG compiler and/or RPG runtime support initializes with file-related status information. Each file defined in the RPG program can have its own unique file information data structure. The format of the information data structure is dependent on the type of file being processed. This chapter will cover only those subfields that are common to all file types. Figure 10-164 contains an example input specification for the information data structure. The field names used are for illustration purposes only.

```
SeqNoIDSName....EIDSInitialvalue++++++++++TFromTo++DField+
     IINFDS       DS
     I                                            1   8 FILE
     I                                            9   9 OPEN
     I                                           10  10 EOF
     I                                           11  150STATUS
     I                                           16  21 OPCODE
     I                                           22  29 ROUTIN
     I                                           30  37 STMNT
     I                                           38  420REASON
     I                                           38  45 RECORD
     I                                           46  52 MSGID
     I                                           53  56 INSNBR
     I                                           67  700DSPSIZ
     I                                           71  720INP
     I                                           73  740OUT
     I                                           75  760MODE
     I                                           81  82 ODPTYP
     I                                           83  92 FNAME
     I                                           93 102 FLIBR
     I                                          103 112 SPNAME
     I                                          113 122 SPLIBR
     I                                        B 123 1240SPNBR
     I                                        B 125 1260RCDLEN
     I                                          129 138 FMEMBR
     I                                        B 147 1480FTYPE
     I                                        B 152 1530LINES
     I                                        B 154 1550COLS
     I                                        B 156 1590RCDCNT
     I                                          160 161 ACCTYP
     I                                          162 162 DUPKEY
     I                                          163 163 SOURCE
     I                                          164 173 UFCBPR
     I                                          174 183 UFCBOV
     I                                        B 184 1850VOLIDO
     I                                        B 186 1870BLKIOL
     I                                        B 188 18900FLINE
     I                                        B 190 1910BLKIOO
     I                                          197 206 PGMDEV
```

Figure 10-164: Example File Information Data Structure

Listed in Figure 10-165 is a description of each information data structure subfield. Information data structure subfields are unique for each information data structure assigned to a file. The subfield names in different information data structures, however, must be unique. For example, the subfield FILE could be called FILE in one INFDS, in another INFDS it might be called FILNAM, and in another INFDS it might be called FNAME.

Subfield	Description
FILE	File name assigned to the information data structure. This is the file name recognized by the RPG program. It may differ from the actual (external) file name.
OPEN	Open indication: 1 = Open; any other value = Closed.
EOF	End of file indication: 1 = EOF.
STATUS	Status Codes. See Figure 10-163 for a list of status codes.
OPCODE	RPG operation code that was used to access the file.
ROUTIN	RPG routine name that was processing the file. See Figure 10-167 for a list of RPG routines.
STMNT	Statement number in the program being run when an error occurred.
REASON	Return code for SPECIAL device files.
RECORD	Record format name being processed for the file.
MSGID	System message ID number.
INSNBR	Compiled code statement number be performed (instruction number).
DSPSIZ	Number of characters that fit on the workstation device.
INP	National language input capability for the workstation device file.
OUT	National language output capability for the workstation device file.
MODE	The preferred national language mode of the workstation device file.
ODPTYP	Type of open data path: DS=display file; DB=database file; SP=spool file.
FNAME	Name of the file recognized by the system. This differs from the subfield FILE, which is the file name as it is known to the RPG program.
FLIBR	Name of the library in which the file is located.

Figure 10-165: INFDS Subfield Description (1 of 2)

Subfield	Description
SPNAME	Name of the spool file (data file name) used for the printer file.
SPLIBR	Name of the library in which the spool file is located.
SPNBR	Spool file number for the printer file.
RCDLEN	Length of the records for the file associated with the INFDS.
FMEMBR	Name of the current member being processed for the database file.
FTYPE	File subtype indicating the type of file.
LINES	Number of lines on the WORKSTN or PRINTER device.
COLS	Number of columns on the WORKSTN or PRINTER device.
RCDCNT	Number of records in the file at open time.
ACCTYP	Type of database file access: KU=Keyed unique; KF=Keyed FIFO, dups allowed; KL=keyed LIFO, dups allowed; AR=Arrival sequence.
DUPKEY	Duplicate key support: D=Dup keys are support; U=Unique keys only.
SOURCE	Source file indicator: Y=File is a SOURCE physical file.
UFCBPR	User file control block parameters.
UFCBOV	User file control block overrides.
VOLIDO	Offset to the location of the volume ID for a diskette or tape file.
BLKIOL	Blocked input/output limit. The maximum number of records that can be sent or received during blocked input/output.
OFLINE	Overflow line for the PRINTER device.
BLKIOO	Blocked input/output offset. The offset from the current data file record to the next data file record.
PGMDEV	The name of the WORKSTN device that is running the program.

Figure 10-165: INFDS Subfield Description (2 of 2)

Predefined INFDS Subfields

There are several subfields that are more easily available through the use of predefined keyword locations. These keywords are used in place of the "from" and "to" locations of the subfields. For example, *FILE can be used in columns 44 to 51 of the input specification to access/define the FILE subfield.

Figure 10-166 contains example input specifications for predefined keyword subfields. These subfields directly correspond to those in Figure 10-164 and Figure 10-165.

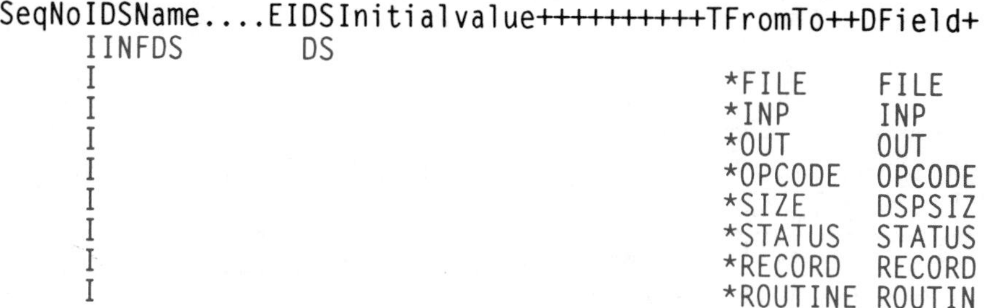

```
SeqNoIDSName....EIDSInitialvalue+++++++++TFromTo++DField+
     IINFDS       DS
     I                                        *FILE    FILE
     I                                        *INP     INP
     I                                        *OUT     OUT
     I                                        *OPCODE  OPCODE
     I                                        *SIZE    DSPSIZ
     I                                        *STATUS  STATUS
     I                                        *RECORD  RECORD
     I                                        *ROUTINE ROUTIN
```

Figure 10-166: Predefined Subfield Keywords

The subfield ROUTIN contains the RPG routine being performed when an exception/error condition occurs. The possible routines are listed in Figure 10-167.

Routine	Description
*INIT	Start of the program (i.e., program initialization).
*GETIN	Get input phase of the RPG cycle.
*DETC	Top of Detail calculations
*DETL	Top of Detail output.
*TOTC	Top of Total-time calculations.
*TOTL	Top of Total-time output.
*OFL	Overflow output.
*TERM	End the program.
pgm name	The name of a called program, such as those used with SPECIAL device files. Note: Only the first eight characters of the program name fit into this subfield.

Figure 10-167: Valid RPG Routine Names for Subfield *ROUTINE

Program Status Error Codes

Most operation codes support status codes. When an operation code generates a program exception/error, the *STATUS subfield in the program-information data structure is updated. Figure 10-168 contains a list of several exception/error status codes. In addition, if the operation code supports an error indicator, that indicator is set on when an error is generated.

For operation codes that do not support an error indicator (e.g., SQRT, ADD, SUB, MULT, and DIV) the program exception/error subroutine (*PSSR) is automatically called when an exception/error is detected; if the routine exists in the program.

Example 142 — Program Status Data Structure used to detect a divide by zero error.

```
SeqNoIDSName....ESDSExternalname..........PFromTo++DField+
0010 IPSDS        SDS
0020 I                                      *STATUS  STATUS

SeqNoCLOn01n02n03Factor1+++OpCodFactor2+++ResultLenDXHiLoEq
0050 C                     Z-ADD5         FACT1   30
0060 C                     Z-ADD0         FACT2   30
0070 C          FACT1      DIV  FACT2     ANSWER  30
0080 C                     MOVE *ON       *INLR
0090 CSR        *PSSR      BEGSR
0100 C          STATUS     IFEQ 0102
0110 C                     Z-ADD999       ANSWER
0120 C                     ENDIF
0130 CSR        ENDPSR     ENDSR
```

Status	Description
00000	No exception/error detected.
00001	Called program ended with LR indicator set on.
00101	Square root of negative number attempted.
00102	Divide by zero attempted.
00121	Invalid array index.
00122	OCCUR operation outside of data structure occurrence range.
00202	Called program failed with halt indicators (H1 to H9) set OFF.
00211	Program specified on CALL or FREE operation on not found.
00221	Called program accessed a parameter that was not passed to it.
00231	Called program failed with one of the halt indicators (H1 to H9) set ON.
00232	Halt indicator (H1 to H9) set ON in current program.
00233	Halt indicator (H1 to H9) set ON and RETRN operation attempted.
00299	RPG formatted dump failed.
00333	Error occurred during DSPLY operation.
00401	Data area specified for IN or OUT opcode not found.
00411	Attributes of data area specified for IN or OUT operation does not match that of the actual data area.
00412	Data area specified for OUT operation was not locked.
00413	Error occurred during IN or OUT operation to a data area.
00414	Security violation occurred while attempting to read a data area.
00415	Security violation occurred while attempting to write to a data area.
00421	Error occurred during UNLCK operation to a data area.
00431	Data area lock detected by another process (program, job, etc.) while attempting to access a data area in this program.
00432	Data area lock detected by another program in the current process (job) while attempting to access a data area in this program.
00907	Decimal data error detected. Bad packed or zoned data found.
09998	Internal failure in RPG or generated runtime routine.
09999	Program exception in an operating system routine.

Figure 10-168: RPG Runtime Program Status Error Codes

Program Status Data Structure

The program status data structure (PSDS) is a data structure that contains information about the program being run and exception/errors that occur. As well as date/time information. A program status data structure is identified by the letters SDS in columns 18, 19 and 20 of the input specification.

Figure 10-169 contains an example input specification for the program status data structure. The field names used are for illustration purposes only.

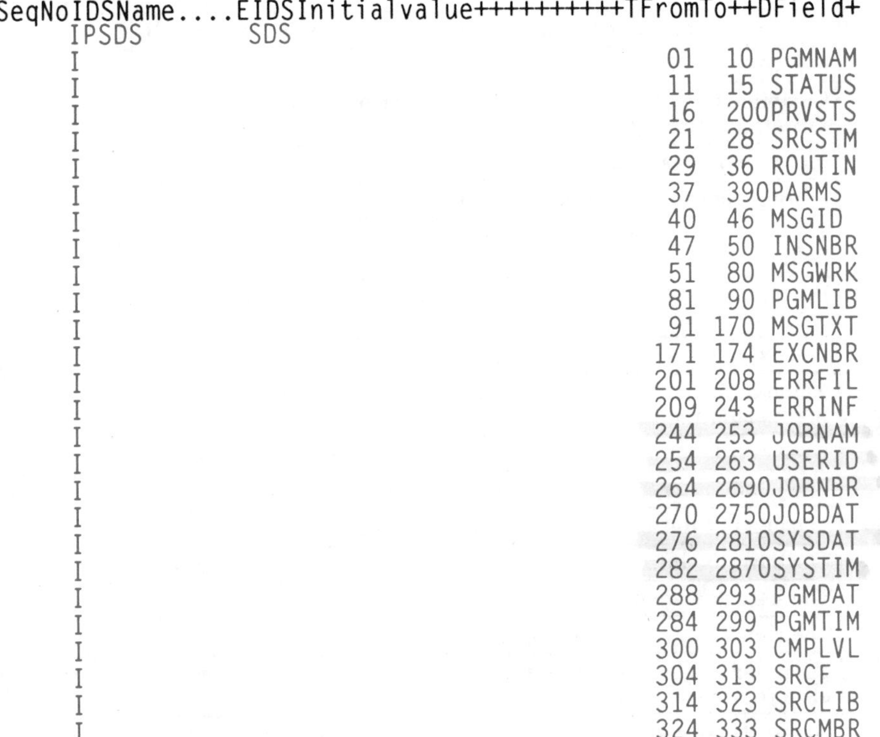

```
SeqNoIDSName....EIDSInitialvalue++++++++++TFromTo++DField+
     IPSDS         SDS
     I                                         01  10 PGMNAM
     I                                         11  15 STATUS
     I                                         16  200PRVSTS
     I                                         21  28 SRCSTM
     I                                         29  36 ROUTIN
     I                                         37  390PARMS
     I                                         40  46 MSGID
     I                                         47  50 INSNBR
     I                                         51  80 MSGWRK
     I                                         81  90 PGMLIB
     I                                         91 170 MSGTXT
     I                                        171 174 EXCNBR
     I                                        201 208 ERRFIL
     I                                        209 243 ERRINF
     I                                        244 253 JOBNAM
     I                                        254 263 USERID
     I                                        264 2690JOBNBR
     I                                        270 2750JOBDAT
     I                                        276 2810SYSDAT
     I                                        282 2870SYSTIM
     I                                        288 293 PGMDAT
     I                                        284 299 PGMTIM
     I                                        300 303 CMPLVL
     I                                        304 313 SRCF
     I                                        314 323 SRCLIB
     I                                        324 333 SRCMBR
```

Figure 10-169: Program Status Data Structure

Figure 10-170 includes a description of each program status data structure subfield. Only one program status data structure can be specified per program.

Subfield	Description
PGMNAM	Name of the program being run
STATUS	Status code. See Figure 10-168 on page 446 for a list of program status error codes.
PRVSTS	Previous status code (if any).
SRCSTM	The statement number in the source member, being run when the exception/error occurred.
ROUTIN	Name of the RPG routine that was running when an exception/error occurred. See Figure 10-172 on page 449 for a list of possible routines.
PARMS	Number of parameters passed to the program when it was called.
MSGID	System message ID number.
INSNBR	Compiled code statement number being performed when an exception/error occurred.
MSGWRK	Message support work area.
PGMLIB	Library containing the program being run.
MSGTXT	Text for the message ID in the MSGID field. Valid when the STATUS code fields = 09999.
ERRFIL	File name on which the last file operation was performed when and exception/error occurs.
ERRINF	File exception/error status information.
JOBNAM	Name of the job (e.g., WORKSTN device ID or actual session/job name) that is running the program.
USERID	User profile name of the user that initialed the program or job.
JOBNBR	The job number that the system assigned to the session.
JOBDAT	The current data, known to the system, when the program was started.
JOBTIM	The current time, known to the system, when the program started.
PGMDAT	The date the program was compiled.
PGMTIM	The time the program was compiled.
CMPLVL	Compiler level—release and modification level of the operating system used to run the compiler.
SRCF	Name of the source file used to compile the program.
SRCLIB	Name of the source file's library used to compile the program.
SRCMBR	Name of the source member used to compile the program.

Figure 10-170: PSDS Subfield Descriptions

There are several subfields that are more easily available through the use of predefined keyword locations. These keywords are used in place of the "from" and "to" locations of the subfields. For example, *PROGRAM can be used in columns 44 to 51 of the input specification to access/define the name of the program.

Figure 10-171 contains example input specifications for predefined keyword subfield locations.

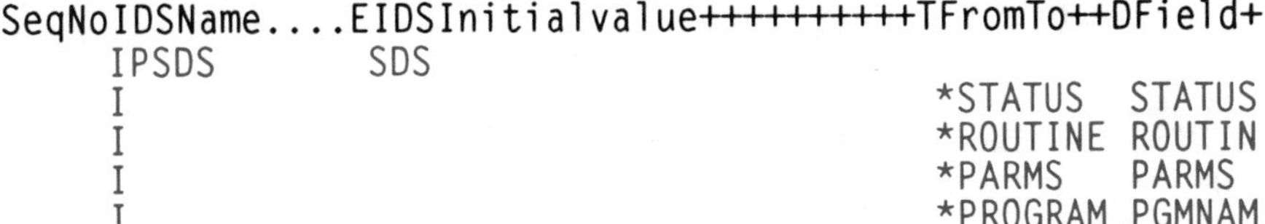

```
SeqNoIDSName....EIDSInitialvalue++++++++++TFromTo++DField+
     IPSDS       SDS
     I                                     *STATUS  STATUS
     I                                     *ROUTINE ROUTIN
     I                                     *PARMS   PARMS
     I                                     *PROGRAM PGMNAM
```

Figure 10-171: Predefined PSDS Keywords

All subfields correspond to the subfields defined in Figure 10-170 and Figure 10-171.

The subfield ROUTIN contains the RPG routine being performed when an exception/error condition occurs. This field is only updated if the RPG cycle is being used. The possible routines are listed in Figure 10-172.

Routine	Description
*INIT	Start of the program (i.e., program initialization).
*GETIN	Get input phase of the RPG cycle.
*DETC	Top of Detail calculations
*DETL	Top of Detail output.
*TOTC	Top of Total-time calculations.
*TOTL	Top of Total-time output.
*OFL	Overflow output.
*TERM	End the program.
pgm name	The name of a called program, such as those used with SPECIAL device files. Note: Only the first eight characters of the program name fit into this subfield.

Figure 10-172: Valid RPG Routines for the Subfield *ROUTINE

Exception/Error Subroutine

The exception/error subroutine is a general exception/error handling routine that traps, corrects, ignores or cancels errors. An exception/error subroutine can be assigned to each file. Each file can have a unique exception/error subroutine or the subroutine can be shared by many files.

A special exception/error subroutine *PSSR (program status subroutine) can be specified in the program to trap all unchecked error conditions—for example, a divide by zero error.

The subroutine *PSSR can be used as the file exception/error subroutine, and it is often used for just that purpose.

File exception/error handling subroutines are specified on the file continuation specification. The subroutine is assigned to a file by the INFSR file continuation keyword. Figure 10-173 illustrates this technique.

The special exception/error handling subroutine *PSSR is called when an error occurs and no file exception/error handling routine is specified. If the subroutine *PSSR is not placed into the RPG program, RPG has its own internal exception/error handling routine, known as the default exception/error handling routine. The default exception/error handling routine is less than elegant in its handling of errors and normally causes the program to end.

Figure 10-173 illustrates the use of a file information data structure and an exception/error subroutine in an RPG program.

```
SeqNoFFilenameIFE.E....Rlen...K.OV....EDevice+RecNbrKKeywrdEntry+EX...UC
     FCUSTINQ CF  E                   WORKSTN
     F                                             KINFDS WSDS
     F                                             KINFSR *PSSR
     F                                             KNUM        01
     FCUSTMASTIF  E           K       DISK

SeqNoIDSName....EIDSInitialvalue+++++++++TFromTo++DField+
     IWSDS        DS
     I                                    *STATUS  STATUS
     IPSDS        SDS
     I                                    *PROGRAM PGMNAM
     I                                     201 208 ERRFIL

SeqNoCLOn01n02n03Factor1+++OpCodFactor2+++ResultLenDXHiLoEq
     C                     WRITEPROMPTER                      Prompt User
     C                     READ CUSTINQ                     58 Wait4TimeOut
     C                     EXSR RTVFKY                        Rtv F-Key
                           .
                           .
      *   Program status (exception/error) subroutine begins here
     CSR          *PSSR    BEGSR
     C            RECURS   CABGE1         ENDPSR              Recursive?
     C                     ADD  1         RECURS
     C            STATUS   IFEQ 01331                         WS Time out
     C            ERRFIL   IFEQ 'CUSTINQ'
     C                     CLOSECUSTINQ                   56
     C                     MOVEL'*CANCL'  RTNPNT  8
     C                     ENDIF
     C                     ELSE
      *                    .
      *                      additional error handling code can go here
      *                    .
     C                     ENDIF
     C                     Z-ADD0         RECURS  30
     CSR          ENDPSR   ENDSRRTNPNT
```

Figure 10-173: Exception/Error Handling with INFDS and *PSSR

Factor 2 of the ENDSR operation of an exception/error handling routine can contain a return point or it can be blank.

If Factor 2 of the ENDSR operation is blank and the subroutine was called with the EXSR or CASxx operation, control returns to the operation following the EXSR or CASxx operation.

If this condition is not met, the program normally cancels. Therefore, for better control of exception/error handling, an INFDS, INFSR and *PSSR are used in conjunction with resulting indicator 2 of a calculation operation code.

The flowchart in Figure 10-174 illustrates the RPG exception/error handling routine. The steps outlined below document the exception/error flowchart.

1. Setup the file information or program status data structure, if specified, with status information.
2. If the exception/error occurred on an operation code that has an indicator specified in positions 56 and 57 of the calculation specifications, RPG sets the indicator, and control returns to the next sequential instruction in the calculations.
3. RPG determines whether the appropriate exception/error subroutine (INFSR or *PSSR) is present in the program.
4. Control passes to the exception/error subroutine (INFSR or *PSSR).
5. RPG determines whether a return point is specified in Factor 2 of the ENDSR operation for the exception/error subroutine. If a return point is specified, the program goes to the specified return point. If a return point is not specified, the program goes to step 6. If a field name is specified in Factor 2 of the ENDSR operation and the content is not one of the RPG-defined return points (such as *GETIN or *DETC), the program goes to step 6. No error is indicated, and the original error is handled as though the Factor 2 entry were blank.
6. If the exception/error subroutine was called explicitly by the EXSR operation, the program returns to the next sequential instruction. If not, the program continues with step 7.
7. If the STATUS code is 1121 to 1126 (see "Program Status Codes" in Chapter 4 for a list of available status codes,) control returns to the next sequential instruction. If not, the program continues with step 7.
8. A message is issued. For an interactive program, the message is sent to the requester (e.g., the workstation user). For a batch program, the message is sent to the computer system operator. If the computer system operator is not available, a default response is used.
9. RPG determines whether the response to the message is to cancel. If the response is to cancel, the program branches to step 11. If not, the program continues with step 10.
10. The program continues processing at *GETIN.

11. RPG determines whether the response to the message is to cancel with a dump. If the response is to cancel with a dump, the program continues with step 12. If not, the program branches to step 13.
12. RPG issues a formatted dump operation.
13. RPG closes all files and sets the return code to indicate that the program ended with an error.
14. RPG frees the program so that it can be called again, and control returns to the calling program.
15. The return code is set, and an error message is issued.
16. Control returns to the calling program.

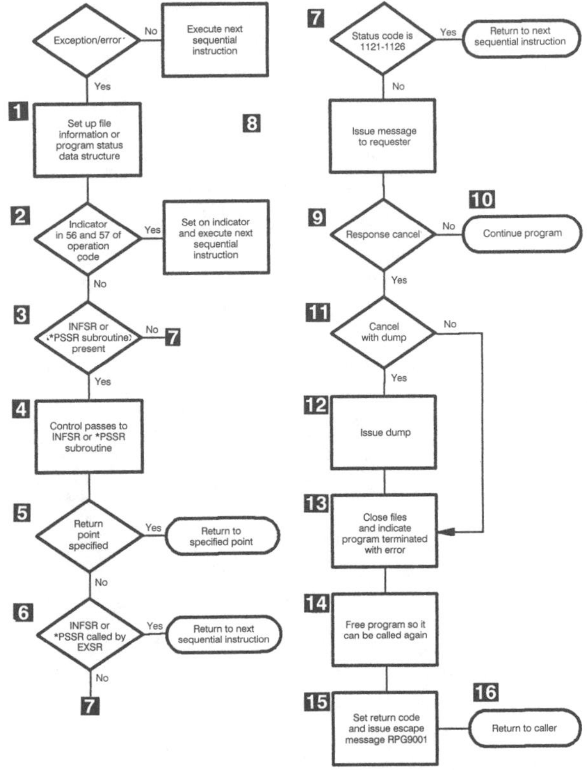

Figure 10-174: RPG Exception/Error Handling Routine

Chapter 11

Array Processing

Array Handling

Arrays are used extensively in RPG. In addition to the typical use of arrays—storing and sorting a group of similar data—arrays have traditionally provided basic string-handling capabilities and a common place to store large literal values.

An array is a collection of similar data elements arranged such that they have a single domain. The individual data elements are referred to as an *array element* and are accessed by using a subscript called an *array index*. Subscripted arrays, that is the array index, refers to the absolute element of an array. For example, STRING,3 refers to the third element of the array named STRING.

RPG supports three types of arrays:

1. Normal arrays
2. Multiple occurring data structures
3. Tables

This section will cover the first two types of arrays.

Normal Arrays

As mentioned earlier, an array is a collection of consecutive data elements. These data elements, known as array elements, are kept in the domain of an array name. Elements within the array are referenced by indexing the array.

Arrays can contain numeric or character data. If an array contains numeric data, that data can be packed, zoned or binary decimal. All array elements have the same data type, that is, all elements are either character or numeric.

To illustrate arrays throughout this section, a graphic containing a series of rows and columns used. That graphic is illustrated in Figure 11-175.

Element	1	2	3	4	5	6
Character						
Zone Digit						

Figure 11-175: Graphic Used to Illustrate Arrays in this Chapter

The row denoted as Element refers to the array element number. The number 3, for example, represents the third element in the array. The row denoted as Character refers to the character value of the array elements. The row denoted as Zone refers to the zone portion of the data in the array elements. The row denoted as Digit refers to the digit portion of the data in the array elements.

For example, an array of 9-digit packed decimal numeric elements is illustrated in Figure 11-176.

Element	1	2	3	4	5	6
Character						
Zone Digit	00000 0000F	00000 0000F	00000 0000F	00000 0000F	00000 0000F	00000 0000F

Figure 11-176: Array of Packed Decimals

A program can reference all the data of an array (i.e., the entire array), or it can refer to a specific array element. To reference an array element, the array name is suffixed with a comma (,) followed by the element number, known as the array index. For example, to refer to the third element of an array named SUM the notation SUM,3 would be used. A field can be used as the array index. This allows reference to variable array elements. For example, the notation SUM,X can be used to refer to a variable array element. The field X is used as the array index.

When a numeric field is used as the array index, the field should not contain decimal positions. Some compilers allow array indexes containing decimal positions—ignoring the digits to the right of the decimal point.

To define an array the extension specification is used. For example, to define a six-element array, SUM, with 9-digit numeric elements, the following extension specification would be used:

Example 143 — Simple Array Declaration

```
SeqNoE....................ArrnamEPRDim+LenPDAAltnamLenPDA
     E                    SUM          6  9P0
```

Input specifications can be used to define array elements. When an array is defined using both extension and input specifications, the array attribute (column 39 of the extension specification) must be left blank for both character and numeric arrays. The array attribute is instead, specified in column 43 of the input specification. For numeric arrays, if column 43 of the input specification is blank, the array elements are defined as zoned decimal. If column 43 contains a 'P', the array elements are defined as packed decimal. (See the example that follows.) Column 43 of the input specifications must be blanks for character arrays.

Example 144 — Redefining an Array on the Input Specifications

```
SeqNoE....................ArrnamEPRDim+LenPDAAltnamLenPDA
     E                    SUM         6  9 0

SeqNoIFormat++NS....Ext-Field+............PFromTo++DField+
     ICUSTOMER
     I                                    P    1  30 SUM
```

When a numeric array is further defined on an input specification, the number of decimal positions (column 52 of the input specification) must be blank.

The "from" and "to" positions of the input specifications for the array must equal the sum of the length of all the elements. In this example, each array element is a 9-digit packed decimal value. Nine digits, when packed, are reduced to five bytes. Therefore, the length of all of the elements for the array is 30 bytes (6 elements times 5 bytes).

Numeric arrays are initialized to zero; character arrays are initialized to blanks. The only exceptions are when an array is also a data structure subfield, or initialized by the *INZSR subroutine. In these situations, the initialization overrides the default.

The array SUM would be susceptible to having blanks as its initial values in the following example. Typically, the letter 'I' would be specified in column 18 of line 20. This causes the data structure to initialize its subfields based on their field attribute.

Example 145 — Numeric array redefined in a data structure

```
SeqNoE....FromfileTofile++ArrnamEPRDim+LenPDAAltnamLenPDA
0010 E                    SUM         6  9 0

SeqNoIDSName....ESDSExt-File++............PFromTo++DField+
0020 IDSDATA     DS
0030 I                                     P    1   30 SUM
```

The data structure DSDATA contains the subfield SUM, which is also a numeric array. Since DSDATA will be initialized to blanks, each (numeric) array element would contain blanks. Graphically, the array SUM would look like this:

Element	1	2	3	4	5	6
Character						
Zone Digit	4444 0000	4444 0000	4444 0000	4444 0000	4444 0000	4444 0000

When the program tries to access any elements of the array, a run-time "decimal data" exception/error may be issued. This error indicates that the elements in the array SUM do not contain valid numeric data.

There are several ways to avoid this condition. Numeric arrays that are also defined as data structure subfields can be initialized to zeros with numeric operations such as Z-ADD or MOVE, or with initialization operations, such as CLEAR. The example that follows illustrates the two most frequently used methods for initializing arrays that are also specified as a data structure subfield.

Example 146 — Two methods for Initializing a decimal array via a data structure

```
SeqNoE....FromfileTofile++ArrnamEPRDim+LenPDAAltnamLenPDA
0010 E                    SUM         6  9 0
0020 E                    TOTAL       7  9 0

SeqNoIDSName....ESDSExt-File++............PFromTo++DField+
0030 IDSDATA      DS
0040 I I                                  P    1  30 SUM
0050 I                                    P   31  65 TOTAL

SeqNoCLOn01n02n03Factor1+++OpCodFactor2+++ResultLenDXHiLoEq
     C                      .
     C*           Additional code goes here
     C                      .
0140 CSR          *INZSR    BEGSR
0150 C                      Z-ADD0         TOTAL
0160 CSR          ENDINZ    ENDSR
```

The array SUM is initialized to zeros by specifying the initialization option for the data structure subfield (column 8 in statement 40). The array TOTAL is initialized via the RPG initialization subroutine, using the Z-ADD operation (line 150).

Element	1	2	3	4	5	6
Character						
Zone Digit	00000 0000F	00000 0000F	00000 0000F	00000 0000F	00000 0000F	00000 0000F

Figure 11-177: Initialized Value of the SUM Array

Element	1	2	3	4	5	6	7
Character							
Zone Digit	00000 0000F	00000 0000F	00000 0000F	00000 0000F	00000 0000F	00000 0000F	00000 0000F

Figure 11-178: Initialized Value of the TOTAL Array

Another technique is to use the MOVE operation to move *ZEROS to the data structure itself. This technique, however, only moves zoned zeros to the data structure. Consequently, invalid data would appear in the array and a "decimal data" exception/error would be issued. Instead of the MOVE operation, a CLEAR operation can be issued to the data structure. CLEAR is "data type aware" meaning it's smart enough to put the proper data into a field, based on the field's data type.

A variation of the first technique is to specify the letter I in column 18 of the data structure specification. This causes the compiler to initialize all data structure subfields to zeros or blanks, based on the data type of the subfield. A numeric array that is also a subfield is initialized with zeros. See the example that follows.

Example 147 — Data Structure Initialization to Initialize an Array to Zero

```
SeqNoE....FromfileTofile++ArrnamEPRDim+LenPDAAltnamLenPDA
0010 E                    SUM        6  9 0

SeqNoIDSName....ESDSExt-File++............PFromTo++DField+
0020 IDSDATA     IDS
0030 I                                    P    1  30 SUM
```

Line 20, in the above example, causes the compiler to set up an initialization area for the data structure. Since the array SUM of the data structure DSDATA is numeric, positions 1 to 30 are initialized to packed zeros.

Loading Array Elements

Array elements can be loaded using three different methods:

1. Loading at compile time.
2. Loading at run-time.
3. Loading at prerun time.

Each of these techniques have wide-spread usage in RPG. The first two, however, are more common place in new programs.

The examples that follow illustrate each of these techniques.

Loading at compile time. To load an array at compile time, place the array data after the last source statement of the program. A double asterisk in columns 1 and 2 is used to identify the start of the array data. For example:

```
SeqNoE....FromfileTofile++ArrnamEPRDim+LenPDAAltnamLenPDA
     E                    ITEMS    1   5  4

SeqNoCLOn01n02n03Factor1+++OpCodFactor2+++ResultLenDXHiLoEq
     C                           .
     C*           Additional code goes here
     C                           .
**
AAAA
BBBB
CCCC
DDDD
EEEE
```

This technique creates a compile-time array. The array data is compiled with the program. The array elements are loaded at compile-time. Graphically, the array would appear as follows:

Element	1	2	3	4	5
Character	AAAA	BBBB	CCCC	DDDD	EEEE
Zone	CCCC	CCCC	CCCC	CCCC	CCCC
Digit	1111	2222	3333	4444	5555

The Character row identifies the "visible" characters stored in the array elements. For example, the first element contains AAAA. The zone and digit portions of the characters are also specified. That is, the letter A is X'C1", B is X'C2' and so on.

Loading at run-time. Perform the following steps: (a) specify the array as a single field of an input file or on a data structure; (b) specify each element of the array as a field of one or more input files; or (c) load the array in the calculation specifications.

Example 148 — Loading a runtime array as a single input field

```
SeqNoFFileNameIPE.E....RLEN...K.OV....EDevice+RecNbrKOptionEntry+
     FPROVNAM IF  F     200             DISK

SeqNoE....FromfileTofile++ArrnamEPRDim+LenPDAAltnamLenPDA
     E                     STATES     50  4

SeqNoIFormat++NSEUDSExternal++............PFromTo++DField+
     IPROVNAM NS  01
     I                                        1 200 STATES

SeqNoCLOn01n02n03Factor1+++OpCodFactor2+++ResultLenDXHiLoEq
     C                      READ PROVNAM                  58  EOF?
     C                      .
     C                      .
     C                      .
```

In Example 148, the file PROVNAM is used to load the array STATES. The array STATES is specified as a fifty element array, each element is four characters in length. The array is loaded at run-time when a record is read from the PROVNAM file.

In this type of situation, the file PROVNAM would typically contain only one record. However, if more than one record existed, each time a new record is read the array would receive the values of that new record.

Example 149 — Loading a runtime array from multiple input fields

```
SeqNoFFileNameIPE.E....RLEN...K.OV....EDevice+
     FQTRSLS  IF  F      30              DISK

SeqNoE....FromfileTofile++ArrnamEPRDim+LenPDAAltnamLenPDA
     E                    QTR          4  7 2

SeqNoIFormat++NSEUINExt-File++............PFromTo++DField+
     IQTRSLS  NS  01
     I                                          1   2 DIV
     I                                    P     3   62QTR,1
     I                                    P    12  152QTR,2
     I                                    P    23  262QTR,3
     I                                    P    27  302QTR,4

SeqNoCLOn01n02n03Factor1+++OpCodFactor2+++ResultLenDXHiLoEq
     C                     MOVE *OFF      EOF     1
     C           EOF       DOWEQ*OFF
     C                     READ QRTSLS                   LREOF?
     C                     MOVE *INLR     EOF
     C           EOF       IFEQ *OFF
     C                     XFOOTQTR       YTDSLS  92
     C                     .
     C           Additional code goes here.
     C                     .
     C                     ENDIF
     C                     ENDDO
```

In Example 149, the file QTRSLS (quarterly sales figures) is used to load the array QTR. Array QTR contains four 7-digit values. Since the values are scattered throughout the record of QTRSLS, each array element is specified on the input specifications.

In this example, the file QTRSLS is read, loading the array QTR with quarterly sales figures for a division. Then, the quarterly sales figures for each division is totaled (XFOOT). Then, processing continues—perhaps printing a report of the figures.

Example 150 — Loading a runtime array via Calculation specifications

```
SeqNoE....FromfileTofile++ArrnamEPRDim+LenPDAAltnamLenPDA
     E                    SUM         5  9P0

SeqNoCLOn01n02n03Factor1+++OpCodFactor2+++ResultLenDXHiLoEq
     C                     Z-ADD6          X
     C                     DO   5          I
     C           X         MULT I          SUM,I
     C                     ENDDO
     C           ENDPGM    TAG
     C                     MOVE *ON        *INLR
```

In Example 150, the array SUM is loaded with the results of several multiplication operations. After the array is loaded it would contain the following data:

Element	**1**	**2**	**3**	**4**	**5**
Character					
Zone Digit	00006 0000F	00002 0001F	00008 0001F	00004 0002F	00000 0003F

Loading at prerun time. To load a prerun time array, define a file name as an array or table by placing an E in column 39 of the File Description specification and the file name in columns 11 to 18 of the extension specification.

Example 151 — Loading a pre-runtime array from a file

```
SeqNoFFileNameIPE.E....RLEN...K.OV....EDevice+RecNbrKOptionEntry+
     FPRINT   O   F     132     OV      PRINTER
     FDIVSALE CT  F       5            EDISK

SeqNoE....FromfileTofile++ArrnamEPRDim+LenPDAAltnamLenPDA
     E    DIVSALE SALES           1   6  5 0

SeqNoCLOn01n02n03Factor1+++OpCodFactor2+++ResultLenDXHiLoEq
     C                         XFOOTSALES,X   TOTAL   90
     C                         EXCPTTOTALS
     C                         Z-ADD0         SALES
     C                         MOVE *ON       *INLR

SeqNoOFilenameEFBASBSAn01n02n03Field+EBEnd+POutputconstant+++++++++++
     OPRINT   E   03             TOTALS
     O                                  +  2 'Sales totals for all'
     O                                  +  1 'divisions:'
     O                           TOTAL 3 +  2
```

In Example 151 the SALES array is loaded with data from the DIVSALE file. The DIVSALE file is defined as a combined table (CT in columns 15 and 16 of the File Description specification). The DIVSALE file is specified as combined (input and output), but could have been input-only or output-only as well. The file is further defined by an extension specification; (and E is specified in column 39 of the File Description specification).

When a prerun-time array is defined, no input/output specifications are allowed for the file being used with the array.

The program begins by adding the elements of the array SALES and producing a total. The XFOOT (cross foot) operation is used to produce the total. The total is printed, and the array is cleared.

Since the DIVSALE file is a combined (input/output) file, the contents of the SALES array is written to the DIVSALE file when the program ends. The data already in the DIVSALE file is replaced with the contents of the SALES array.

Multiple Occurrence Data Structures

Multiple occurrence data structures function similar to arrays; however, there are several operational differences between arrays and multi-occurrence data structures. The following list of items defines the characteristics of multi-occurrence data structures:

1. They are defined with input specifications.
2. They can be up to 9999 bytes in length.
3. They can contain up to 9999 elements or occurrences.
4. Each occurrence can be defined by subfields.
5. The occurrence of data structure is set and retrieved by the OCUR operation.
6. An array can be used as a subfield, providing two-dimensional array capability.

The following example application illustrates a multiple occurrence data structure used as a multidimensional array.

Example Application — Quarterly Sales Report

Suppose several divisions for a company exist, creating a need for a report containing a matrix of quarterly sales figures.

The file DIVSALES contains sales data for each division. DIVSALES is made up of three fields:

DIVNBR	Division number
QTR	Quarter that sales were made
QTRSLS	Quarterly sales

The DIVSALE file contains multiple records for each of several divisions, and one or more record for each quarter. (Our sample data contains only one record for each quarter's sales per division.)

Figure 11-179 illustrates the data contained in the file DIVSALE.

DIVNBR	QTR	QTRSLS
01	01	1000.00
01	02	1200.00
01	03	1500.00
01	04	900.00
02	01	2300.00
02	02	5700.00
02	03	6300.00
02	04	1400.00
03	01	32000.00
03	02	54000.00
03	03	1500.00
03	04	65000.00

Figure 11-179: Data contained in Database File DIVSALE

Using RPG program-defined printer output specifications or an externally described printer device file, the report should be formatted with multiple rows and columns. See Figure 11-180.

```
*... ... 1 ... ... 2 ... ... 3 ... ... 4 ... ... 5 ... ... 6 ... ... 7 ...
    Div     -------- Quarterly Sales Figures --------                Percent
    Nbr         First      Second       Third      Fourth       Total  of Total
     01     12345.67-   12345.67-   12345.67-   12345.67-   12345.67-    12.345
     02     12345.67-   12345.67-   12345.67-   12345.67-   12345.67-    12.345
     03     12345.67-   12345.67-   12345.67-   12345.67-   12345.67-    12.345
            --------    --------    --------    --------    ========
 Totals->   12345.67-   12345.67-   12345.67-   12345.67-   12345.67-

 % of Sales  12.345      12.345      12.345      12.345
```

Figure 11-180: Report Format/Layout

An array overlaying a multiple occurrence data structure can be used to produce this report's matrix. The example program code on the following pages can be used to produce the report featured in Figure 11-180. The program code is featured in sections. Each section is explained with comments and narrative as needed.

After all sections of the program have been presented, a complete program listing is featured in Figure 11-181 beginning on page 472.

```
SeqNoFFileNameIPE.E....RLEN...K.OV....EDevice+RecNbrKOptionEntry+
     FPRINTER O   F     132      OV      PRINTER
     FDIVSALE IF  E                      DISK

SeqNoE....FromfileTofile++ArrnamEPRDim+LenPDAAltnamLenPDA
     E                   QS            4  7 2                Qtr Sales
     E                   QTOT          4  9 2                Qtr Totals
     E                   QP            4  5 3                Qtr Percent

SeqNoIDSName....EIDSInitialvalue+++++++++TFromTo++DField+
     IDIVS       IDS                           10
     I                                      P   1    30QS

SeqNoCLOn01n02n03Factor1+++OpCodFactor2+++ResultLenDXHiLoEq
     C                      Z-ADD3         NBRDIV  30           Set # of Div
      *    Set the file to the first record to be used.
     C                      READ DIVSALE                  LR
      *    Define grand total and sub-total fields with the
      *    attributes of the quarterly sales figures.
     C           *LIKE      DEFN QTRSLS    TOTAL + 2
     C           *LIKE      DEFN QTRSLS    SUBTOT+ 2
      *    Fill the DIVS data structure with the
      *    quarterly sales from each division.
     C           *INLR      DOWEQ*OFF
     C           DIVNBR     OCUR DIVS
     C                      ADD  QTRSLS    QS,QTR
     C                      ADD  QTRSLS    TOTAL
     C                      READ DIVSALE                  LR
     C                      ENDDO
```

At this point, the data structure DIVS would be filled with each division's quarterly sales figures. The annual sales for all divisions is stored in the subfield TOTAL.

The next step will be to calculate the total sales for each division and for each quarter. Each quarter's sales are accumulated in a second array named QTOT (quarterly totals). Then, the percentage of total sales for each division is calculated.

```
SeqNoCLOn01n02n03Factor1+++OpCodFactor2+++ResultLenDXHiLoEq
     C                         DO   10         X        30
     C              X          OCUR DIVS
      *    Add up the elements in the array producing
      *    the total for this division.
     C                         XFOOTQS         SUBTOT
      *    Add the individual quarterly sales for this
      *    division to the total quarterly sales array.
     C                         ADD  QS         QTOT
      *    Calculate the percentage of total sales for this
      *    division using the formula D/T*100 (division sales
      *    over totals sales times 100).
     C              SUBTOT     DIV  TOTAL      PERCNT  53
     C                         MULT 100        PERCNT  53
```

Next, the detail lines are printed with each division's quarterly sales. At this point, the report output would be added.

```
SeqNoCLOn01n02n03Factor1+++OpCodFactor2+++ResultLenDXHiLoEq
      *    Print the divisions sales figures.
     C                         EXCPTDETAIL
     C                         ENDDO
```

```
SeqNoOFilenameEFBASBSAn01n02n03Field+EBEnd+POutputconstant++++++++++++
     OPRINTER E  102              HEADER
     O                                   +  4 'Div'
     O                                   +  2 '---------'
     O                                   +  1 'Quarterly Sales Figures'
     O                                   +  1 '---------'
     O                                   +  4 'Percent'
     O         E  1               HEADER
     O                                   +  4 'Nbr'
     O                                   +  7 'First     Second'
     O                                   +  6 'Third     Fourth'
     O                                   +  7 'Total   of Total'
     O         E  1              DETAIL
     O                           DIVNBR  +  5
     O                           QS,1   L +  4
     O                           QS,2   L +  2
     O                           QS,3   L +  2
     O                           QS,4   L +  2
     O                           SUBTOTL  +  2
     O                           PERCNT3  +  4
```

The final step involves printing the totals for each quarter and calculating the percentage of total sales for each quarter.

```
SeqNoCLOn01n02n03Factor1+++OpCodFactor2+++ResultLenDXHiLoEq
     *   Calculate the percentage of sales for each
     *   quarter using the formula (QS/T)*100 (quarterly
     *   sales over totals sales times 100).
     C           QTOT      DIV  TOTAL     QP
     C                     MULT 100       QP
     *   Print the quarterly totals
     C                     EXCPTTOTALS
     C                     MOVE *ON       *INLR            End program

SeqNoOFilenameEFBASBSAn01n02n03Field+EBEnd+POutputconstant+++++++++++
     O        E  1               TOTALS
     O                                  + 11 '--------'
     O                                  +  3 '--------'
     O                                  +  3 '--------'
     O                                  +  3 '--------'
     O                                  +  3 '========'
     O        E  1               TOTALS
     O                                  +  1 'Totals->'
     O                           QTOT,1L +  2
     O                           QTOT,2L +  2
     O                           QTOT,3L +  2
     O                           QTOT,4L +  2
     O                           TOTAL L +  2
```

Figure 11-181 contains a listing of the entire program. Most comments have been removed to reveal the program source code more directly.

```
SeqNoFFilenameIFE.E....Rlen...K.OV....EDevice+RecNbrKKeywrdEntry+EX...UC
     FPRINTER O   F     132      OV      PRINTER
     FDIVSALEIF   E                      DISK

SeqNoE....FromfileTofile++Array+EprDim+LenPDAAltnamLenPDAComments+++++++++
     E                    QS           4  7 2                QtrDiv Sales
     E                    QTOT         4  9 2                Qtr Totals
     E                    QP           4  5 3                Qtr Percent

SeqNoIDSName....EIDSInitialvalue++++++++++TFromTo++DField+
     IDIVS        IDS                          10
     I                                       P   1   30 QS

SeqNoCLRN01N02N03Factor1+++OpCodFactor2+++ResultLenDXHILOEQComments+++++++
     C                     Z-ADD3         NBRDIV  30          Set # of Div
     C                     READ DIVSALE                     LR Read data
     C           *LIKE     DEFN QTRSLS    TOTAL + 2           Define TOTAL
     C           *LIKE     DEFN QTRSLS    SUBTOT+ 2           Define SubTL
     C           *INLR     DOWEQ*OFF                          Do till EOF
     C           DIVNBR    OCUR DIVS                          Set DS Occur
     C                     ADD  QTRSLS    QS,QTR              Add to qtr
     C                     ADD  QTRSLS    TOTAL               Add to total
     C                     READ DIVSALE                     LR Get next Rec
     C                     ENDDO
     C                     DO   NBRDIV    X       30          Prt each Div
     C           X         OCUR DIVS                          Set DS Occur
     C                     XFOOTQS        SUBTOT              Sum Qtr Sale
     C                     ADD  QS        QTOT                Add to qtr
     C           SUBTOT    DIV  TOTAL     PERCNT  53          Computer Div
     C                     MULT 100       PERCNT  53          % of sales.
     C                     EXCPTDETAIL                        Print sales
     C                     ENDDO
     C           QTOT      DIV  TOTAL     QP                  Compute Qtr
     C                     DIV  100       QP                  % of sales
     C                     EXCPTTOTALS                        Print totals
     C                     MOVE *ON       *INLR               End program
```

Continued on next page

Figure 11-181: Quarterly Sales Report Program (1 of 2)

Continued from the previous page

```
SeqNoOFilenameEFBASBSAn01n02n03Field+EBEnd+POutputconstant+++++++++++
     OPRINTER E  102           HEADER
     O                                + 4 'Div'
     O                                + 2 '--------'
     O                                + 1 'Quarterly Sales Figures'
     O                                + 1 '--------'
     O                                + 4 'Percent'
     O        E  1             HEADER
     O                                + 4 'Nbr'
     O                                + 7 'First     Second'
     O                                + 6 'Third     Fourth'
     O                                + 7 'Total   of Total'
     O        E  1             DETAIL
     O                         DIVNBR + 5
     O                         QS,1  L + 4
     O                         QS,2  L + 2
     O                         QS,3  L + 2
     O                         QS,4  L + 2
     O                         SUBTOTL + 2
     O                         PERCNT3 + 4
     O        E  1             TOTALS
     O                                +11 '--------'
     O                                + 3 '--------'
     O                                + 3 '--------'
     O                                + 3 '--------'
     O                                + 3 '========'
     O        E  1             TOTALS
     O                                + 1 'Totals->'
     O                         QTOT,1L + 2
     O                         QTOT,2L + 2
     O                         QTOT,3L + 2
     O                         QTOT,4L + 2
     O                         TOTAL L + 2
```

Figure 11-181: Quarterly Sales Report Program (2 of 2)

Chapter 12

Tools and Techniques

The RPG language, while it is not the easiest language to create "black box" functions, does provide the facilities to create very useful utilities, tools, and techniques specifically for use with other RPG programs.

This chapter illustrates serveral techniques written in RPG, including:

1. Stack Manipulation
2. Sentence (word) Parsing

Stack Manipulation

Stack manipulation has proven to be one of the most useful features of any language. A stack provides the programmer with a place to store (i.e., PUSH) data and then later retrieve (i.e., POP) the data.

A stack could be depicted as a stack of dishes (i.e., stack entries). Each time a new dish is placed onto the stack of dishes, the stack grows. When a dish is removed, it is taken from the top of the stack—lowering reducing the entries on the stack. This technique is known as last in, first out, or LIFO, processing.

With a program stack, a program PUSHes data onto the stack—the stack grows. When the program needs data from the stack, it POPs the data from the top of the stack—the stack shrinks.

This kind of processing is useful in string manipulation, such as parsing infix notation or passing a variable number of parameters between programs. (By passing the stack, the parameter never changes; only the data and quantity of data on the stack changes.)

RPG does not directly provide support for stack manipulation. However, the stack and stack manipulation can be simulated with RPG code and, unlike most languages that only allow a few bytes to be placed on the stack, an RPG stack routine can be created to support data of virtually any size.

To implement stack support in an RPG program, an array must be defined and two subroutines must be included in the program.

```
SeqNoE....FromfileTofile++Array+EprDim+LenPDAAltnamLenPDAComments+++++++++
     E                    $S         200 10                        Stack Array
```

This array specification defines the $S array. $S is used as the stack. Up to 200 entries may be placed onto this stack. Each entry can be up to 10 characters in length, although the stack can be almost any size. If a larger or smaller stack is required, the number of elements for $S should be adjusted.

In addition to the array, several stack field names must be defined to take advantage of stack support. The table that appears in Figure 12-182 lists the definitions for each of the stack field names.

Field	Type	Description
SI	Dec(5,0)	Stack index. Contains the index of the array element that will be used by the next PUSH or POP operation. In other words, SI always "points" to the top-of-stack.
TOS	Dec(5,0)	Top of stack limit. Contains the maximum number of stack entries permitted. In most cases, 200 entries is adequate. The value in this field is constant and should reflect the number of array elements allowed in the $S array.
TOSMSG	(*)	Top of stack message constant. The type and length of this field should match that of an array element of the stack array. This field contains a constant that the programmer defines to indicate when a PUSH or POP operation will exceed the top-of-stack. For example, if TOS=200, then the 200th successive PUSH operation will cause the PUSH subroutine to move the constant contained in TOSMSG to the field STACK. This will indicate an error condition, and the program should react properly.
STACK	(*)	Stack data. This field contains the data that was just PUSHed to or POPed from the stack. The type and length of this field should match that of an array element of the stack array.
$S	(*)	Stack array. This array contains the stack data. The array is used by the PUSH and POP subroutines to hold the stack entries. As stated earlier, the number of elements within this array should correspond to the value specified for the field TOS. The length of the array elements is determined by the requirements of the data that will be placed onto the stack.

Figure 12-182: Push/Pop Stack Field Definitions

To put data onto the stack, the data must be copied to the field STACK with the MOVE operation; then, the PUSH subroutine is called. Figure 12-183 illustrates the PUSH subroutine.

```
SeqNoCLOn01n02n03Factor1+++OpCodFactor2+++ResultLenDXHiLoEq
0001 CSR            PUSH      BEGSR
      *    Push data onto the stack.
0002 C              SI        IFGE TOS                          If top-stack
0003 C                        MOVE TOSMSG       STACK           Send TOS Msg
0004 C                        ELSE
0005 C                        ADD  1            SI              Increment SI
0006 C                        MOVE STACK        $S,SI           Put to stack
0007 C                        ENDIF
0008 CSR                      ENDSR
```

Figure 12-183: Stack PUSH Subroutine

The subroutine PUSH *pushes* stack entries onto the stack. Line 2 first tests for the top-of-stack limit. If the PUSH operation would cause the stack limit to be exceeded (line 2), the field TOSMSG is moved into the field STACK (line 3). If the limit will not be exceeded, the stack index field SI is incremented (line 5), and the contents of the field STACK is copied to the next stack array element (line 6).

To remove data from the stack, the POP subroutine is called. Upon completion, the field STACK will contain either the top-of-stack message or the data that was in the top stack entry, i.e., that in the array element $S,SI. Figure 12-184 illustrates the POP subroutine.

```
SeqNoCLOn01n02n03Factor1+++OpCodFactor2+++ResultLenDXHiLoEq
0001 CSR            POP       BEGSR
      *    Pop data off of stack.
0002 C              SI        IFLE 0                            Bottom Stack
0003 C                        MOVE TOSMSG       STACK           Send TOS Msg
0004 C                        ELSE
0005 C                        MOVE $S,SI        STACK           Pop stack
0006 C                        SUB  1            SI              Decrement SI
0007 C                        ENDIF
0008 CSR            ENDPOP    ENDSR
```

Figure 12-184: Stack POP Subroutine

The subroutine POP *pops* stack entries off the top of the stack. Line 2 first tests for the bottom-of-stack limit. If the POP operation would cause the stack limit to be exceeded (line 2), the field TOSMSG is moved into the field STACK (line 3). If the limit is not exceeded, the contents of the array element at the stack index ($S,SI) is copied to the field STACK (line 5). Then the stack index field SI is decremented.

Parsing a Group of Words

A primary use for a stack is in parsing. Parsing is a technique used to separate independent elements from a string of data. For example, the phrase PARSE A GROUP OF WORDS, when parsed, would consist of five independent words.

If parsing phrases were required, a parsing routine would need to be written to handle a large number of words; for example, an entire paragraph.

The logic behind this type of parsing routine is very basic:

1. Get a word.
2. If word exists, push word to stack.
3. If more words, branch to step 1.

Steps 2 and 3 are, in fact, quite easy. The PUSH routine has already been developed and branching should be second nature.

Step 1, however, is a little more difficult, but certainly not too terribly challenging. It simply requires the use of array processing. Figure 12-185 contains the RPG code necessary to perform step 1. This entire process is illustrated in Figure 12-187 and in Figure 12-188 the compiler listing generated from the DSPWRD program is featured.

```
SeqNoE....FromfileTofile++Array+EprDim+LenPDAAltnamLenPDAComments++++++++
0001 E                    STG      256  1                  Phrase

SeqNoCL0n01n02n03Factor1+++OpCodFactor2+++ResultLenDXHiLoEq
0002 CSR         GETWRD    BEGSR
     *     Retrieve the next word in the phrase.
     *           Input:  the array STG  (will be altered upon exit)
     *           Output: the field WORD (will contain the next word)
0003 C                     Z-ADD1         X       50          Init X to 1
0004 C           X         DOWLT256                           Find first
0005 C           STG,X     ANDEQ*BLANK                        character of
0006 C                     ADD  1         X                   next word in
0007 C                     ENDDO                              the phrase.
0008 C                     MOVE *BLANKS   SAVSTG256
0009 C                     MOVEASTG,X     SAVSTG              Save string
0010 C                     MOVEASAVSTG    STG                 Restore Stg
0011 C           X         DOWLT256                           Look for...
0012 C           STG,X     ANDGT*BLANK                        next blank
0013 C                     ADD  1         X                   Increment X
0014 C                     ENDDO                              Loop back up
0015 C                     MOVE *BLANKS   SAVSTG
0016 C                     MOVEASTG,X     SAVSTG              Save string
0017 C                     MOVEA*BLANKS   STG,X               Blank extra
0018 C                     MOVEASTG       WORD    12          Get the Word
0019 C                     MOVEASAVSTG    STG,1               Restore Stg
0020 CSR                   ENDSR
```

Figure 12-185: Retrieve Next Word from Phrase

Lines 4 to 7 search the array STG for the first non-blank character. This is the first step in left justifying the phrase. Lines 9 and 10 shift the string to the left in preparation for the next step.

Lines 11 to 14 search the array STG for the next blank character or the end of the array. This step locates the end of (last character in) the word that will be isolated.

Lines 16 and 17 blank out any data beyond the word that will be isolated. Line 18 moves the isolated word to field WORD.

Line 19 restores the remainder of the phrase onto the array STG.

To illustrate this technique, a phrase can be processed by a program that used both the PUSH/POP subroutines and the GETWRD subroutine.

In the following example, the phrase 'Parse a Group of Words' is passed to the DSPWRD program.

```
call DSPWRD 'Parse a Group of Words'
```

Is passed to the DSPWRD program. After the phrase is parsed, the stack will contain an entry for each word in the phrase as illustrated in Figure 12-186.

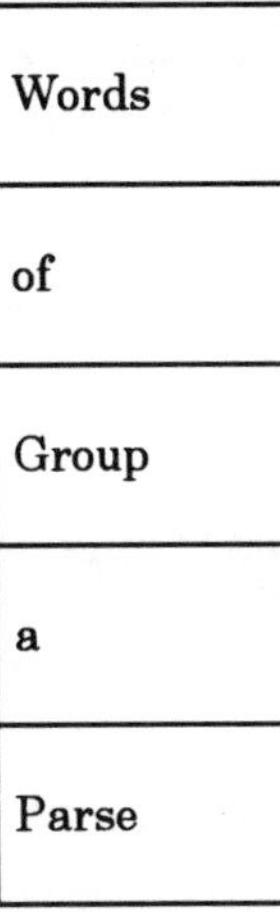

Figure 12-186: Contents of Stack After Parsing Has Completed

Figure 12-188, beginning on pages 486 that follow, illustrates the output from the RPG compiler for the RPG program DSPWRD. Figure 12-187 contains the entire DSPWRD source program that performs the word parsing routine.

```
*****************************************************************
*   Program:   DSPWRDS                                          *
*   From:      "The Modern RPG Language"                        *
*              by Robert Cozzi, Jr. COPR. 1988 and 1990         *
*                                                               *
*   Purpose:   To illustrate a parsing technique using          *
*              PUSH and POP subroutines with a pseudo stack.    *
*                                                               *
*   Input:     A sentence or list of words separated by         *
*              one or more blanks--not to exceed 256 bytes.     *
*                                                               *
*   Output:    Using DEBUG, set a break point at statement      *
*              ENDPGM.  Then display the stack variable $S.     *
*              Each word of the input sentence should be        *
*              contained in its own array element of $S.        *
*                                                               *
*   Author:    R. Cozzi, Jr.                                    *
*                                                               *
*   Date:      7 July 88                                        *
*                                                               *
*   Revised:   21 August 90                                     *
*   Purpose of revision:                                        *
*              Altered code to include named constants and      *
*              *FIRST (*INZSR) subroutine.                      *
*                                                               *
*   Revised:   21 December 92                                   *
*   Purpose of revision:                                        *
*              Removed ON and OFF named constants               *
*              Utilized *ON and *OFF                            *
*              Utilized ENDDO and ENDIF                         *
*****************************************************************
E                    STG        256  1
E                    $S         200 12
 *  Top of Stack message
I                  '**TOS**'              C         TOSMSG
 *  Maximum stack entries (top of stack)
I                  200                    C         TOS
IPSDS         SDS
I                                         *PROGRAM  PGMNAM
I                                         *PARMS    PARMS
```

Figure 12-187: RPG Source Code for DSPWRD Program (1 of 4)

```
 /SPACE
C           *ENTRY    PLIST
C                     PARM           PHRASE256         Phrase to parse
 /SPACE
C           PARMS     IFGE 1                           If PHRASE, then
C           PHRASE    ANDNE*BLANKS                     Move the PHRASE
C                     MOVEAPHRASE    STG               to an array
C                     EXSR GETWRD                      Parse next word
C           WORD      DOWNE*BLANK                      More words?
C           STACK     ANDNETOSMSG                      Top of STACK??
C                     MOVELWORD      STACK             PUSH WORD onto
C                     EXSR PUSH                        the STACK
C           STACK     CASNETOSMSG    GETWRD            Top of STACK??
C                     END                              Parse next word
C                     ENDDO
C                     ENDIF
 /SPACE
 *   This GOTO ENDPGM statement is required in order to       *
 *   force the CPF and OS/400 debugger to allow the label     *
 *   as a break-point.                                        *
C                     GOTO ENDPGM
C           ENDPGM    TAG
C                     MOVE *ON       *INLR             End of Program
```

Figure 12-187: RPG Source Code for DSPWRD Program (2 of 4)

```
 /EJECT
CSR          *INZSR    BEGSR
 *  Initialize/declare work fields
C                      Z-ADDO         X        50         Misc counter
C                      Z-ADDO         SI       50         Stack index
C                      MOVE *BLANKS   WORD    12          Next word
C                      MOVE *BLANKS   SAVSTG256           Saved string
C                      MOVE *BLANKS   STACK   12          Stack value
CSR          ENDINZ    ENDSR
 /SPACE
CSR          GETWRD    BEGSR
 *  Parse out next word from the phrase stored in STG.
C                      Z-ADD1         X
C            X         DOWLT256                           Find first
C            STG,X     ANDEQ*BLANKS                       non-blank
C                      ADD  1         X                   string position
C                      ENDDO
C                      MOVE *BLANKS   SAVSTG
C                      MOVEASTG,X     SAVSTG              Left Adjust
C                      MOVEASAVSTG    STG                 the phrase
 /SPACE
C            X         DOWLT256                           Find next
C            STG,X     ANDGT*BLANKS                       blank position
C                      ADD  1         X                   in the string
C                      ENDDO
 /SPACE
C                      MOVEASTG,X     SAVSTG     P        save remainder
C                      MOVEA*BLANKS   STG,X               clear excess
C                      MOVEASTG       WORD                Store the WORD
C                      MOVEASAVSTG    STG                 Shift balance
CSR                    ENDSR                              of string.
```

Figure 12-187: RPG Source Code for DSPWRD Program (3 of 4)

```
 /SPACE
CSR           PUSH      BEGSR
 *   Push data onto the stack.
C             SI        IFGE TOS                              If top of stack
C                       MOVELTOSMSG    STACK      P           Send TOS msg
C                       ELSE
C                       ADD  1         SI                     Increment SI
C                       MOVELSTACK     $S,SI      P           Push onto STACK
C                       ENDIF
CSR                     ENDSR
 /SPACE
CSR           POP       BEGSR
 *   Pop data off of stack.
C             SI        IFLE 0                                Top of stack,
C                       MOVELTOSMSG    STACK      P           Send TOS msg
C                       ELSE
C                       MOVEL$S,SI     STACK      P           POP from stack
C                       SUB  1         SI                     Decrement SI
C                       ENDIF
CSR                     ENDSR
```

Figure 12-187: RPG Source Code for DSPWRD Program (4 of 4)

To see the results of the DSPWRD program, a string must be passed to the program. The interactive debug utility can be used to view the PHRASE field and the $S array. A breakpoint can be set at the ENDPGM statement label.

Compiler Listing from DSPWRD

To compile DSPWRD run the following CL command on the AS/400.

CRTRPGPGM PGM(DSPWRD) SRCFILE(QRPGSRC) SRCMBR(DSPWRD) 

A listing similar to the one featured in Figure 12-188 is generated.

```
5738RG1 V2R2M0  920925              IBM SAA RPG/400                         RPGBOOK/DSPWRD     Page  0001
Compiler . . . . . . . . . . . . . . :   IBM SAA RPG/400
Command Options:
  Program  . . . . . . . . . . . . . :   RPGBOOK/DSPWRD
  Source file  . . . . . . . . . . . :   RPGBOOK/QRPGSRC
  Source member  . . . . . . . . . . :   DSPWRD
  Source listing options . . . . . . :   *SOURCE    *XREF      *GEN       *NODUMP    *NOSECLVL *NOSRCDBG *NOLSTDBG
  Generation options . . . . . . . . :   *NOLIST    *NOXREF    *NOATR     *NODUMP    *NOOPTIMIZE
  Source listing indentation . . . . :   *NONE
  Type conversion options  . . . . . :   *NONE
  SAA flagging . . . . . . . . . . . :   *NOFLAG
  Generation severity level  . . . . :   9
  Print file . . . . . . . . . . . . :   *LIBL/QSYSPRT
  Replace program  . . . . . . . . . :   *YES
  Target release . . . . . . . . . . :   *CURRENT
  User profile . . . . . . . . . . . :   *USER
  Authority  . . . . . . . . . . . . :   *LIBCRTAUT
  Text . . . . . . . . . . . . . . . :   *SRCMBRTXT
  Phase trace  . . . . . . . . . . . :   *NO
  Intermediate text dump . . . . . . :   *NONE
  Snap dump  . . . . . . . . . . . . :   *NONE
  Codelist . . . . . . . . . . . . . :   *NONE
  Ignore decimal data error  . . . . :   *NO
  Allow null values  . . . . . . . . :   *NO
Actual Program Source:
  Member . . . . . . . . . . . . . . :   DSPWRD
  File . . . . . . . . . . . . . . . :   QRPGSRC
  Library  . . . . . . . . . . . . . :   RPGBOOK
  Last Change  . . . . . . . . . . . :   01/28/93  13:51:26
  Description  . . . . . . . . . . . :   Display a parsed group of words
```

Figure 12-188: Compiler Listing for DSPWRD Program (1 of 6)

This page of the compiler listing contains the parameters and options specified for the compiler. Each parameter and option can be specified by the program when the program is compiled. Normally, only the source file name, source file library and source member are changed. The optimize parameter, however, can improve performance when large arrays are used.

```
5738RG1 V2R2M0  920925                IBM SAA RPG/400                        RPGBOOK/DSPWRD      Page  0002
SEQUENCE                                                                              IND     DO    LAST
NUMBER     *...1....+....2....+....3....+....4....+....5....+....6....+....7...*   USE     NUM   UPDATE
                      S o u r c e   L i s t i n g
    100    *****************************************************************                  01/28/93
    200    *   Program:   DSPWRDS                                             *                  01/28/93
    300    *   From:      "The Modern RPG Language"                           *                  01/28/93
    400    *              by Robert Cozzi, Jr. COPR. 1988 and 1990            *                  01/28/93
    500    *                                                                  *                  01/28/93
    600    *   Purpose:   To illustrate a parsing technique using             *                  01/28/93
    700    *              PUSH and POP subroutines with a pseudo stack.       *                  01/28/93
    800    *                                                                  *                  01/28/93
    900    *   Input:     A sentence or list of words separated by            *                  01/28/93
   1000    *              one or more blanks--not to exceed 256 bytes.        *                  01/28/93
   1100    *                                                                  *                  01/28/93
   1200    *   Output:    Using DEBUG, set a break point at statement         *                  01/28/93
   1300    *              ENDPGM.  Then display the stack variable $S.        *                  01/28/93
   1400    *              Each word of the input sentence should be           *                  01/28/93
   1500    *              contained in its own array element of $S.           *                  01/28/93
   1600    *                                                                  *                  01/28/93
   1700    *   Author:    R. Cozzi, Jr.                                       *                  01/28/93
   1800    *                                                                  *                  01/28/93
   1900    *   Date:      7 July 88                                           *                  01/28/93
   2000    *                                                                  *                  01/28/93
   2100    *   Revised:   21 August 90                                        *                  01/28/93
   2200    *   Purpose of revision:                                           *                  01/28/93
   2300    *              Altered code to include named constants and         *                  01/28/93
   2400    *              *FIRST (*INZSR) subroutine.                         *                  01/28/93
   2500    *                                                                  *                  01/28/93
   2600    *   Revised:   21 December 92                                      *                  01/28/93
   2700    *   Purpose of revision:                                           *                  01/28/93
   2800    *              Removed ON and OFF named constants                  *                  01/28/93
   2900    *              Utilized *ON and *OFF                               *                  01/28/93
   3000    *              Utilized ENDDO and ENDIF                            *                  01/28/93
   3100    *****************************************************************                  01/28/93
           H                                                                                              *****
   3200    E                    STG        256  1                                                 01/28/93
   3300    E                    $S         200 12                                                 01/28/93
   3400     *  Top of Stack message                                                               01/28/93
   3500    I                 '**TOS**'              C         TOSMSG                              01/28/93
   3600     *  Maximum stack entries (top of stack)                                               01/28/93
   3700    I                 200                    C         TOS                                 01/28/93
   3800    IPSDS         SDS                                                                      01/28/93
   3900    I                                         *PROGRAM PGMNAM                              01/28/93
   4000    I                                         *PARMS   PARMS                               01/28/93
   4200    C             *ENTRY    PLIST                                                          01/28/93
   4300    C                       PARM           PHRASE256          Phrase to parse              01/28/93
   4500    C             PARMS     IFGE 1                            If PHRASE, then      B001    01/28/93
   4600    C             PHRASE    ANDNE*BLANKS                      Move the PHRASE       001    01/28/93
```

Figure 12-188: Compiler Listing for DSPWRD Program (2 of 6)

This page contains the first page of the compiled source. It contains mostly comments about the program, the author and the program's creation/revision dates. In addition, the arrays, named constants and the program status data structure used by the program are listed here.

```
5738RG1 V2R2M0  920925              IBM SAA RPG/400                         RPGBOOK/DSPWRD     Page  0003
SEQUENCE                                                                            IND      DO     LAST
NUMBER     *...1....+....2....+....3....+....4....+....5....+....6....+....7...*   USE      NUM    UPDATE
    4700  C                    MOVEAPHRASE    STG                 to an array                001    01/28/93
    4800  C                    EXSR GETWRD                        Parse next word            001    01/28/93
    4900  C          WORD      DOWNE*BLANK                        More words?               B002    01/28/93
    5000  C          STACK     ANDNETOSMSG                        Top of STACK??             002    01/28/93
    5100  C                    MOVELWORD      STACK               PUSH WORD onto             002    01/28/93
    5200  C                    EXSR PUSH                          the STACK                  002    01/28/93
    5300  C          STACK     CASNETOSMSG    GETWRD              Top of STACK??             002    01/28/93
    5400  C                    END                                Parse next word            002    01/28/93
    5500  C                    ENDDO                                                        E002    01/28/93
    5600  C                    ENDIF                                                        E001    01/28/93
    5800   *    This GOTO ENDPGM statement is required in order to          *                       01/28/93
    5900   *    force the CPF and OS/400 debugger to allow the label        *                       01/28/93
    6000   *    as a break-point.                                           *                       01/28/93
    6100  C                    GOTO ENDPGM                                                          01/28/93
    6200  C          ENDPGM    TAG                                                                  01/28/93
    6300  C                    MOVE *ON       *INLR               End of Program                    01/28/93
```

Figure 12-188: Compiler Listing for DSPWRD Program (3 of 6)

This page contains the main-line calculations of the program. The /EJECT compiler directive is used before line 3500 and after line 5600 too allow these statements to be isolated on a separate page. Note the "DO NUM" column on the right-hand side of the compiler listing. This column indicates the nesting level and beginning and ending of the structured operations (i.e., DO, IF-THEN-ELSE, DOWxx, and DOUxx).

```
5738RG1 V2R2M0  920925               IBM SAA RPG/400                      RPGBOOK/DSPWRD     Page  0004
SEQUENCE                                                                             IND      DO    LAST
NUMBER   *...1....+....2....+....3....+....4....+....5....+....6....+....7...*   USE      NUM   UPDATE
     CSR         *INZSR    BEGSR                                                               01/28/93
      *  Initialize/declare work fields                                                        01/28/93
     C                     Z-ADD0         X        50        Misc counter                      01/28/93
     C                     Z-ADD0         SI       50        Stack index                       01/28/93
     C                     MOVE *BLANKS   WORD    12         Next word                         01/28/93
     C                     MOVE *BLANKS   SAVSTG256          Saved string                      01/28/93
     C                     MOVE *BLANKS   STACK   12         Stack value                       01/28/93
     CSR         ENDINZ    ENDSR                                                               01/28/93

     CSR         GETWRD    BEGSR                                                               01/28/93
      *  Parse out next word from the phrase stored in STG.                                    01/28/93
     C                     Z-ADD1         X                                                    01/28/93
     C           X         DOWLT256                          Find first               B001     01/28/93
     C           STG,X     ANDEQ*BLANKS                      non-blank                 001     01/28/93
     C                     ADD  1         X                  string position           001     01/28/93
     C                     ENDDO                                                      E001     01/28/93
     C                     MOVE *BLANKS   SAVSTG                                               01/28/93
     C                     MOVEASTG,X     SAVSTG             Left Adjust                       01/28/93
     C                     MOVEASAVSTG    STG                the phrase                        01/28/93
     C           X         DOWLT256                          Find next                B001     01/28/93
     C           STG,X     ANDGT*BLANKS                      blank position            001     01/28/93
     C                     ADD  1         X                  in the string             001     01/28/93
     C                     ENDDO                                                      E001     01/28/93
     C                     MOVEASTG,X     SAVSTG      P      save remainder                    01/28/93
     C                     MOVEA*BLANKS   STG,X              clear excess                      01/28/93
     C                     MOVEASTG       WORD               Store the WORD                    01/28/93
     C                     MOVEASAVSTG    STG                Shift balance                     01/28/93
     CSR                   ENDSR                             of string.                        01/28/93

     CSR         PUSH      BEGSR                                                               01/28/93
      *   Push data onto the stack.                                                            01/28/93
     C           SI        IFGE TOS                          If top of stack          B001     01/28/93
     C                     MOVELTOSMSG    STACK       P      Send TOS msg              001     01/28/93
     C                     ELSE                                                       X001     01/28/93
     C                     ADD  1         SI                 Increment SI              001     01/28/93
     C                     MOVELSTACK     $S,SI       P      Push onto STACK           001     01/28/93
     C                     ENDIF                                                      E001     01/28/93
     CSR                   ENDSR                                                               01/28/93

     CSR         POP       BEGSR                                                               01/28/93
      *   Pop data off of stack.                                                               01/28/93
     C           SI        IFLE 0                            Top of stack,            B001     01/28/93
     C                     MOVELTOSMSG    STACK       P      Send TOS msg              001     01/28/93
     C                     ELSE                                                       X001     01/28/93
     C                     MOVEL$S,SI     STACK       P      POP from stack            001     01/28/93
     C                     SUB  1         SI                 Decrement SI              001     01/28/93
     C                     ENDIF                                                      E001     01/28/93
     CSR                   ENDSR                                                               01/28/93
         * * * * *   E N D   O F   S O U R C E   * * * * *
```

Figure 12-188: Compiler Listing for DSPWRD Program (4 of 6)

This page contains the initialization subroutine (*INZSR) which is used to define several variables used by the PUSH/POP subroutines (also featured on this page). The subroutine GETWRD (Get next word) searches through the string of words to locate the next word. Once located, GETWRD isolates the word by storing it in the field WORD. That field is then "pushed" onto the stack by the PUSH subroutine, which is called by the main-line calculations.

```
 5738RG1 V2R2M0  920925               IBM SAA RPG/400                          RPGBOOK/DSPWRD     Page  0005
                               C r o s s   R e f e r e n c e
 Field References:
         FIELD         ATTR     REFERENCES (M=MODIFIED D=DEFINED)
         $S(200)       A(12)     3300D
           $S,SI                10200M 11100
         *ENTRY        PLIST     4200D
         *INLR         A(1)      6300M
         *INZSR        BEGSR     6500D
         ENDINZ        ENDSR     7200D
         ENDPGM        TAG       6100   6200D
         GETWRD        BEGSR     4800   5300    7400D
         PARMS         Z(3,0)    4000D  4500
 * 7031  PGMNAM        A(10)     3900D
         PHRASE        A(256)    4300D  4600    4700
 * 7031  POP           BEGSR    10600D
 * 7031  PSDS          DS(39)    3800D
         PUSH          BEGSR     5200   9600D
         SAVSTG        A(256)    7000D  8100M  8200M  8300    9000M  9300
         SI            P(5,0)    6800D  9800   10100M 10200   10800  11100   11200M
         STACK         A(12)     5000   5100M  5300    7100D  9900M 10200   10900M
                                11100M
         STG(256)      A(1)      3200D  4700M  8300M  9200    9300M
           STG,X                 7800   8200   8600    9000   9100M
         TOS           CONST     3700D  9800
         TOSMSG        CONST     3500D  5000   5300    9900  10900
         WORD          A(12)     4900   5100   6900D   9200M
         X             P(5,0)    6700D  7600M  7700    7800   7900M  8200    8500
                                 8600   8700M  9000    9100
         *BLANK        LITERAL   4900
         *BLANKS       LITERAL   4600   6900   7000    7100   7800   8100    8600
                                 9100
         *ON           LITERAL   6300
         0             LITERAL   6700   6800  10800
         1             LITERAL   4500   7600   7900    8700  10100  11200
         256           LITERAL   7700   8500
 Indicator References:
         INDICATOR  REFERENCES (M=MODIFIED D=DEFINED)
         LR           6300M
       * * * * *   E N D   O F   C R O S S   R E F E R E N C E   * * * * *
```

Figure 12-188: Compiler Listing for DSPWRD Program (5 of 6)

This page contains the program cross-reference list. Each field, data structure, data structure subfield, indicator, array, array element, literal value, named constant and label is listed along with the statements on which they are referenced. When a statement number is followed by the letter D, that means the item is defined on that statement. When a statement number is followed by the letter M, that means the item is modified on that statement. When a statement number is followed by a blank, that means the item is used (referenced) by the source line.

```
5738RG1 V2R2M0  920925                IBM SAA RPG/400                      RPGBOOK/DSPWRD     Page  0006
                        M e s s a g e   S u m m a r y
* QRG7031 Severity:  00   Number:    3
        Message . . . . :   The Name or indicator is not referenced.
     * * * * *   E N D   O F   M E S S A G E   S U M M A R Y   * * * * *
5738RG1 V2R2M0  920925                IBM SAA RPG/400                      RPGBOOK/DSPWRD     Page  0007
                          F i n a l   S u m m a r y
Message Count:  (by Severity Number)
          TOTAL    00     10     20     30     40     50
              3     3      0      0      0      0      0
Program Source Totals:
   Records . . . . . . . . . . :   114
   Specifications  . . . . . . :   65
   Table Records . . . . . . . :   0
   Comments  . . . . . . . . . :   40
PRM has been called.
Program DSPWRD is placed in library RPGBOOK. 00 highest Error-Severity-Code.
        * * * * *   E N D   O F   C O M P I L A T I O N   * * * * *
```

Figure 12-188: Compiler Listing for DSPWRD Program (6 of 6)

These are the final two pages of the compilation. They contain a summary of the messages (error or otherwise) that were identified in the source listing.

The final summary contains the count of each message and its severity. A severity of 30 or higher is generally to high to compile the program. A severity of 10 or 20 is usually fine to allow the compiler to create the program. Use the GENLVL parameter of the CRTRPGPGM to control program generation severity levels. The default is 9.

A severity of 20 is usually an acceptable severity, but this level can cause problems. Unless specified differently, a severity of 20 will prevent the compiler from compiling the program.

A severity of 10 is normally unreferenced field names or indicators.

The severity level of messages replaces the WARNING ERRORS, TERMINAL ERRORS, and CAUTIONS used by older compilers.

Appendix A

Decimal Data Errors and the AS/400 RPG Compiler

Decimal Data Overview

Decimal data is at the heart of most business applications. Floating point and binary numbers are not as precise as decimal data. With the possible exception of the banking industry, floating point and binary fields are not used in the vast majority of business applications. This appendix describes decimal data errors, and illustrates how the system handles decimal data errors when IGNDECERR(*YES) is specified when an RPG program is created.

There are two forms of decimal data:

1. *Zoned* — Occupying 1 byte for every digit declared.
2. *Packed* — Occupying approximately 1 byte for every 2 digits declared.

The AS/400 is strict when it comes to valid decimal data. The predecessor of the AS/400, the System/38, had no mechanism to handle invalid decimal data—RPG programs written for System/38 had to completely control the handling of invalid decimal data messages, or they stopped running.

Because much of the data contained on the AS/400 has been "migrated" from other systems, such as the System/36, the ability to easily handle invalid decimal data has become a requirement. The ability to handle decimal data errors is available in RPG, but we are still waiting for the "easy" part.

Decimal data errors occur during program runtime when a packed or zoned decimal field contains data that is invalid. An example of invalid data can be a packed decimal field containing blanks, or the letters 'ABCD'. This is clearly not valid numeric data and causes a decimal data error to be generated.

Fix Decimal Data Errors

The System/36 compatible RPGII compiler that is provided on the AS/400 supports an option to fix decimal data errors. The parameter keyword is as follows:

```
FIXDECDTA(*YES | *NO)
```

The default, FIXDECDTA(*YES), causes invalid decimal data to be "corrected" by the low-level interface of the operating system. This low-level interface, referred to as *licensed internal code* (VLIC), contains routines to change incorrect decimal data before presenting the data to the application program.

This provides some degree of relief for RPGII programs processing data that has been migrated from the System/36 to the AS/400. FIX DECIMAL DATA, however, is not supported by the AS/400 RPGIII compiler.

Ignore Decimal Data Error

The AS/400 RPGIII compiler provides an option to ignore decimal data errors. The CRTRPGPGM command supports the IGNDECERR parameter as follows:

```
IGNDECERR(*NO | *YES)
```

The default option, IGNDECERR(*NO), causes decimal data errors to generate an exception/error. In this situation the default RPG exception/error handling routine is called when an error occurs. If the *PSSR subroutine is specified in the RPG program, that subroutine is called when the exception/error occurs. The default is an appropriate option for anyone using AS/400 database with valid data.

The other option, IGNDECERR(*YES), causes all decimal data errors to be handled by the underlying licensed internal code (VLIC). The VLIC handles IGNORE DECIMAL DATA ERROR very differently from the FIX DECIMAL DATA process.

IGNORE DECIMAL DATA ERROR processes data errors by eliminating the bad data from the operation, (i.e., ignoring it). When invalid decimal data appears in a field specified in Factor 1, Factor 2, or the Result field, a *decimal data error* exception occurs. Depending on the operation being performed, however, the error is handled differently. For example, the ADD and SUB operations throw away the invalid value, while the MULT and DIV operations are canceled (i.e., not performed).

IGNDECERR(*YES) is appropriate for very few situations, such as programs that do not process data from a file or where accuracy in the result field is not critical.

Typically, IGNDECERR(*YES) is used in programs with data structures that contain numeric subfields. Since data structures, by default, are initialized to blanks, decimal data errors can occur.

To correct this type of decimal data error in data structures, most programs have been modified to include the recent *initialization* function. By specifying the letter 'I' in column 18 of the data structure specification, the data structure is initialized to blanks and zeros, based on the data type of each subfield. This can virtually eliminate this type of decimal data error.

Database File Models

The IBM System/34 and System/36 use a *flat file system*. All files are linear, or non-relational. This is in sharp contrast to the System/38 and AS/400 *relational database management system*, where fields are used to define the representation of the file.

When a file is created with the flat file model, its records are created as one large "field". There are no database field definitions. On the System/36, field definition is available only though IDDU (interactive data definition utility). While this definition utility is useful, it is not integrated into the System/36 operation system and compilers.

When a file is created with the relational model, its records are created as a collection of columns, known as *fields* to RPG programmers. The record length is calculated by the sum of the lengths of the fields. In essence, the record length becomes unimportant to the application developer.

When moving from a flat file system, such as the System/36, to a relational database system, such as the AS/400, several data integrity problems can arise.

- When an RPG program writes a record using the System/36 flat file model, only the fields specified in the RPG Output specification are written to the file. The remainder of the record is padded with blanks.
- When a file from the System/36 flat file model is moved to the AS/400, the file is generally created with one large field. The length of this field equals that of the file's record length.

Decimal data errors can occur when a record is read from a file (i.e., during a CHAIN, READ, or RPG cycle input operation). When this occurs, if IGNDECERR(*YES) is specified, the record is returned, but the invalid data is not copied into the input fields. This can present a major problem. Since the data causing the decimal data error is not copied to the input fields, the input fields retain the current data. This means that the input field in question contains data from the previous "good" record.

Since RPG initializes input record formats based on field data type, should the first record read contain a decimal data error, the input field whose data generated the decimal data error will be zero. Again, only if IGNDECERR(*YES) is specified when the program is created.

Zoned Decimal Data

Zoned decimal is a carry-over from the old 80-column punch card era. Essentially, each digit of a decimal number occupies 1 byte of a zoned decimal field. The top 4 bits (the *zone*) are set on in a normal zoned decimal number. The default hexadecimal value for the zone is X'F'. The bottom 4 bits (the *digit*) of the byte represent the numeric value. For example a value of 3 would be X'F3', a value of 4 would be X'F4' and so on.

The sign (sometimes referred to as the *status*) of a zoned decimal field is stored in the top 4 bits of the rightmost byte of a zoned decimal field. The sign can be X'C' or X'D' for negative values (X'D' is the default), and X'A', X'B', X'E', or X'F' for positive values (X'F' is the default). The dual negative signs are a result of the way the COBOL language sets the bits for negative values. COBOL uses X'C' for its negative sign; RPG and other AS/400 languages use X'D'. Both are supported by all AS/400 languages and system functions.

The diagram below illustrates the storage for a typical 5-position zoned decimal field. The value of the field below is set to 3741.

Byte Position	1	2	3	4	5
Zone	F	F	F	F	F
Digit	Ø	3	7	4	1

The digit portion of a zoned decimal field identifies the numeric value. The zone portion of each byte (except the sign byte) can contain any value. During an RPG operation the zone of each byte (except the sign byte) is set on (i.e., set to B'1111' or X'F'). This includes mathematical, move, copy, and output operations.

The zone of a zoned decimal field is ignored (except for the sign). Consequently, operations on zoned decimal fields are forgiving when some invalid data appears. For example, a 5-position zoned decimal field with a value of 3741 can appear as follows:

Byte Position	1	2	3	4	5
Zone	A	8	8	D	E
Digit	Ø	3	7	4	1

This value is tolerated because the zone portion of a zoned decimal field is ignored. The sign is also tolerated because it is between X'A' and X'F' (i.e., X'E'). When this zoned decimal field is used, the operating system translates the zone of each byte (except for the sign) to X'F'. Consequently the value is treated as though it were coded as X'F0F3F7F4E1'.

The sign of a zoned decimal field is handled a little more strictly. The zone portion of the rightmost byte (i.e., the sign of the zoned value) must be one of the following:

Zone Value (in hex)	Zone Value (in binary)	Sign (status)	Description
X'F	B'1111'	+	All bits are on, the sign is positive. (DEFAULT)
X'D'	B'1101'	–	Bit 2 is off, the sign is negative. (DEFAULT)
X'A'	B'1010'	+	Bits 1 and 3 are off, the sign is considered positive.
X'B'	B'1011'	+	Bit 1 is off, the sign is considered positive.
X'C'	B'1100'	–	Bits 2 and 3 are off, the sign is negative.
X'E'	B'1110'	+	Bit 3 is off, the sign is considered positive.

Valid Signs for a Zoned Decimal Field

Zoned Decimal Data Errors

There are two situations that cause decimal data errors for a zoned decimal field:

1. When a sign value other than X'A' to X'F' is used. Any other value, that is X'0' to X'9', in the sign location generates a decimal data error.
2. When any digit in the zoned decimal field contains a value other than X'0' to X'9' a decimal data error is issued. Any other value, that is X'A' to X'F', in the digit location generates a decimal data error.

This creates a problem with the use of zoned decimal fields in data structures. A zone decimal data structure subfield is, by default, initialized to blanks, which is a X'40'. This is, by its very nature, invalid decimal data.

There are several methods to prevent this type of decimal data error, including:

1. Move zeros or some other valid numeric value into the subfield prior to using the subfield in another operation.
2. Clear the subfield with the CLEAR operation code. The CLEAR operation is a "smart" opcode, in that it is context sensitive. When it is used on a decimal field, it is smart enough to move zeros into the field.
3. Clear the data structure containing the subfield with CLEAR operation code. The CLEAR operation moves either blanks or zeros to each data structure subfield, based on the data type of the subfield. Since, however, data structure subfields can, and often do, overlap one another, the CLEAR operation can cause a decimal data error to occur in a later operation. The CLEAR operation clears subfields in the order they appear in the RPG program (not their location within the data structure). Therefore, should both a zoned decimal subfield and a character subfield occupy the same physical location, the subfield that appears last in the RPG Input specifications will dictate the value stored in those positions within the data structure.
4. Specify that the data structure containing the subfield be initialized at program start time. This can be accomplished by specifying an 'I' in column 18 of the data structure specification. Again, subfields are initialized based on their appearance in the RPG Input specifications, so the criteria for the CLEAR operation also applies here.
5. Specify that the subfield be initialized based on its data type at program start time. This can be accomplished by specifying an 'I' in column 8 of the RPG statement that defines the subfield.

Options 4 and 5 are the easiest to implement. They require no changes to the program's Calculation specifications, and require that only one additional character be added to the program. Options 2 and 3 can be just as easy, and should be used where appropriate. Option 1 is the most commonly used technique. This is because the other options were not originally available in RPGIII. Option 1, however, is now the last choice for inserting the correct initial value into data structure subfields.

Packed Decimal Data

A packed decimal field occupies 1 byte for every 2 digits, except for the rightmost digit, which shares its byte with the *sign*. Two formulas are used to calculate the number of bytes that a packed decimal field occupies. They are as follows:

```
If the declared length is an odd number of digits, then:
         bytes = (declared length + 1 ) / 2

If the declared length is an even number of digits, then:
         bytes = (declared length + 2 ) / 2
```

Consider a 5-position packed decimal field with 4 decimal positions. Using the above formula to calculate the number of bytes occupied, gives:

```
         bytes = (5 + 1) / 2
```

The number of bytes occupied by this packed decimal field is 3. Note that the number of decimal positions (4 in this example) has no impact on the bytes occupied.

The diagram below illustrates the storage allocation of a 7-position packed decimal field, with 2 decimal positions. The value is set to 0.

Byte Position	**1**	**2**	**3**	**4**
Bits 0-3 (in hex)	Ø	Ø	Ø	Ø
Bits 4-7 (in hex)	Ø	Ø	Ø	F

Each number of a decimal value is coded into its binary form when copied to a packed decimal field. The values are copied starting with the sign, then the numeric digits are copied, starting with the rightmost number and continuing to the left.

The diagram that follows illustrates a 7-position packed decimal field with 2 decimal positions. The field is set to 1207.38 with a positive sign.

Byte Position	1	2	3	4
Bits 0-3 (in hex)	Ø	2	7	8
Bits 4-7 (in hex)	1	Ø	3	F

This spelunking storage technique is the most common format for decimal data on the IBM AS/400. In fact the operating system (i.e., the low-level VLIC) has been optimized to handle packed decimal data.

Although the sign is stored in bits 4 to 7 of the rightmost byte for packed decimal fields, and in bits 0 to 3 of the rightmost byte for zoned decimal fields, it is handled basically the same for both.

The sign for a packed decimal field (i.e., bits 4 to 7 of the rightmost byte) must be X'A' to X'F', with X'F' being the default value for a positive sign, and X'D' being the default value for a negative sign. The diagram below describes the valid signs for a packed decimal field.

Sign (in hex)	Sign (in binary)	Sign (symbol)	Description
X'F	B'1111'	+	All bits are on, the sign is positive. (DEFAULT)
X'D'	B'1101'	–	Bit 2 is off, the sign is negative. (DEFAULT)
X'A'	B'1010'	+	Bits 1 and 3 are off, the sign is considered positive.
X'B'	B'1011'	+	Bit 1 is off, the sign is considered positive.
X'C'	B'1100'	–	Bits 2 and 3 are off, the sign is negative.
X'E'	B'1110'	+	Bit 3 is off, the sign is considered positive.

Valid Signs for a Packed Decimal Field

Packed Decimal Data Errors

There are two situations that cause decimal data errors for a packed decimal field:

1. When a sign value other than X'A' to X'F' is used. Any other value, that is X'0' to X'9', in the sign location generates a decimal data error.
2. When bits 0 to 3 or 4 to 7 of any position (except the sign) contain a value other than X'0' to X'9'. Any other value, that is X'A' to X'F', generates a decimal data error.

Conditions for Decimal Data Errors

Depending on the conditions where a decimal data error occurs results will vary. In most situations, however, the result can be predicted. There are two primary conditions under which decimal data errors occur. They are:

1. On a read to a database file (externally described or program described).
2. On an operation code that uses a field containing invalid numeric data in Factor 1, Factor 2, or the Result field.

When the IGNDECERR(*YES) operation is specified for RPGIII program, decimal data errors are ignored by the RPG program. The results of the program, however, may differ from what is expected.

Decimal Data Error Upon an Input Operation to a Database File

When a record is read from a database file, its data is copied to an "input buffer." This buffer is separate from the file's Input specifications. After the data from the file is copied to the input buffer, it is copied on a field by field basis, to the input area of the program. The input area is essentially the file's Input specifications.

At the point at which data is copied from the input buffer to the input area, decimal data errors can occur. For example, if a packed decimal field named AMOUNT is going to be set to blanks due to the data stored in the file being blank, the VLIC code running-the copy operation detects this as a decimal data error.

At this point, since IGNDECERR(*YES) is specified, the copy operation is canceled, and control transfers to the next instruction. The invalid decimal data is not copied into the input area and therefore, the input field contains zero.

For example, an item master file (ITEMMAST) containing two fields:

```
SeqNoAAn01n02n03T.Name++++++RLen++TDcBRowColKeywords+++++++++++++++++++
     A          R ITEMREC
     A            ITMNBR         7P 0       COLHDG('Item' 'Number')
     A            ITMDSC        20A         COLHDG('Item' 'Description')
```

In the example that follows, the ITEMMAST file described above contains three records. The first and third contain data that causes decimal data errors. The second record contains good data. These records are illustrated below.

Record 1 — A record with a bad item number

Byte Position	1...v....1....v....2....
Character	ƀƀƀƀThis is an item desc
Zone	4444E88A48A48948A89488A8
Digit	000038920920150935404523

Record 2 — A record with a good item number

Byte Position	1...v....1....v....2....
Character	....This is a 3741 item
Zone	0071E88A48A484FFFF48A894
Digit	034F38920920103741093540

Record 3 — Another bad item number

Byte Position	1...v....1....v....2....
Character	ƀƀƀƀAnother bad record
Zone	4444C99A8894888498899844
Digit	000015638590214095369400

The ITMNBR field is located over the first 4 bytes of the record. In records 1 and 3 those positions contain X'40's (blanks). This, of course, is invalid decimal data.

Read all the records in the ITEMMAST file

```
SeqNoFFilenameIFE.E....Rlen...K.OV....EDevice+RecNbrKKeywrdEntry+EX...UC
0001 FITEMMASTIF                       DISK

SeqNoCLRN01N02N03Factor1+++OpCodFactor2+++ResultLenDXHILOEQ
0002 C             *INLR      DOUEQ*ON
0003 C                        READ ITEMREC                LR
0004 C                        ENDDO
```

Since ITEMMAST is an externally described file, no Input specifications are required in the source program. The RPG compiler automatically imports the field descriptions—generating the Input specification at compile-time.

When the program is run, two decimal data errors occur. One for record 1, and one for record 3. RPG does not return data to input fields that corresponde to the decimal data error field; the fields retain their current value.

The diagram that follows illustrates what happens when this RPG program is run. The Do Until loop will iterate 4 times; once for each record in the file and one additional time when it receives the end-of-file indication and the LR indicator is set on. Note the Data Returned columns. They illustrate the value that is contained in the fields after the READ operation is performed.

	ITMNBR		ITMDSC		
Operation	Value in Input Field	Data Returned	Value in Input Field	Data Returned	Status of *INLR
1st READ	0	No	This is an item desc	Yes	*OFF
2nd READ	3741	Yes	This is a 3741 item	Yes	*OFF
3rd READ	3741	No	Another bad record	Yes	*OFF
4th READ	3741	No	Another bad record	No	*ON

When the end-of-file condition is reached (upon the 4th READ operation in this example), no data is returned to the input area. Consequently, the data from the last record in the file is retained in the input fields. This phenomenon has nothing to do with decimal data errors, however.

Decimal Data Errors During Calculation Specifications

When Factor 1, Factor 2, or the Result field of an operation code contains a packed or zoned decimal field and that field contains invalid decimal data, a decimal data error is generated.

If IGNDECERR(*YES) is specified, then depending on the operation code, the value is either ignored or the operation is canceled.

When the operation ignores the decimal field, it is, essentially, treated as 0. For example, consider the following:

The field named AMT contains invalid decimal data. It is a 5-position zoned decimal field, with 2-decimal positions. The field contains blanks as illustrated below.

AMT is a 5-position zoned decimal field with 2 decimal positions: ZONED(5,2)

Byte Position	1...v
Character	ƀƀƀƀƀ
Zone	44444
Digit	00000

Another field, TOTAL, is a 9-position packed decimal field, with 2 decimal positions. In the example that follows, the value 333 is added to the AMT field. The result is stored in the TOTAL field. Then the value 222 is multiplied by AMT. Again, the result is stored in the TOTAL field.

```
SeqNoIDSName....EIDSInitialvalue+++++++++++TFromTo++DField+
0001 IDATA        DS                                 5
0002 I                                         1     50AMT
0003 I                                         1     5 VALUE

SeqNoCLRN01N02N03Factor1+++OpCodFactor2+++ResultLenDXHILOEQ
0004 C            333      ADD  AMT       TOTAL   92            TOTAL = 333
0005 C            222      MULT AMT       TOTAL                 TOTAL = 333
```

Lines 1 to 3 define the DATA data structure and the AMT and VALUE subfields. The data structure is initialized to blanks (column 18 contains a blank). Therefore the AMT subfield is set to X'4040404040' when the program starts. The VALUE subfield occupies the same storage location as AMT, but it is a character field.

When line 4 is performed, a decimal data error is generated. The ADD operation performs as much of the ADD as possible. It adds 333 to the TOTAL field; but it cannot add AMT to TOTAL. Therefore, after line 4 is performed, the TOTAL field is equal to 333.

When line 4 is performed, a decimal data error is generated again. The MULT operation is canceled. Nothing is performed. Therefore, the Result field (i.e., TOTAL) retains its current value.

Avoiding Decimal Data Errors

To avoid this basic type of decimal data error, the data structure named DATA can be initialized based on the data type of its subfields. By specifying the letter 'I' in column 18 of line 1, the data structure is initialized when the program is first called.

In order for the initialization to be effective, however, the order of the subfields must be changed. Lines 2 and 3 must be swapped. This technique is illustrated in the RPG source code that follows:

```
SeqNoIDSName....EIDSInitialvalue++++++++++TFromTo++DField+
0001 IDATA        IDS                                 5
0002 I                                          1    5 VALUE
0003 I                                          1    50AMT
```

As an alternative, without changing the statement sequence, the AMT data structure subfield can be initialized independent of the rest of the data structure. By specifying the letter 'I' in column 8 of the AMT statement, the subfield is initialized based on its data type. See line 2 in the RPG source code that follows:

```
SeqNoIDSName....EIDSInitialvalue++++++++++TFromTo++DField+
0001 IDATA         DS                                 5
0002 I I                                        1    50AMT
0003 I                                          1    5 VALUE
```

Note that the data structure statement (line 1) does not contain the initialization control in column 18.

A third, and final option is to clear the field using an operation code. The example that follows illustrates several techniques for clearing a field, prior to it use.

```
SeqNoIDSName....EIDSInitialvalue++++++++++TFromTo++DField+
0001 IDATA         DS                                 5
0002 I                                          1    50AMT
0003 I                                          1    5 VALUE

SeqNoCLRN01N02N03Factor1+++OpCodFactor2+++ResultLenDXHILOEQ
0004 C                     CLEARAMT
0005 C                     Z-ADDO         AMT
0006 C                     MOVE *ZEROS    AMT
```

In this example, the DATA data structure is not initialized. Therefore, the AMT subfield contains blanks when the program is called.

The CLEAR operation (line 4) sets the value of AMT to its default initial value, based on its data type. In other words, it clears the fields by moving zeros to it.

The Z-ADD operation (line 5) does essentially the same task as line 4, but forces a zero into the field. Line 6, (the MOVE operation) uses the *ZEROS figurative constant to accomplish the same task.

Appendix B

DDS Subfile and Window Keyword Summary

DDS Overview

The Data Description Specification language (DDS) is the de facto standard for user interface handling on the IBM AS/400. DDS is somewhat similar to RPG in that it is columnar and utilizes indicators. But it also supports keywords and parameters for controlling data attributes.

It is not the intent of this appendix to define or even review the DDS language. That would take several hundred pages, and is far beyond the scope of this book. This appendix simply serves as a quick reference guide to the DDS keywords that support subfiles and windowing.

Subfile Keyword Summary

Since it inception in 1980, DDS has supported the concept of a ***subfile***. A subfile is a special type of record format within a display device file. It is optimized to handle multiple lines of like data. The data is normally displayed on the WORKSTN device on successive lines. Each line typically has an identical format (with some flexibility). The number of lines sent to the WORKSTN device can exceed the physical limit of the device. When the number of lines exceeds the physical limit, the operating system inserts the word "More..." at the bottom of the display and handles the scrolling of the list on the display.

To an RPG program, a subfile is treated very similar to a database file record. So similar, in fact that many operations normally reserved for database input/output are used to access subfile records.

There are two components in a subfile: (1) The subfile control record; and (2) The subfile detail record.

The subfile control record, as the name implies, contains the controls, descriptions and other attributes of the subfile. For example, the maximum number of records the subfile can contain (known as *subfile size*), the number of records to display at one time (known as *subfile page*), the name of the subfile detail record format that is controlled by the control record, and when and how the subfile control and detail records are displayed.

To a user of the AS/400, subfiles are a way of life, virtually every "Work with ..." display contains a scrollable list of items. That scrollable list is a subfile. For example, the WRKOBJ (work with objects) display lists a set of object names, type, library, attribute and text description. Below the list the word "More..." or "Bottom" is displayed. When "More..." appears, the ROLL or PAGE keys on the keyboard can be used to scroll the list of object names up or down. When "Bottom" appears, the end or *bottom* of the list is displayed.

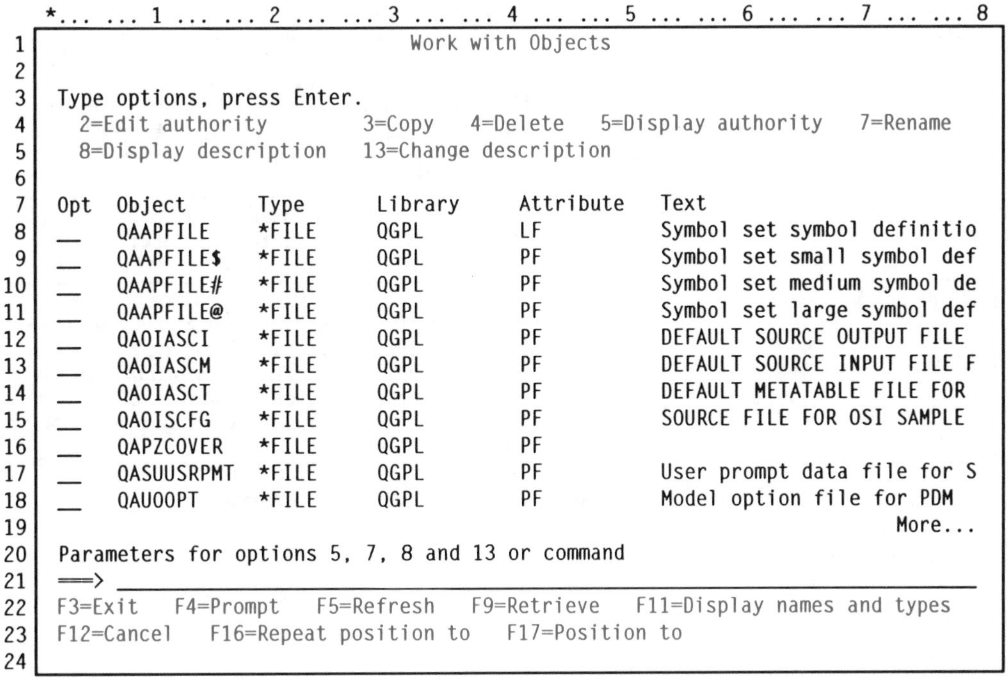

```
                                 Work with Objects

 Type options, press Enter.
   2=Edit authority         3=Copy   4=Delete   5=Display authority   7=Rename
   8=Display description    13=Change description

 Opt  Object       Type       Library     Attribute   Text
 __   QAAPFILE     *FILE      QGPL        LF          Symbol set symbol definitio
 __   QAAPFILE$    *FILE      QGPL        PF          Symbol set small symbol def
 __   QAAPFILE#    *FILE      QGPL        PF          Symbol set medium symbol de
 __   QAAPFILE@    *FILE      QGPL        PF          Symbol set large symbol def
 __   QAOIASCI     *FILE      QGPL        PF          DEFAULT SOURCE OUTPUT FILE
 __   QAOIASCM     *FILE      QGPL        PF          DEFAULT SOURCE INPUT FILE F
 __   QAOIASCT     *FILE      QGPL        PF          DEFAULT METATABLE FILE FOR
 __   QAOISCFG     *FILE      QGPL        PF          SOURCE FILE FOR OSI SAMPLE
 __   QAPZCOVER    *FILE      QGPL        PF
 __   QASUUSRPMT   *FILE      QGPL        PF          User prompt data file for S
 __   QAUOOPT      *FILE      QGPL        PF          Model option file for PDM
                                                                         More...
 Parameters for options 5, 7, 8 and 13 or command
 ===> ____________________________________________________________________________
 F3=Exit   F4=Prompt   F5=Refresh   F9=Retrieve   F11=Display names and types
 F12=Cancel   F16=Repeat position to   F17=Position to

```

Diagram B-1: Work with Objects Subfile Display

Each piece of data in the Work with Objects display is a field in a subfile detail record, subfile control record, or a normal display file record.

Keyword	Parameters	Description
SFL	none	Identifies the record format as a subfile detail record. For most subfiles, this is the only keyword applicable to a subfile detail record. The message displaying subfile also supports the SFLMSGRCD, SFLMSGKEY, and SFLPGMQ keywords.
SFLNXTCHG		Causes the subfile detail records to be read by the READC operation regardless of whether or not the operator changes data in the record.
SFLCSRPRG		Identifies that the cursor is to progress to the next subfile record after exiting this field. The cursor is positioned into the same field in the next subfile record. This keyword allows the normal cursor progression of left-to-right and top-to-bottom to be overridden to top-to-bottom and left-to-right.

Diagram B-2: Subfile Detail Record Keywords

Keyword	Parameter	Description
SFLCLR		Clears an existing subfile of its detail records. The records are removed from the subfile.
SFLCTL	*subfile detail format*	Identifies this record format as a subfile control format; also, names the subfile detail format being controlled by this control record.
SFLCSRRRN	*record number of cursor*	Returns, via RPG input, the subfile record number that contains the cursor. The parameter must be a field name defined in DDS as a 5-position signed numeric field with 0 decimal positions. The field usage must be hidden.
SFLDLT		Deletes the subfile from the list of active subfiles. The data in the subfile control and detail records is no longer accessible by the program.
SFLDROP	*function key*	Directs the subfile to be displayed without folding. The subfile is displayed, and if its detail record is wider than the physical display device, the data that exceed the physical size is not displayed. This is known as *subfile drop*. The Function Key parameter can be used to assign a function key that controls switching between folded and drop modes. Also see the SFLFOLD keyword.
SFLDSP		Controls whether or not the subfile detail records are displayed when the subfile control record is displayed. A controlling indicator can be used to switch between displaying and not displaying the detail records. If this keyword is not specified, the subfile detail record is displayed on every output operation to the subfile control record.
SFLDSPCTL		Controls whether or not the subfile control record is displayed during an output operation. A controlling indicator can be used to switch between displaying and not displaying the control record. If this keyword is not specified, the subfile control record is displayed on every output operation to the subfile control record.

Diagram B-3: Subfile Control Record Keywords (1 of 4)

Keyword	Parameter	Description
SFLEND	*MORE *PLUS	Controls the display of More... and Bottom below the subfile detail records. This indicates whether or not the subfile can be scrolled to the next page. When no more records are available, Bottom is displayed. A controlling indicator is required for this keyword. Traditionally, N99 is used to control the keyword, and then, that indicator is not used in the RPG program. There are two forms of this keyword, the keyword itself, which causes the More... and Bottom to be replaced by a + and blank respectively. And the parameter form that allows the type of identification to be specified. SFLEND(*MORE) causes More... and Bottom to be displayed; while SFLEND(*PLUS) causes the + and blank to be used.
SFLENTER	*function key*	Causes the Enter key to be mapped to the RollUp (pagedown) key. When Enter is pressed, subfile support causes the subfile to scroll to the next subfile page. When the last page of the subfile is displayed and Enter is pressed, the subfile support passes the Enter key along to the RPG program. A function key can be specified as a parameter, for example, SFLENTER(CF10), to provide an alternative "Enter" key. The function key F1 becomes the Enter key to the RPG program.
SFLFOLD	*function key*	Directs the subfile to be displayed folding. The subfile is displayed, and if its detail record is wider than the physical display device, the data that exceed the physical size is displayed on subsequent lines until the entire subfile detail record is displayed. This is known as *subfile fold*. The Function Key parameter can be used to assign a function key that controls switching between folded and drop modes. Also see the SFLDROP keyword.
SFLINZ		Causes the subfile detail records to be initialized to their low values. That is character fields are set to blanks and numeric fields are set to zero. Input-only fields with default values are set to their default values. In addition if the SFLRNA (subfile record not active) keyword is NOT specified, the subfile detail records are activated.

Diagram B-3: Subfile Control Record Keywords (2 of 4)

Keyword	Parameter	Description
SFLLIN	*spaces*	Causes the subfile to occupy multiple columns with the same data. Typically this keyword and style of subfile is used when only a few (1 to 4) fields of information are to be displayed. Those fields are repeated horizontally across the display until the display is filled. The *spaces* parameter controls the spacing between the columns of information.
SFLMODE	*mode*	Returns the mode of the subfile. The parameter must be a field defined in DDS as a 1-position character field. The field's usage must be hidden. The field will return, via RPG input, a value of 1 if the subfile is in drop mode, or a value of 0 if the subfile is in fold mode.
SFLPAG	*page size*	Controls the number of subfile detail records that appear on the display simultaneously. Typically this value is less than or equal to the value specified for the SFLSIZ keyword. This value also controls the scroll value, that is the number of records the system scrolls the display when a roll key is pressed (unless the SFLROLVAL keyword is also specified).
SFLRCDNBR	*CURSOR*	Controls which subfile pageis displayed. The displayed page is calculated by the value specified for the field assigned to this keyword. The field must be a 4-position zoned decimal field, with 0 decimal positions. The page number of the record number specified in this field is displayed. If the operation CURSOR parameter is specified, the cursor of the display is positioned on the first input-capable field for the record.
SFLRNA		SFLRNA and SFLINZ can be used together to initialize and avoid activating the subfile detail records. Records can be written by the RPG program, and the additional records can receive data from the operator.

Diagram B-3: Subfile Control Record Keywords (3 of 4)

Keyword	Parameter	Description
SFLROLVAL		Controls the number of subfile detail records that are scrolled when a roll key is pressed. The number of records to scroll must be specified in a 4-position zoned decimal field, with 0 decimal positions.
SFLSIZ	*subfile size*	Controls the total number of records in the subfile. Typically, this value is used in one of three ways. (1) To establish that the subfile size is equal to the subfile page size (see the SFLPAG keyword). (2) To indicator that the subfile size is greater than the page size, and that it is a multiple of the page size (e.g., page=12, size=48). And (3) To indicator that the subfile size is 1 greater than the page size (page=12, size=13). These three techniques are the most common for SFLSIZ. The first is referred to as *page equals size*. The second and a *normal subfile*. And the third as *optimized subfile*. The term optimized subfile simply means that subfile support only has to deal with the minimum number records that will be displayed. For example, in a normal subfile, if page size is 12 and subfile size is 1000, subfile support has to manage those 1000 unused records. When subfile page size is 12 and subfile size is 13, the system will still allow records to be added to the subfile, but avoids allocating storage and managing those 1000 records until they are actually used by the program.

Diagram B-3: Subfile Control Record Keywords (4 of 4)

DDS WINDOW Keywords

AS/400 DDS has always been able to "do windows". These windows are text-based, that is they are not graphical user interfaces as on most other systems, but rather character-based windows.

Recently, the AS/400 system began recognizing the need for windowing and included DDS keywords to support them. There are three DDS keywords that support windowing, and a fourth that, indirectly contributes to clean and pleasant switch between windows. They are as follows.

Keyword	Parameter	Description
WINDOW	*row, col, width, height, [*NOMSGLIN | *MSGLIN]* **DFT, width, height, [*NOMSGLIN | *MSGLIN]*	Identifies the format as a window control record. The format is display in a window whose size is specified on this keyword. Other formats can reference this record format name to inherit the properties of this window and be included within its border. The *row* and *col* parameters can be variable names and set via the RPG program. For example: WINDOW(&ROW &COL 50 10 *NOMSGLIN) The *row* and *col* parameters can be replaced with the *DFT parameter. When *DFT is specified, the position of the window is determined by the system, based-on the cursor location. The parameter *NOMSGLIN, when specified, avoids reserving one of the window's lines for status messages. The *MSGLIN parameter is the default. Essentially *MSGLIN and no parameter are the same.
WINDOW	*format name*	This form of the WINDOW keyword is used to reference a window format as the primary window frame. The format on which this form of the keyword is used appears within the window border of the format named as the parameter. For example, if format FMT38 contains the following: WINDOW(&ROW &COL 50 10 *NOMSGLIN) And format FMT400 contains the following: WINDOW(FMT38) FMT400 is displayed within the window border of FMT38. That is the field positions for format FMT400 are relative to the window border for format FMT38.

Diagram B-4: DDS Windowing Keywords (1 of 2)

Keyword	Parameter	Description
WDWBORDER	**COLOR* **DSPATR* **CHAR*	Identifies the window's border attributes. To specify the border attribute, the parameter is specified followed by the appropriate value. For example: WDWBORDER((*COLOR BLU) (*CHAR '********'))
RMVWDW		Clears all formats from the display that have been output with the WINDOW keyword. The format containing the RMVWDW keyword is then written to the display.
USRRSTDSP		Causes the display device to act more appealing to the eye. Less screen blanking occurs, and screen images overlap each other without excessive "blinking".

Diagram B-4: DDS Windowing Keywords (2 of 2)

WINDOW Keyword Overview

The WINDOW keyword has two formats: window definition and window reference. The window definition format is used to define the window size, and border attributes. The window reference format references an existing window definition format, and optionally overrides the window border attributes.

Window Definition Keyword Syntax

There are two formats for the WINDOW keyword:

```
WINDOW(starting-line starting-column lines columns [*NOMSGLIN | *MSGLIN])

WINDOW(*DFT  lines  columns  [*NOMSGLIN | *MSGLIN])
```

Parameter	Description
starting line	The line number where the window's top left corner is to be positioned. This parameter can be a variable name. The variable must be a DDS program/parameter field (i.e., a data type of P) and contain an ampersand prefix. For example &ROW. When a variable is specified, it must be defined as a 3 position signed numeric field with 0 decimal positions.
starting column	The column number where the window's top left corner is to be positioned. This parameter can be a variable name. The variable must be a DDS program/parameter field (i.e., its *usage* must be P) and the name must contain an ampersand prefix. For example &COL. When a variable is specified, it must be defined as a 3 position signed numeric field with 0 decimal positions.
*DFT	This value can be used in place of starting line number and starting column number. The system determines where to position the window on the display.
number of lines	The number of usable lines occupied by the window. This value does not include the 2 lines required for the window border. A literal value must be specified for this parameter. If *NOMSGLIN is specified, all lines specified by this parameter are available to the application program. If *NOMSGLIN is not specified, the last line in the window is reserved for use by the system.
number of columns	The number of columns available to the window. This value does not include the 6 columns required for the window border and border attributes. A literal value must be specified for this parameter.
*NOMSGLIN	This optional parameter controls whether or not the last line of the window is reserved for use by the system. If specified, the last line of the window is available to the application. If not specified, the last line is reserved by the system and used to display status messages.

Diagram B-5: WINDOW Keyword Parameter Definition

Window Reference Keyword Syntax

The syntax for the window reference keyword is as follows:

```
WINDOW(name-of-format-containing-window-definition-record)
```

The one and only parameter must be the name of a record format that contains a window definition record. That is the referenced format contain the window definition form of the WINDOW keyword. The format is included within the window border of the based-on format.

The border attributes can be overridden by simply specifying a new WDWBORDER keyword with the window reference format.

Restricted Keywords

The following DDS keywords cannot be used on the same record format as a WINDOW keyword.

Keyword	Description
ALWROL	Roll the display up when this format is written
ASSUME	Assume "this" format is already on the display
BLKFLD	Fold text at a blank when it wraps at the end of the display
ERRSFL	Error subfile (only ignored, not verboten)
KEEP	Keep the format on the display after closing the file
MNUBAR	Pulldown menu bar
MSGLOC	Message line location (only ignored, not verboten)
PULLDOWN	Pulldown menu option
SFL	The format is a subfile (although SFLCTL can be specified)
USRDFN	The format contains 5250 data stream commands

Diagram B-6: DDS Keywords Restricted from WINDOW Formats

The KEEP and ASSUME keywords are not really required because the USRRSTDSP keyword is more flexible and provides similar support. The SFL (subfile detail record) keyword is not allowed, but the SFLCTL (subfile control record) keyword is allowed. The subfile detail record will follow the control record into the window border area, therefore, a subfile can appear within a window.

Example WINDOW Keyword Usage

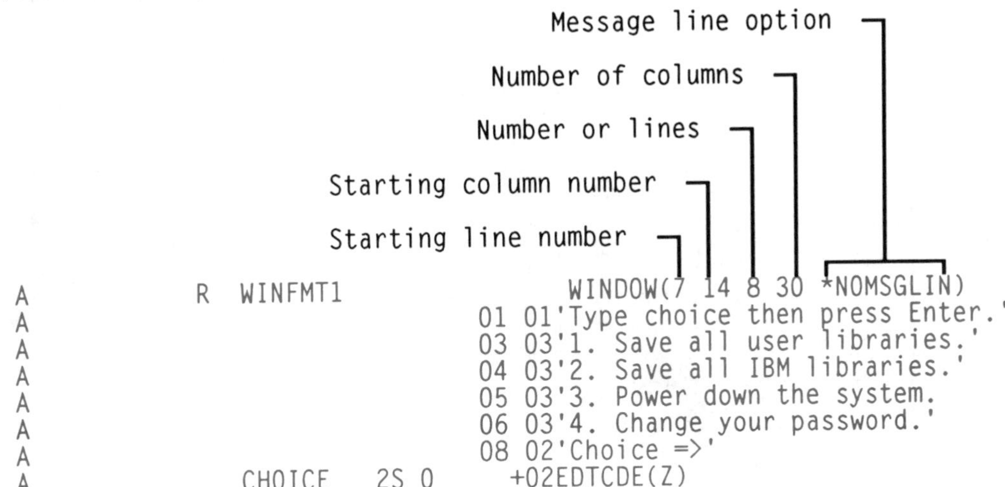
Message line option
Number of columns
Number or lines
Starting column number
Starting line number
A   R WINFMT1   WINDOW(7 14 8 30 *NOMSGLIN)
A   01 01'Type choice then press Enter.'
A   03 03'1. Save all user libraries.'
A   04 03'2. Save all IBM libraries.'
A   05 03'3. Power down the system.
A   06 03'4. Change your password.'
A   08 02'Choice =>'
A   CHOICE   2S 0   +02EDTCDE(Z)

Diagram B-7: DDS Source Illustrating the Use of the WINDOW Keyword

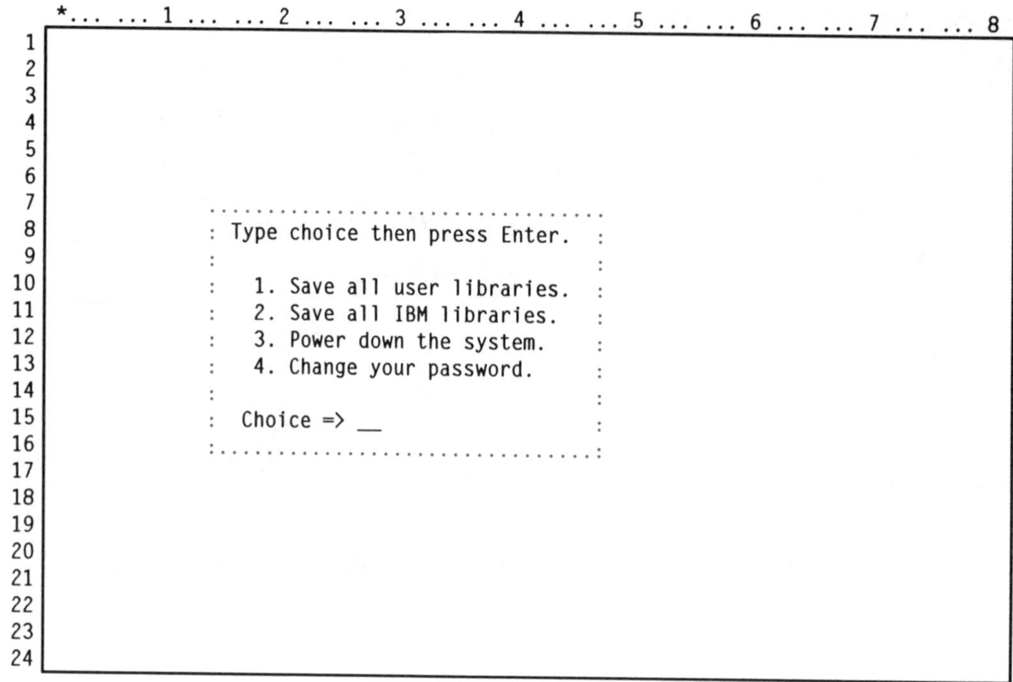

Diagram B-8: Display Panel Illustrating a Window

Since no WDWBORDER keyword is specified in the DDS, the default border character set is used.

WDWBORDER Keyword Overview

The WDWBORDER is used to define the window's border. The border occupies two additional rows and 6 additional columns beyond the window size. While the keyword has an unusual format, it can be specified more than once per record format.

Window Border Syntax

```
WDWBORDER((ctrl-parm1 options) (ctrl-parm2 options) (ctrl-parm3 options))
```

The control parameters and their options are described in the table that follows.

Parameter	Options	Description
*COLOR	BLU GRN WHT RED TRQ YLW PNK	One color can be specified for the window border. The color applies only to color display devices. The color is ignored, and is superseded by the *DSPATR parameter. An example use of *COLOR follows: `WDWBORDER( (*COLOR BLU) )`
*DSPATR	RI HI ND CS UL BL	One display attribute can be specified for the window border. The display attribute is used on both color and monochrome display devices. The default attribute is HI for monochrome displays, and normal (i.e., not special attribute) for color displays. An example use of *DSPATR follows: `WDWBORDER( (*DSPATR HI) )`
*CHAR	*any 8 characters*	The window border is made up of 8 characters. They are: 1. Top left corner. 2. Top row border. 3. Top right corner. 4. Left column border. 5. Right column border. 6. Bottom left corner. 7. Bottom row border. 8. Bottom right corner. An example use of *CHAR follows: `WDWBORDER((*CHAR '...::::.:'))`

Diagram B-9: WDWBORDER Parameter Options

Example Usage of the WDWBORDER Keyword

```
A          R WINFMT1                  WINDOW(7 14 8 30 *NOMSGLIN)
A                                     WDWBORDER( +
A                                       (*CHAR  '********') +
A                                       (*COLOR BLU) +
A                                       (*DSPATR HI))
A                                 01 01'Type choice then press Enter.'
A                                 03 03'1. Save all user libraries.'
A                                 04 03'2. Save all IBM libraries.'
A                                 05 03'3. Power down the system.
A                                 06 03'4. Change your password.'
A                                 08 02'Choice =>'
A            CHOICE    2S 0        +02EDTCDE(Z)
```

Diagram B-10: DDS Source Illustrating the Use of the WDWBORDER Keyword

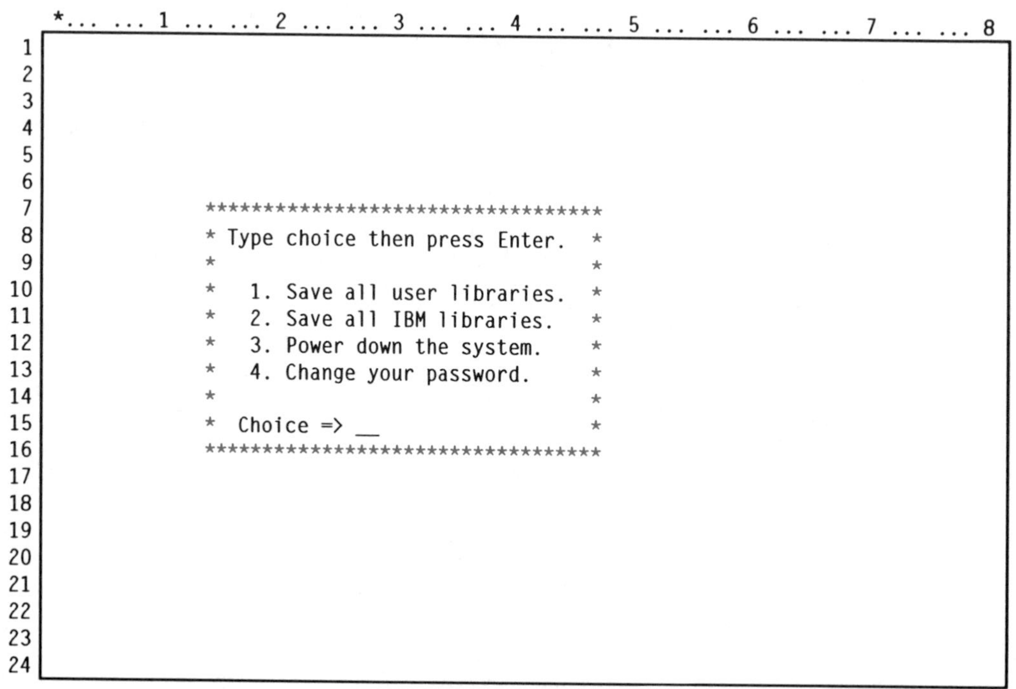

Diagram B-11: Display Panel Illustrating How a Custom Window Border Appears

Since a WDWBORDER keyword is specified, a custom border character set is used.

The WDWBORDER can appear multiple times—once for each parameter; or all parameters can appear within a single WDWBORDER keyword.

Window Border Character Identification

The diagram below illustrates the window border character positioning.

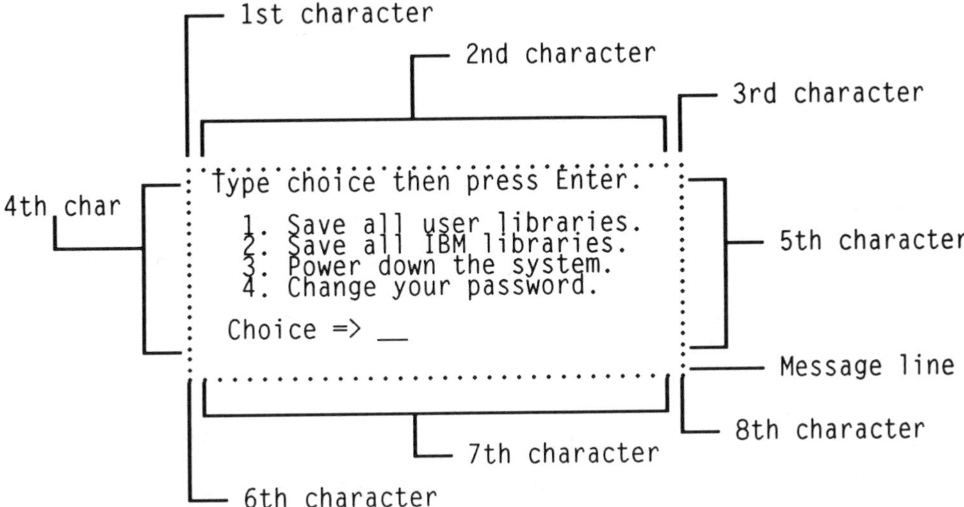

Diagram B-12: Display Panel Illustrating Window Border Character Positioning

In the examples that follow, several common window border character patterns are illustrated. The DDS WDWBORDER keyword that is used to generate the border patterns window border appears above each border.

```
WDWBORDER((*CHAR '...::::.:'))    WDWBORDER((*CHAR '********'))

  ............                      ************
  :          :                      *          *
  :          :                      *          *
  :          :                      *          *
  :          :                      *          *
  :..........:                      ************

WDWBORDER((*CHAR '+-+||+-+'))     WDWBORDER((*CHAR '12345678'))

  +----------+                      122222222223
  |          |                      4          5
  |          |                      4          5
  |          |                      4          5
  |          |                      4          5
  +----------+                      677777777778
```

Diagram B-13: Common Window Border Patterns

Multi-Format Windows

Multi-format windows use the WINDOW(format) form of the WINDOW keyword to allow multiple formats within the same window. The example that follows illustrates the structure of the multi-format window.

Example DDS illustrating the structure of a multi-format window

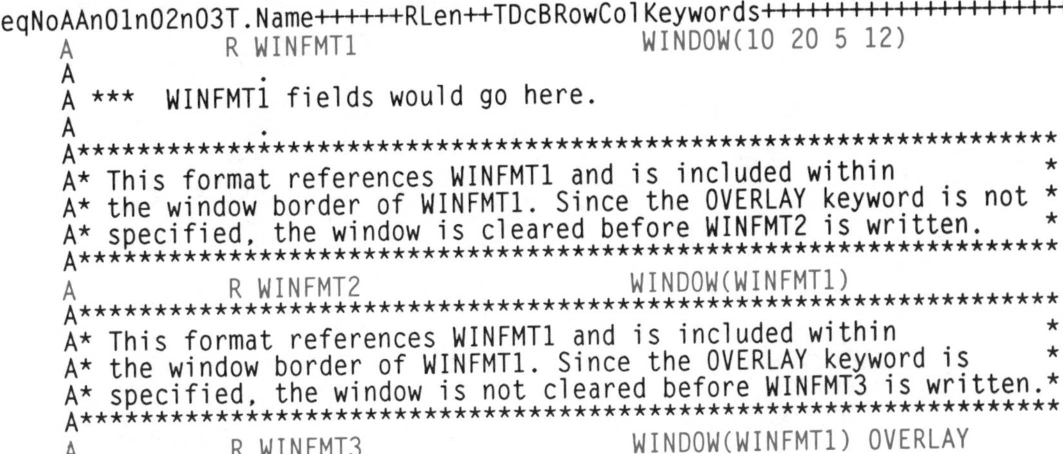

```
SeqNoAAn01n02n03T.Name++++++RLen++TDcBRowColKeywords+++++++++++++++++++++
     A          R WINFMT1                   WINDOW(10 20 5 12)
     A            .
     A ***  WINFMT1 fields would go here.
     A            .
     A*****************************************************************
     A* This format references WINFMT1 and is included within         *
     A* the window border of WINFMT1. Since the OVERLAY keyword is not *
     A* specified, the window is cleared before WINFMT2 is written.    *
     A*****************************************************************
     A          R WINFMT2                   WINDOW(WINFMT1)
     A*****************************************************************
     A* This format references WINFMT1 and is included within         *
     A* the window border of WINFMT1. Since the OVERLAY keyword is     *
     A* specified, the window is not cleared before WINFMT3 is written.*
     A*****************************************************************
     A          R WINFMT3                   WINDOW(WINFMT1) OVERLAY
```

The OVERLAY keyword can be used to cause the display to overlay the other existing formats in the window. If OVERLAY is not specified, writing the format to the window causes the entire window to be cleared before the format is written.

The example DDS that follows illustrates a multi-format window, window reference formats and output data for the window.

The RPG code that follows the DDS, illustrates how RPG handles writing window formats to the display.

Example DDS illustrating the use of a multi-format window

```
SeqNoA.........R.Format++++RLen++PDcULinColKeywords+++++++++++++++++++++
     A          R WINAAA                       WINDOW(4 6 16 60)
     A                                         WDWBORDER( +
     A                                          (*DSPATR HI))
     A                                    01 01'Window AAA Line 1.'
     A                                    02 01'Window AAA Line 2.'
     A                                    03 01'Window AAA Line 3.'
     A                                    04 01'Window AAA Line 4.'
     A                                    05 01'Window AAA Line 5.'
      ****
     A          R WINBBB                    WINDOW(WINAAA) OVERLAY
     A                                    06 08'Window BBB Line 1.'
     A                                    07 08'Window BBB Line 2.'
     A                                    08 08'Window BBB Line 3.'
     A                                    09 08'Window BBB Line 4.'
     A                                    10 08'Window BBB Line 5.'
      ****
     A          R WINCCC                    WINDOW(WINAAA) OVERLAY
     A                                    11 12'Window CCC Line 1.'
     A                                    12 12'Window CCC Line 2.'
     A                                    13 12'Window CCC Line 3.'
     A                                    14 12'Window CCC Line 4.'
     A                                    15 12'Window CCC Line 5.'
```

Example RPG code to display multi-format windows

```
SeqNoCSRn01n02n03Factor1+++OpCodFactor2+++ResultLenXHHILOEQ
     C                     WRITEWINAAA
     C                     WRITEWINBBB
     C                     WRITEWINCCC
```

RPG handles windows no differently than any other type of format. In fact, RPG doesn't need to consider whether a format is in a window or occupies the entire display screen. The only consideration is when variable row and column numbers are controlled. Then, RPG must manipulate these values appropriately.

The example display panel that follows, illustrates how the multi-format window would appear on the display. The window formats in this example were written by the RPG code listed above.

Example multi-format window output from an RPG program

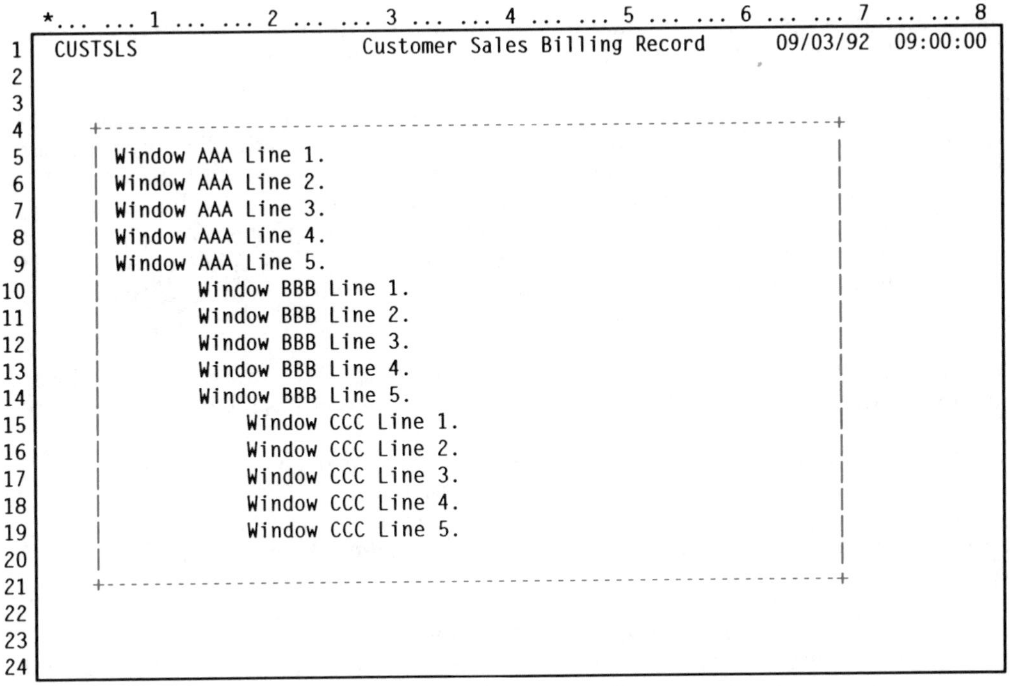

```
*... ... 1 ... ... 2 ... ... 3 ... ... 4 ... ... 5 ... ... 6 ... ... 7 ... ... 8
 CUSTSLS                    Customer Sales Billing Record      09/03/92  09:00:00


     +----------------------------------------------------------------+
     | Window AAA Line 1.                                             |
     | Window AAA Line 2.                                             |
     | Window AAA Line 3.                                             |
     | Window AAA Line 4.                                             |
     | Window AAA Line 5.                                             |
     |        Window BBB Line 1.                                      |
     |        Window BBB Line 2.                                      |
     |        Window BBB Line 3.                                      |
     |        Window BBB Line 4.                                      |
     |        Window BBB Line 5.                                      |
     |            Window CCC Line 1.                                  |
     |            Window CCC Line 2.                                  |
     |            Window CCC Line 3.                                  |
     |            Window CCC Line 4.                                  |
     |            Window CCC Line 5.                                  |
     |                                                                |
     +----------------------------------------------------------------+



```

Diagram B-14: Multi-format Window

Including a Subfile Within a Window

Using a subfile inside a window provides the ability to display two or more subfiles side by side. This capability does not exist without windowing.

To include a subfile within a window requires only that the subfile control record contain both the SFLCTL and WINDOW keywords. The WINDOW keyword can be either the window definition format, or a window reference keyword. No other special coding is required. By simply including the WINDOW keyword in the subfile control record, the subfile appears within the domain of the window. Be certain not to include the subfile detail record in the window, however. This is not allowed by DDS. The subfile detail record will appear within the window defined with the subfile control record.

The positions within the subfile control record and subfile detail record are the same as that of other window fields; they are relative to the window's top left corner.

The subfile page size must be one less than the number of lines in the window. When the subfile is scrolled up or down, only the data within the window is scrolled; data outside the window is not altered. This is in contrast to traditional subfiles where the enter subfile detail line is scrolled regardless of whether the data is part of the subfile detail record.

The example DDS that follows, illustrates how to specify a subfile within a DDS window. Following the source code is an example display panel, featuring the subfile and window. The window overlaps the existing display to provide a more desirable effect. Note that the DDS that follows does not include source for the background display format.

Example DDS for a subfile-in-a-window

```
SeqNoA.........R.Format++++RLen++PDcULinColKeywords++++++++++++++++++++++
     A         R CARDS                          SFL
     A           SEQ            2S 00  3  3 EDTWRD(' 0.')
     A           CRDTXT        25A  0  3 +1
     A         R SFLWIN                        SFLCTL(CARDS)
     A                                         WINDOW(12 24 5 32 *NOMSGLIN)
     A                                         WDWBORDER( +
     A                                         (*CHAR  '+-+||+-+') +
     A                                         (*COLOR BLU) +
     A                                         (*DSPATR HI))
     A                                         SFLPAG(2) SFLSIZ(8)
     A  21                                     SFLDSPCTL SFLDSP
     A N21                                     SFLCLR
     A N29                                     SFLEND(*MORE)
     A                                     1  1 'Select Type of Credit Card:'
     A           CHOICE         2S 0    + 2 EDTCDE(Z)
```

Example output of a subfile-in-a-window

```
*... ... 1 ... ... 2 ... ... 3 ... ... 4 ... ... 5 ... ... 6 ... ... 7 ... ... 8
 CUSTSLS                        Customer Sales Billing Record      09/03/92  09:00:00


    Customer . . . . . .      11496
                              Science Application International Corp.
                              1157 Meachum Road
                              Schaumburg, IL  60177

    Area Code/Phone . . .     (708) 555-1212

    Credit Card . . . . .     __                         F4=List
                         +-----------------------------------+
    Last called on  . .  | Select Type of Credit Card:  __   |
                         |                                   |
    Next call date  . .  |   1. VISA/MasterCard (VS)         |
                         |   2. Master Card (MC)             |
    Person to contact .  |   3. American Express (AX)        |
                         |   4. Discover (DC)                |
                         |                          More...  |
                         +-----------------------------------+

    F3=Exit   F4=Prompt   F12=Cancel


```

Considerations for Subfiles in Windows

- Subfile control records can be located within a window record format.
- Subfile detail records must fit within the dimensions of the window (i.e., width, height).
- SFLDROP can be used to allow larger records.
- The plus sign (+) for more data, appears to the right of the subfile detail record's data.
- The '+' overlaps the data, if data fills the entire window.
- Use the SFLEND(*MORE) option to display "More..." instead of the '+'.
- Subfile page (SFLPAG) must be 1 less than the number of window lines.
- The last line of a window is reserved for status messages unless *NOMSGLIN is specified.

INDEX

INDEX

P

R

S

Titles currently available from Cozzi Research include:

Title	Author	ISBN
The Modern RPG Language *With Structured Programming*	Cozzi	0-9621825-0-8
CL Programming for the AS/400	Veal	0-9621825-2-4
The Modern RPG Language *Reference Summary*	Cozzi	0-9621825-3-2

Additional copies of these titles may be ordered directly from the publisher.

29 W 120 Butterfield Road
Suite 101
Warrenville, IL 60555
U.S.A.

Phone: 1 (800) 552-9404
Outside the U.S.A. call: (708) 393-4474
24 hour FAX: (708) 393-2936

Titles currently available from Cozzi Research include:

Title	Author	ISBN
The Modern RPG Language *With Structured Programming*	Cozzi	0-9621825-0-8
CL Programming for the AS/400	Veal	0-9621825-2-4
The Modern RPG Language *Reference Summary*	Cozzi	0-9621825-3-2

Additional copies of these titles may be ordered directly from the publisher.

29 W 120 Butterfield Road
Suite 101
Warrenville, IL 60555
U.S.A.

Phone: 1 (800) 552-9404
Outside the U.S.A. call: (708) 393-4474
24 hour FAX: (708) 393-2936